THE
CHRISTIAN
TRAVEL
PLANNER

Kevin J. Wright

Thomas Nelson
Since 1798

NASHVILLE   DALLAS   MEXICO CITY   RIO DE JANEIRO   BEIJING

Published in Nashville, Tennessee, by Thomas Nelson. Thomas Nelson is a trademark of Thomas Nelson, Inc.

Thomas Nelson, Inc. titles may be purchased in bulk for educational, business, fund-raising, or sales promotional use. For information, please e-mail SpecialMarkets@ThomasNelson.com.

Although every effort is made to provide accurate information, we live in a fast-changing world. We ask readers to call to our attention any outdated information by e-mailing Kevin J. Wright at the World Religious Travel Association at info@religioustravelassociation.com.

Scripture references marked KJV are taken from The King James Version of the Bible.

Scripture references marked NKJV are taken from The Holy Bible, The New King James Version®. © 1982 by Thomas Nelson, Inc. Used by permission. All rights reserved.

HOLY BIBLE: NEW INTERNATIONAL VERSION®. © 1973, 1978, 1984 by International Bible Society. Used by permission of Zondervan Publishing House. All rights reserved.

Library of Congress Cataloging-in-Publication Data

Wright, Kevin J., 1972–
    The Christian travel planner / Kevin J. Wright.
      p. cm.
    Includes bibliographical references and index.
    ISBN 978-1-4016-0374-8
    1. Tourism—Religious aspects. 2. Christian pilgrims and pilgrimages. I. Title.
G156.5.R44W75 2008
910.4088'27—dc22

2007041975

Printed in the United States of America
08 09 10 11 12 RRD 8 7 6 5 4 3 2 1

To Katherine

CONTENTS

LIST OF ILLUSTRATIONS

Maps

FOREWORD

Most of my career has been spent helping Christians depart from their everyday lives to meet God in new and refreshing ways. As a director with Campus Crusade for Christ's Conference Ministry at Arrowhead Springs, California, for many years, I was involved in developing or overseeing nearly six thousand Christian retreats, conferences, and events. During a nearly ten-year period of time, week after week I saw over half a million Christians leave the cares and stresses of work and home behind to have what I call a "mountaintop" experience with God.

There is no doubt, something happens to us when we put ourselves in an environment that is 180 degrees from our day-to-day life. Whether it is at a Christian retreat center, on a tour abroad, a Christian cruise, or a family vacation, this change in environment allows us to quiet the din of our everyday lives and meet God in new and refreshing ways. Over the years I have seen marriages restored, families strengthened, and career- and ministry-weary individuals re-energized. Most importantly, as a result of these getaways, I have seen lives refreshed with renewed clarity and rededicated to a closer relationship with the Lord. This is my definition of a "mountaintop" experience.

Because Christian travel provides an endless variety of opportunities for individuals to experience these "mountaintops" in their own lives, it has been the mission of my company, Christian Travel Finder, to make this a reality for as many people as possible. I share that vision with Kevin J. Wright, and he is a kindred spirit in this pursuit.

For the last few years, unbeknownst to each other, Kevin and I have been on parallel paths in bringing Christian travel to a place of general awareness among both Christian consumers and the travel trade. Consequently, we both began to be quoted regularly in the same articles and media featuring the phenomenal growth and development of faith-based travel. It was only a matter of time before our journeys intersected. After getting to know Kevin, my deep admiration and respect for him made it easy to partner with him in launching the World Religious Travel Association—an association dedicated to educating and equipping the faith-based travel planner as well as the travel suppliers who offer these very special travel programs.

The launch of WRTA and the subsequent release of *The Christian Travel Planner* come at a pivotal time in the growth of Christian travel. Christians today are demanding more travel options that are family friendly and enrich their faith. Christians have had great success in driving the corporate world to offer products that reflect their values, so it is no surprise that faith-based travel is on the rapid rise. Christian travel is following in the footsteps of three major Christian consumer segments: Christian music, books, and films. It wasn't long ago that we would have been astounded at the idea of *The Purpose-Driven Life* becoming one of the best-selling books of all time and of Christian books representing 20 percent of Wal-Mart's book sales. Equally astounding would have been the thought that Christian music would outsell jazz and classical music combined and that *The Passion of the Christ* would become one of the highest grossing films of all time, subsequently giving birth to numerous faith-based subsidiaries of movie studios.

Faith-based travel is one of the fastest growing segments in travel. According to the World Tourism Organization, more than 300 million people embark on religious travel annually around the globe. The number of Americans traveling abroad for pilgrimage and spiritual purposes has grown by almost 30 percent in the past few years alone, according to the U.S. Office of Travel and Tourism Industries. And some estimates place the religious travel industry at 18 billion dollars worldwide.[1] This growing economic clout of Christians is capturing the travel industry's attention in a huge way. As a result, major tour and travel companies are rapidly developing new products to meet this growing demand. Many Christians now define an "all-inclusive" vacation as one that includes an emphasis on faith. So travel companies seeking to meet the needs of this segment are providing travelers with many new options.

Christian travel is not an entirely new concept, so why the sudden growth? It seems lectures or travelogues don't quite cut it with this new generation of travelers. They don't want to be told about their faith; they want to experience it for themselves. They want to explore where Jesus was baptized and where Paul preached. They want to see the country where they have supported missionaries for years. They are the ones planning where their next church conference or retreat will go for the weekend, and they are choosing cruise ships over hotel ballrooms. This new generation is seeking to explore the world and experience different cultures. Most importantly, they are looking to bring their faith and the Bible alive through their travels.

The next five to ten years will prove to be a most exciting time for Christian travel. One of the factors that will contribute to the growth of faith-based travel in the coming years will be the new U.S. passport laws that will require travelers to Mexico, Canada, and the Caribbean to possess a passport. With only an estimated 30 percent of United States citizens possessing a passport, this new requirement will encourage some of the 70 percent without passports to secure one. This will open up a whole new world for faith-based travelers to explore.

Most Christians are not aware of the variety of Christian travel options available to them. Many may think that Christian travel is defined solely as a trip to the Holy Land or a mission trip. Kevin J. Wright's *The Christian Travel Planner* comes along at precisely the right time as Christians are now faced with a plethora of new experiences from which to choose. Kevin combines his passion for faith-based travel with the in-depth foundational knowledge and expertise needed to assist travelers in the pursuit of their life-long Christian travel adventures.

In *The Christian Travel Planner*, Kevin provides the seasoned traveler, the group planner, or anyone new to Christian travel altogether with a storehouse of information detailing the wide array of travel experiences available so they can choose which will provide the best backdrop for their next "mountaintop" experience.

Honnie Korngold
Christian Travel Finder, President

ACKNOWLEDGMENTS

I n writing a book of this magnitude, I have many people to thank. First and foremost, I extend my sincerest appreciation, thanks, acknowledgment, and compliments to Katherine. This book is not only dedicated to her but is also a result of her tremendous work, research, and contributions. Simply put, she made this book possible through her dedicated assistance. Whenever I think of *The Christian Travel Planner*, I will always think of Katherine.

At the top of my list of thanks is also, of course, Honnie Korngold—my colleague at the World Religious Travel Association and president of Christian Travel Finder. I couldn't ask for a more treasured, wiser, or more virtuous business partner.

I would like to thank my good friends Jennifer Love and Kathy Swezy, who together designed all the maps. As both are the "best of the best" graphic designers within the tourism industry, it is simply a privilege to have their tremendous work included in this travel guidebook.

I also extend my deepest gratitude to Christine Moore: my publicist, business advisor, and dear friend. She has assisted me in multiple ways, from providing research and information to offering insightful advice, guidance, and suggestions.

And, of course, there is Amee Estill and Jackie Coronado—two of my closest friends and colleagues. They are the heart and soul of this new generation of Christian travel. They are the two greatest ambassadors for Christian tourism throughout the world— blessed are those companies who reap the rewards of Amee and Jackie's services.

Many thanks go out to Jesse Reeves, who edited the book prior to my submitting it to Thomas Nelson. I first met Jesse when he interviewed me for a Christian travel article; today he is my number one "go-to guy" for editing and proofing.

I would also like to thank the many tourist boards, travel companies, and Christian destinations and attractions that provided us with much-needed information, photographs, and insight regarding their respective destinations and organizations. In many ways their material serves as the foundation of this travel guidebook.

Special thanks to the following companies, organizations, and individuals who supplied personal stories and testimonies for this book including Christian Travel Finder www.christiantravelfinder.com, Jordan Tourism Board www.seejordan.org, Faith Travel

Development Consulting www.faithtraveldevelopment.com, Cruise Holidays of Grand Rapids www.cruiseholidays.com/sail, His 2 Overcome Adventure Ministries www.his2overcome.org, Reformation Tours www.reformationtours.com, Luminora Cruise & Land-Tour Vacations www.luminora.com, Saint Francis Pilgrimages www.stfrancispilgrimages.com, Sweet Magnolia Tours www.sweetmagnoliatours.com, Adventures in Missions www.adventures.org, The World Race www.theworldrace.org, and World Mission Tours www.womito.com.

I would like to express my gratitude for all my friends, colleagues, associates, contacts, and partners in Christian and faith-based tourism. This includes the many members of the World Religious Travel Association. Your love of and involvement in this industry have served as motivators for this much-needed guidebook.

And lastly, I would like to thank my family. My mom is the greatest enthusiast when it comes to Christian travel; more than anybody, she truly understands the enormous value and benefits such trips bring to one's life and faith. My dad is the one who opened my eyes to the wonderful field of tourism at a young age; today tourism is my life and career. And Patti is the person who has shown me the true nature of Christian hospitality, which is the premise of this handbook.

To all these people and to anyone else who has assisted me with this book in one form or another—I thank you. And so do all Christian travelers. Because of you, the world of Christian tourism is now that much richer. And for that I give all thanks and praise to the good Lord Himself.

A NEW ERA

Each year more than 200 million Christians embark on trips around the world.[1] Christians visit places ranging from Mt. Sinai, where Moses received the Ten Commandments, to Bethany-beyond-the-Jordan, where John the Baptist baptized Jesus, and to Turkey and Greece, where the apostle Paul preached the Good News. In addition, Christians journey throughout Europe each year visiting the Vatican, the Reformation sites in Germany, and even C.S. Lewis's home, *The Kilns*, in England. At the same time, Christians are traveling for missionary purposes to Africa, South America, Eastern Europe, Russia, and Asia.

But that's not all. Tens of thousands of Christians embark on faith-based cruises each year. Hundreds of thousands step away from their normal daily routines to spend time on retreat or at a monastery. Several million people make a stop each year at Christian attractions such as biblical parks, theaters, museums, and welcome centers. Mega-churches themselves draw similar-sized crowds to their choral and drama performances. Christian music festivals themselves attract a staggering 22 million attendees from coast to coast and throughout the world.[2] Nearly 8 million people are involved in Christian camps and conferences,[3] and a whopping 15 million attend Christian conventions, crusades, and rallies.[4]

Christian travel is in a category all its own. Imagine being with family, friends, or church members atop Mt. Nebo, the very place where Moses viewed the Promised Land. Picture yourself sailing through the paradise-like Caribbean waters while listening to your favorite Christian speakers and artists. Envision embracing the "toughest vacation you'll ever love" by devoting your time and services to short-term missions. All of these experiences have the potential to dramatically impact your life and faith in a single moment—with profound and lasting effects.

In short, Christian travel provides a benefit virtually unmatched by any other ministry: it enables you to experience your faith *physically*. There is no greater feeling than being in the places where the most pivotal events of our faith took place. Only through travel can you stand, for example, in the very same spot where the apostle Paul stood and delivered a speech to the people of Athens at Areopagus (Acts 17:22). It's one thing to read or hear this Scripture passage in the comfort of your air-conditioned church, it's quite another to read, hear, *and stand* in the very site of the Scripture passage while fighting the blistering heat and mugginess of Athens. By physically experiencing places of faith through travel, biblical and historical Christian events become *real places* with *real people* and *real meaning.* The same experience applies to mission trips and other forms of Christian travel and vacations.

But that's not all. Christian travel enables you to experience your faith not only physically but also spiritually, socially, intellectually, and emotionally. No other Christian ministry provides such unique benefits. This is just one reason why more than fifty thousand church travel programs exist today and why religious travel lies at the heart of worldwide tourism.

Welcome to the new era of Christian vacations! This exciting new era combines Christian faith, fun, and fellowship with travel. Christians are journeying together with their churches and ministry groups in greater numbers than ever before. And they are embarking on a greater *variety* of Christian travel experiences than ever before. It's not uncommon for faith communities today to offer everything from Holy Land trips to short-term mission opportunities to Christian attraction visits to retreat getaways to leisure vacations. What does this all mean? Christians have found a new travel partner in recent years—each other!

As president of the World Religious Travel Association, it is with great joy that I present this travel planner. I've written this handbook for anyone interested in Christian tourism, including the individual traveler, group planner, and pastor or religious leader. The book is designed to be user-friendly and can assist you in not only choosing the right Christian trip but also in making plans to embark on it. In addition, *The Christian Travel Planner* can help your faith community begin or enrich its travel ministry program.

What about you? Have you considered taking a Christian vacation? With so many options to choose from today, there's never been a better time to consider such a trip. With this Christian trip and vacation planner, you'll have the knowledge at your fingertips to design or choose a trip that's just right for you. No matter what your desires, *The Christian Travel Planner* will enable you to prepare for such memorable and possibly life-changing experiences.

As Saint Augustine once said, "The world is a book, and those who do not travel read only a page."[5] My great hope is that for your next trip, you will think *Christian vacation* first. There is no better way to enjoy faith, fun, and fellowship than through travel— and this time, you can return home refreshed and rejuvenated in mind, body, *and soul.*

May God bless and enrich your travels,
Kevin J. Wright

PART ONE

FAITH, FUN, AND FELLOWSHIP

CHAPTER ONE

CHRISTIAN TRAVEL OF YESTERDAY

CREDIT: TURKISH CULTURE AND TOURISM OFFICE, NEW YORK

Christian travel and general tourism are inextricably linked. Worldwide tourism as we know it today has its roots in faith-based travel. The earliest known days of leisure tourism date to the Egyptian Empire when religious festivities drew outside visitors. As people streamed into the city for celebrations, local businesses sprang up to meet the travelers' demands for lodging, food, guides, and transportation. This led to the birth of today's tourism industry.

In later years, the Greeks entered the arena of tourism. Tourist destinations for the Greeks included thermal baths and sacred sites. Greek religious festivals were also major attractions and later became sports and leisure outings. One of the world's earliest and largest tourist events was the Olympic Games in 776 BC, heavily promoted throughout ancient Greece. As in Egypt, hospitality-type services and businesses developed around the Games to assist the many visitors. Two centuries later, the Greek citizen Herodotus, the world's earliest travel writer, visited lands stretching from Athens to Egypt and Asia and reported on religious sites and events.

In Scripture, Deuteronomy 16:16 speaks of the Jews traveling on pilgrimage to the feasts: "Three times a year all your males shall appear before the LORD your God in the place which He chooses: at the Feast of Unleavened Bread, at the Feast of Weeks, and at the Feast of Tabernacles; and they shall not appear before the LORD empty-handed." Mosaic Law required every Jewish male to observe each feast, including the Feast of Unleavened Bread (Passover), the Feast of Weeks (Pentecost), and the Feast of Booths (Succot). Exodus 23:17 and 34:23 also speak of similar pilgrimage acts.

Shiloh served as one of the first destinations for celebrating the Jewish feasts. Then, once Solomon built the Temple around 1000 BC, Jerusalem became the prime pilgrimage site. The Babylonian exile increased Jewish travel around 586 BC, and Herod's rebuilding of the Temple (approximately 20 BC) further heightened mass pilgrimages.

During the period of Roman domination from 27 BC to AD 476, travel flourished as people journeyed throughout the Empire. People traveled for a variety reasons: religious, trade, political, military, communication, and leisure. And don't forget the Magi, who traveled from the East for the birth of the Savior: "Now after Jesus was born in Bethlehem of Judea in the days of Herod the king, behold, wise men from the East came to Jerusalem, saying, 'Where is He who has been born King of the Jews? For we have seen His star in the East and have come to worship Him.'" (Matthew 2:1–2)

Jesus traveled many times from Galilee to Jerusalem on pilgrimage, and much of the Gospel of John is centered on these travels (John 2:13, John 5:1, John 7:2–3, John 10:22–23, John 11–19). We also know that Jesus journeyed with his family to Jerusalem as a child to observe the feasts: "His parents went to Jerusalem every year at the Feast of the Passover. And when He [Jesus] was twelve years old, they went up to Jerusalem according to the custom of the feast. When they had finished the days, as they returned, the Boy Jesus lingered behind in Jerusalem" (Luke 2:41–43).

After the death of Jesus, the apostles and disciples embarked on travels throughout the Roman Empire to spread the gospel of Jesus Christ. Among the most ardent travelers was the apostle Paul, who embarked over a span of several years on three missionary journeys to modern-day Greece, Turkey, Syria, and Rome. Other apostles made similar trips, including the apostle Thomas who, according to tradition, traveled to the Far East and preached in India.

Around AD 300, the Holy Land became one of the top destinations for travel. Three of the most famous pilgrims of this era are Helena, mother of the Emperor Constantine; Egeria, a woman (possibly a nun) from the western Roman Empire; and an unknown traveler called the Bordeaux Pilgrim.

Helen traveled in the fourth century to Jerusalem where she is said to have discovered the cross upon which Jesus Christ died. Egeria traveled throughout Egypt, Israel, and Syria, most likely during the fourth century, and she also wrote a travel diary (today called *Itinerarium Egeriae* or "The Travels"). The unknown Bordeaux Pilgrim (from Bordeaux, France) was an anonymous Judeo-Christian traveler who made a trip to Jerusalem in AD 333 and wrote what is essentially the first pilgrimage travel guide. His chronicle included such travel information as descriptions of churches, monuments, landmarks, distances, and even tips on where to eat dinner! His works are known as the *Itinerarium Burdigalense.*

As time passed, Christian holy days became the norm for taking time off from work (the very word "holiday" comes from these medieval days of religious celebration and leisure). With the fall of the Roman Empire in the fifth century though, roads became fraught with danger, and people stayed within the confines of their communities. This led to people spending leisure time at home rather than traveling.

By the Middle Ages, long-distance travel again became vogue. As in earlier centuries, pilgrimages were one of the top reasons for making a journey. During this time, many people traveled in groups for both safety and community. Jerusalem, Rome, Canterbury, and Walsingham (England) became top tourist destinations.

The seventeenth century introduced a revolutionary new form of travel called *The Grand Tour*. In order to complete their education, young men from aristocratic families journeyed around Europe visiting many of the great cultural centers. This concept of group travel foreshadowed today's concept of mass tourism. The Industrial Revolution and the inventions of the railway and steamboat eventually brought travel to the middle class. In fact, in 1749, the first European travel guidebook was written.

In the midst of all this, missionary travel began to grow in earnest as well. Christian missionaries began traveling around the globe, even to the New World and the Far East. During this time, some of the first organized Protestant missionary activities were launched from Greenland to the West Indies. William Carey founded the British Baptist missions and became essentially the grandfather of modern missions. Catholic religious orders such as the Franciscans, Dominicans, and Jesuits also embarked on missionary travels around the world.

In 1841, a Methodist preacher by the name of Thomas Cook began what is recognized today as the first escorted tour company. In order to increase the number of people attending his religious Temperance Society meetings, Thomas organized group travel to his gatherings in Britain. From these religious gatherings, he then expanded the planned itineraries to other destinations. With a business firmly in place, Thomas offered the first overseas trip in 1861, and then in 1869, he led one of the first organized group trips to the Holy Land. The birth of escorted travel had officially begun.

At the start of the twentieth century, travel had become a mainstay not only in Europe but also throughout other parts of the world, including America. Christian travel began to take a backseat to other forms of travel as people traveled for the purpose of leisure, culture, health, or adventure. Near the end of the century, tourism expanded from an emerging market into one of the largest, fastest-growing sectors of the global economy.[1]

Because of the improvements in transportation, including air travel, religious travel experienced a rebirth in the 1960s and again in the 1980s. A few companies and organizations even began specializing in Christian and missionary travel. During this same period, many people embarked on Christian retreats, which resulted in the expansion of guesthouses and conference centers. Christian camps also became a virtual rite of passage for many youth and a mainstay of American life.

By the end of the twentieth-century, Christian crusades and rallies had evolved from a phenomenon into a way of life for the Christian church. Billy Graham and T.D. Jakes, among others, attracted hundreds of thousands into packed stadiums and other major sports venues to share Christian faith and fellowship. The sheer volume of visitors to these events often "took over" those cities. World Youth Day was also born during this time, attracting millions of young adults from around the globe to see the Pope and share in Christian festivities every two or three years. Mega-events such as these unofficially brought to a close this era of Christian travel and ushered in a new and much more dynamic era for the twenty-first century.

CHAPTER 2

CHRISTIAN TRAVEL
OF TODAY

CREDIT: JORDAN TOURISM BOARD NORTH AMERICA

The new millennium immediately set a new standard in faith-based tourism when some Christian denominations declared AD 2000 a Jubilee year (Holy Year) and encouraged religious travel throughout the world. Many Christian sites and destinations received record numbers of pilgrims in the year 2000. Rome doubled its number of visitors from 10 million to 20 million, while the number of tourists to visit Italy increased to a record high of 41 million visitors.[1] Israel and Egypt also set records by welcoming 2.4 million and 5.2 million travelers respectively.[2,3]

In recent years, a new form of missionary travel has grown tremendously in popularity. What is it? Short-term missions, also commonly referred to as STMs. With trips ranging from a few days to two years in length, this form of travel has become extremely popular with youth groups, churches, and individuals.

The terrorist attacks in America on September 11, 2001, brought worldwide tourism to a virtual standstill. However, Christian travel was one of the quickest to rebound. During this time of grief, many churches and communities shared and expressed their solidarity by traveling together. In addition, people of faith were open to journeying again despite the uncertainties of war, economy, and terrorism. Many Christians traveled with implicit trust in God and God's protection.

In the spring of 2004 history's most prolific traveler, Pope John Paul II, died. The late pontiff took more than two hundred trips to more than one hundred countries, each time highlighting the faith, history, and culture of his destination. This provided unprecedented media coverage of holy sites around the world including his historic visit to Jerusalem in 2000. From 2004 to 2006, Christian travel began garnering even further national and worldwide media attention. Major outlets including the CBS *Early Show*, *TIME*, *USA TODAY*, *Wall Street Journal*, *New York Times*, *Los Angeles Times*, and dozens of others featured stories on the growth and expansion of faith-based travel.

The travel industry itself began making religious travel a key topic at major conventions and conferences. During this same time, many tourist boards and companies launched new faith-based travel programs and initiatives. Christians also began starting their own travel agencies in greater numbers. Many top quality Christian attractions have arisen since 2001, and the construction of new ones continues to this day. Even the Vatican is getting involved: It launched its own low-cost charter airline in August 2007 to transport Christian pilgrims to holy sites throughout Europe and the biblical lands. And in 2008 the World Religious Travel Association hosted the first-ever international tradeshow and educational conference on faith tourism.

Christian travel is set for explosive growth in the years ahead. As awareness of Christian vacations has increased, so has the number of people turning to these types of trips. In fact, in November 2006, the Travel Industry Association of America released its findings that one in four travelers is currently interested in "spiritual vacations."[4]

To meet the growing demand, churches and religious organizations are now launching travel ministries and programs in greater numbers. Pastors and leaders have recognized that Christian travel and vacations offer a fabulous opportunity to build fellowship and faith. As a result, the future of Christian tourism is tremendously bright and poised to reclaim its rightful place as the cornerstone of worldwide tourism.

Throughout history Christian travel has traditionally been understood as travel to a holy site or travel with a spiritual intent. Pilgrimages, which include trips to the biblical lands, and missionary travel, such as overseas travel to spread the Christian faith and assist with humanitarian needs, are the two forms most closely associated with this understanding of Christian travel.

In the past two decades though, this twofold understanding has expanded to include a third type of travel: leisure travel with fellowship intent. This includes everything from Christian cruises to leisure vacations to attending Christian events. It even includes adventure and active vacations such as youth ski trips. This newest form of travel has grown to become enormously popular with the Christian community.

Today the Christian church is beginning to recognize travel as ministry. Think of the JESUS Film Project developed by Campus Crusade for Christ, which has had more than six billion viewings worldwide since 1979.[5] How was such an achievement possible? Thousands of Christians traveled the globe sharing the film on nearly every continent in the past several decades.

It is for reasons such as this and others that Christian travel is in many ways the *par excellence* of outreach ministry. Think of a typical church or Christian organization. What ministries does it offer? You will find programs for adults, families, youth, small groups, hospitality, music, social events, prayer, worship, faith education, and Scripture studies. These are the same outreach ministries found on many Christian trips and vacations.

But the question remains: Why would anybody embark on a Christian trip in today's world of glitzy vacations and destinations such as Las Vegas? The answer is simple: Only Christian travel provides rest and relaxation for the mind, body, *and* soul. Only Christian vacations enable you to experience faith, fun, and fellowship to the fullest.

Christians embark on travel together for three primary reasons: *to enrich their lives, to experience fellowship, and to deepen their faith*. First, Christian travel enriches life because it enables the traveler to see the world and explore the beauty of God's creation firsthand. It also provides an opportunity for the traveler to experience different cultures, cuisines, and geographies. More importantly, Christian travel fosters inspiration, joy, and a renewed sense of hope in life. Some Christian travelers receive a new direction or purpose in life, while others experience healing—whether spiritual, emotional, or physical.

Second, Christian travel nurtures fellowship. It is where friendships are born, strengthened, or rekindled. Just imagine sailing across the Sea of Galilee singing alleluias with your church community and experiencing the bonds created from such a powerful moment. Or imagine attending a crusade in a professional sports stadium with seventy thousand Christians, all of whom are singing praises to Jesus. What happens? Fellowship. Church members form unbreakable bonds with each other through these powerful and emotional experiences. Christian communities return home from these trips and vacations with strengthened ties and a shared sense of purpose.

The third, and possibly greatest, reason for Christian travel is the *deepening* of faith it produces. Christian travel enables travelers to be in the presence of sacred lands, events, and people; these experiences often enliven and enrich one's faith dramatically. For example, those who enter the cave where John the Evangelist wrote the Book of Revelation often exit with greater assurance and conviction of their faith. Experiences like these are similar to putting prescription glasses on and letting your faith come into clearer focus. It is common for many people to commit or recommit their lives to Jesus while on a Christian trip. For such reasons, Christian travel has earned its rightful place as "ministry" in the twenty-first-century church.

TRAVEL OPPORTUNITIES

What Christian travel experiences exist today? I have created five categories for the different types of Christian travel available today: pilgrimages and tours, missionary travel, fellowship vacations, Christian events and retreats, and Christian attractions.

PILGRIMAGES AND TOURS

Pilgrimage is an important concept in the Christian spiritual life. Many Christians view life itself as a pilgrimage; that is, a journey to God. In the world of travel, a Christian pilgrimage is a journey to a holy site with a spiritual intent or purpose.

Although there is no biblical mandate to embark on a pilgrimage, many Christians have done so throughout the centuries for various reasons. Some seek to rediscover the

CREDIT: ISRAEL MINISTRY OF TOURISM

Tours and pilgrimages are the heart of Christian travel.

origins of Christianity, while others wish to touch the very places where Jesus and the apostles walked. For many, such a trip becomes a turning point in their lives and their commitment to Christ. Many also return home with a renewed spirit and enriched knowledge of Scripture and Christian history (and even theology). And no Christian pilgrimage is complete unless there is a conversion to Christ. As the fourth-century theologian Jerome affirmed, "It is not sufficient merely to go on pilgrimage. Its success depends upon the pilgrim's ability to journey in faith, with a new heart and with a will to conversion."[6]

In today's world, Christian pilgrimages are more dynamic than ever before. These trips often combine a spiritual focus with traditional sightseeing and enjoyment. For example, you may spend a morning walking through the ruins of Corinth in Greece (Book of Acts), while the afternoon is spent exploring the famed city of Athens and its ancient monuments (such as Mars Hill where Paul spoke to the local population, Acts 17:22), and in the evening you might enjoy Greek cuisine and fellowship with your church members.

As Christian pilgrimages remain a venerable tradition in the third millennium, you should consider making it a priority to embark upon at least one major Christian pilgrimage in your life. One thing is guaranteed, it *will* be a life-changing experience.

MISSIONARY TRAVEL

If tours and pilgrimages are the heart of Christian travel, then missions are its lifeblood. Missionary travel is indispensable to Christian faith, theology, and tradition.

Today missionary travel remains as popular as ever. Consider the United Methodist Church: it recently reported an increase from twenty thousand mission volunteers in the early 1990s to one hundred and ten thousand participants and workers today.[7] In total, several million Christians embark on mission trips each year, whether short or long term. This is just one of the many signs that missionary travel remains alive and well in the Christian church.

The most popular form of missionary travel and work today is short-term missions. These are trips typically consisting of anywhere from a few days to two years. Such experiences can take place in North America or at the farthest reaches of the globe.

The primary purposes of missionary travel are Christian evangelism, church planting (establishing churches in Christian and non-Christian communities), and assisting with the humanitarian needs of the local population. In many ways, the apostle Paul is the prime example of a Christian missionary. During his missionary journeys, the apostle Paul spread the gospel, established new Christian communities, and assisted the needs of the local population.

CREDIT: ©ISTOCKPHOTO.COM/SEAN WARREN

Missionary travel is the lifeblood of Christian travel.

Today, the opportunities to embark on a mission trip are numerous. Hundreds of organizations exist for this very purpose. In addition, thousands of missionary travel possibilities are available, depending on the type of work you want to do, the experience you are seeking, the length of time you can spend, and the location you desire. If you feel a "calling" to engage in such a trip, do not ignore it. Read the chapter on missions in part two and then pick up the phone and call a missionary agency. Within a few months to a year, you could be in a foreign country spreading the gospel of Jesus Christ!

FELLOWSHIP VACATIONS

The newest and possibly fastest-growing segment of Christian travel today is fellowship vacations. What is a fellowship vacation? Simply put, it is a leisure vacation that is embarked upon for the primary purpose of sharing fellowship and mutual interests. In recent years, we have seen a tremendous increase in churches and religious groups traveling together on fellowship vacations. These trip experiences fall primarily into one of three categories: *leisure, cruises,* and *adventure.*

CREDIT: ©ISTOCKPHOTO.COM/JOELLE GOULD

Christians travel together on leisure vacations.

The first and possibly most popular segment of fellowship vacations is *leisure vacations.* Like any other sector of the population, many Christians enjoy traveling for no reason other than the recreation and pleasure it brings. These faith community trips can include anything from sightseeing in Washington D.C., to relaxing at the beach in Florida, to watching entertainment shows in Branson, Missouri.

What are the benefits of a Christian leisure vacation? For one, these trips provide an outlet for people of faith to join other like-minded people in their travels. In addition, these particular leisure trips can take on a Christian character and focus. For example, while traveling through the Canadian Rockies on a tour, groups can talk about the majesty and awe of God who created such magnificent wonders. Prayer and worship can be openly shared among the travelers and integrated into the trip. That is the beauty of a Christian leisure vacation. You will find such experiences nowhere else.

One of the newest categories of Christian fellowship vacations is Christian cruises. Today, tens of thousands of Christians embark on faith-based cruising each year. What is behind the growth of this form of Christian travel? In short, cruises have become one of the world's most favorite vacations. Not only do cruises represent the essence of a holiday to many, they are also quite inexpensive. For these reasons and more, approximately 10 million North Americans embark on cruises each year, with 15 percent of all Americans being cruise trip veterans.[8]

Because Christianity is about meeting people where they are and taking the Gospel to the ends of the earth, many churches and religious organizations have learned that taking the Gospel to the high seas is a winning combination. As a result, today there are more than a dozen full-ship Christian charters that take place annually (a full-ship charter is where an entire ship is hired exclusively by a group). If you have never been on a Christian cruise, you might consider it. Many rate it as one of the best vacations of their lives. There are many Christian cruise opportunities and destinations to choose from—don't miss the boat!

One of the smaller but growing segments of Christian tourism is adventure and active trips. Currently most of these tours and activities take place in North America or near one's hometown. Along with church- or ministry-sponsored local hiking or biking trips, among the most popular vacations in this category are Christian wilderness journeys, adventure camps, and active ranches. One of the most fascinating hidden gems of Christian adventure trips is the Christian African safari. Most people are surprised to learn that such faith-based safari opportunities exist, but they do. Whether you choose hiking, biking, or an African safari for your church or ministry adventure trip, one thing is certain—you will experience fellowship like never before!

CHRISTIAN EVENTS AND RETREATS

Christians have congregated for various events, meetings, and gatherings since the time of Jesus. Some came together for prayer and worship, while others came together for decision-making meetings. Still others met for the purpose of learning or reflection. In most cases, though, Christians congregated in order to seek refreshment and renewal not only in their personal lives but also in their communal lives. Today is no different. Christians continue to gather at conferences, crusades, rallies, retreats, and Christian camps in the hopes of personal and communal renewal.

Christian conventions and rallies are possibly the most popular form of Christian travel and gatherings today. When you take into account the number of people who attended Billy Graham's crusades and Pope John Paul's World Youth Days in the past few decades, these numbers outweigh almost any other faith-based vacation category. On multiple occasions, more than a million people came together for these events. Christian gatherings can take place for any rea-

CREDIT: ©ISTOCKPHOTO.COM/CLAYTON HANSEN

Retreats are a mainstay of Christianity.

son, but the most common include denominational convention meetings, educational seminars, music concerts, youth conferences, political cause movements, and association and affinity group events.

CREDIT: ©ISTOCKPHOTO.COM/LYA CATTEL

Fifteen million Christians attend conventions annually.

Christian retreats comprise another popular segment of Christian travel. People can embark on such experiences individually or with friends, family, or one's ministry or church group. Retreats can take place at a guesthouse, conference center, or even a monastery. Just as every type of Christian vacation provides certain benefits, retreats can arguably provide the greatest source of personal renewal. If there is one type of Christian travel experience every person should embark upon often, it is a personal or communal retreat.

Finally, if Christian pilgrimages are the heart of Christian travel and missions are its lifeblood, then what are Christian camps? These experiences are the *genesis* of Christian travel because Christian camps often serve as the first taste of a faith-based vacation for many youth. Better still, many young people walk away from these experiences with wonderful memories, and these experiences serve as the beginning of a lifelong commitment to Jesus. For this reason alone, everyone should be given an opportunity to attend a Christian camp at least once while growing up.

CHRISTIAN ATTRACTIONS

We all know about Disneyland, the Broadway theater district, and the Louvre Museum. But where are the Christian attractions? I have great news for you—these places now exist.

CREDIT: SIGHT & SOUND THEATRES

Christian attractions like Sight & Sound Theatres® draw hundreds of thousands of visitors per year.

Since the turn of the millennium, a number of top Christian attractions and facilities have sprung up. One of the foremost is the Holy Land Experience in Orlando, Florida. This biblical park debuted in 2001 and today receives more than two hundred thousand visitors a year. And not far from this venue is Wycliffe's interactive biblical center WordSpring Discovery Center (launched in 2002) and Campus Crusade for Christ's JESUS Film Project Master Studio. Each of these places offers experiences that rival similar, but secular, attractions.

This is a new trend in Christian travel—the availability of high quality Christian attractions and entertainment venues. Today you can choose from a variety of Christian facilities, including museums, theaters, welcome centers, and theme parks. Best of all, many offer first-class products and services. If you are looking for a Christian theatre experience, look no further than Sight & Sound Theatre's biblical performances, which are attended by more than eight hundred thousand people each year in Strasburg, Pennsylvania and Branson, Missouri.[9] Other top-quality Christian performances include The Great Passion Play in Eureka Springs, Arkansas, and The Miracle Theater in Pigeon Forge, Tennessee. With so many top-drawer Christian attractions available today, you might find yourself opting for miracles instead of Mickey.

READY TO START PLANNING YOUR CHRISTIAN TRIP?

Now that you know the five types of Christian travel experiences, you are ready to begin planning your next Christian vacation. But many questions still remain: Which Christian trip might be right for you? What are some of the most popular destinations? How much should you budget? When should you go and for how long? Who can assist you with travel arrangements? Part two of this book will address these questions and much more. So turn the page and begin planning your memorable trip!

PLANNING YOUR TRAVEL

CHAPTER 3

CHRISTIAN PILGRIMAGES
AND TOURS: BIBLICAL LANDS

CREDIT: JORDAN TOURISM BOARD NORTH AMERICA AND RON STERN

Is a pilgrimage to the biblical lands right for me?

It is the dream of many Christians to walk in the lands of the Bible. In many ways it is the crème de la crème travel experience for believers, and most Christians state that such trips become pivotal moments in their life and faith. The majority of Christians travel with their churches and faith communities to the Holy Land. A trip to the biblical lands takes you away to another time and place and right into the heart of Scripture and salvation history. Simply put, no other travel experience compares to a trip like this. If you are ever blessed with an opportunity to visit the Holy Land, pack your bags at once and go! Your life will never be the same.

BIBLICAL LANDS "AT A GLANCE"

TRIP SUMMARY

Typical length: 8–14 days
Average cost per day: $200–$300
Total average cost: $2,000–$4,000
Distance from home: direct flights from New York are approximately ten to thirteen hours long
Variety of pilgrimages: many
When to go: any time of the year; spring and fall typically offers the smallest crowds and the best weather
Why go: you feel a calling or receive an opportunity to embark on a Holy Land pilgrimage
Whom to go with: not individually; travel with a group
Which biblical destination to choose: since you may only visit the biblical lands once or twice in your life, choose a trip that combines several countries

DEMANDS AND BENEFITS

Spiritual focus: high
Fellowship opportunities: many
Physically demanding: low to moderate
Intellectually stimulating: very
Emotionally rewarding: very
Culturally enriching: very

What is the relevance of pilgrimages to the biblical lands?

The Judeo-Christian faith has a long history of pilgrimages, of the faithful traveling to holy sites for a religious or spiritual purpose, and the Bible is full of pilgrimage stories. The word "pilgrim" comes from the Latin *peregrines*, which means "foreigner" or a person traveling from abroad or in a foreign place. It also means "wanderer."[1] Over time, the word "pilgrim" came to describe someone who traveled in response to a call of faith—that is, a traveler on a faith journey.

For this reason, Abraham is recognized as one of the first pilgrims in Scripture. God called him to pick up his belongings and journey to another land chosen by God. Centuries later, Abraham's descendants embarked on pilgrimage to the Promised Land from Egypt (the Exodus). Jesus himself traveled on pilgrimage to Jerusalem many times for the feasts, including with his parents as a child.

Today is no different. Christians continue to travel on faith journeys, and to embark on pilgrimages to the biblical lands is to embark on a venerable and cherished tradition of the Christian faith.

Why should I embark on a pilgrimage to the biblical lands?

The predominant reason to engage in such a journey is to deepen one's faith and personal relationship with Jesus Christ. That is the goal of every biblical pilgrimage. Other reasons include seeking inspiration or renewal in one's spiritual life, fulfilling the desire to walk where Jesus and other biblical figures did, and the yearning to gain a deeper understanding and knowledge of Scripture and salvation history. Regardless of your reason for embarking on a biblical pilgrimage, one thing is certain—few other experiences in life will be as rewarding or fulfilling as a biblical pilgrimage.

CHOOSING A BIBLICAL PILGRIMAGE

How can I choose the right biblical destination for me?

Five biblical lands most often visited by North Americans are Israel, Jordan, Egypt, Turkey, and Greece. Because it is fairly impractical to explore each of these destinations on one single trip, you will need to decide which countries you will visit. Because of the distance involved, your choice in most cases comes down to visiting either the areas of Greece and Turkey or the lands of Israel, Jordan, and Egypt.

With that in mind, here are the four guidelines to use when deciding which biblical travel destinations are right for you:

- desire to visit sites related to the Old Testament
- desire to visit sites related to the Gospels and life of Jesus
- desire to visit sites related to the New Testament
- desire to visit sites related to the Bible "as a whole"

If your interest lies mostly with the Old Testament, Egypt is an excellent option, along with Israel and Jordan. If your desire is primarily to touch the ground upon which Jesus walked, then consider a trip to Israel and Jordan. If you wish to explore the sites of the New Testament and those related to the missionary journeys of the apostle Paul, then Turkey and Greece are your calling. If you want to experience the whole Bible and are willing to take two trips, you might consider taking one trip to Israel, Jordan, and Egypt and then take a second trip to Turkey and Greece.

What are the advantages and disadvantages of visiting the biblical lands?

Advantages

- receiving deep emotional joy (and sometimes healing) by being where Jesus walked
- closer, more personal relationship with Jesus Christ
- increased knowledge of the Bible
- experience of biblical (and Middle Eastern) culture
- greater understanding of salvation history
- clearer picture of biblical geography
- expanded knowledge of the Jewish faith (which Jesus belonged to)
- tasting and enjoying Middle Eastern cuisine
- better insight into the challenges, struggles, and political issues of the Middle East
- enriched fellowship among fellow church or ministry members

Disadvantages

Although visiting the lands of the Bible is a dream come true for many, this is not a reason to ignore the potential challenges of such a trip. First, there is the cost. A trip to the Holy Land will cost several thousand dollars; however, the cost pales in comparison to the life- and faith-changing experiences one receives.

The second and possibly greatest disadvantage to a trip to the Holy Land is the changing security conditions within the destination. Unfortunately, it is a reality that a change in security conditions can jeopardize your travel plans at a moment's notice. For this reason, it is imperative to travel with reputable companies and always to purchase travel insurance.

Is it safe to travel in the biblical lands?

The question most often asked by Christians interested in visiting the biblical lands is: Is it safe for travel? To answer this, let's begin by stating that most people carry an inaccurate image of the biblical lands. The vast majority of tourism and pilgrimage sites in the biblical lands have a very long history of safety. As tourism remains a major pillar of the economy in this region, the countries go to great lengths to ensure the safety of all travelers. Millions of North Americans travel each year to the biblical lands and return home safely with wonderful memories and tremendous experiences.

The safety issue is best summarized by the many similar comments that I hear often from companies specializing in biblical trips: Our greatest challenge with Holy Land trips is not ensuring the safety and security of our groups but rather educating and informing travelers to the actual conditions of the destination and how safe it really is. We hear over and over again that travelers feel very safe during their journeys and they are very happy nobody talked them out of embarking on such a life-changing experience.

With the above said, before embarking on any trip to biblical lands or anywhere in the world, you should always do your homework and become a well-informed traveler or group leader so that you will make the right decisions when it comes to planning, preparing, and choosing a trip.

What is the average biblical trip length?

Most biblical trips are one to two weeks in length. Shorter trips of seven to ten days typically involve visiting one or two countries, while longer trips of eleven to fourteen days will often include visits to at least two countries.

How much does a biblical pilgrimage cost?

The cost of a biblical pilgrimage can vary based on the type of company you are traveling with, airfare arrangements, quality of accommodations, number of meals, and other expenses such as activities or events. An estimated cost for a typical biblical lands trip including airfare from New York (or your hometown) ranges from about $2,000 to $4,000. In general, an average trip is about ten days and costs roughly $3,000. Although it's very hard to give an exact figure, an estimated average per day cost for a biblical land trip is in the range of $200 to $300. This depends, however, upon the factors discussed above, including your own personal spending habits and the prevailing domestic and worldwide economic conditions.

What does the cost of an escorted tour to the biblical lands include?

A biblical lands trip through an escorted tour operator or travel agent costs $2,000 to $4,000 and often includes:

- round-trip airfare from a New York-area airport (and sometimes the airfare from your hometown airport as well)
- accommodations: first-class or superior tourist class
- meals: breakfast and most dinners daily
- touring by first-class, air-conditioned motor coach
- services of a professional tour director and local guides
- sightseeing: admission (entrance) fees to key or important sights
- airport transfers at your destination
- hotel taxes
- porterage (luggage handling)
- "goodies," such as flight bag and touring wallet, from the travel company

What costs are typically not included in a biblical lands escorted tour?

These are the costs most often not included when purchasing a trip from a travel company or agency:

- airfare from your airport to New York area airport
- lunches, snacks, and beverages
- tips to your tour director, local guides, driver, and hotel personnel (estimated total per day is $5–$10)
- airport taxes (estimated cost is $200–$500)
- travel insurance (estimated cost is $100–$200)
- personal items and souvenirs

PREPARING FOR YOUR BIBLICAL PILGRIMAGE

Should I travel independently or with a group to the biblical lands?

Before you make any travel preparations, the first question you need to ask yourself is whether you will travel independently or with a group. There are a few exceptions, but it is highly recommended that most Christians travel with a group. There are many reasons for traveling with others, such as fostering greater fellowship, security issues, language barriers, great cultural differences, and the changing political climate.

If you choose to travel with a group, you will need to choose the type of group travel you want. The three most common group travel options are to join a trip scheduled by your own faith community, to join a trip scheduled by a travel company, and to lead your own group trip.

If you choose the first option, little planning is involved other than contacting the leader of your faith community trip and inquiring about the itinerary, price, dates, etc. In the second and third options, your primary trip preparation lies in choosing the right trip for you or your group. How can you do that? Contact one or more travel companies (or your favorite one) and ask for their brochure or list of biblical tours. After reviewing the itineraries, you simply choose the one that is best for you or your group. If you are the group travel leader and cannot find an itinerary that matches what you are looking for, you can often customize a trip.

What are the three most important trip components?

The three most important criteria to consider are budget, dates, and itinerary. Regarding the budget, you should determine what you are willing to spend on a trip. Remember, a budget should include not only the obvious costs such as airfare, hotels, meals, and sightseeing but also the often unforgotten or hidden costs such as airport taxes, tips (gratuities), insurance, health (vaccinations), souvenirs, and the like. As for dates, you should look at your calendar and find the month or period of the year that works best for you (or your group) regarding your availability for a trip. You should also keep in mind the ideal travel periods of each respective country (i.e., an ideal time to visit Egypt is spring or fall). Finally, you should develop a record of those biblical sites (found in this chapter) that you wish to visit. From this list, you can then either choose or design your ideal itinerary.

What should I ask a tour operator or travel agent?

- Do you offer both scheduled and customized Christian trips to the biblical lands?
- Does your company have a Web site and brochure so I can learn more about your organization and trips?
- How many years has your company been in business and operating trips to the biblical lands?
- What professional associations and organizations does your company belong to? (World Religious Travel Association [WRTA], National Tour Association [NTA], American Society of Travel Agents [ASTA], Cruise Lines International Association [CLIA], etc.)

- Does your company offer a consumer protection plan and/or general public liability insurance?
- What are your most popular biblical lands trips? Are there any special upcoming trips?
- Are there any discounts or savings programs I should be aware of?
- How can I earn a free trip as a group leader or organizer?
- What is the process of signing up for a trip with your company?
- Is there anything else I should know regarding my plans to embark on a biblical trip with your company?

How can I make the most of my biblical pilgrimage?

This may be the most important trip of your life. To make sure you are prepared, you'll want to:

- Choose the right biblical trip and time of year for visiting.
- Dress and pack appropriately; wear comfortable shoes.
- Take time to learn about the destination, culture, and maybe even the language you will be immersing yourself in and experiencing.
- Find out if any holidays or special events are taking place during your trip.
- Start a biblical pilgrimage study or discussion group with other travelers.
- From the moment you sign up for a trip, begin reading and reflecting on the Scripture passages that refer to the sites you will be visiting.
- Pray about your upcoming trip on a daily basis; get others to pray for your pilgrimage as well.
- Begin a travel journal several months prior to your trip; continue writing in it during and after your biblical pilgrimage.
- Do not carry the expectation that you must see everything.

Let God be your biblical pilgrimage guide

One of the keys to making the most of your biblical trip is to let God be your ultimate Guide in your travels. Let Him lead and direct you to the people and places He desires you to visit and experience. That also means handing over any challenges to Him as well, such as the airline's losing your luggage when you arrive. No matter what happens, remember that God is in control and has called you personally on a biblical pilgrimage to the Holy Land—just as He called Abraham and Moses on pilgrimage several millennia ago. To embark on a holy trip such as this is to respond to a great calling in faith.

Therefore hear, O Israel, and be careful to observe it, that it may be well with you, and that you may multiply greatly as the LORD God of your fathers has promised you—'a land flowing with milk and honey.'

DEUTERONOMY 6:3

Now after Jesus was born in Bethlehem of Judea in the days of Herod the king, behold, wise men from the East came to Jerusalem.

MATTHEW 2:1

CREDIT: ©ISTOCKPHOTO.COM/CLAUDIA DEWALD

Walk in the footsteps of Jesus in Israel.

Why should I visit?

Israel is the Promised Land of the Bible. It is home to several thousand years of Judeo-Christian history, events, and figures. Israel is not only the foundation of the Bible, but it is also its heart and soul. And, it is the land where the Savior of the world—Jesus Christ—was born, lived, died, and rose again. Israel is sacred land. Today, it is a dream of millions of Christians around the globe to visit Israel and follow in the footsteps of Jesus.

What can you expect on a trip to Israel? First and foremost, you will experience and discover most of the "Who's Who" and "Where's Where" in the Bible. You may also find that a lifetime of religious teaching and sermons come to life and take on a whole new meaning. Everything you've previously learned about the Christian faith becomes three-dimensional. What you've learned in church will take on a whole new meaning, from Abraham to Moses to the Israelites to King David to Solomon to the prophets to Caesar to Mary to Jesus to Pontius Pilate to the apostles. Best yet, after returning home from a trip to Israel, you will have renewed inspiration in life, an enlivened personal faith, and an enriched love for Jesus Christ.

If you have not yet been to Israel, wait no longer—make this the year you embark on the journey of a lifetime. Ask your pastor if he or she will lead a trip for your church or congregation. You might even consider serving as the leader or organizer of your group trip. There is no better way to experience fellowship than on a church trip to the Holy Land.

CONTACT INFORMATION FOR ISRAEL

Tourist Offices: Israel Ministry of Tourism, www.goisrael.com; Palestinian Ministry of Tourism and Antiquities, www.visit-palestine.com

Embassy: www.israelemb.org

Other Helpful Web Sites: Christian Information Center (Jerusalem), www.cicts.org; Franciscan Custody of the Holy Land, www.custodia.org; Bethlehem, www.bethlehem-city.org

What do I need to know?

Religion. About 75 to 80 percent of the population is Jewish, 15 percent is Muslim, and almost 2 percent is Christian. Islam is the predominant religion in the Palestinian Territories.

Language. Hebrew (biblical language) and Arabic are the official languages of Israel. English is widely spoken, especially in tourist areas. Many road and commercial signs are in Hebrew, Arabic, and English. Arabic is the language of the Palestinian Territories.

Climate. In general, Israel features a warm climate. Summers are long, warm, and dry, lasting from April through October. Winters are fairly mild and last from November through March; however, the hill regions such as Jerusalem can range from cool to cold during this time. Rainfall is heavier in the north, with the arid, desert south receiving very little precipitation. In short, the coastal and northern sections feature hot, dry summers and cool, rainy winters, while the southern and eastern regions have more desert-like conditions.

When to visit Israel. When thinking of the best time to visit Israel, you should consider four factors: weather, crowds, Christian holidays, and price. If you would like to visit Israel during the best weather months, consider the spring (April to May) or fall (September to October). You might also consider March and November when temperatures are still fairly mild, but there's a bit more rain. In terms of crowds, the busiest times are summer, and the fewest tourists are found in winter. Spring and fall bring fairly steady groups of tourists, but it's typically not overcrowded. Christian holidays are a very popular time to visit, especially Easter week. Winter typically offers the least expensive prices, yet not all tourist facilities are open, or they may be operating with limited hours. Summer tends to bring the highest prices.

Clothing. There are three simple keys to remember for travel clothes in Israel: casual, layered, and modest or conservative clothing (for religious sites). For the summer, dress lightly and prepare for warm temperatures. In the winter, bring an umbrella and warm clothing, especially for central and northern Israel. For spring and fall, dress in layers. It is a good idea to bring a light jacket for most times of the year. Women might consider bringing a shawl or scarf to wrap around their bare shoulders or legs (when wearing shorts). And don't forget a hat, sunglasses, and maybe some sunscreen.

ISRAEL TRAVEL PLANNING
Airport: Tel Aviv: www.iaa.gov.il/Rashat/en-US/Airports/BenGurion
Train: National rail service: www.israrail.org.il
Bus: Egged, www.egged.co.il (or www.egged.co.il/Eng); Dan Bus Company, www.dan.co.il; Metrodan, www.metrodan.com
Car (driving directions): EMap: www3.emap.co.il

Traveler's tip

The designation of Palestinian Territories refers primarily to those areas or regions, including the West Bank and Gaza Strip, that fall under the jurisdiction of the Palestinian Authority. Some of the Christian sites featured in this chapter are located in Palestinian Territories including Jerusalem, Bethlehem, Hebron, Ramallah, Nablus, Sebastia, Jordan River, Dead Sea, and Jericho.

A Never-To-Be-Forgotten Pilgrimage

I had a feeling that this pilgrimage was going to turn out to be one that falls in the category of "Never to Be Forgotten" and I was right. We saw and visited more historical and holy places than most come across in a lifetime. Jerusalem, Nazareth, Gethsemane, Caesarea, Mount Carmel, Cana, and Masada became real, not just places that I read about in the Bible. I can't for the life of me single out a specific place or happening which was the highlight of our pilgrimage because all of the Holy Land is a highlight. The Lord has been good to me; He has allowed me to travel and experience many places in this world. I know of no other journey, out of the ordinary experiences or destination of your dreams, that even comes close to a pilgrimage to the Holy Land. I earnestly believe that the journey opened wide my eyes and enhanced my appreciation of the Bible. It strengthened my faith and increased my love of Jesus Christ. It is this strengthened faith and love for our Savior that keeps urging me to return again and again to this truly Holy Land. —*Henry*

JERUSALEM: THE HOLY CITY

Now Jesus, going up to Jerusalem, took the twelve disciples aside on the road and said to them, "Behold, we are going up to Jerusalem, and the Son of Man will be betrayed to the chief priests and to the scribes; and they will condemn Him to death.

MATTHEW 20:17-18

Why should I visit?

Around 1000 BC, King David captured the city, brought the Ark of the Covenant here, and declared Jerusalem the capital of Israel. Several decades later, Solomon built the First Temple, which was demolished by Nebuchadnezzar in 586 BC, at the same

In Jerusalem, touch the sites where Jesus was crucified and resurrected;
pictured is the Church of the Holy Sepulchre.

time that he exiled the Jews to Babylon. In 538 BC the Jews returned, and in 445 BC the Second Temple was built.

About a hundred years later in 332, Alexander the Great captured the city, but in 167 BC the Jews gained independence. In AD 63, the tides changed again as the Romans captured Jerusalem (and ruled until AD 324). In 37 BC Herod the Great became king and subsequently enriched the city and Temple.

Almost forty years later, Jesus of Nazareth was born in Bethlehem. Because of the events of the subsequent thirty-three years, Jesus's life and ministry have become synonymous with Jerusalem. Throughout his life, Jesus made frequent journeys and pilgrimages here.

Jesus lived out his Passion in Jerusalem. During the last week of his life, he triumphantly entered the capital city on a donkey (celebrated today as Palm Sunday). Jerusalem became the site of the Last Supper (Passover Seder meal) on Mount Zion and was where he spent the night praying in the Garden of Gethsemane before being arrested. His trial before Pontius Pilate took place here, as did the verdict that he be executed by way of crucifixion. After being flogged, Jesus carried his cross along the Via Dolorsa (Way of the Cross) to the top of Calvary Golgotha where he was crucified and died. You know the rest of the story—and it happened here!

In subsequent centuries, Christians traveled to Jerusalem from throughout the Roman Empire to walk in the same places as Jesus did. In the fourth century, the mother of Emperor Constantine, Helena, embarked on a trip to Jerusalem. Soon thereafter she ordered the construction of churches in the area, including the Church of the Holy Sepulchre. In the remaining years and throughout the Middle Ages, Jerusalem served as the primary destination for Christian pilgrims.

Today, the story is no different. Jerusalem remains one of the holiest places on earth and a premier destination for Christians. Today, more than 2 million people each year visit the sites related to Jesus's life, death, and resurrection in Jerusalem.

What should I see and do?

The primary sites in Jerusalem for Christian visitors are listed below and are broken down by the various sections of Jerusalem.

The Christian Quarter and Church of the Holy Sepulchre

The Christian Quarter includes one of the holiest sites in Christendom—the Church of the Holy Sepulchre, the place where, according to many Christian traditions, Jesus died on the cross, was buried, and rose again.

- Church of the Holy Sepulchre: According to many Christian denominations, this is the actual site of Jesus's crucifixion and the empty tomb. Many Christian communities are represented here including Coptic, Greek Catholic, Greek Orthodox, Roman Catholic, Lutheran, and Russian Orthodox. Inside the church are Golgatha (Calvary) and Christ's tomb.
- Lutheran Church of the Redeemer: Many come here for the views from the bell tower—but you must climb the 177 steps first!
- Christian Quarter Road: The main shopping thoroughfare and market of religious items and handicrafts.

The Mount of Olives and Gethsemane

The Mount of Olives and Gethsemane are the sites of Jesus's final hours before his arrest and crucifixion. The best views of Jerusalem are from here as well—take your camera! Here are the other sites you can visit:

- The Mount of Olives summit offers spectacular panoramic views of Jerusalem.
- Church (Mosque) of the Ascension: According to one tradition, this is the place where Jesus ascended into heaven.
- Church of All Nations (Basilica of Agony): This church is built at the reputed site where Jesus prayed during the night of his agony.
- The Garden of Gethsemane: The garden is the place of Christ's arrest, leading to his crucifixion.
- Church of Mary Magdalene: This church was built in honor of Mary Magdalene, one of the first disciples to see the resurrected Christ.
- Pater Noster Church: Constructed over the site where Jesus is said to have taught the Lord's Prayer, the church features the Lord's Prayer in over 45 languages.
- Dominus Flevit Chapel (Our Lord Weeping): This chapel commemorates Jesus's weeping over Jerusalem.

Visit the Mount of Olives and Gethsemane, where Jesus prayed prior to his arrest in the garden.

- Cave of Gethsemane: The cave is the traditional site of Christ's betrayal by Judas.
- Tomb of the Virgin Mary: Sometimes called the Church of the Assumption, it is the reputed grave of Mary, the mother of Jesus.
- Mount of Olives Jewish Cemetery: One of the holiest cemeteries in Judaism, it rests on Mount Olivet.

The Temple Mount (Mount Moriah)

The Temple Mount is one of the holiest sites for the three monotheistic faiths of Christianity, Judaism, and Islam. Situated in the eastern section of the Old City, the First Temple and Second Temple were built at this site.

- The Dome of the Rock: The First and Second Temples stood here, and the Dome is erected over the site where, according to an ancient tradition, Abraham almost sacrificed his son.
- The Western Wall: The wall is part of the retaining wall that once supported the platform of the Second Temple. Today it is Judaism's holiest site. Jesus taught and worshiped in this area.
- The Mosque of Al Aqsa: This mosque is the third holiest shrine in Islam.

Muslim Quarter

- Monastery of the Flagellation: This monastery is built on the traditional site where Jesus was flogged.
- Convent of the Sisters of Zion: This convent is believed to be at the site of Pontius Pilate's judgment hall.

- The Via Dolorosa: According to tradition, the Via Dolorosa is the mile-long route Jesus took from Pontius Pilate's judgment hall (Convent of the Sisters of Zion) to Calvary-Golgatha (Church of the Holy Sepulchre).
- Church of Saint Anne: The church is believed to be built over the place where the grandparents of Jesus (Anne and Joachim) lived; the supposed remains of their house lie in the crypt.
- Saint Stephen's Gate: According to one tradition, this is where the first Christian martyr, Saint Stephen, was stoned to death.

The Citadel

- The Citadel: The Citadel, also commonly called the Tower of David, is a site of world prominence and serves as one of Jerusalem's best known landmarks. At this site, King Herod built a palace in 24 BC. Today the Citadel houses the Tower of David—Museum of the History of Jerusalem (www.towerofdavid.org.il).

Mount Zion

- Mount Zion: Revered by Christians, Jews, and Muslims alike, Mount Zion is believed to be the site of David's tomb and is synonymous with the final days of Christ.
- Cenacle or Hall of the Last Supper (Room of the Last Supper): The traditional site of the Upper Room where Jesus shared his last meal with his disciples, it is also where the Holy Spirit descended at Pentecost.
- King David's Tomb: Below the Room of the Last Supper is the site believed to house the tomb of King David.
- Church (or Crypt) of the Dormition Church: The church is built on the site where Mary, the mother of Jesus, "fell into eternal sleep."
- Lutheran Cemetery: This cemetary includes the burial site of Oscar Schindler, who became well known through the 1993 Hollywood movie *Schindler's List*.
- Saint Peter in Gallicantu: This church is built over the traditional site where Peter denied Jesus three times.

Modern Jerusalem and New City

- The Garden Tomb: Many Christian denominations believe this to be the authentic Calvary and tomb of Jesus.

- Israel Museum: Home to the Shrine of the Book, it houses the Dead Sea Scrolls.
- Yad Vashem: This is Israel's national museum of the Holocaust.
- Ein Kerem (also known as Ein Karem): Ein Kerem means the spring (ein) of the vineyard or olive grove (kerem). This site is the possible birthplace of John the Baptist. Both the Church of Saint John the Baptist and Church of the Visitation can be visited.

Bethany and Bethphage

Located on the eastern slope of the Mount of Olives, Bethany was the home of Mary, Martha, and Lazarus, as well as Simon the leper.

- Franciscan Church (of Lazarus): This church is built over what is believed to be the home of Lazarus, Martha, and Mary.
- Tomb of Lazarus: Near the church and down twenty-six steps is the tomb of Lazarus, where Jesus brought him back to life.
- Bethpage Church: The Franciscan monastery is located at the site where Jesus mounted his donkey for his triumphal entry into Jerusalem (on the first Palm Sunday).

Traveler's tip

Israel's weekly day of rest is Saturday, the Sabbath. As such, many services such as banks, businesses, and public institutions close from sundown on Friday through sunset on Saturday. Be sure to plan accordingly.

How much time should I spend?

You should plan anywhere from two to five days in Jerusalem. Many Christian groups spend about three or four days in Jerusalem and use the capital as a main city from which to embark on nearby daily excursions (such as to Masada and the Dead Sea).

How can I get there?

Location. Jerusalem is the capital of Israel and is located atop a mountain chain running through the center of the country. The Mediterranean Sea lies to the west, Egypt and the Red Sea to the south, Jordan to the east, and Lebanon and Syria to the north. The lowest point on earth (the Dead Sea) lies about fifteen miles east of Jerusalem.

By Plane. Israel's main airport, Ben Gurion International Airport, is located about nine miles south of Tel Aviv and thirty miles west of Jerusalem. The airport receives flights from about fifty airlines from around the world, including nonstop flights from North America. El Al is Israel's national airline.

By Train. Israel Railways provides service on two train routes: Tel Aviv north to Nahariyya (via Netanya, Haifa, Acre, etc.) and Tel Aviv south to Rehovot (via Kfar Chabad). You can catch the train to Jerusalem from Tel Aviv, but you must change in Beit Shemesh (disembark in Jerusalem at the Malha Station, then take a bus or taxi to city center). Similar to bus service, trains do not operate on the Sabbath or major holidays.

By Boat. Israel is accessible by ship via its ports of Haifa, Ashdod, Eilat, or the Tel Aviv Marina.

By Bus. The bus service is the primary means of public transportation in Jerusalem and throughout Israel. It is cheap, efficient, and goes to nearly all cities and towns. It's important to note that most bus lines do not operate on the Sabbath (Friday evening to Saturday evening). To reach the Palestinian city of Bethlehem, you must catch the bus from the Jerusalem bus station of Salah a-Din (near the Rockefeller Museum).

The following are the primary bus services in the country:

- Egged Bus Cooperative: operates most inter-city bus lines and urban services
- Dan Cooperative: services Tel Aviv
- Independent bus companies operate in Nazareth

By Car. As the capital of Israel, Jerusalem is easily accessible by car from throughout Israel, especially with its excellent road system and network. From the Ben Gurion International Airport, take Highway 1 to Jerusalem. The other road leading from the north into Jerusalem is the Ayalon Highway, Israel's only motorway. Driving in Israel is fairly easy due to its well marked roads and signage in English.

By Taxi. Taxis are widely available throughout Jerusalem and the country. If you would like to save money, one of the best options is to take a "sherut," a shared taxi (minivan) that carries up to ten people and is about half the cost of a private taxi. If you're trying to reach Jerusalem from the airport, the Nesher Company (Tel 02-623-1231; Fax 02-6241114) provides shared taxi service. Shared taxis are an excellent option if you're traveling to the Palestinian cities such as Bethlehem.

What lodgings are available?

Jerusalem has a wide selection of hotels ranging from the simple to five-star luxury. For a special experience you might consider staying at a Kibbutz Hotel (a kibbutz is a collective farm or settlement). Today the Kibbutz Hotels Chain (www.kibbutz.co.il) is Israel's largest network of hotels, holiday villages, and country lodgings. Through these accommodations, you get an insider's experience of kibbutz life. Many of these places can be found throughout Israel's countryside, while others are situated near historic, archaeological, and geographical sites. Some Christian denominations offer

Christian accommodations as well; prices are typically low to moderate. For more information about these lodgings, contact the Christian Information Center at www.cicts.org. For other accommodations throughout Israel, visit www.zimmeril.com.

It came to pass in those days that Jesus came from Nazareth of Galilee, and was baptized by John in the Jordan.

MARK 1:9

CREDIT: ISRAEL MINISTRY OF TOURISM

From the Church of the Beatitudes, view the Sea of Galilee and the area where Jesus spent much of his public ministry.

Why should I visit?

Aside from visiting Jerusalem, many Christian groups spend a good portion of their time in northern Israel. Many significant biblical cities and towns from Scripture can be visited in this area, with the Sea of Galilee being among the most prominent. Jesus spent much of his life in northern Israel including growing up in Nazareth and then preaching and ministering in Galilee. Today northern Israel not only offers the visiting Christian a plethora of places to visit related to Jesus and the Gospels but also provides one of the most beautiful and tranquil settings in Israel.

What can I see and do?

BETHSAIDA Although only ruins remain, Bethsaida (meaning "house of fishing") is a popular site along the Christian tour route. Located on the northeast coast of Galilee on the road to Caesarea Philippi, Bethsaida was the home of apostles Andrew and Philip and was where Jesus cured a blind man and fed five thousand through the miracle of the loaves and fishes. Jesus also rebuked the town for not receiving him. *(Matthew 11:21, Mark 6:45, Mark 8:22, Luke 9:10, Luke 10:13, John 1:44, John 12:21)*

BETH SHAN (BETH-SHEAN, BEIT-SHEAN, BET-SHAN, BET SHE'AN) Recognized as one of the major cities of the Decapolis (the ten prominent cities of ancient Rome), Beth Shan was an important city located on a main caravan route. Near this ancient city lies Mount Gilboa, the place where King Saul and his sons were killed by the Philistines; their bodies were then hanged from the city gates of Beth Shan. With many excavations and ruins to see, Beth Shan serves as one of Israel's most popular and important archaeological sites with its twenty levels of ancient settlements. While there, you can view or explore the Roman theater, streets, baths, mosaics, shops, columns, and church ruins. *(1 Samuel 31:8–13; 2 Samuel 21:12; 1 Kings 4:12)*

CAESAREA PHILIPPI (BANIAS/PANIAS) Caesarea Philippi (Caesarea of Philippi) is possibly the most northern point that Christ traveled, about 120 miles north of Jerusalem. Originally a worship site of the Greek god Pan, the city of Panias (Banias in Arabic) was later rebuilt, enlarged, and renamed by the son of King Herod (Philip). The center was renamed to Caesarea Philippi, to distinguish it from the port Caesarea. It is here that Peter identified Jesus as the Messiah. Although there are no major sites from the time of Jesus in the area to explore, most groups simply spend their time sightseeing the city. The ruins of the former Greek Shrine to Pan in the national park can be visited. *(Mark 8:27; Luke 9:18; Matthew 16:13)*

CANA (KEFER KANA) Cana is located just a few miles from Nazareth on the road to Tiberias. As one of the most visited Christian sites in northern Israel, Cana is the place of Jesus's first miracle when he changed water into wine at a wedding. In addition to exploring the site, you can visit the Cupola dedicated to Bartholomew (John 21:2), as well as the Roman Catholic and Greek Orthodox churches dedicated to the miracle. *(John 2:1–11, 4:46–54, 21:2)*

CHORAZIN With its ruins located just north of Capernaum, Chorazin is a hilltop community that Christ scolded for its unbelief. At the time it served as an important Jewish town. One of the area's best preserved ancient synagogues can be visited. *(Matthew 11:21; Luke 10:13)*

CAPERNAUM A must-see on every Christian tour itinerary, Capernaum served as the primary place of Jesus's ministry and teachings in the Galilee region. Many Gospel events and miracles took place here including Jesus's healing of the apostle Peter's mother-in-law. He gave the discourse on the Bread of Life while preaching in the local synagogue in

CREDIT: ©ISTOCKPHOTO.COM/EARTHMANDALA

Visit the ruins at Capernaum, where Jesus performed miracles.

Capernaum. The ruins and excavations of Capernaum can be visited, including a well-preserved ancient synagogue. Other sites include Saint Peter's Catholic Church, the Franciscan monastery, and the Greek Orthodox Church. *(Matthew 4:13; Mark 1:21–31; Luke 10:15; John 2:12)*

JORDAN RIVER The Jordan River is where Jesus was baptized by John the Baptist. Many other biblical events took place in or near the river including John the Baptist's preaching, Naaman being cured of his leprosy, and Elijah striking the waters to pass over it. Many Christians come here to be baptized in the same river where Jesus's baptism took place. Today the primary site to visit is at Kibbutz Kinneret (Yardenit), the point at which the Jordan flows out of the Sea of Galilee. The original baptism site (Kasr Al-Yahud) is only accessible a few times a year by visitors. *(Joshua 3; 2 Samuel 17:22; 2 Kings 2; Jeremiah 12:5; Matthew 3:5–6; Mark 1:9; John 1:28)*

MEGIDDO Megiddo was a royal city of the Canaanite tribe and served as the site of several biblical battles. King Solomon built a large fortified city here, the ruins of which can be visited. Today it is best known as Armageddon, the final biblical battle site between "good and evil." *(Joshua 12:21; Judges 1:27; 1 Kings 1 9:15; 2 Kings 9:27; 2 Chronicles 35:22)*

MOUNT OF BEATITUDES Integral to any Christian tour is a visit to the Mount of Beatitudes, the place of Jesus's famed sermon (often referred to as the Sermon on the Mount). On a hilltop perch overlooking Galilee, the Mount of Beatitudes, with its church and gardens, offers wonderful views of Capernaum, Tabgha, and the surrounding area. *(Matthew 5:1)*

MOUNT CARMEL Overlooking the Mediterranean, Mount Carmel is best known as the site where the prophet Elijah battled the prophets of Ba'al. Other biblical events that took place here include Saul's setting up a monument after his victory over Amalek. Along with seeing the bustling city of Haifa, Christian tourists can visit Mount Carmel and Elijah's cave. Other sites to consider visiting include the Stella Maris Church and Monastery (Schola Prophetarun), as well as the Muhraqa, the Carmelite monastery. *(Joshua 12:22;1 Kings 18:19–20; Isaiah 35:2; 1 Samuel 15:12)*

MOUNT TABOR A number of Old Testament events took place at or around Mount Tabor; however, the site is most famous for being the place where, according to tradition, Jesus transfigured himself before the apostles Peter, James, and John. Afterward, he conversed with Moses and the prophet Elijah. At the top of Mount Tabor is the (Catholic)

Church of the Transfiguration and its nearby monastery. The summit provides breathtaking views of the Sea of Galilee and Nazareth. *(Joshua 19:12, 22; Judges 4:6—14; Matthew 17:1—13; Luke 9:28—36)*

NAZARETH Because it is where Jesus spent his childhood, Nazareth is one of the most beloved New Testament towns from the Bible. He lived here for about thirty years with his parents Joseph and Mary before embarking on his ministry. Jesus also preached in his home synagogue. Another "must" for Christian tours, Nazareth offers a number of sites to see and explore including the Basilica of the Annunciation, Church of Saint Gabriel, Mary's Well, Synagogue Church, and the Leap of the Lord—where the local population tried to throw Jesus off a cliff. *(Matthew 2:22—23; Mark 1:9; Luke 1:26; John 1:45—46; Acts 2:22)*

SEA OF GALILEE The highlight of many Christian trips to northern Israel includes a visit to the Sea of Galilee. Many prominent Gospel events took place here including Jesus calming the storm, walking on water, multiplying the loaves and fishes, the large catch of fish, and the calling of Peter, Andrew, James, and John to be fishers of men. Jesus also appeared here after his resurrection and commissioned the apostle Peter to spread the Good News. With dozens of holy sites and sea-shore shrines to visit and explore, the Sea of Galilee has so much to offer for the visiting Christian. One of the most popular activities is sailing across the Sea of Galilee just as Jesus did almost two thousand years ago. Many Christian groups stay overnight in Tiberas, the largest city on the Sea of Galilee and one of the four holy cities of Judaism. Nearby at Ginossar and the Yigal Allon Museum is a two-thousand-year-old fishing boat, which was discovered during the drought of 1985. *(Matthew 4:18; Mark 3:7—9; Luke 5:1—11; John 6:1)*

TABGHA Located in the Sea of Galilee area, Tabgha is the traditional site of Jesus's feeding the five thousand people through the multiplying of loaves and fishes. He also appeared here after his resurrection. Several sites to visit here are the Church of the Multiplication of the Loaves and Fishes, the Octagon Pool, and the Church of Saint Peter. *(Mark 6:30—44; Matthew 14:13—21)*

TIBERIAS Considered one of the four holiest cities of Judaism, Tiberias is the most prominent city along the Sea of Galilee. The son of Herod the Great, Herod Antipas, built the spa town to honor the Roman Caesar Tiberias (who ruled from AD 14-37). Most Christian visitors to northern Israel stay overnight in Tiberias. *(John 6:1, 23)*

Other places you may wish to visit in northern Israel include:

ACRE (AKKO) Considered one of the oldest cities in the world, Acre was known in the Old Testament as Accho or Acco. The apostle Paul stopped in Acre briefly while traveling to Jerusalem. In later years, it served as the Crusaders' last capital of the Holy Land. Some of their buildings and structures can still be visited. *(Judges 1:31)*

EN DOR Located near Mount Tabor, En Dor is home to the witch that King Saul visited when the Lord did not answer him. Today you can explore the local archaeological museum. *(1 Samuel 28:7–25)*

HAZOR (HATZOR) An ancient city originally referred to in nineteenth-century BC Egyptian writings, Hazor was captured by Joshua and the Israelites. In later years, Solomon rebuilt it and made it one of his chariot cities. Today you can view Israel's largest tell (archaeology hill or site), which exposes five thousand years of history and civilization. *(Joshua 11)*

HORNS OF HITTIN Although not mentioned in Scripture, the Horns of Hittin played a key role in the history of Christianity. In AD 1187, Saladin defeated the Crusaders which marked the end of the first Crusader kingdom in the Holy Land and the beginning of Muslim influence. (Note: If you'd like to watch a Hollywood movie about this story, see the 2005 film *Kingdom of Heaven*).

JEZREEL VALLEY Jezreel Valley divides Israel from east to west and, since antiquity, has served as a land bridge for armies ranging from the Pharaohs of Egypt to the Israelites to the Crusaders to the Turks. Many other biblical events also took place here, especially from the books of Kings. *(Judges 6:1–33)*

KISHON RIVER Also known as the "waters of Megiddo," the Kishon River is located at the foot of Mount Carmel and is the site where Elijah had the prophets of Ba'al killed. *(Judges 5:21; 1 Kings 18:40)*

MAGDALA (MIGDAL, MAGADAN) Located on the western shore of the Sea of Galilee, this small town is the birthplace of Mary Magdalene. *(Matthew 15:39; Luke 8:2; John 20:1)*

MOUNT GILBOA Two Scripture events took place here: (1) Saul and his sons were killed by the Philistines, and (2) David wrote and sang a canticle about the deaths of Saul and his sons. The area earned international attention when *TIME* magazine recognized it as being one of the most beautiful places on earth. *(1 Samuel 31:1–2; 2 Samuel 1:19–27)*

SEPPHORIS (SEPHORIS, ZIPPORI) Sepphoris (Zippori in Hebrew) is believed to be the hometown of Jesus's grandparents, Joachim and Anne, as well as his mother Mary. Today you can visit the Franciscan Church of Saint Anne, the grandmother of Jesus.

Why should I visit?

Bethlehem and Jerusalem are not the only cities in central Israel that figure in the life of Jesus. Jericho is another prominent biblical city in the area and is, in fact, one of the oldest cities in the world. Most Christian groups spend a majority of their time in northern and central Israel.

CREDIT: ©ISTOCKPHOTO.COM/PETER SPIRO

Explore Bethlehem, Jericho, and Hebron (seen here) in Israel.

What can I see and do?

BETHLEHEM Bethlehem is one of Christianity's most famous and beloved cities. Located in the Palestinian Territories, Bethlehem is home to several prominent Scripture events including Jesus's birth. It is also where Jacob's wife Rachel died while giving birth to Benjamin, where King David was born and anointed by Samuel, and the place where Herod ordered all new baby boys to be put to death. The prophet Micah foretold that the Messiah would be born in Bethlehem. Just south of Bethlehem are the Pools of Solomon, which have provided water to Jerusalem for three thousand years and are considered an engineering feat of their time.

There is much to see in Bethlehem. Along with just being in the presence of Jesus's birth city, you can visit the Church of the Nativity (with a large star marking the traditional birthplace of the baby Jesus), the Chapel of the Milk Grotto, Shepherds' Fields (the caves are in nearby Bet Sahur), and Rachel's Tomb. Bethlehem is only five miles south of Jerusalem. *(Genesis 35:18–19; 1 Samuel 16; Micah 5:2; Matthew 2; Luke 2)*

CAESAREA Caesarea, established by Herod the Great in 25 BC, was the capital of the Roman province of Judea during Jesus's life. Biblically speaking, it was the home of Cornelius (Acts 10:1) and the place where the first gentiles converted. It was also in Caesarea where Pontius Pilate lived, where the apostles Paul and Philip preached, and where Paul spent two years in prison prior to being shipped off to Rome. Caesarea offers a number of sites to explore, including its hippodrome, Crusader fortress, and ancient Roman theater with its outstanding acoustics. *(Acts 8–12, 21, 23)*

VALLEY OF ELAH The Valley of Elah is most famous for being the place where David defeated Goliath. You can put your hand in the very same creek from which David selected his rock that killed Goliath. *(1 Samuel 17:1–2)*

HEBRON-KIRYAT ARBA One of the four holy cities of Israel, Hebron is home to several prominent Old Testament events and places including the place where Abraham came to live, where he bought a cave as the burial site of his family, where David was anointed King of Israel and reigned for seven years, and where the tombs of Abraham, Sarah, Isaac, Leah, Jacob, and Rebecca are located. The main attractions here are the nearby communities of Kiryat Arba and the Machpelah Cave, which is the most ancient Jewish site in the world and the second holiest place for Jewish people after the Temple Mount in Jerusalem. *(Genesis 23, 25:8–10; Joshua 10:36-37; 2 Samuel 2:1–4)*

JERICHO Known as "the city of palm trees," Jericho is considered one of the oldest—if not the oldest—cities on earth. Moses viewed Jericho from Mount Nebo, and Jericho was the first city captured by the Israelites after crossing into the Promised Land. Most Christian groups visit Elisha's Church and the archaeological tell of ancient Jericho. Some tour groups also visit the nearby monasteries such as the Monastery of Saint John (Kasr El-Yahud). *(Joshua 2–6; 2 Kings 2)*

SHECHEM The biblical city of Shechem (present-day Nablus) is best known as the place where God appeared to Abraham and said He was giving this land to his descendants. It is also home to other biblical events and people. It is the location of Joseph's tomb and is also where Abraham pitched his tent when passing through. Jacob purchased a plot of land here (Jacob's Well), and Joshua renewed his covenant with God. The Samaritan people originated here, and Jesus met the Samaritan woman at Jacob's Well and spoke of living waters. Key sites to visit include Jacob's Well, the tomb of Joseph, Canaanite city walls, El Birith Temple (Judges 9:46), and the Crusader church. *(Genesis 12:6–7, 33:18–19; Joshua 24; 1 Kings 12)*

Other places you may wish to visit in central Israel include:

ABU GHOSH The Ark of the Covenant laid here (in former Kiriat Yearim) for twenty years before King David brought it to Jerusalem. Today you can visit the Benedictine Monastery of the Ark and the Church of Notre Dame, said to be built where the Ark of the Covenant once resided. *(Genesis 23:2)*

APHEK (AFEK; ANTIPATRIS) Two key biblical events took place here: the Philistines captured the Ark of the Covenant at Aphek, and the apostle Paul passed through here while en route to Caesarea for trial. *(1 Samuel 4:1–11; Acts 23:31)*

ANATHOTH Anathoth (today's Anata) was the birthplace and hometown of the prophet Jeremiah. *(Jeremiah 1:1)*

ASHDOD Recognized as one of the five Philistine cities, Ashdod is where the Ark of the Covenant was brought by the Philistines after they battled the Israelites. The apostle Philip baptized the Ethiopian near here. *(1 Samuel 5:1)*

BETHEL Meaning "House of God," Bethel served as one of the royal cities of the Canaanites. It's possibly best known for being the place where Jacob dreamed of the ladder. *(Genesis 28:19, 31:13; Judges 21:19; 1 Kings 13:11; 2 Kings 2:2; Joshua 12:16)*

BET SAHUR Located between Jerusalem and Bethlehem, Bet Sahur (Shepherds' Fields) is where an angel of the Lord appeared to the shepherds and told them about the birth of Jesus. *(Luke 2:8–21)*

DOTHAN Dothan is where Joseph found his brothers tending their flocks (only to be sold into slavery by his brothers), and it is where the Syrian army tried to capture Elisha, only to be captured by him instead. *(Genesis 37:17; 2 Kings 6:13)*

EMMAUS Emmaus is of course the site of the well-known biblical passage where Jesus met the disciples "on the road to Emmaus" and opened their eyes to Scripture. The exact location has not yet been determined. *(Luke 24:13–35)*

GERIZIM AND EBAL Israel gathered together on the Mounts of Gerizim and Ebal. In the Book of Deuteronomy, a blessing is placed on Mount Gerizim and a curse on Mount Ebal. Much of Israel can be viewed from the summit of Mount Gerizim. *(Joshua 8:33; Deuteronomy 11:29–30)*

JAFFA As part of Israel's largest metropolis, Jaffa (modern-day Joppa) appears in Scripture several times. It is the place where the Cedars of Lebanon were unloaded prior to being shipped to Jerusalem for the building of the Temple, and it is also where Jonah left for Tarshish, where Tabitha was healed by Peter, and where Peter had a vision prompting him to expand his ministry to the gentiles. *(2 Chronicles 2:15–16; Acts 9–10)*

JUDEAN DESERT One of the more popular sites in this area is the "modern" Inn of the Good Samaritan between Jericho and Jerusalem. Other places to visit include the local monasteries. *(Luke 10:30–37)*

SAMARIA (SEBASTE, SAMRON) Better known as Samaria in biblical times, the city played a prominent role in the Book of Kings. For one, it was here that King Omri originally built Samaria on a hill in 885 BC, which became a capital of the northern Jewish nation of Israel. Many Jews avoided traveling through Samaria from Galilee to Judea (or vice versa) due to the poor reputation and feelings for Samarians, but it was here that Jesus spoke to the Samarian woman about the living water. It is also here where the Holy Spirit was poured out, resulting in the conversion of the Samaritans. Today there is much to see including the ruins of the ancient Samaria with its theater, the Roman Forum, an acropolis, and the Temple of Augustus. *(1 Kings 16:23–28; 2 Kings 17:5–6; Luke 17:11; John 4; Acts 8:5–25)*

SHARON VALLEY Renowned for its majesty and beauty, Sharon Valley is a wild, fertile plain ideal for grazing sheep and cattle. Measuring about ten miles wide by thirty miles long, the area runs from the mountains of Mount Carmel in the north to Tel Aviv. Isaiah 35:2 speaks of the Sharon Valley as blooming with vegetation and as the "excellence of Carmel and Sharon." *(Isaiah 35:2)*

SOUTHERN ISRAEL: THE DEAD SEA AND OTHER CHRISTIAN SITES

Why should I visit?

Southern Israel is significant not only scripturally but also geographically and historically. Geographically speaking, the Dead Sea, the lowest place on earth, is located here, and historically speaking, southern Israel is important because it is where the Jews defended themselves against the Romans.

What should I see and do?

THE DEAD SEA At more than one thousand three hundred feet below sea level, the Dead Sea is a geographical wonder because it is the lowest place on earth. Referred to as the Salt Sea in Scripture, the Dead Sea is located near the southern end of the Jordan Valley. Sodom and Gomorrah are believed to have been located at its southern edge. A majority of Christian tours to Israel include a visit to the Dead Sea. Many people take the opportunity to get in the water and float on it! *(Genesis 14:3; Deuteronomy 3:17; Joshua 3:16)*

MASADA During the time of Jesus, King Herod built a fortress atop Masada ("Masada" means fortress in Hebrew). A UNESCO World Heritage Site today, Masada is the place where the Jews held out against the Romans in AD 73 before committing mass suicide. In addition to visiting the top of Masada, you can visit the Kibbutz Almog with its Museum of the Scrolls, the excavations of Qumran, and David's Gorge at Ein Gedl.

CREDIT: ©ISTOCKPHOTO.COM/NOEL POWELL

Climb to the top of Masada, which overlooks the Dead Sea.

NEGEV DESERT The Negev Desert is mentioned several times in Scripture as the place where the Israelites wandered in the desert. Most Christian groups simply drive the biblical desert. *(Genesis 20:1, 24:62; Isaiah 30:6)*

Other places you may wish to visit in southern Israel include:

BEERSHEBA (BEERSHEVA) Both Abraham and Isaac resided here. Abraham made a covenant here with Abimelech, and Isaac dug a well here. *(Genesis 26:33)*

EZION GEBER The children of Israel camped here on their way from Mount Sinai. Today the modern resort city of Eilat lies here. *(Numbers 33:35-36)*

Then the LORD spoke to Moses that very same day, saying: "Go up this mountain of the Abarim, Mount Nebo, which is in the land of Moab, across from Jericho; view the land of Canaan, which I give to the children of Israel as a possession."

DEUTERONOMY 32:48–49

This all happened at Bethany on the other side of the Jordan, where John was baptizing.

JOHN 1:28 (NIV)

CREDIT: JORDAN TOURISM BOARD NORTH AMERICA

Discover the wilderness where John the Baptist preached and the river where Jesus was baptized.

Why should I visit?

Jordan is synonymous with the lands of the Bible and plays a prominent role in Scripture from the Old Testament to the New Testament. Only here can you find the lives and stories of Abraham, Job, Jacob, Moses, Joshua, Ruth, Elijah, Elisha, David, John the Baptist, Jesus, and the apostle Paul all tied together in one place. Only here can you stand at the very same site where Moses viewed the Promised Land, walk in the wilderness where John the Baptist preached, and stand in the river where Jesus was baptized.

This is the land where the "Plains of Moab" existed for centuries, where Moses led the Israelites before entering the Promised Land, where Jacob wrestled with the angel of God, where Lot's wife turned into a pillar of salt, where Job suffered (and then was rewarded), and where Elijah ascended to heaven.

Jesus himself spent time in Jordan, preaching and healing. This is where he cured a man by sending his evil spirits into a herd of swine then plunging them into the sea. It is also where he called his first disciples and where the Trinity was first revealed during Jesus's baptism. For these reasons and more, Jordan is called by some as the "cradle" of Christianity.

Today, many of the same sites and places spoken about in the Bible can be visited and explored. With its rich biblical history beginning in Genesis, Jordan offers one of the best places to begin one's biblical lands trip. As the NBC *Today Show* travel editor Peter Greenberg states, "A visit to Jordan transforms the pages of the Bible into a living, breathing world, where you can walk, touch and live the places that the printed word alone can't convey." To miss Jordan would be to miss large segments of Scripture. That is why Jordan continues to remain a top travel choice for Christian tour groups and individual travelers.

What do I need to know?

Religion. The country is predominantly Muslim (more than 90 percent Sunni Muslim). About 5 percent of the population is Christian, many of whom are Greek Orthodox.

Language. Arabic is the official language, yet English is widely spoken especially in tourist areas.

Climate. Jordan features a Mediterranean and desert climate throughout most of the country. Summers are generally very hot and dry (except evenings can be cool in some places, so be sure to bring a sweater or shawl). Winters are wet and considered cool to cold in parts of Jordan (a good coat is usually a must). Spring and fall have quite pleasant temperatures. Rainfall across the country ranges from two inches in the desert to more than thirty inches in the northern hills.

When to visit Jordan. Jordan is a place that can be visited any time during the year, even in winter. Spring and fall are wonderful times to visit Jordan because the weather is quite enjoyable, the crowds are smaller, and airfare to Jordan is typically less expensive. Although Easter can have more crowds, it is a magnificent time to visit because of the Holy Week events and activities. Summer can be quite warm and a little more crowded.

Clothing. As Jordan is a predominately Muslim country, both men and women should dress modestly or conservatively, particularly in rural areas. Although many Jordanian women cover their hair, arms, and legs (per the local dress customs), Western women do not have to abide by this; however, it is strongly recommended that you not wear revealing clothing. Shorts are not typically worn by locals but are common for tourists. It is okay to wear a swimsuit at designated places such as a hotel pool.

Transportation. Jordan's capital city of Amman serves as the country's main international airport. Royal Jordanian, the national airline, flies direct between Amman and numerous destinations throughout the Middle East and around the world, including Chicago, Montreal, New York, and Toronto. A ferry/bus service runs from Amman to Cairo, and a boat service runs between Aqaba (Jordan) and Nuweiba (Egypt). In Jordan the most common method of transportation is by bus—JETT Bus Company being among the most prominent (book reservations in advance with JETT). Another option is the large number of private or charter bus companies that operate throughout the country. There is only one passenger train (Hejaz Railway), so rail service is the least used method of transportation. Taxis are inexpensive and often the most convenient form of transportation in Jordan. As Jordan is a relatively small country, getting around is fairly easy.

HELPING JORDAN THROUGH TOURISM

By visiting Jordan as a tourist, you are doing much more than just exploring sacred sites and archeological treasures. You are helping build the local economy of the people and raising their standard of living. Tourism lies at the heart of the national economy of Jordan. It contributes almost one billion dollars to the country's economy and accounts for approximately 10 percent of its gross domestic product (GDP). As the country's largest export sector and second largest private sector employer, tourism plays a vital role in Jordan's economy, and Jordan is seeking to double its visitors in the near future. By visiting Jordan, know that you are contributing to the well-being of its people and the country.

JORDAN TRAVEL PLANNING

Airport: Amman www.jcaa.gov.jo/Airports/queen_alia.htm
Train: Jordan Hejaz Railways, www.jhr.gov.jo
Boat: AB Maritime, www.abmaritime.com.jo
Bus: JETT Bus Company (no Web site), Telephone (962) 6-562-2430 or Fax (962) 6-560-5005
Car: Jordan features a very good and expanding road system. As the country is small, getting around the country and finding towns and places is relatively easy. Road signs are in English and Arabic.

The Difference between Seeing the Movie in Black and White and Seeing It in Color

I'm delighted with just how historically rich Jordan is—coming to Jordan is the difference between seeing the movie in black and white and seeing it in color. Suddenly, the images are sharper. Being able to stand on the hill where most likely John the Baptist lived and baptized and where Elijah walked is powerful. I'll never forget that. —*Marshall Shelley, Editor,* Christian History *(Christianity Today publication)*

Jordan Should Not Be Overlooked

While Christians and Jews often think of the Holy Land in terms of Israel and Palestine, the country of Jordan should not be overlooked. Those who want to walk where Jesus walked or to tread the path that Moses blazed can find food for their souls in Jordan, Holy Land East. —*Tony Cartledge, Editor of* Biblical Recorder *and ordained pastor*

BETHANY BEYOND THE JORDAN

Then Jesus came from Galilee to John at the Jordan to be baptized by him.

MATTHEW 3:13

Why should I visit?

What would it be like to stand in the wilderness where John the Baptist preached or in the waters where Jesus was baptized? If you visit Bethany Beyond the Jordan, you can share in these two powerful and emotional experiences. Considered one of the most sacred sites of Christianity, Bethany Beyond the Jordan receives more than 1 million pilgrims each year who come to wade in the very same waters that Jesus did. In fact, many Christians consider only Jerusalem and the Church of the Nativity in Bethlehem as holier places than the baptism site of Jesus.

However, that is not all that Bethany Beyond the Jordan offers. The area is also home to several other prominent biblical events including the prophet Elijah's ascent into heaven. It is here where Elijah parted the Jordan River, walked across it with his anointed successor, the prophet Elisha, and then ascended into heaven in a chariot of fire. Today the hill associated with this Old Testament event is known Elijah's Hill (commonly referred to in Arabic as Jabal Mar Elias or Tell Mar Elias). Christian pilgrims dating back to the fourth century are known to have visited the sacred site, and their writings about Elijah's Hill exist to this day.

Today Bethany Beyond the Jordan is home to the twenty-five acre Baptism Archaeological Park, one of the best preserved and eco-friendly Christian sites in the Holy

CREDIT: JORDAN TOURISM BOARD NORTH AMERICA & JIM PITTS

Wade in the waters at Bethany Beyond the Jordan; be baptized for the first time.

Land. The area offers the Christian visitor a chance to stand in the very same places where Jesus, John the Baptist, Joshua, Elijah, and Elisha all once stood.

CONTACT INFORMATION FOR BETHANY BEYOND THE JORDAN

General Information: The Jordan Ministry of Tourism & Antiquities, www.tourism.jo/Baptism_Site/Baptism_Site.asp; The Jordan Tourism Board, www.seejordan.org

The Baptism Site of Jesus Christ: Bethany Beyond the Jordan, JORDAN

Tel: (962) 5-3590360

Fax: (962) 5-3590361

E-mail: baptismsite@wanadoo.jo

Web Site: www.baptismsite.com

Other Helpful Information: Volunteer vacations, also known as voluntourism, are a growing segment for travel opportunities to Jordan. For more information visit the Jordan Tourist Board Web site.

What should I see and do?

The twenty-five-acre Baptism Archaeological Park features a visitor center and seventeen Christian sites, about half of which are located in the vicinity of Elijah's Hill (near the entrance of the Park) and the other half located near the Jordan River on the lower basin of Bethany Beyond the Jordan. The most popular activity for the visitor is wading in the baptismal waters. The following is a description of what you will find at the Baptism Archaeological Park.

THE BAPTISMAL WATERS AND POOLS

The number one reason most people come to Bethany Beyond the Jordan is to immerse themselves in the same baptismal waters as Jesus did two thousand years ago. Tour groups visiting the park usually hold religious services at the Jordan River or the several baptism pools located throughout the site. Near the church is the access point to the Jordan River, where guests can wade, get baptized, or simply enjoy the waters. Connected to this entrance of the Jordan River is a baptismal font where groups can pray before entering the water. There are also several other baptismal pools located in the park; the water in all the baptismal pools is channeled from the Jordan River.

In addition to enjoying the Jordan River, visitors can explore the following sixteen archaeological and historical sites of Bethany Beyond the Jordan:

SOUTHERN SIDE OF WADI AL-KHARRAR
(ON OR NEAR THE VICINITY OF ELIJAH'S HILL)

1. Elijah's Hill: One of the most popular sites of the park is Elijah's Hill. This is where, according to tradition, the prophet Elijah ascended into heaven. A sanctuary lies atop it, the same one that has attracted pilgrims for centuries. In AD 570, the Piacenza pilgrim left behind the following description: "This is the place where . . . Elijah was taken up (to heaven)."
2. Rhotorios Monastery: This Byzantine monastery dates from the fifth to sixth century.
3. Northern Church: The Northern Church's main attraction is the mosaic floor.
4. Western Church: The Western Church features several interesting ruins including the semi-circular apse and lamp niches carved into the walls.
5. Prayer Hall: Considered the oldest building within the park, the facility is believed to have once served as an ancient place of prayer.
6. Water System: Constructed during the fifth to sixth century, the water system includes a pool, cistern, and basins.
7. The Pools: Ancient baptismal pools dating from the third to fourth century. Steps leading into the pool can be viewed, as can the channels that carried the water.
8. The Church of John Paul II: One of the original churches of the area dating from the fifth to sixth century, it was renamed to commemorate Pope John Paul II's visit to Bethany Beyond the Jordan in 2000.

NORTHERN SIDE OF WADI AL-KHARRAR
(NEAR THE BANKS OF THE JORDAN RIVER)

9. The Pilgrims Station: Built between the fifth and sixth centuries for the growing number of visiting pilgrims, this ancient inn once featured guestrooms, an open courtyard, and a water pool.
10. Ancient Pool: Located near the banks of the Jordan River, this pool of antiquity once served as the largest baptism pool in the area and could accommodate up to three hundred people.
11. John the Baptist Spring: For centuries this spring served as a source of drinking refreshment for pilgrims, as well as a place of baptisms.
12. Cave Cells: Built into the upper layers of the cliffs, these caves were once the residential site for monks, which included special cave prayer rooms and niches.
13. Laura: The Laura is a foundation of collective ancient (individual) hermit cells located near Elijah's Hill. Monks once prayed, lived, and provided hospitality services to visiting pilgrims here.
14. Saphsaphas: Filled with many stories and traditions, the Saphsaphas feature caves that were turned into churches and living cells for hermits.

15. Site of Saint Mary of Egypt: According to tradition, this saint spent almost fifty years of her life in prayer, penance, and fasting here.
16. John the Baptist Church: Recent archaeological discoveries unveiled the ruins of a sixth-century church; today the area is believed to be where early Christians built a church at the traditional site of Jesus's baptism.

CHURCHES AND SERVICE INFORMATION

Christian tour groups that come here usually hold their own baptismal or worship services, which must be arranged in advance with the Baptism Archaeological Park (by themselves or through their tour operator/travel agent).

How much time should I spend?

You should plan on spending a minimum of half a day to allow time for both wading in the Jordan River and visiting other key sites at the Baptism Archaeological Park.

How can I get there?

Location. Bethany Beyond the Jordan is about thirty miles west of Amman and six miles north of the Dead Sea.

By Plane. The nearest airport is in Amman, about forty-five minutes away by road.

By Train. There is no train service to Bethany Beyond the Jordan.

By Bus. Currently there is no regular public bus service to Bethany Beyond the Jordan. Minibuses, however, do provide transportation to the Visitor Center, which is located about 1 mile from the primary sites of the Baptism Archaeological Park. A free shuttle bus takes people from the visitor center to the baptism site every fifteen to twenty minutes. The shuttle bus stops at Parking 1 (Elijah's Hill and John Paul II Church), Parking 2 (baptism pools and caves), and Parking 3 (Saint John Church, Greek Orthodox church, and the river).

By Car. Travel along the Dead Sea Highway until you reach the Suwaymeh Intersection; turn right and head north following the signs to Bethany Beyond the Jordan.

By Taxi. Taxis are inexpensive and are often the most convenient and efficient form of transportation in Jordan, so it is a good idea to take a taxi to Bethany Beyond the Jordan if you are traveling independently.

What lodgings are available?

As Bethany Beyond the Jordan does not have any hotels, most visitors stay overnight in nearby Amman or the Dead Sea area. Both of these places offer a wide variety of lodging options, from simple to luxury.

Then Moses went up from the plains of Moab to Mount Nebo, to the top of Pisgah, which is across from Jericho. And the LORD showed him all the land of Gilead as far as Dan, all Naphtali and the land of Ephraim and Manasseh, all the land of Judah as far as the Western Sea, the South, and the plain of the Valley of Jericho, the city of palm trees, as far as Zoar.

DEUTERONOMY 34:1–3

Why should I visit?

One of the most revered sites in Jordan is Mount Nebo. From this place, Moses viewed the Promised Land, and into it he brought the Israelites after leading them out of Egypt and wandering in the desert for forty years. The Israelites camped here prior to entering the Land of Canaan, and Moses died and was buried here. For all these reasons, Mount Nebo is recognized as one of the most sacred and prominent sites of the Old Testament.

What can you expect when visiting Mount Nebo? Like Moses, you can view the Dead Sea, Jordan River Valley, Jericho, and in the distance, Jerusalem from its summit. Today a memorial lies here commemorating the prophet's death and burial place. You can also view the ruins of churches dating back to the fourth century.

Among the most significant sites to see at Mount Nebo today is the Serpentine Cross, a representation of the bronze serpent lifted up by Moses in the desert. God promised that all who looked upon the raised serpent would be saved from the deadly plague, which God had sent to kill the rebellious Israelites. Today it also symbolizes the cross upon which Jesus died and that all who look upon him will be saved. Interestingly, the symbol of the raised serpent is in modern times the icon of the health, medical, and ambulatory services in the United States.

If you are planning a trip to the Holy Land, be sure to include Mount Nebo in your itinerary. Only here can you get a real sense of what it must have been like for Moses and the Israelites to view the Promised Land. Few places in the world offer such an authentic biblical experience.

CONTACT INFORMATION FOR MOUNT NEBO

Mount Nebo (Franciscan Archaeological Institute, affiliated with
  the Franciscan Custody of the Holy Land)
P.O.Box 2 Faysaliyah
17196 Madaba (JORDAN)
E-mail: mtnebo@go.com.jo
The Jordan Tourism Board lists information about Mount Nebo at www.seejordan.org.

What should I see and do?

You can view the Promised Land (as Moses did) from Mount Nebo. You can take in spectacular views from the platform in front of the church, which on a clear day can sometimes include the rooftops of Jerusalem and Bethlehem. (The peak of Mount Nebo is about three thousand feet.) Be sure to visit:

- Moses Memorial Church with its beautiful mosaics; built on the grounds of a sixth-century basilica and monastery
- Monument of the Serpentine Cross
- Spring of Moses located almost one mile east of Mount Nebo
- Groups can celebrate religious services in the modern chapel presbytery

How much time should I spend?

You should budget several hours at Mount Nebo.

How can I get there?

Location. Mount Nebo is located about five miles west of Madaba and about twenty-five miles from Amman.

By Plane. The nearest airport is in Amman.

By Train. There is no train service to Mount Nebo.

By Bus. There is bus service to nearby Madaba from Amman and other cities. Once at Madaba, you will need to take a taxi to reach Mount Nebo.

By Car. From Madaba, drive west and follow the signs for Mount Nebo; the drive is about ten minutes.

By Taxi. If you are traveling independently, taxi is the best (and primary) way to reach Mount Nebo.

What lodgings are available?

Although the nearest town is Madaba, most people stay overnight in Amman or the Dead Sea area and make a day excursion to Mount Nebo.

MORE BIBLICAL SITES OF JORDAN

ANJARA is an ancient city that is home to a cave where Jesus, his mother Mary, and the disciples are said to have rested during a journey from Jerusalem to Galilee. Today the cave is enshrined by a large church known as Our Lady of the Mountain. Anjara is located in the hills of Gilead east of the Jordan Valley, about thirty minutes from Jerash.

AMMAN The capital of Jordan today is Amman, known in biblical times as Ammon or Rabath Ammon. Today you can visit the city's many ruins, as well as the archaeological museum located in the Citadel. *(Deuteronomy 2:37)*

AS SALT (SALT) One of the best-known figures of Scripture is Job. In the city of Salt lies the shrine and tomb of Job, the man who endured great suffering only to be rewarded by God for his faithfulness. Salt is also home to the tombs of Jethro, father-in-law of Moses, and Jad (Gad) and Asher, sons of Jacob. *(Job 1–42)*

CREDIT: JORDAN TOURISM BOARD NORTH AMERICA & JIM PITTS

Experience the Roman Empire when visiting Jerash, one of the best-preserved ancient cities.

JERASH The ancient city of Jerash, a Decapolis city in the area where Jesus and his disciples drew large crowds, is recognized as one of the best-preserved cities of the Roman Empire. The ruins feature the Triumphal Arch and Street of Columns, as well as tracks of chariot wheels in the ground. Referred to in the Bible as the "region of the Garasenes," Jerash is the country's most important historical destination outside of Petra. *(Luke 8:26)*

KARAK The biblical name for Karak is Qer Harreseth and is mentioned in Scripture as the place where the Syrians went before they settled in the area north of Palestine. Karak is best known for its Crusader castle. Featured in the movie *Kingdom of Heaven*, Karak fell to Saladin and the Muslims in 1188. Today you can explore the castle and its many underground halls and passageways. *(Amos 9:7)*

MADABA Although Madaba played a role in Old Testament times (known as "Medeba"), today it is best known as being the City of Mosaics. The number one attraction is the Church of Saint George, which features a sixth-century mosaic map of Jerusalem and the Holy Land. With 2 million pieces of colored stone, it is the oldest map of the Holy Land in any form. Many more mosaics can be found throughout Madaba, including at the archaeological museum and park, as well as at the Church of the Apostles. *(Numbers 21:30)*

MUKAWIR (MACHAERUS) Mukawir is the imposing hilltop fortress of Herod Antipas, where John the Baptist was imprisoned and beheaded after Salome's fateful dance. Today you can view the ruins of the fortress and take in the windswept vista as you contemplate the pivotal biblical drama that took place here. Mukawir is located about thirty miles from Madaba. *(Mark 6:17)*

PELLA Pella is believed to be near the Old Testament site of Penuel where Jacob wrestled with God. *(Genesis 32:24, 25)*

PETRA The number one tourist attraction in Jordan is Petra, the rose-red city carved out of rock by the Nabateans, who controlled the ancient trade routes in this area. Although not everybody may recognize the city by name, many people do recognize Petra for its appearance in the movie *Indiana Jones and the Last Crusade*. Today the place remains one of the greatest wonders of the ancient world. A UNESCO World Heritage Site today, Petra is connected to Scripture via the Exodus itinerary. Moses and the Israelites are said to have passed through the Petra area in ancient Edom. Be sure to visit Petra's most famous monument, The Treasury—located at the end of the winding siq (the main entrance at Petra). *(Numbers 20:11)*

TALL MAR ELIAS is believed to be the former biblical place of Tishbe, the home of the prophet Elijah. Located near the ruins of a village known as Listib, the site later became home to two churches built upon the tel (hilltop) at the end of the Byzantine period. Today Tall Mar Elias features architectural remains spread around the hill's summit. *(1 Kings 17:1)*

THE DEAD SEA The Dead Sea is almost synonymous with the Holy Land. Referred to primarily as the "Salt Sea" in Scripture, this body of water appears a number of times in the Old Testament and served as host to several biblical cities, including the infamous Sodom and Gomorrah. As the lowest place on earth, the Dead Sea is known today for its health benefits and attracts people from around the world to its spa resorts. *(Genesis 14:3)*

LOT'S CAVE Near the Dead Sea lies the Sanctuary of Lot, near modern-day Safi (biblical Zoar). Here you will find Lot's cave where he and his daughters sought refuge. It is

Take a swim in the Dead Sea, referred to in the Bible as the Salt Sea.

also where you will see a dried pillar of salt, which local tradition says is the remains of Lot's wife. According to the Book of Genesis, God punished Lot's wife by turning her into a pillar of salt when she disobeyed His command not to look back at Sodom during their escape. *(Genesis 19:30)*

THE PLAINS OF MOAB The Plains of Moab figure prominently in Scripture, especially in the Old Testament. It is where Moses and the Israelites arrived after their Exodus and where Joshua prepared to cross the river into Canaan. Today you can view several archaeological mounds that have been identified with biblical sites. *(Joshua 3:1)*

UMM AR-RASAS Umm Ar-rasas is a city cited in both the Old and New Testaments. In addition to its ruins, the main attraction today for visitors is the Church of Saint Stephen. Inside you will find the largest (preserved) mosaic floor in Jordan, an artwork featuring images of twenty-seven biblical cities. *(Genesis 13:18)*

UM QUAIS (UMM QAYS) The well-preserved Decapolis city of Gadara (modern-day Umm Qais) is home to the miracle of the Gadarene swine (when Jesus cast out the evil spirits of a man and threw them into a herd of pigs that ran down the hill and were drowned in the Sea of Galilee). *(Matthew 8:28–34)*

EGYPT: MOSES, MOUNT SINAI, AND THE OLD TESTAMENT

In the third month after the children of Israel had gone out of the land of Egypt, on the same day, they came to the Wilderness of Sinai.

EXODUS 19:1

Why should I visit?

If you want to understand the Bible and life of Moses, there is no better place to visit than Egypt where a number of key events in the Old Testament took place, including God's appearance to Moses in the Burning Bush. Egypt is where the pharaohs kept the Israelites in slavery and captivity prior to the plagues sent by God. It is also home to the Sinai Peninsula, the wilderness where the Israelites wandered for forty years.

CREDIT: ©ISTOCKPHOTO.COM/STEVEN ALLAN

Hike to the top of Mount Sinai, where God gave Moses the Ten Commandments.

With its rich biblical history, Egypt is an ideal travel destination for the Christian visitor and is often included on many Christian trips to the Holy Land. The primary highlight is a visit to Mount Sinai, the mountain where Moses received the Ten Commandments. Some Christian tour groups combine a visit to Egypt with Jordan or Israel (or all three countries), thus providing for a full biblical immersion experience. Whether you visit Egypt alone or in combination with other countries, one thing is certain: you will walk away not only with a much greater insight into the "Cradle of Civilizations" but also with a much richer understanding of Scripture and the Old Testament.

CONTACT INFORMATION FOR EGYPT

Tourist Office: The Egypt Tourist Authority, www.egypttourism.org
Embassy: www.egyptembassy.net; www.embassy.org/embassies/eg.html
Other Helpful Web Sites: Egypt Travel Help Centre, www.ask-aladdin.com;
  Association of Egypt Travel Businesses on the Internet, www.touregypt.net

What do I need to know?

Religion. The official state religion is Islam. About 90 percent of the population is Sunni Muslim, and the majority of the remaining 10 percent is Christian (mostly Coptic Christian).

Language. Arabic is the official language, although English and French are widely spoken (especially among the educated).

Climate. Egypt is mostly a desert environment with hot, dry summers and moderate winters.

When to visit Egypt. The most popular time to visit Egypt is mid-October to May, as the weather is typically at its best. However, this part of the season is also more expensive, and reservations need to be made in advance. Spring can be quite nice, although the Khamsin Wind (a southerly, hot wind that blows across Egypt) can kick up in March and April, though it typically lasts only a few days at a time. May through October offers smaller crowds, making it easier to see and photograph the sites. However, the temperatures can range from high to scorching.

Clothing. As Egypt is primarily a Muslim country, you should dress modestly. Wearing shorts or having bared shoulders, by men or women, is generally discouraged and usually accepted only at beach resorts.

EGYPT TRAVEL PLANNING

Airport: Cairo, www.cairo-airport.com

Train: Sleeping trains, www.sleepingtrains.com; for train schedules, www.seat61.com/Egypt.htm or www.ask-aladdin.com and then click on the train schedule links.

Boat: AB Maritime, www.abmaritime.com.jo; International Fast Ferries SAE, www.internationalfastferries.com; for ferry schedules, www.ask-aladdin.com and then click on the ferry timetable links (or visit www.ask-aladdin.com/ferries.html).

Bus: For bus schedules visit: www.ask-aladdin.com and then click on the bus schedule links (or visit: www.ask-aladdin.com/bus_schedules.htm).

Car: Although it is possible to rent a car in Egypt, driving is usually not recommended due to higher than normal hazards. If traveling independently, consider other alternatives such as private transportation.

ONE MOUNTAIN, MANY NAMES

Mount Sinai goes by many names. Here are a few:

- Mount Horeb (biblical term)
- Holy Peak (term used by the monks at Saint Catherine's Monastery)
- Jebel Musa (Modern Arabic term meaning the Mount of Moses)
- Mount Moses (English term)
- Other terms include Gebel Musa, Jebel Musa, Jabal Musa, and Mount Musa

I Learned So Much about the Old Testament

I will never forget my trip to Egypt and Israel. My favorite part of the Egypt portion was visiting Mount Sinai, where Moses came face to face with God! The number one highlight for me personally was seeing the Burning Bush. Word has it that this is the only kind of bush growing in the entire Sinai Peninsula and that every time someone tries to transplant a branch of it to another place, they fail. As for the monastery and church itself, what struck me most was its ancient beauty. The library was also an incredible experience with all its centuries-old manuscripts ... I especially enjoyed this as I am a big book lover and historical buff anyway. If I were to summarize my trip to Mount Sinai and Egypt as a whole, I would say that it has not only enriched my faith immensely but has also motivated me to learn and study the Old Testament in much more depth. Best yet, whenever I read the passage now about Moses and the Israelites camping out at Mount Sinai ... I can say that I've been there! —*Brian*

MOUNT SINAI AND SAINT CATHERINE'S MONASTERY

Then the LORD *came down upon Mount Sinai, on the top of the mountain. And the* LORD *called Moses to the top of the mountain, and Moses went up.*

EXODUS 19:20

CREDIT: ©ISTOCKPHOTO.COM/DADDYBIT

At Saint Catherine's Monastery see the Burning Bush.

Why should I visit?

Of all the Christian destinations in Egypt, Mount Sinai is considered the most significant because it is where God appeared in a burning bush to Moses and also where He delivered the Ten Commandments. In this vicinity, the children of Israel wandered in the desert for forty years. Today Saint Catherine's Monastery serves as the "custodian" of the remote pilgrimage destination of Mount Sinai. Tens of thousands of Christians travel from around the world each year to stand at the very site where God told Moses to remove his sandals, for the prophet was standing on holy ground. Mount Sinai appears numerous times in Scripture: Exodus 19, 24, 31, 34; Leviticus 7, 25–27; Numbers 3, 28; Nehemiah 9; Acts 7; and Galatians 4.

The Christian presence at the site began in the fourth century. According to one tradition, the mother of Constantine the Great, Empress Helena, commissioned a church to be built at Mount Sinai after her visit there around AD 330. About two centuries later in AD 527, Emperor Justinian ordered a much larger church, monastery, and fortress to be built at Mount Sinai. In subsequent centuries, the monastery and nearby area were named after Saint Catherine, a young Christian girl from Alexandria who died a martyr in the fourth century. The monastery itself remains one of the oldest active Christian abbeys in the world.

A great center of pilgrimage for fifteen centuries, Saint Catherine's Monastery in recent years has garnered international attention for its extraordinarily rich collection of religious treasures, art, and artifacts. Its most famous asset is the library of ancient manuscripts and icons, which is second only to the Vatican itself. In total, the monastery houses more than two thousand icons including some that are more than one thousand five hundred years old. A selection of these can be viewed by the general public in this small museum.

All the notoriety has led UNESCO to designate Saint Catherine's Monastery a World Heritage Site. The ancient monastery has recently been featured in publications ranging from the *New York Times* to *Parade* magazine. Located in the stark, natural beauty of the southern Sinai Peninsula and desert, the monastery today receives as many as one thousand visitors in a day.

CONTACT INFORMATION FOR MOUNT SINAI
Tourist Office: Saint Catherine's Village, www.st-katherine.net; Saint Catherine's Monastery, www.sinaimonastery.com

CONTACT INFORMATION FOR SAINT CATHERINE'S MONASTERY
Saint Catherine's Monastery
South Sinai, EGYPT
Tel/Fax (secretary of the Monastery): (2069) 347-0349

What should I see and do?

The two most typical activities when visiting Mount Sinai are exploring Saint Catherine's Monastery and hiking to the summit of Mount Sinai (although not everyone does this due to the physical fitness requirements). The monastery itself is open from 9 AM to 12 PM daily except Fridays and Sundays and Christian Coptic holy days. While at Mount Sinai, be sure to visit:

- The Basilica of Transfiguration: Very rich in icons and art, the Church of Transfiguration's most significant treasure is its sixteenth-century mosaic featuring the transfiguration of Jesus.
- Chapel of the Burning Bush: Considered one of the more sacred sections of the monastery, the chapel incorporates the original fourth-century church and is built upon the roots of the Burning Bush (which now grows outside the church).
- The Burning Bush: Among all the sites to visit at the monastery, the most popular is the Burning Bush. A rare species of the rose family called Rubus Sanctus, the bush is believed to be a direct descendent of the bush in which God appeared to Moses.
- The Library: Possibly the most "treasured" area of the monastery is the library which contains more than six thousand manuscripts. Among its most prized possessions are the Codex Syriacus and Codex Sinaiticus, some of the world's oldest translations of the Bible.
- Sacristy: This houses a well preserved and world famous collection of religious paintings, icons and artifacts that the monastery has collected over time.
- Moses Well: Located outside the walls is the Moses Well, the monastery's main water source. It is the reputed meeting place of Moses and his future wife, Zipporah.
- Monastery Garden: Also outside the walls is the monastery garden, which includes a variety of fruit and vegetables such as plums, apricots, and olives. The monastery cemetery is located here as well.
- Museum (Sacred Sacristy): Open to the public, visitors can explore the monastery museum featuring Christian icons and artifacts dating centuries back. The museum provides a glimpse of the monastery's spiritually and culturally rich collection of icons, artwork, and biblical manuscripts.

HIKING MOUNT SINAI

One of the most popular activities while visiting Mount Sinai is hiking to its summit, just as Moses did many centuries ago. The climb itself takes two to three hours, depending on the time of day and one's pace. Believe it or not, the most popular time for hiking Mount Sinai is during pre-dawn hours. The reason? To be at the summit in time for the breathtaking and unforgettable sunrise. To accomplish this, most visitors begin their journey around 3 AM at the base of Mount Sinai. Following along the Path of Moses (Arabic: Sikket Sayidna Musa) to the mountain's 7,498-foot peak, hikers scale a stairway totaling 3,750 steps (carved out by a monk performing a penance, according to one tradition). Once at the top, travelers are in for an awe-inspiring experience as the summit is one of the highest points in the Sinai region. Many mark this event as one of the most spectacular and spiritual experiences of their life.

What you need to know before hiking: The early morning climb can be very cold and you must dress accordingly for the excursion. Also, plan to take a little extra time because most of the hike up takes place in the dusk, thus slowing you down.

When you are near the summit at Elijah's Basin, look for the cypress trees. According to tradition, those who accompanied Moses waited here while the prophet climbed the summit alone. Once at the mountaintop, look for the cave on the north side of the Chapel of the Holy Trinity, which Moses is said to have visited.

Camel ride, anyone? If you would like to experience being at the top of Mount Sinai yet are unable to make most of the physical journey (or simply don't want to), you can instead ride up on a camel—which is an event in itself! In this case, you will not be traveling along the Path of Moses but rather the Camel Path.

How much time should I spend?

If you will be hiking to the top of Mount Sinai and visiting the monastery, plan a full day, including an overnight stay in the area. If you will only be visiting the monastery, then budget about half a day. If you are traveling from Sharm el-Sheikh to Mount Sinai as an excursion, dedicate a full day to include driving time.

How can I get there?

Location. Saint Catherine's Monastery is located in the southern part of Sinai Peninsula about 130 miles west of Nuweiba on the Red Sea coast. Cairo is 275 miles from Saint Catherine's village.

By Plane. The closest major airport is in Sharm el Sheikh. Egypt Air has daily flights from Cairo, Alexandria, and Luxor.

By Train. Mount Sinai is not accessible by train. Sharm el-Sheikh is also not accessible by train from Cairo.

By Boat. The nearest ports are at Nuweiba and Sharm el Sheikh. Nuweiba has daily ferries from Aqaba, Jordan; the car ferry is three hours, and the "fast" ferry is one hour. Sharm el Sheikh has ferry service with Hurghada.

By Bus. There is a daily East Delta bus service from Cairo (Turgoman Bus Station) to Saint Catherine's village departing in the morning and arriving in the evening (eight to nine hour trip). Buses depart Saint Catherine's Village for Cairo at 6 AM (times can change) opposite the mosque. There is also frequent bus service to Saint Catherine's village from Sharm el Sheikh and Dahab (and vice versa). Once you're at Saint Catherine's village, take a taxi for the two miles to the monastery. If you're traveling first to Sharm el-Sheikh from Cairo, there is frequent daily service including an overnight bus (the trip takes about seven hours).

By Car. Saint Catherine's Village is about nintey miles (or two hours) from Dahab, which provides the only road to Mount Sinai. Gas is available at the monastery for your car.

By Taxi. Taxi and transportation companies provide one of the most convenient methods of traveling to Saint Catherine's Monastery. Services are provided from Dahab (ninety miles), as well as Sharm el Sheikh, Taba, and Nuweiba (all of which are about 130 miles away). Many local travel agents can also arrange day or short excursions to Mount Sinai.

What lodgings are available?

Visitors have two major lodging options: stay overnight either in Mount Sinai with limited accommodations or in Sharm el Sheikh (three hours away) with a greater variety of resort and hotel options. If you plan to hike Mount Sinai in the early morning hours, you should stay overnight in Mount Sinai.

Saint Catherine's Monastery Guesthouse

Telephone: (69) 347-0353
Fax: (69) 347-0543; (69) 347-0343
E-mail: sinai@tedata.net.eg

Located right next to the monastery (just outside its walls), Saint Catherine's Monastery Guesthouse provides fifty-two rooms including single, double, and dormitory accommodations. There is also a restaurant that serves breakfast and dinner. The lodging experience is described by most as simple yet comfortable. Although there is no charge, you should give a donation and bring a gift such as cakes or sweets.

Other options in Mount Sinai near the monastery

Catherine Plaza Hotel www.catherineplaza.com; Daniella Village www.danielahotels .com; Other hotels at Saint Catherine's include Morgenland Village, Tourist Village, and the dormitory El Milga Bedouin Camp (www.sheikmousa.com).

Travel planning

www.cairocitytourist.com

Why should I visit?

Although sometimes forgotten, Egypt is home to an ancient Christian heritage. It is here where the Holy Family took flight, where Saint Mark spread the Gospel in Alexandria and established a church, and where a thriving monastic community sprang up. As such, Christian historical sites can be found throughout Egypt to this day, ranging from places where the Holy Family is said to have stayed (or traveled through) to ancient monasteries to centuries-old churches. Although some Christian travelers will spend their entire trip visiting religious and historical sites throughout Egypt, most will just visit Mount Sinai and Cairo.

What can I see and do?

Among the more popular Christian sites visited in Cairo are:

- The Hanging Church (El Muallaqa): The church's name comes from its nave, which hovers above the passageway. It is the most famous church in Cairo.
- Church of Abu Serga and the Crypt of the Holy Family: This is the place where the Holy Family is believed to have sought shelter.
- Church of the Holy Virgin: This church dates from the eleventh century
- The Coptic Museum (www.copticmuseum.gov.eg): This museum is an excellent place to learn Christian history and heritage in Egypt.

Wadi Natroun and the Coptic Christian monasteries

Outside of Cairo to the northwest lie the well-known Wadi Natroun monasteries, some of which date to the fourth century. Many Christian groups will include a day excursion to these ancient monasteries.

Travel planning

http://www.touregypt.net/holyfamily1.htm; www.touregypt.net/featurestories/journey.htm

Why should I visit?

Although Mount Sinai is usually the primary attraction for Christians traveling to Egypt, sites related to the Holy Family are often of interest as well. In fact, some groups build their entire tour itineraries around following "in the footsteps of Jesus, Mary, and Joseph" and their flight to Egypt. Retracing the traditional route of the Holy Family's journey can take more than a week.

What can I see and do?

Two of the most common sites relating to the Holy Family's flight to Egypt are The Church of Abu Serga (Saint Sergius) and the Crypt of the Holy Family, which lies in Old Cairo. According to various Christian traditions, Jesus and his parents took refuge here. Other similar places of interest relating to the Holy Family can be explored, including in Tal Basta, Sakha, Matariya, Maadi, and elsewhere. Ask your tour operator or travel agency about integrating these Christian sites into your Egypt trip.

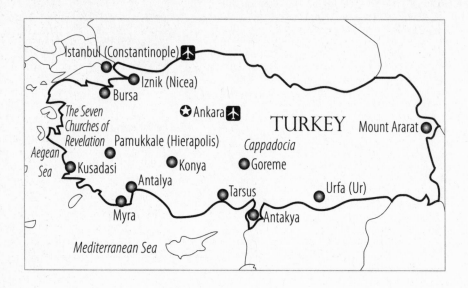

Why should I visit?

Turkey is home to the Seven Churches of Revelation. It is here that the first Christian community began (in Antioch) and where the term "Christians" was first applied. Turkey has served as the site of about half of the ecumenical councils of the Christian church; the Nicene Creed was written and adopted in Nicea (modern day Iznik). Tarsus is the birthplace of the apostle Paul. And Noah's ark is believed to rest on Mount Ararat in eastern Turkey. One of the great churches of Christendom, the Hagia Sophia, was located in Constantinople. The bishop of Bari, better known as Saint Nicholas (as in Santa Claus) is from southern Turkey. Several prominent early church fathers come from Cappadocia, including Saint Basil the Great. Selcuk is the reputed burial place of the apostle John. Mary, the mother of Jesus, is believed to have spent her last days in Ephesus, Turkey. Abraham originally resided in modern-day Turkey before embarking on his pilgrimage to the land of Canaan. The apostle Paul visited many sites in Asia Minor while on his three missionary journeys.

Many people do not realize that Turkey is one of the most prominent and biblically-based destinations in the world, but that is slowly changing. In recent years, more Christians are discovering that some of the most significant events and sites of our faith lie in the land formerly known as Asia Minor. In many ways, it is from southern Turkey

CREDIT: ©ISTOCKPHOTO.COM/GRAPHIXEL

In Turkey, visit the Seven Churches of Revelation.

that the Christian faith spread to the rest of the world. The Vatican itself recognized the importance of this fact and, in 1963, designated the Church of Saint Peter (Saint Peter's Grotto) in Antioch as the world's first cathedral. It was in this city and church that the apostles and first Christians gathered and set out on their missionary journeys. As a result, many new Christian communities were founded, including the Seven Churches of Asia Minor (also known as the Seven Churches of Revelation). Today, much of the Christian faith that has been handed down to us comes from the people, places, and events that took place over the past two millennia in Asia Minor. Wait no longer, pack your bags and head for the biblically rich land of Turkey!

CONTACT INFORMATION FOR TURKEY

Tourist Office: Turkey Ministry of Culture and Tourism, www.tourismturkey.org; www.turizm.gov.tr; www.kultur.gov.tr

Embassy: www.turkishembassy.org

Other Helpful Web Sites: www.biblicalturkeyguide.com

What do I need to know?

Religion. The vast majority of the Turkish population is Muslim, most of who are Sunni. All other faiths comprise only about 1 to 2 percent of the population. Turkey is officially a secular state that recognizes along with Islam the following three minority religious communities: Greek Orthodox Christians, Armenian Orthodox Christians, and Jews.

Language. The official language is Turkish. Many other languages are also spoken in certain sections of the country including Kurdish, which is spoken by almost 10 percent of the population. English is often spoken by those working in tourism, as well as the younger people.

Climate. Turkey is a large country with a wide variety of climates and geographical regions. If you plan to visit Istanbul, the western coast (Izmir, Ephesus, etc.), or the central interior of Turkey, you can pretty much plan on the following: very to extremely hot summers with temperatures above 100°F regularly; spring and fall temperatures can range from warm to quite cool, so dress in layers and bring a good jacket and sweater.

When to visit Turkey. Spring and fall (April to June; September to October) are considered the best times to visit Istanbul and western Turkey, both price- and weather-wise. Summer (July through mid-September) is the hottest and most crowded time to visit.

Clothing. Turkish summers are typically very hot, so dress accordingly—but bring a light sweater or jacket for cooler evenings in some locations. During the spring and fall, dress in layers for cooler weather. Casual clothing is appropriate for most sightseeing; however, you should wear pants or long skirts when entering churches and religious places.

TURKEY TRAVEL PLANNING

Airport: Istanbul, Izmir, www.ataturkairport.com; www.adnanmenderesairport.com; Ankara, www.esenboga.com

Train: Turkey rail, www.tcdd.gov.tr/tcdding/index.htm or www.tcdd.gov.tr

Bus: Varan, www.varan.com.tr; Ulusoy, www.ulusoy.com.tr; Havas, www.havas.com.tr.

Car (driving directions): www.viamichelin.com; www.mapquest.com

We Feel Like Scripture Scholars Now!

We recently returned from our Christian trip to Turkey, which included visiting sites stretching from Antakya to Cappadocia to the Seven Churches of Revelation. It turned out to be one of the greatest travel experiences for us. We thoroughly enjoyed the two weeks of visiting biblical places and historical sites, as well as immersing ourselves in Turkish culture, cuisine, and its people. The entire trip opened our eyes to just how much of the New Testament and the early Christian church lies in Turkey—which was a big surprise to us. We learned and experienced so much biblical history that we almost feel like Scripture scholars now!
—*Jim and Michelle*

Why should I visit?

Few places in the world offer such religious and historical importance and intrigue as does Istanbul. Home to a long and glorious yet sometimes turbulent history, Turkey's largest city has served as the seat of power for the Roman Empire (fourth century), Byzantine Empire (fifth century to fifteenth century), Latin Empire (thirteenth century), and Ottoman Empire (fifteenth century to early twentieth century). As a result, the former capital remains today a city of timeless treasures and provides a cultural atmosphere not found anywhere else in the world. Although the city has had different names over the years, Istanbul has been the official title since the edict of 1930.

CREDIT: TURKISH CULTURE AND TOURISM OFFICE, NEW YORK

In Istanbul, see the Hagia Sophia, formerly one of the greatest churches in Christendom.

Located at the intersection of two continents (in fact, the only city in the world built on two continents), between AD 324 and AD 330 the emperor Constantine the Great transferred his headquarters from Rome to Byzantium and renamed it Constantinople. As the capital of three major empires, the city is inextricably linked to Christianity. One of the great churches of Christendom, the Sancta Sophia (today the Hagia Sophia or Ayasofya Museum), once stood here. Constantinople also served as the site of three Ecumenical councils (AD 381, AD 553, AD 680), as well as a fourth one in AD 879 during the

Byzantine Empire. The Crusaders passed through here in the thirteenth century. Today, Istanbul still plays a key role within several major branches of Christianity. For example, the Patriarch of Constantinople serves as the supreme and primary authority of the Greek Orthodox Church.

If you are planning to visit Turkey and the Seven Churches of Revelation or retrace the apostle Paul's journeys through Asia Minor, a trip to Istanbul is a must for any itinerary. As one of the world's former great capitals, a visit here will provide you with tremendous insight into a city that has placed an indelible mark on the history of Christianity—and the world itself. Welcome to where the "East meets the West."

CONTACT INFORMATION FOR ISTANBUL
Tourist Office: Istanbul, www.istanbul.com
Other Helpful Web Sites: Ecumenical Patriarchate (Orthodox Christian Church), www.ecupatriarchate.org

What should I see and do?

The most prominent sites in Istanbul for the Christian visitor are:
- Hagia Sophia (Ayasofya Museum): Built in the fourth century, this famed landmark of Istanbul served as one of Christendom's great churches prior to being converted into a mosque and later a museum. Today it is the city's number one attraction for the Christian visitor and all tourists in general.
- Church of Saint Saviour in Chora (Kariye Museum): A Greek Orthodox Church from the eleventh to fourteenth centuries, today it is a museum famous for its Byzantine frescoes and mosaics.
- Saint Irene Church: The site of the Second Ecumenical Council in AD 381, today it is a museum, and special permission must be secured in advance to enter.
- The monastery of Saint John of Studius: The oldest church in Istanbul and one of the most famous monasteries from the Byzantine era, today only the ruins can be viewed.
- Greek Orthodox Patriarchate Church (Aya Yorgi Fener): This church is the worldwide headquarters of the Greek Orthodox Church.

How much time should I spend?

Ideally you should plan on a minimum of one to three full days in Istanbul to include visiting both Christian and traditional tourist sites.

How can I get there?

Location. Istanbul is situated literally at the crossroads of where Asia meets Europe. Within Turkey itself, it is located at the northwestern tip. Once in Istanbul, you might consider purchasing the Akbil (electronic) transit pass, which makes it very convenient for getting around the city.

By Plane. The main airport is Istanbul Atatürk Airport, located more than ten miles west of the city center. Flights from around the world arrive in Istanbul daily.

By Train. Istanbul is accessible by train from Europe, Turkey, and eastern countries. Trains coming from Europe arrive at Sirkeci rail station; trains coming from Asia stop at Haydarpasa station.

By Boat. Istanbul is accessible by both ferry and ship. Some of the major cruise lines dock here. Ferry services are used both within the city and to reach other places outside of Istanbul.

By Bus. Buses are the best and least expensive forms of transportation around the city. Two types of bus systems exist in Istanbul, one operated by the municipality and the other by private sector. You can go virtually anywhere in the city by bus. There is also excellent bus service from Istanbul to other cities throughout Turkey (and vice versa).

By Metro. Istanbul has two main metro lines, both of which can be quite useful in traveling around to certain sections of the city quickly and efficiently.

By Tram. Istanbul has the following two tram services, which are excellent options for getting around town: Istiklal Caddesi and Eminonu/Kabatas-Zeytinburnu.

By Car. Driving inside Istanbul is not recommended. Simply park your car and use alternative forms of transportation. Reaching Istanbul by road from either Greece or southern Turkey is very easy as signs to Istanbul are well marked.

By Taxi. Taxis are very plentiful in Istanbul and serve as a major form of transportation in the city and as one of the best ways to get around town. Shared taxis (called Dolmus) are an excellent option as well and are less expensive.

By Foot. In spite of almost a dozen options of how to get around town, walking is sometimes the best way to get around Istanbul—especially for short distances.

What lodgings are available?

Istanbul truly offers nearly every imaginable form of accommodation ranging from youth hostels to the most luxurious hotels. Finding a good, quality hotel that fits your budget is very easy as your options are virtually unlimited. Many brand name and chain hotels are in Istanbul.

Travel planning

http://www.kultur.gov.tr/EN, search for "Iznik" within the Web site

Why should I visit?

The biblical city of Nicea, or modern-day Iznik, is best known as being the site of the first ecumenical council (or conference) of the Christian church. Referred to as the Council of Nicea, the gathering took place in AD 325 at the request of Constantine the Great, who had only about ten years earlier recognized Christianity as the official religion throughout the empire. The council gave birth to the Nicene Creed, the established doctrine set forth for the Christian church throughout the world. Today, it remains the primary and underlying statement of Christian faith and belief. In the end, Nicea served as the site of not only the first ecumenical council in AD 325, but also the seventh ecumenical council in AD 787.

What can I see and do?

Although the actual place (Senatus Palace) where the council took place lies under Lake Iznik, there are other sites to explore. For example, the ruins of Saint Sophia Cathedral, the site of the second ecumenical council can be visited.

How can I get there?

Iznik is located about fifty miles northeast of Bursa at the eastern tip of Lake Iznik. The best way to reach Iznik is by ferry; if you are coming from Bursa, bus is the best transportation.

SEVEN CHURCHES OF REVELATION

John, to the seven churches which are in Asia: Grace to you and peace from Him who is and who was and who is to come . . .

REVELATION 1:4

THE SEVEN CHURCHES OF REVELATION

✝ Bergama
✝ Akhisar
✝ Izmir
✝ Sart
✝ Alasehir
Aegean Sea
✝ Ephesus
✝ Eskihisar

TURKEY

Why should I visit?

The Seven Churches of Revelation are early Christian communities located in modern-day western Turkey to whom the apostle John wrote letters during his exile on Patmos Island. These writings are included in the last book of the Bible—Revelation. Also referred to as the Seven Churches of the Apocalypse or the Seven Churches of Asia Minor, the biblical communities include Ephesus, Smyrna (modern-day Izmir), Pergamum (modern-day Bergama), Thyatira (modern-day Akhisar), Sardis (modern-day Sart), Philadelphia (modern-day Alasehir), and Laodicea (modern-day Eskihisar).

The opening of Revelation begins with:

CREDIT: TURKISH CULTURE AND TOURISM OFFICE, NEW YORK

Walk the same streets that the apostles Paul and John did in Ephesus.

I, John, both your brother and companion in the tribulation and kingdom and patience of Jesus Christ, was on the island that is called Patmos for the word of God and for the testimony of Jesus Christ. I was in the Spirit on the Lord's Day, and I heard behind me a loud voice, as of a trumpet, saying, "I am the Alpha and the Omega, the First and the Last," and, "What you see, write in a book and send it to the seven churches which are in Asia: to Ephesus, to Smyrna, to Pergamos, to Thyatira, to Sardis, to Philadelphia, and to Laodicea" (Rev. 1:9–11).

When speaking of "churches" in this biblical passage, John is primarily referring to communities or groups of Christians, not necessarily buildings. Hence, embarking on a tour of the Seven Churches means you will be visiting the cities or vicinities of these former Christian communities, not always their respective physical structures per se. The point of such a trip is more about what you experience and learn about the Seven Churches of Revelation, rather than what you see.

With that in mind, the best thing about visiting the Seven Churches of Asia Minor is that it offers one of the best experiences of what first-century Christianity must have been like. And your understanding and appreciation for the Book of Revelation will dramatically increase, as will your overall knowledge and comprehension of the Bible. That alone is worth the price of visiting Turkey.

EPHESUS/SELCUK (AND KUSADASI): THE LOVELESS CHURCH

(Acts 18–19; Revelation 2:1–3)

Travel planning

Selcuk tourist office: www.selcuk.gov.tr

Why should I visit?

If there is one Turkish city which should top the list for Christian travelers, it is Ephesus. Recognized as one of the former great cities of the Western world, Ephesus played a prominent role in early Christianity. It served as the site of several ecumenical councils, and it was one of the Seven Churches of Revelation that John the Evangelist addressed in his letters. While praising the community's fortitude and perseverance, the apostle also reprimanded the Christian citizens for "forsaking their first love" and urged them to return to their love for Christ.

In the late first century AD, Ephesus was the fourth largest city in the Roman Empire and served as the administrative center for Asia. In size and importance, it was comparable to Rome in Italy, Corinth in Greece, Alexandria in Egypt, and Antioch in Syria. The apostle Paul preached and worked here for several years. Mary, the mother of Jesus, and the apostle John are said to have lived here as well. Today the towns of Ephesus and Selcuk are visited by hundreds of thousands of Christians each year traveling on "Footsteps of Apostle Paul" tours to Greece (with a cruise stop in Ephesus), as well as on "Seven Churches of Revelation" tours through Turkey. It is a "must" for any Christian visitor to Turkey.

What should I see and do?

Ephesus (sometimes called or written as Efes) and nearby Selcuk are exceptional places to visit with their rich Christian and historical sites. The following are sites most often included on Christian tours to these two towns:

EPHESUS

- The House of Mary (Meryemana Kultur Parki): According to tradition, the mother of Jesus spent her last days here in Ephesus at this house. Located five miles from the center of Ephesus, it can only be reached by taxi (not regular city bus service).

- Basilica of the Virgin Mary: This is the site of the Third Ecumenical Council, held in AD 431.
- Great Theater: The apostle Paul delivered a sermon here to the local population during his missionary journeys.
- Library of Celsus: This ancient library and mausoleum serves as the landmark of Ephesus.

SELCUK

- Basilica of Saint John: Once a great church, today the ruins house the reputed burial site of John the Evangelist. It is located at the foot of Ayasoluk Hill near the center of Selcuk and just two miles from Ephesus.
- Ephesus Museum: This museum features many artifacts from excavations at Ephesus and the Basilica of Saint John.

How can I get there?

Ephesus is located on the western coast of Turkey, just two miles west of Selcuk and almost ten miles inland from the port city of Kusadasi. As one of Turkey's most popular tourist destinations, Ephesus is easily accessible by car, bus, and taxi. Minibuses run frequently during the tourist season between Kusadasi, Ephesus, and Selcuk. Taxi service to Ephesus from Kusadasi is relatively inexpensive and is a popular option. Train service is available to Selcuk; however, bus is often the preferred method of transportation.

What lodgings are available?

Most people visit Ephesus either as a shore excursion while on a tour of the Greek Isles or while on a land tour of Turkey. If the latter, most people stay overnight in nearby Kusadasi, which has a wide variety of hotel and accommodation options.

IZMIR (BIBLICAL CITY OF SMYRNA): THE PERSECUTED CHURCH
(Revelation 2:8–11)

Travel planning
Izmir tourist office: www.izmirturizm.gov.tr

Why should I visit?
Izmir is the uncrowned capital and the "pearl" of the Turkish Aegean area. With its magnificent coastline and some of the country's most beautiful beaches, the city is a

very popular tourist and cruise line destination. Izmir is also home to the biblical and ancient city of Smyrna. In his letter to the community at Smyrna, John encourages the faithful to accept suffering and persecution, even to the point of death. He assures them that they will be rewarded and earn the "crown of life." One of the best known early Christians from Smyrna is Polycarp, the city's second century bishop who was martyred here. Smyrna is the only Church of Revelation that has possessed an active Christian community since the time of John's writings.

What should I see and do?

The site most often visited is the Roman agora, the ancient marketplace of Smyrna. In addition, many Christian groups visit Saint Polycarp Church because it is not only the oldest church in Izmir, but it also represents the city's role as one of the Seven Churches of Revelation. You might also consider visiting the Izmir Archaeological Museum.

How can I get there?

Izmir is located on the Aegean Sea of western Turkey, about thirty-five miles north of Ephesus. It is accessible by a variety of transportation methods. The Izmir Adnan Menderes Airport is about ten miles from the city center, receives flights from throughout Europe, and has daily flights to/from Istanbul and other Turkish cities. Izmir is also accessible by train (main station is Basmane) and bus service from throughout Turkey. Once in Izmir, there is both bus and subway transportation. Izmir can also be reached by ferry including from Venice, Italy.

What lodgings are available?

With a population of almost 4 million and as a major tourist destination site, Izmir offers virtually every type of accommodation imaginable. Many Christian groups stay here and use it as a "hub city" to make daily excursions to the other Seven Churches of Revelation.

PERGAMUM (BIBLICAL CITY OF BERGAMA): THE COMPROMISING CHURCH *(Revelation 2:12–17)*

Why should I visit?

In his letter to the biblical city of Bergama, John commends the church for holding fast to the faith; however, he rebukes them for tolerating and accepting false teachings. Pergamum today is a small Turkish village. In its day, Bergama was a prominent political and cultural center that had many temples to pagan gods including Asklepios, the god of healing. For this reason, the city served as one of the region's most prominent places of pagan pilgrimage.Because of the cult of Asklepios, the city became well-known for health and medicine. Several famed medical doctors of antiquity were born and worked here including Hippocrates and Galenus, who wrote about five hundred medical books. Today the village offers a number of excavated sites that can be visited; it is also home to several healing mineral springs.

What should I see and do?

The two main sites to visit are the Asklepion of ancient Pergamum and the Acropolis. You might also consider visiting the Red Basilica and the archaeology museum.

How can I get there?

Bergama is located sixty miles north of Izmir. The best way to reach Bergama is by bus. Once you arrive in Bergama, however, you will need to get a taxi or walk to get around (no bus service exists inside Bergama).

What lodgings are available?

Because few accommodations exist, most people make a day trip here from Izmir.

AKHISAR (BIBLICAL CITY OF THYATIRA): THE CORRUPT CHURCH
(Revelation 2:18–29)

Travel planning

Akhisar tourist office: www.akhisar.com

Why should I visit?

Located in a fertile valley of Asia Minor, Akhisar served as a prosperous trading center during its day and was an opportune place for missionary work and evangelism. John included Thyatira as one of the Seven Churches of Revelation. The smallest of the seven Christian communities, it was both praised and reprimanded by him in his letter. After complimenting the people on their love, faith, service, and perseverance, the apostle chastised them for tolerating the prophetess Jezebel and her teachings. Although Akhisar does not feature as many ruins or archaeological sites as other places, it does offer the wonderful feeling and experience of being in the very same place as the original biblical community.

What should I see and do?

There are very few ruins and remains to see in Akhisar. The primary sites of ancient Thyatira lie within an enclosed area of Akhisar's city center.

How can I get there?

Akhisar is sixty miles east of Izmir, which has the closest major airport. As Akhisar is situated on the main highway from Istanbul to Izmir, there is frequent regular bus and train service to Akhisar from throughout Turkey including Izmir, Istanbul, Ankara, and other major cities.

What lodgings are available?

Some people who are traveling independently will stay overnight here while on a tour of the Seven Churches, as it's a long drive from Izmir.

SARDIS (BIBLICAL CITY OF SART):THE DEAD CHURCH
(Revelation 3:1–6)

Why should I visit?

Sardis once served as the capital of the prominent Lydia kingdom and is recognized as one of the great and legendary cities of the ancient world. A wealthy city in its time, its citizens were known for their prestige in business and economics. The area was also the site of the prominent Sanctuary of Artemis. In later years, the city served as home to a flourishing Jewish community and one of the largest synagogues in antiquity. As one of the Seven Churches of Revelation, its citizens were rebuked for having the reputation of being alive physically but dead spiritually. In short, he accused them of not living out the Gospel. He did acknowledge that some were living faithfully and had not "soiled their clothes," and he comforted them by acknowledging that their names were in the book of life.

What should I see and do?

The should sites to visit in Sardis include the ruins of a Jewish synagogue, Byzantine church, shops, gymnasium, and the Temple of Artemis.

How can I get there?

Sardis and its ruins lie about fifty five miles east of Izmir. It is located on the main Izmir-Salihli-Ankara highway, about an hour-and-a-half driving distance from Izmir. Bus service is available to the village of Sart from nearby towns including Izmir (departing from Yeni Garaj station in the direction of Salihli, take the bus heading to Salihi). Train service is available from Izmir (Basmane station) but is not the preferred method of transportation because it is typically not as convenient or efficient as the bus.

What lodgings are available?
Most people make a day trip to Sardis from Izmir.

ALASEHIR (BIBLICAL CITY OF PHILADELPHIA): THE FAITHFUL CHURCH
(Revelation 3:7–13)

Why should I visit?
Alasehir was known in antiquity as Philadelphia, the "city of brotherly love." Located along an important trading route that overlooked the Persian Royal Road, Alasehir was one of the earliest cities to adopt the faith. In later years, it became one of the Seven Churches of Revelation that John wrote. In his letter, the apostle acknowledged their "little strength" yet encouraged them to endure patiently and remain loyal. Alasehir and Smyrna were the only two Churches of Asia Minor that John did not condemn nor that speak of negatively. Although the city was almost completely destroyed in the earthquake of AD 17, Alasehir exists today, and the village has a population of about forty thousand.

What should I see and do?
Although ancient Philadelphia is a virtual must on any Churches of Revelation tour, only the ruins of a Byzantine church, wall, and frescoes can be seen.

How can I get there?
Alasehir is located about eighty miles east of Izmir and twenty miles southwest of Sardis. It is accessible by bus and train from nearby larger cities. Private bus service or taxi is also a common way to reach the site for those who are traveling independently. You might consider hiring a local travel agent to arrange an excursion for you to Alasehir, as well as to the other Seven Churches of Revelation such as nearby Sardis.

What lodgings are available?
Although lodging opportunities exist in Alasehir, most Christian groups stay overnight in Izmir, which is eighty miles to the west and features every kind of accommodation from hostel to five-star hotels.

ESKIHISAR (BIBLICAL CITY OF LAODICEA): THE LUKEWARM CHURCH
(Revelation 3:14–20)

Travel planning

Denizli-Pamukkale tourist office: www.pamukkale.gov.tr/tr

Why should I visit?

Located at the crossroads of a major trading route in the ancient world, Laodicea became known as the "Metropolis of Asia." Recognized as a prominent banking center, it also gained fame as a medical city. Home to a medical school, the ancient biblical city became well known for the treatment of both eye and ear problems. All of this wealth and

CREDIT: TURKISH CULTURE AND TOURISM OFFICE, NEW YORK

Take a dip in the famed hot mineral springs of Pamukkale.

commerce led to Laodicea's becoming a very prosperous city. A number of apostles and disciples worked as missionaries here including Paul, Philip (who was martyred here), John, Luke, and Timothy. The apostle John wrote to the local faith community at Laodicea and accused them of being lukewarm in their faith, neither "hot nor cold."

Near Laodicea lies the ancient city of Hierapolis. A UNESCO World Heritage Site, the city is built above the famed Pamukkale hot springs, also known as the "cotton castle" or "white castle." As one of Turkey's most popular tourist sites, many people come here from around the world to relax in the aesthetically beautiful and mineral-rich healing waters. For Christians, another draw here is the Martyrium of Apostle Philip—the memorial built at the site of the apostle's death.

What should I see and do?

In ancient Laodicea, you will find the ruins of a basilica, theater, stadium, cistern, aqueduct, and other remnants from the Roman period. In nearby Hierapolis, you can visit the Martyrium of Apostle Philip and then afterward relax in the healing springs at Pamukkale.

How can I get there?

The ruins of Laodicea are located below a hill near the village of Eskihisar (with its citadel on the hilltop) and just four miles from the large city of Denizli, thirteen miles from Pamukkale, and 110 miles southeast of Izmir. The primary way to reach the ruins is by taxi from one of the nearby cities such as Pamukkale or Denizli; these latter two cities are easily accessible by bus and train from throughout Turkey.

What lodgings are available?

If you wish to overnight in the area, Denizli offers a wide variety of lodging options.

Paul and Barnabas also remained in Antioch, teaching and preaching the word of the Lord, with many others also.

ACTS 15:35

Why should I visit?

As Asia Minor plays a prominent role in Scripture, there are literally dozens of biblical sites and cities to visit in modern-day Turkey. Most of the places are often visited on tours of the Seven Churches of Revelation, missionary journeys of the apostle Paul, the New Testament, or early Christianity in general. As there are so many Christian places in Turkey, it is virtually impossible to explore them all on any given tour. When planning or booking your trip to this great land, you might consider including some of the following biblical and Christian sites.

CREDIT: TURKISH CULTURE AND TOURISM OFFICE, NEW YORK

Explore the caves of Cappadocia, once home to a thriving ancient Christian kingdom.

ANTAKYA (BIBLICAL CITY OF ANTIOCH) *(Acts 11:26)*

Why should I visit?

As the place where the faithful first received the name "Christians," Antioch shares a prized spot in Christianity. It is also the place from which the apostle Paul and others

CREDIT: TURKISH CULTURE AND TOURISM OFFICE, NEW YORK

Discover Saint Peter's Church, where the faithful were first called "Christians."

began their missionary journeys. Ecumenical church councils were held here, and it's where what may be the oldest Christian church in the world lies. Many prominent and influential Christians have gathered or ministered from the city, including the apostles Peter and Paul and the early church father and bishop Ignatius of Antioch.

What should I see and do?

The most significant site to visit is the Cave Church Saint Peter, also known as Saint Peter's Grotto. The early Christians gathered, worshiped, and ministered here.

How can I get there?

Antakya is located in south-central Turkey, slightly more than ten miles from the Syrian border. It is easily accessible by road or bus; however, there is no train service. Saint Peter's Grotto is located just two miles northeast of the city center. The best way to reach it is by taxi or walking.

What lodgings are available?

Antakya offers a wide variety of accommodations ranging from budget to luxury.

CAPPADOCIA *(Acts 2:9, 1 Peter 1:1)*

Why should I visit?

What looks almost like an attraction taken right out of Disneyland in inland Turkey is the fantasy-like landscape of Cappadocia. An ancient Christian kingdom, this land of carved-rock dwellings once housed an entire metropolis complete with more than six hundred churches, chapels, monasteries, and hermits. As early as the second century, persecuted Christians escaped here for shelter in the rock formations. The society produced several prominent Christian figures during its heyday including the Cappadocian Fathers and Saint Basil the Great (AD 329–379). Because the residents of the time painted and decorated the inside walls with frescoes, today the rock-cut churches and monasteries of the region feature a treasure trove of Christian art. Although people lived in the caves until the 1950s, today it is primarily a tourist site.

What should I see and do?

There are several sites or "sections" to explore at Cappadocia. The capital is Nevsehir and makes for a great starting point to tour the area. The most popular attraction in Cappadocia is the Goreme Open-Air Museum, a UNESCO World Heritage Site. Here you can visit the cone-headed pillars of tuff which once housed a bustling monastic community. Inside are some of Cappadocia's best frescoes and works of art. Other areas to visit include Zelve with its hermit cave dwellings, Derinkuyu and Kaymakli with their ancient underground cities, Soganli that provides donkey tours of the rock-cut churches, Avanos with its pottery and ceramics, and Cavusin (about a mile from Goreme) where Christian missionaries once lived. The Urgup area of Cappadocia is the primary gathering place for tourists with its many hotels and restaurants.

How can I get there?

Cappadocia is one hundred miles southeast of Ankara, with Goreme as the main tourist site. To reach Cappadocia, you will need to take a bus from Ankara or another nearby city to Goreme or Nevsehir. Although there is no rail service to Goreme or Nevsehir, you can take the train to Ankara, Konya, or Kayseri and then complete your journey to Cappadocia by bus.

What lodgings are available?

Cappadocia is a wonderful place to overnight with a wide variety of options, many of which beautifully reflect the geography and landscape of the area—you can even enjoy elegant and comfortable accommodations built as cave dwellings. Price levels vary from budget to high-end. Goreme serves as the center of tourism and lodging for the region.

TARSUS *(Acts 21:39)*

Travel planning

Tarsus tourist office: www.tarsus.gov.tr

Why should I visit?

Tarsus is best known in the Christian world as being the birthplace of the apostle Paul. Located in south-central Turkey, the city was also the home of Marc Anthony and Cleopatra in the first century. Tarsus is mentioned several times in Scripture, specifically in the Book of Acts. Today it is primarily a commercial and industrial city.

What should I see and do?

The main site of significance for the Christian visitor is Saint Paul's Well, which is believed to be located on the site of the apostle's house. There is also the Church of Saint Paul, built in the 1800s.

How can I get there?

Tarsus is fifteen miles from Mersin and is accessible by bus and train. The nearest major airport is at Adana.

What lodgings are available?

As one of the largest cities in Turkey, Adana offers many lodging facilities including hotels (budget to high-end), guesthouses, pensions, and hostels.

OTHER BIBLICAL CITIES IN TURKEY

- **Antioch in Pisidia:** Paul preached in this city and synagogue.
- **Antioch on the Orontes:** While here, Paul reported to the elders.
- **Antalya:** Paul sailed for Antioch from here.
- **Assos:** Luke waited here for Paul to arrive from Troas.
- **Colossae:** Paul wrote to Philemon to free Onesimus.
- **Derbe:** Paul was kept safe from persecution while in Derbe.
- **Konya (biblical city of Iconium):** This is the place where Paul met Timothy; it served as one of the Ecumenical council sites of the early church. For more information visit www.konya.bel.tr.
- **Lystra:** Lystra is the disciple Timothy's hometown and the place where Paul was stoned by a mob.
- **Miletus:** Paul said farewell to the Ephesian leaders.
- **Mount Ararat:** This is where Noah's ark is believed to rest.
- **Myra:** Although not necessarily a biblical city, it is here where Saint Nicholas (as in "Santa Claus") lived and ministered as a bishop.
- **Patara:** This is the harbor in which Paul changed ships.
- **Perge:** Paul and Barnabas visited the Agora; Paul spoke here on first missionary journey.
- **Seleucia:** Paul and Barnabas departed from this ancient harbor.
- **Urfa (Ur):** Ur is the location of the cave of Abraham.

Paul's First Missionary Journey: Acts 13:1–15:35
Paul's Second Missionary Journey: Acts 15:36–18:22
Paul's Third Missionary Journey: Acts 18:23–21:17

Why should I visit?

One of the most popular tours for Christians is retracing the missionary journeys of Paul. Although the apostle made three missionary trips, the route taken by most Christians is following the apostle's second missionary trip through Greece and parts of Turkey. This takes you to the biblical cities of Athens, Corinth, Thessaloniki, Philippi, Kavala, Patmos Island, and Ephesus (Turkey) among others.

Much of the popularity of this trip has to do with Paul's prominence in the New

Retrace the journeys of the apostle Paul through Greece and Turkey.

Testament. A large part of Acts is devoted to Paul's travels and missionary activities, and the New Testament features a number of letters written by Paul to the various church communities. Another reason for the trip's popularity is the inclusion of visiting Patmos Island, the place where John wrote the Book of Revelation. All this, combined with the fact that many of the places visited by Paul, John, and the other apostles can still be explored today, makes this a coveted tour.

If you plan to embark on such a trip, prepare yourself by reading, watching, and studying everything about the life of the apostle Paul and his missionary journeys. By doing so, you will get the most out of your experience, and the New Testament will come alive like never before.

CONTACT INFORMATION FOR GREECE
Tourist Office: Greece Tourist Authority: www.gnto.gr
Embassy: www.greekembassy.org
Other Helpful Web Sites: Hellenic Ministry of Culture, www.culture.gr;
   Church of Greece: www.ecclesia.gr

What do I need to know?

Religion. According to the constitution of Greece, the country's official religion is Greek Orthodox. Almost the entire population is Greek Orthodox Christian.

Language. The official language is Greek; however, many people also speak English—especially in tourist areas.

Climate. Most of the country features a temperate climate of hot, dry summers with mild, wet winters. Greece has three distinct types of weather:

- Mediterranean (Greek Isles): hot, dry summers with mild, wet winters
- Alpine (Mountain areas of northwestern Greece): colder weather with snow in winter

- Temperate (central and east Macedonia and Thrace): hot, dry summers with cold, damp winters

When to visit Greece. Summer provides the most available services and amenities yet at the highest cost. Fall and spring can be quite pleasant weather-wise, but services are often cut back slightly. However, prices are usually better at this time. Few church groups travel here in the winter.

Clothing. In tourist areas, Greece is rather casual with clothing. However, visits to monasteries, churches, and religious centers typically require modest to conservative clothing. The latter means no shorts (for men or women), no bare shoulders, and in general no clothing that reveals too much skin. At resorts, hotels, and beaches, you can wear swimsuits and shorts. Spring and fall require a sweater and light jacket. Winter necessitates warm clothing. Be sure to bring an umbrella if you're traveling any time other than the summer months.

Transportation. Athens and Thessaloniki are easily accessed by international flights. Once in Greece, there are multiple transportation venues. Bus is one of the most common modes for getting around—the network is fairly extensive and prices are reasonable. The intercity bus system in Greece is "KTEL" (hallmarked by green-colored buses) and can be found in virtually every city. Rail is another option; however, service is limited and restricted primarily to transportation between larger cities. Renting a car in Greece is relatively inexpensive, and mopeds and scooters are readily available. However, due to the high accident rate (especially among tourists) of moped/scooter-riders, only experienced riders should consider this option. Another excellent choice for getting around Greece is via ferry or boat. If you plan to visit an island near the mainland, a ferry is your best option. For islands further away from the mainland, you may consider a short flight from Athens or Thessaloniki. Or maybe better yet, like many Christian tour groups and travelers, consider embarking on a several day cruise that combines visiting sites of faith (i.e. Patmos Island) with traditional Greek island sightseeing.

GREECE TRAVEL PLANNING
   Airport: Athens: www.aia.gr; Thessaloniki, www.hcaa-eleng.gr/thes.htm
   Train: Hellenic Railways: www.ose.gr
   Boat: Greece ferries, www.greekferries.gr, www.ferries.gr
   Bus: National and intercity bus services, www.ktel.org
   Car (driving directions): www.viamichelin.com; www.theaa.com;
      www.mapquest.com

What Was My Favorite Place?

What we next experienced as Christians, we will never forget. We boarded our ship and sailed into a beautiful sunset that bathed the skyline of Venice behind us a bright gold. It was a fitting scene that put a visual exclamation mark on our experiences in Italy. The next eight days would take us where the apostle Paul journeyed on his second and third missionary trips preaching the gospel of Jesus Christ. We began in Greece, visiting Patras, Corinth, Athens, Kavala, Philippi, and Thessaloniki. Then it was on to Turkey where we visited Dikili, Pergamum, and Kusadasi. Our final stop was Patmos Island (in Greece) where we visited the cave in which the apostle John wrote the Book of Revelation. All of these places sounded familiar to most Christians and created reality in depicting events in the lives of people who lived on the heels of the life of Christ. These amazing locations on our tour brought to life the magnitude of these cities and the sophisticated way of their cultures. In spite of these attributes it was encouraging to understand the challenges Paul faced dealing with their pagan ways of worship and the response he received by most that gives us hope of eternal life today. What was my favorite place? Selfishly, Mars Hill in Athens because I was asked to give devotions to a tour group of forty. Anyone who has taught or preached would feel the same way about speaking at the very same spot where Paul spoke some two thousand years ago! Personally, I was moved at a site near Philippi where Lydia lived and sold her purple cloth. She accepted Paul's message about Christ and was the first convert baptized in Europe. She was the reason the message spread throughout Europe and the reason behind our having that message today, the Good News. Why should you retrace Paul's journeys? You will be able to grasp the regions he traveled. It will put into perspective the enormity of what he and others faced to make the Gospel available to us today. It will amaze you that these were sophisticated cultures with deep-seated pagan worship trends. Finally, you and your friends will be bonded together with the common thread of hope that the Good News is alive and well! —*Pastor Roger*

ATHENS

Then Paul stood in the midst of the Areopagus and said, "Men of Athens, I perceive that in all things you are very religious; for as I was passing through and considering the objects of your worship, I even found an altar with this inscription: TO THE UNKNOWN GOD."

Acts 17:22–23

In Athens, visit Mars Hill, where Paul delivered his sermon about the UNKNOWN GOD.

Why should I visit?

After preaching in Veria (biblical Berea), Paul sailed to Athens alone and arrived around AD 50, while Timothy and Silas remained in Macedonia. At the time of Paul's arrival, Athens was the most important city in ancient Greece. As he did in other towns and places, the apostle made a beeline for the local synagogues and began preaching about Jesus Christ.

As the local population was steeped in idolatry, Paul confronted their beliefs head on. The apostle's most famous sermon took place at the Areopagus where he spoke about the UNKNOWN GOD and nature of God. As many Athenians were philosophers, they listened to him and questioned whether he was promoting or educating about false gods. In his preaching, Paul spoke about God, life, and the resurrection of the soul. Among his converts were Dionysius and Damaris (Acts 17:22–34). After spending time in Athens, Paul left for Corinth.

CONTACT INFORMATION FOR ATHENS

Tourist Office: Athens, www.cityofathens.gr (click on English version upper left)
General Information: Athens Guide, www.athensguide.org; Athens City Tourist, www.athenscitytourist.com
Bus: Athens Urban Transport Organization, www.oasa.gr
Other Helpful Information: An outstanding Web site for travel planning to Christian sites in Greece is www.culture.gr, which is the Hellenic Ministry of Culture Web site. You can search for virtually any Christian site by clicking on the "Archeological sites" Web link on the Homepage. For example, you can search for sites in Athens such as "Acropolis of Athens" and "Ancient Agora of Athens."

What should I see and do?

After arriving at Mars Hill, you can choose from one of three paths to reach the top. The Areopagus is located just west of the Acropolis. You can climb to the top of Mars

Hill and stand at the site where Paul delivered his sermon. Near the steps is a plaque commemorating the apostle Paul's visit to the Areopagus, to includes the text of Paul's sermon reproduced in Greek. Other sites include the Agora and the ancient market of Athens where Paul also spoke and preached to the local population (it is located at the foot of the hill). You can also visit the Church of the Holy Apostles, built in honor of the apostle's preaching in the local marketplace. And of course, you can explore the famed ruins of the Parthenon.

How much time should I spend?

You probably only need an hour or two to explore much of Mars Hill, longer if you plan to visit the Acropolis, Parthenon, and other sites.

How can I get there?

Location. Athens is five miles inland from Piraeus, its main port (located on the Saronic Gulf, an arm of the Aegean Sea). Mars Hill is located northwest of the Acropolis.

By Plane. The new Athens Eleftherios Venizelos International Airport is state-of-the-art, very user friendly, and easily accessible to the city. Athens receives flights from all over the world daily.

By Train. Getting to Athens by train is extremely easy because it's the final destination for many train runs. The main station is about thirteen miles north of the city center at Arharnon; from here you can connect with suburban trains to the city center and the port Piraeus. To reach Mars Hill, it's easiest to switch to the Metro (see below).

By Boat. Athens's main port is Piraeus and is one of the most popular ports throughout the Aegean Sea. You can arrive at Athens by ferry from many of the Greek Isles. Once at Piraeus, you can take the city train, bus, metro, or taxi into the city center or the Acropolis.

By Bus. The national bus company is KTEL, and bus stations are found in Athens and the vast majority of cities in Greece. Bus service is a popular choice of travel in Greece.

By Metro and Trams. The Metro is one of the best ways to get around Athens and to reach the Acropolis and Mars Hill. Another option includes the trams.

By Car. Renting a car in Athens or Greece can be fairly expensive. Caution must also be used on the roads as Greece has a higher rate of accidents than other European countries. Because driving in Athens can be difficult and exhaustive, it is recommended to reach the Acropolis and Mars Hill by Metro, bus, or walking versus driving there yourself.

By Taxi. Taxis are plentiful throughout Athens and one of the best ways to get around town, including to Mars Hill. One interesting difference about Greek taxis is that they are allowed to pick up other passengers heading in your direction until the taxi is full. Catching a taxi to Mars Hill is a great idea.

What lodgings are available?

As one of the most prominent and major tourist destinations in the world, Athens provides a wide selection of hotels ranging from extreme budget to luxury.

EXCURSION TO CORINTH (ACTS 18:1–18)

Travel planning

Visit www.culture.gr, click on Archaelogical sites, Alphabetical Index, and then search for "Corinth."

Why should I visit?

After spending time in Athens, Paul departed the city and traveled to Corinth in AD 50. In total, he spent about a year-and-a-half here spreading the Gospel. As one of the most cosmopolitan and bustling cities of ancient Greece, Corinth figured heavily in Paul's missionary work. Among his first and many converts was Crispus, a chief synagogue official. (Crispus's entire family was also baptized.) While in Corinth, Paul met and became friends with Aquila and Priscilla. Together they worked as tentmakers and preached to the local people. At one point, Paul received for "Ancient Korinthos" a vision in which the Lord told him he would not be

CREDIT: ©ISTOCKPHOTO.COM/STEVE MAEHL

Visit the ruins of Corinth where Paul preached and worked with Aquila and Priscilla.

harmed in Corinth (Acts 18:4–10). However, he did run into problems when people began accusing him of improper teachings, especially in regard to worshiping God. When he was brought before the court, the area's Roman governor, Gallio, dismissed the case and advised that he did not want to become involved in the religious issues of the day. Several of Paul's writings and letters in the New Testament are closely associated with Corinth. He wrote several epistles to the Thessalonians and Romans while here. After leaving the city, he also wrote to the Corinthians. More than five years later, Paul returned to Corinth in AD 57 and stayed in the house of Gaius.

What should I see and do?

The major place to visit is the Ancient Corinth site and museum, which is filled with many ruins. You must purchase a ticket to gain entrance. At the center of the park is the ancient agora and bema (city's place of judgment) where Paul appeared before Gallio. Many other sites can be visited as well including the Temple of Apollo, Temple of Octavia, and more. While at the bema, read the Scripture passage from Acts 18:12–17.

How can I get there?

Corinth is located about fifty miles west of Athens, on a narrow isthmus connecting the Peloponnese and the Balkan Peninsula. Ancient Corinth is located about four miles from the city of Corinth. Bus and taxi service is available to ancient Corinth. If you take the train to Corinth from Athens, you will need to switch to bus or taxi service to reach ancient Corinth.

EXCURSION TO CENCHREAE (ACTS 18:18)

Why should I visit?

After preaching and ministering in Corinth for eighteen months, Paul visited Cenchreae. As Scripture says, it is here where he completed a vow and had his head shaved. Located about two miles south of Isthmia, Cenchreae served as the eastern port and shipping harbor for Corinth. From here Paul sailed to Ephesus.

What should I see and do?

The ancient harbor remains of Cenchreae are still visible today in the modern-day small town of Kechries (Kechriais).

How can I get there?

Cenchreae is located six miles east of Corinth. Unless you're with a tour group, taking a taxi to Kechries (Cenchreae) is probably easiest. Or best yet, embark on a local daily tour of the ancient Corinth and Cenchreae sites.

Travel planning

Visit www.culture.gr, click on Archaeological sites, Alphabetical Index, and then search for "Meteora."

CREDIT: GREEK NATIONAL TOURISM ORGANIZATION

You can explore these famed monasteries built upon geographical wonders.

Why should I visit?

Combine a geographical wonder with the marvel of ingenious monks and what do you get? The breathtaking Meteora monasteries in central Greece. Spectacular geographical formations protrude several thousand feet into the air, only to be crowned by "gravity-defying" monastic buildings and residences resting atop them. For this reason, Meteora means "hovering or suspended in air." Together the giant rocks and monasteries create a twin wonder. Monks settled in the area in the eleventh century and then began building the first of twenty-four monasteries in the fourteenth century. In the 1920s, steps leading to the monasteries were cut. Today only six monastic sites remain, and although a few monks and nuns staff them, they are primarily museums.

What should I see and do?

Recognized as a UNESCO World Heritage Site, Meteora can be visited by pilgrims and tourists alike. Along with enjoying spectacular views, guests can explore the monasteries' religious treasures, wall paintings, icons, and libraries rich in old manuscripts. The six monasteries include:

• Megalo Meteoro (Great Meteoron): most popular monastery

- Varlaam: very friendly monks here often chat with visitors
- Roussanou: active convent with very pleasant nuns who sometimes offer guests sweets
- Agios Nikolaos (Saint Nicholas): features wonderful frescoes and is typically the least populated monastery of Meteora
- Agia Triada (Holy Trinity): has a "winch," which was used to pull up monks and supplies
- Agios Stefanos (Saint Stephen): active convent with a museum; usually sells embroideries.

How can I get there?

The two closest villages to Meteora are Kalambaka and Kastraki (where most people stay overnight, unless they make a day trip from Athens or Thessaloniki). From Athens, you can take the train to Kalambaka via Volos (switching to narrow gauge train) or the bus to Kalambaka via Trikala. Other options include hiring a taxi to drive you around to all monasteries (this is typical) or asking a local travel agent to arrange a small tour for you.

THESSALONIKI

These were more fair-minded than those in Thessalonica, in that they received the word with all readiness, and searched the Scriptures daily to find out whether these things were so.

ACTS 17:11

Why should I visit?

Thessaloniki is the second-largest city in Greece and the capital of Macedonia. Located in the northern section of the country, Thessaloniki not only features places connected to Paul's missionary journeys but is also within close proximity of other towns that offer the same. As a big city with many amenities, Thessaloniki makes for the perfect "overnight hub" and launching pad for daily excursions elsewhere.

When Paul came to Thessaloniki around AD 50, the town embraced him and Silas along with their message about Jesus Christ. However, the friendly welcome quickly wore out as some individuals began rising up against them. According to Scripture, a mob broke out and began rioting. The disorderly crowd then headed for Jason's house, a local who housed the apostle and Silas. After the city officials caught wind of the

CREDIT: ©ISTOCKPHOTO.COM/IVO VELINOV

Witness the Roman agora where the apostle Paul's preaching caused a riot.

events, Paul and Silas escaped Berea during the night. However, Paul never forgot the Thessalonians and wrote several letters to them. In time, the city became a thriving Christian community as a result of Paul's visit.

CONTACT INFORMATON FOR THESSALONIKI
Tourist Office: www.saloniki.org
Municipality of Thessaloniki: www.thessalonikicity.gr
Museums of Macedonia: www.macedonianmuseums.gr
Other Helpful Information: Visit www.culture.gr and then click on Archaeological Sites, Alphabetical Index, and then search for "Ancient Thessaloniki."

What should I see and do?

Thessaloniki features a few key sites related to Paul's visit including:

- The Roman Agora: This is where the apostle preached.
- Roman forum: The riot which broke out due to Paul's teachings occurred here.
- Vladtadon Monastery: This is the location of Jason's house where Paul stayed during his visited to Thessaloniki.
- Arch of Galeirus: This is the start of Via Egnatia, once a key Roman highway which the apostle would have traveled upon.
- Saint Demetrios Church: Although not directly connected to the apostle Paul, the church is the largest in Greece and is renowned for its stunning mosaics and frescoes.

How much time should I spend?

You should budget a few hours to half a day for visiting the Christian sites of Thessaloniki. If you wish to visit other tourist sites of Thessaloniki or wish to simply explore on your own, then plan a full day.

How can I get there?

Location. Thessaloniki is located in northern Greece and is situated fairly close to many other key towns and sites related to the apostle Paul (see the excursions on the following pages).

By Plane. The Thessaloniki airport is about ten miles outside the city and is well serviced from many other Greek cities including Athens. It is typical for many church tour groups to fly into Athens and then connect on a flight to Thessaloniki to begin their tour.

By Train. Thessaloniki has outstanding train connections throughout Greece and Europe. The trip is from Athens is about six hours long. The train can be used for some daily apostle Paul excursions; however, a combination of bus and taxi is probably your best bet (for example, Kavala does not have a train station).

By Bus. Thessaloniki is easily accessible by bus and has plenty of service to other cities, including those relating to the apostle Paul. For example, there is frequent daily bus service to Kavala (slightly more than a two-hour trip). The bus trip from Athens is about seven hours.

By Car. As a main city in northern Greece, Thessaloniki is easily accessible from other cities. It connects to other towns in northern Greece via its major national road 2 (E90). From Athens, it's about five to six hours driving time along the scenic national highway. Thessaloniki is four hundred miles from Istanbul.

By Taxi. Taxis are plentiful in Thessaloniki and are often willing to conduct special tours around the city for you.

What lodgings are available?

As the second largest city in Greece and an important tourist destination, Thessaloniki features hotels to suit virtually any taste.

EXCURSION TO AMPHIPOLIS (ACTS 17:1)

Travel planning

Visit www.culture.gr, click on Archaeological Sites, Alphabetical Index, and then search for "Early Christian Amphipolis" and "Amphipolis."

Why should I visit?

Although Amphipolis receives only scant attention in Scripture, it does at least receive mention. Paul passed through this town on his way to Thessaloniki. In later years, Amphipolis became an important Christian city complete with an Episcopal see (seat of the bishop), as evidenced by its basilicas and ruins. Amphipolis lies along the ancient Egnatian Way, a key road running west-east across northern Greece.

What should I see and do?

The Christian Amphipolis includes the site of the acropolis of ancient Amphipolis. Excavations today feature four basilica ruins and a rotunda church, all of which are believed to date from the sixth century. You will probably also see the Lion of Amphipolis, the same one the apostle Paul most likely saw during his travels through the area.

How can I get there?

Amphipolis is located thirty-five miles west of Philippi and situated near the route of the modern National Road 2 (E90) from Philippi to Thessaloniki. From Thessaloniki, head toward Kavala on E90 for about fifty-five miles. Just past the Strymon River Bridge, on your left on the lowlands, are the ruins of ancient Amphipolis.

EXCURSION TO APOLLONIA (ACTS 17:1)

Why should I visit?

Similar to Amphipolis, Apollonia received its biblical fame as a city that Paul passed through on his way to Thessaloniki. At the time of the apostle, Apollonia was considered to be a city of size and importance in Macedonia and was located along the main Egnatian Way.

What should I see and do?

At the Apollonia archaeological site is a large rock with a tablet that states that Paul preached here (sometimes referred to as the apostle Paul's Pulpit). Near the north side of the Apollo temple was the bema of the apostle Paul, a spring believed to be the sacred fount of the apostle himself.

How can I get there?

Apollonia is located about forty miles east of Thessaloniki along the national road 2 (E90), and thirty-five miles southwest from Amphipolis. Bus service is available from Thessaloniki.

EXCURSION TO KAVALA (NEAPOLIS) (ACTS 16:9-11)

Travel planning

www.kavala.gr

Why should I visit?

The apostle Paul first stepped on European soil around AD 50 at Neapolis, the port city at the time for Philippi. Although Neapolis was later renamed Christoupolis (city of Christ) during the Byzantine era, the port's modern name is Kavala. Today it serves as the primary seaport in eastern Macedonia. Paul also sailed from Neapolis (Philippi's port) at the end of his third missionary journey, as recorded in Acts 20:6.

CREDIT: ©ISTOCKPHOTO.COM/BLADE KOSTAS

Kavala is where Paul arrived on European soil around AD 50.

What should I see and do?

The main site to visit is the Church of Saint Nicholas, which features a mural commemorating Paul's arrival because the apostle is believed to have come ashore here. There is also an archaeological museum with an excellent collection of artifacts from Neapolis, Philippi, and Amphipolis, all three places visited by Paul.

How can I get there?

Kavala is less than ten miles from the ancient city of Philippi. Regular bus service is available from Thessaloniki and Philippi to Kavala. Ferry service is also available to Kavala. There is no train service, however, to Kavala.

EXCURSION TO PHILIPPI (ACTS 16:9–40)

Travel planning

Visit www.culture.gr and then click on Archaeological Sites, Alphabetical Index, and then search for "Ancient Christian Philippi" and "Philippi."

Why should I visit?

Philippi is the first place in Europe where the apostle Paul and Silas preached and gained their first convert, Lydia. It is also where Paul cast out an evil spirit and landed in jail. While he was in prison, an earthquake struck and the jail foundations were jarred loose and opened the doors. Paul was set free. The first person he spoke with was his jailer, who asked to be baptized along with his family. Although Paul and Silas were summoned before the magistrates, when the latter heard that they were Roman citizens, the two were set free and asked to leave the city. Afterwards Paul and Silas visited the house of Lydia and then departed for Thessaloniki. Due to the apostle's close ties with the Philippians, Paul wrote several letters to them and visited the city several more times between AD 56 and 64.

CREDIT: ©ISTOCKPHOTO.COM/CHRISTOPHER JONES

Touch the Roman water cistern where the apostle Paul was imprisoned.

What should I see and do?

Philippi should be included on any apostle Paul tour to Greece. As there is so much to see and do at ancient Philippi, here are the top sites to visit:

- Paul's Prison: Roman water cistern where the apostle was imprisoned
- Ruins of three Christian basilicas
- Marketplace: where Paul and Silas were brought before the judge
- Octagon Church: incorporates a first-century Christian church dedicated to Paul
- Memorial and place of Lydia's baptism near the river and beside a small church (about half a mile north of town)
- Other places include the great theater, walls, Roman forum, and Archaeological Museum of Philippi with artifacts from early Christianity.

How can I get there?

Philippi is less than ten miles from Kavala on Road 2 (which connects Kavala and Drama). Frequent bus service is also available, as well as ferry service from Piraeus and North Aegean islands (both ferry and high-speed boats).

EXCURSION TO SAMOTHRACE (SAMOTHRAKI) (ACTS 16:11–12)

Travel planning

www.samothraki.gr

Why should I visit?

In the northeast Aegean Sea near the western coast of Turkey is the island of Samothrace. It is best known biblically as the place where Paul dropped anchor in AD 49 or AD 50 on his second missionary journey before continuing to Macedonia and the northern coast of Greece.

What should I see and do?

An original early Christian basilica was built at the ancient port Paleopolis to commemorate Paul's visit. Today only scant remains of the ruins can be found. Very few apostle Paul tours typically include Samothrace on their itineraries.

How can I get there?

Samothrace is accessible by ferry from Kavala, Alexandroupolis, Lavrion, and East Aegean islands.

EXCURSION TO VERIA (BEREA) (ACTS 17:10–15)

Why should I visit?

In the first century AD, Berea possessed a thriving Jewish community. Paul, Silas, and Timothy traveled to Berea and began preaching here after being persecuted in Thessaloniki. As the people of Berea were much more receptive to their message, Paul characterized the locals as being nobler than the Thessaloniki citizens. However, once word reached Thessaloniki of Paul's whereabouts and doings, his enemies from the previous city came to stir up trouble. Shortly after, Paul left for the coast while Silas and Timothy stayed in Berea to continue preaching and spreading the Gospel. In total Paul visited Berea three times: twice on his second missionary journey (AD 49–52) and once on his third missionary journey (AD 53–58). The biblical town of Berea (also Beroea) is today called Veria or Veroia. Berea is called "Little Jerusalem" by some people.

What should I see and do?

Paul's Bema is the monument commemorating the site where Paul preached to the local people in AD 54.

How can I get there?

Veria is forty-five miles southwest of Thessaloniki on road 4.

I, John, both your brother and companion in the tribulation and kingdom and patience of Jesus Christ, was on the island that is called Patmos for the word of God and for the testimony of Jesus Christ.

REVELATION 1:9

Why should I visit?

"Dear visitor, the place you have just entered is sacred." This is the inscription that greets you at the entrance of the Cave of the Apocalypse, the very site where John the apostle is said to have written the Book of Revelation, the last book of the Bible. Considered one of the more sacred sites in the Christian world, the cave is also commonly referred to as the Holy Grotto of the Revelation.

Exiled to Patmos in AD 95 by the Roman emperor Domitian, the apostle (also known as John the Evangelist, John the Divine, and John the Theologian) made the island his home for two years. Within the cave, you can see the threefold fissure in the ceiling, believed to represent the trinity and a mark of God's presence.

At the top of the island is the Monastery of Saint John the Divine, also known as Saint John the Theologian. Founded in 1088, the monastery was originally built as a fortress, and it towers over the island both physically and spiritually. One of the most impressive aspects of Saint John the Divine is its library, considered one of the most important in all of Christendom. The monastery's treasury is also home to a prized collection of icons, manuscripts, and other religious artifacts. In summer 2006, UNESCO declared both the monastery and the cave World Heritage Sites.

Christian groups often visit Patmos Island while either retracing the missionary journeys of Paul through Greece or when traveling through Turkey and visiting the Seven Churches of Revelation. No matter which tour you take, the Cave of the Apocalypse always serves as a highlight.

CONTACT INFORMATION FOR PATMOS ISLAND

Tourist office: www.patmos.gr (click on English version upper left)

What should I see and do?

The Cave of the Apocalypse and the Monastery of Saint John are the island's primary Christian attractions. The cave itself is located about halfway up the island and is under the custodianship of the Greek Orthodox Church. Once you arrive at the grotto, be sure to pick up the brochure that provides excellent descriptions and insights about the cave. After walking down the forty-plus stairs into the grotto, you will be inside the very cave where John wrote the Book of Revelation. Look for the "rock pillow" where the apostle rested his head for sleep, as well as the "rock table" where Prochoros transcribed what John dictated. After a visit to the cave, you may wish to proceed to the top of the island. Here you can join a guided tour of the Monastery of Saint John or simply visit its treasury.

CREDIT: ©ISTOCKPHOTO.COM/MARK WEISS

On Patmos Island visit the cave where the apostle John wrote the Book of Revelation, and tour the famed monastery at the top (seen here).

How much time should I spend?

About two hours can be spent visiting both the cave and monastery; the cave itself needs only about thirty minutes.

How can I get there?

Location. Located forty miles off Turkey's west coast, Patmos is a small island measuring about ten miles long and six miles wide.

By Boat. Patmos is accessible by ferry from many of the islands with daily service from Athens and Rhodes. To travel by ferry between Kusadasi Turkey and Patmos, you must change in Samos. It is also accessible by ferry from Piraeus (Athens).

By Bus. There is bus service from the base of the island to both the monastery and cave.

By Taxi. A taxi can also be used to reach the monastery or cave and is one of the best and easiest ways to get there.

By Moped. One of the most exciting ways to travel the island and reach the cave and monastery is by moped.

By Walking. If you're traveling independently, one of the best ways to reach the cave and monastery is by walking. It is a twenty-minute walk to the cave and a forty-minute walk to the monastery from the cobbled path that begins from the main road in Hora.

What lodgings are available?

Most Christian groups traveling to Patmos travel aboard a cruise, which provides accommodations. When booking your cruise, be sure to ask about cabin choices (inside or outside, etc.). The island itself does offer a variety of accommodation options as well.

EXCURSION TO RHODES (ACTS 21:1)

Travel planning

Visit www.culture.gr, click on Archaeological Sites, Alphabetical Index, and then search for "Lindos," "Medieval City of Rhodes," or "Acropolis of Rhodes."

Why should I visit?

Paul landed here on this third missionary journey and probably only spent one night. The capital of the Greek Islands, Rhodes is also home to the Venetian Castle (built by the Knights of Saint John) and provides a wonderful glimpse of medieval architecture.

What can I see and do?

At the base of the Acropolis is Saint Paul's Bay, where the apostle dropped anchor before continuing to Ephesus. Along with visiting the castle built by the Knights of Saint John, visitors can also explore the many beautiful Byzantine churches.

How can I get there?

Rhodes is the largest of the Dodecanese Islands and is located in the southeastern Aegean Sea (near Turkey). The island is easily accessible by very frequent ferry service from many islands, as well as from Athens's port Piraeus.

CHAPTER 4

CHRISTIAN PILGRIMAGES AND TOURS: EUROPE

CREDIT: ©ISTOCKPHOTO.COM/LUKE DANIEK

Is a Christian pilgrimage to Europe right for me?

When you think of a European trip, what comes to mind? If you're like most people, you probably imagine exploring the continent's fascinating history, heritage, culture, and cuisine. For the Christian though, Europe offers something even greater: almost twenty centuries of Christian heritage, history, and faith, including the roots of many Christian denominations. You can visit sites ranging from the Vatican to Martin Luther's church and C.S. Lewis'ss home. If you would like to immerse yourself in Christian history and faith while enjoying some of the world's great historical events, cultures, cuisines, and personalities, then a pilgrimage to Europe might be right for you. And best of all, it's a destination you can journey to any time of the year, with a group or on your own.

EUROPE "AT A GLANCE"

TRIP SUMMARY
Typical length: 6–14 days
Average cost per day: $200–$350
Total average cost: $2,000–$4,000
Distance from home: direct flights from New York to Europe are approximately six to nine hours in length
Variety of pilgrimages: many
When to go: any time of the year; spring and fall typically offer the smallest crowds and the best weather
Why go: To learn more about the Christian faith while experiencing European culture and history
Whom to go with: alone, with a few friends, or in a group
Which Christian European destination to choose: visit the country or region that most appeals to you for its Christian sites, European culture, history, and personal or denominational heritage

DEMANDS AND BENEFITS
Spiritual focus: high
Fellowship opportunities: many
Physically demanding: low to moderate
Intellectually stimulating: very
Emotionally rewarding: very
Culturally enriching: very

What is the relevance of a pilgrimage to Europe?

A Christian journey to Europe is a journey to discover and explore the heart of our post-biblical Christian heritage. Much of the Christian faith that we know today is a combination of events, movements, personalities, and the culture of the past twenty centuries in Europe.

Europe is home to many prominent holy sites, shrines, and places of faith for various Christian denominations; and it is the one place you can discover the best of traditional Christian art, architecture, literature, and music. Those who do take advantage of the opportunity to explore Christian Europe return home with a much greater passion, appreciation, knowledge, understanding, and love for the Christian faith. If you wish to discover the Christian faith of today, there's no better place to begin your journey than in Europe.

Why should I embark on a pilgrimage to Europe?

Some people embark on pilgrimages to Europe for spiritual purposes, while others go for intellectual, social, physical, or emotional reasons. You might consider visiting Europe on a Christian pilgrimage if you want to:

- explore firsthand the roots of our Christian faith
- discover in person the immense contributions of Christianity to Western civilization
- seek inspiration from some of Christianity's greatest men, women, and saints
- learn about Christians who sacrificed everything for the Gospel of Jesus Christ and changed the world
- visit holy sites and shrines
- search for spiritual or emotional healing
- vacation in Europe while visiting sites of faith
- combine a physically active vacation with a pilgrimage (hiking the Santiago de Compostela trail, for example)

CHOOSING A CHRISTIAN EUROPEAN PILGRIMAGE

How can I choose the right European pilgrimage for me?

Once you know the reasons why you wish to visit Europe on a pilgrimage, you are ready to decide which trip is right for you. In general, there are three major types of Christian European pilgrimages:

1. A journey to the roots of your particular Christian faith or denomination
2. A visit to a place that is home to a significant Christian event or person
3. A trip to a holy site, church, cathedral, or shrine

Most Christian European pilgrimages include some aspect of all three components. For example, a trip to Scotland might include visits to Iona Abbey, Saint Giles Cathedral, and John Knox's home, while a trip to Italy may include Rome and the Vatican, Assisi (Saint Francis), and visits to cathedrals in Florence or Venice. You can decide what works best for your interests.

What are the advantages and disadvantages of Christian European tours?

Advantages

- great destination for traveling independently or with a group
- many English-speaking people, especially in tourist areas
- hundreds of Christian sites to choose from
- opportunity to explore your own Christian denomination roots
- provides tremendous insight into Christian history
- ability to combine a pilgrimage with vacation
- offers fascinating culture and cuisine
- possible ancestral ties to Europe
- excellent transportation facilities, venues, and roads
- quite safe as a destination

Disadvantages

- can be very expensive, especially when the value of the U.S. dollar declines
- heavily populated with tourists especially during the summer or high tourism season
- overnight flights to Europe can be long and uncomfortable in coach class
- long lines at popular venues such as the Vatican Museums
- travel throughout Europe often requires changing hotels every few nights and "living out of a suitcase"
- trips to some areas of Europe (i.e. Eastern Europe) may feature more limited facilities and possibly fewer people who speak English

What is the average pilgrimage trip length?

Most trips average ten days; however, some can be as short as five or six days if you're visiting only one city (such as London or Rome), while other "grand European" pilgrimage tours covering several countries can last as much as fourteen days or longer.

How much does a Christian European tour cost?

As with biblical pilgrimages, a Christian European trip cost will vary greatly depending on your travel choices. First of all, the overall cost will be dictated by whether you travel alone or with a group tour. If you plan to travel independently and very cheaply, you might be able to budget anywhere from $150 to $250 a day. However, if you plan to stay at first-class to superior tourist class hotels found on many escorted pilgrimage tours, eat meals in restaurants (or hotels), rent a car and the like, then you should budget the same amount per day as a group tour, which can range from an estimated $200 to $350.

If you are traveling on a group trip, a mid-range estimate is $2,000 to $4,000. The less expensive trips will primarily consist of those one-week or less trips to one city in Europe (i.e. a six-day trip to London or Rome), while the more expensive trips will be your typical two-week tours. As with biblical pilgrimages, in general you should budget an average of about $3,000 for a trip to Europe (including airfare). However, depending on the value of the U.S. dollar against the Euro, this amount can quickly rise. Because of this, European pilgrimages can sometimes cost slightly more than biblical pilgrimages.

What does the cost of a Christian European tour include? What costs are typically not included?

As the costs included on a Christian European pilgrimage tour will often be quite similar to those on an escorted biblical tour, please see the Biblical Lands chapter (p.24) for the answer to these questions.

PREPARING FOR YOUR CHRISTIAN EUROPEAN PILGRIMAGE

Should I travel independently or with a group to Europe?

Europe is one of the great overseas destinations perfectly suited for independent or group travel.

Although visiting Europe with your church or faith community offers many benefits (greater fellowship and camaraderie), independent travel is also satisfying. Independent travel is made possible by Europe's ease of transportation, excellent tourist facilities, and wide variety of accommodations, as well as the fact that English is widely spoken and Europe is generally a safe destination. How can you arrange such travels? Most independent travelers research and plan trips by themselves. One of the most popular trip planning resources for travelers to Europe is Rick Steve's *Europe through the Back Door* (www.ricksteves.com). Of course, you can always rely on the services of a travel agent.

Group Travel

How or where can you join or arrange a group trip to Europe? You typically have the option of joining a trip scheduled by your own faith community or by a travel company, or leading your own group trip. The first option is the most common form of travel to Europe by Christians because it requires the least amount of planning and preparation. If one's church or faith community isn't offering a pilgrimage to Europe, many Christians will then turn to companies or organizations that offer trips on a scheduled basis. Researching and finding the right tour company, as well as choosing a particular tour, is where most of the planning is involved. The third option is the most time consuming because you take on the role of organizing a group trip for your faith community or group. Regardless of the scenario you choose, you can find a list of resources for companies and organizations specializing in pilgrimage trips to Europe in appendix A.

What trip preparations should I make for my Christian European pilgrimage?

As trip preparations for a Christian European pilgrimage or tour are quite similar to the process for planning a Holy Land trip, please refer to the Biblical Lands chapter for guidance and answers to your questions. You will also find there the top ten tips for making the most of your Biblical pilgrimage, which can easily be adapted to your Christian European pilgrimage as well.

How can I combine the best of a pilgrimage with a vacation?

Once you decide to embark on a Christian journey to Europe, make certain your trip includes both pilgrimage and vacation elements: be sure to dedicate a good portion of your time to visiting key Christian sites and places of history but also immerse yourself in European culture. Enjoy the cuisine, the people, and the general culture it offers. By doing so, you will find that you truly are refreshed and reenergized in body, mind, and soul when you return home. As with biblical pilgrimages, make sure to hand the reigns of your trip over to God. Let Him show you the people, places, and experiences that He wants you to encounter. This way, you can ensure yourself the trip of a lifetime.

So, as much as is in me, I am ready to preach the gospel to you who are in Rome also.

ROMANS 1:15

Why should I visit?

Rome is inextricably linked with the history of Christianity. The city is mentioned frequently in the Book of Acts and Romans and played a key role in the early days of the church. Although Jesus's death took place one thousand five hundred miles from Rome, Rome played a role in his crucifixion. Pontius Pilate, a Roman, served as the local governor of the Judea Province from AD 26 to 36, which included overseeing Jesus's death in AD 33. After the resurrection of Christ, the apostles took advantage of the extensive and well-kept Roman roads and traveled throughout the empire spreading the Gospel message. Paul wrote letters to the Romans and, according to Acts, spent two years under house arrest in Rome.

During the subsequent centuries of persecution, many of the faithful began meeting, worshiping, and burying their fellow Christians in underground Roman cemeteries, later known as the catacombs. The emperor Constantine's recognition of

CREDIT: ©ISTOCKPHOTO.COM/BILL GROVE

Rome is the spiritual headquarters of the Roman Catholic Church.

Christianity as an official religion via the Edict of Milan in AD 313, led to the construction of churches and basilicas throughout Rome and the empire, including Saint Peter's Basilica on Vatican Hill, reportedly on the site of the apostle Paul's grave. Ten million people each year continue to make the trip to Rome to explore the great churches of Christendom, saunter through the catacombs, see the sites of Christian martyrdom, gaze upon the great works of art, and attend the General Audience to see the Pope.

CONTACT INFORMATION FOR ROME

Tourist Office: Italy, www.italiantourism.com; Rome, www.romaturismo.it

Vatican Tourist Information: The Vatican, www.vatican.va

Information Office for Pilgrims and Tourists in Saint Peter's Square: (Located in front of Saint Peter's Basilica, to the left—next to the post office): Tel (3906) 698-84466; Fax (3906) 698-85100

Embassy: Italian Embassy, www.ambwashingtondc.esteri.it; Vatican Embassy, www.vatican.usembassy.gov

Other Helpful Web Sites: Saint Peter's Basilica, www.stpetersbasilica.org; Santa Susanna (American church), www.santasusanna.org; U.S. Bishop's Office for Visitors to the Vatican, www.pnac.org/general/visiting_vatican.htm

What do I need to know?

Religion. Italy is synonymous with Roman Catholicism. More than 90 percent of Italians are Roman Catholics, with the remaining 10 percent Protestant Christian, Jewish, or Muslim.

Language. Italian is the official language of the country and the main language spoken in Rome. You will find some local Romans, especially those in tourism, who speak English (either fluently or at least enough to understand).

Climate. Just a few things to remember: August is unbearably hot with temperatures over 95°F and with very heavy humidity. Spring and fall brings mild temperatures, while winter is marked with fairly damp weather and temperatures around 50°F. It can rain virtually any day of the year in Rome and sometimes with a downpour. Bring an umbrella.

When to visit Rome. The primary tourist season lasts from Easter to the fall. The most pleasant times to visit are the spring and autumn as the weather can be quite nice. Summer brings stiflingly hot temperatures (especially August) as well as large crowds of tourists. Though winter weather isn't ideal, prices are lower and crowds are smaller. The very best overall months for visiting are April through June or late September through October.

Clothing. If you're traveling in the summer, dress lightly and be prepared for warm temperatures. Remember to bring light pants or long skirts for visiting Saint Peter's Basilica, Vatican Museums, and other churches (no shorts or bare shoulders are permitted for men or women). Dress in layers for spring and fall and dress warmly for the winter. And don't forget to bring good, comfortable walking shoes (after a full day of touring Rome on its cobblestone streets, you will understand why).

Transportation. Rome is very easy to get around. The most popular transportation methods include walking and using the two Metro Lines (Linea A is red and Linea B is blue), buses, and trams. The two most important things to keep in mind when using public transport is to buy your ticket in advance (you can't buy it aboard public transport) and validate your ticket before embarking on the public transport.

That Summer Would Change My Life

When I was nineteen years old, I made my first journey to Florence, Italy, to study Italian. I had no idea then how that summer would change my life. It happened on a day excursion to nearby Assisi, where I discovered one of the greatest and most beloved Christian Saints—Saint Francis of Assisi. I was immediately struck by the archaic beauty of Assisi—her timeless stone walls, cobblestone streets, the travertine church facades. However, after I heard the story of Francis, I thought surely he must be one of the most faithful Christians in the history of the church: his humility, radical poverty, immense faith, peaceful spirit. As I was struck by the ancientness of the city, I was impressed by the fact that there were still men and women following this poor, humble Saint in an unbroken line of eight hundred years! That day in Assisi led me to re-commit my life to Christ. —*Bret*

ROME TRAVEL PLANNING
General trip planning: Enjoy Rome: www.enjoyrome.com
Airport: Leonardo da Vinci/Fiumicino International Airport: www.adr.it

Train: Tren Italia (Train Italy), www.trenitalia.com/en/index.html; Italian Rail, www.italianrail.com

Bus: Atac, www.atac.roma.it; Cotral, www.cotralspa.it; SIT Bus Shuttle, www.sitbusshuttle.it and www.sitbus.com

Car (driving directions): www.viamichelin.com, www.theaa.com, www.mapquest.com

Wonder and Awe

We flew to Rome and spent three days touring everything the human eye would want to see—from the Catacombs to the view atop Saint Peter's Basilica. The timeless history of Rome filled our minds with wonder and awe. The art of Leonardo DaVinci and sculptures of Michelangelo were spectacular. We saw the Pope and experienced communion at the Vatican. As Protestants, we were appreciative of the Catholic Church and its holy place in history. The sights, sounds, and tastes of Rome will remain as a fond memory to each of us. —*Pastor Roger*

ROME

Why should I visit?

Throughout the centuries, Rome has witnessed its share of prominent historical events and people. The Roman historian Tacitus wrote that the emperor Nero blamed the Christians in AD 64 for the great fire that destroyed a good portion of Rome. As a result, Christians became a target for persecution, which lasted for the next three centuries. In the catacombs they met, worshiped, and even buried their dead. Rome is where two thousand years of history remains intertwined with faith. It is the city where apostles, saints, reformers, kings, queens, nobility, and everyday Christians from around the world have walked its streets.

What should I see and do?

With so many spectacular sites to see, be sure you visit:

- Basilica of Saint Mary Major (Santa Maria Maggiore): Built on the Esquiline Hill in AD 352, this Papal Basilica is said to hold the relics of Jesus's manger.

- Basilica of Saint John Lateran (San Giovanni in Laterano): This Papal Basilica serves as the cathedral of Rome, the home church for the Bishop of Rome (the Pope).
- Holy Stairs: According to tradition, Jesus climbed these same stairs to reach Pilate's Palace.
- Ancient Appian Way: The oldest road in Rome, it features the Chapel of Domine Quo Vadis.
- Catacombs: Visit the Christian catacombs of Saint Callisto, San Sebastiano, and Saint Domitilla.
- Basilica of Saint Paul Outside the Walls: One of the five Papal Basilicas, this church is believed to be built upon the relics of the apostle Paul.
- Porta San Sebastiano: This is the gate where Rome's most ancient road exits the city.
- Circus Maximus: The largest stadium in ancient Rome, which held chariot races, it also served as the site of many Christian martyr deaths.
- Colosseum: Serving as the landmark symbol of Rome, the ancient amphitheatre could accommodate fifty thousand spectators during its heyday.
- Arch of Constantine: The arch was built in AD 312 by the senate to honor Constantine's liberation of Rome at the Battle of Milvian Bridge.

CATACOMBS

One of the most popular sightseeing activities (and a "must") for Christians is exploring the catacombs—the ancient underground Roman cemeteries located outside the original city center. Both Christians and Jews used the catacombs from the second century through the fifth century. As the years passed, the underground sites evolved from being primarily burial places to actual places of Christian gathering and worship. To learn more about the catacombs visit the official Web site at www.catacombe.roma.it.

TO ARRANGE YOUR VISIT OR GUIDED TOUR TO THE CATACOMBS CONTACT:
Catacombe di San Callisto
Via Appia Antica 126
00179 ROMA (Italy)
E-mail: scallisto@catacombe.roma.it
Tel: (3906) 513-01-51; (3906) 513-01580
Fax: (3906) 513-01-567

How much time should I spend?

You should plan to spend about three days visiting Rome. The following is a typical itinerary for most Christian tour groups (or individuals) visiting Rome:

Day 1: Arrive in Rome and spend remainder of day at leisure.

Day 2: Tour "Christian Rome" in the morning and early afternoon. Remainder of day at leisure.

Day 3: Tour Saint Peter's Basilica, Sistine Chapel, and Vatican Museums. Some groups will integrate the Pope's General Audience into this day. (Note: Days 2 and 3 can, of course, be reversed).

How can I get there?

Location. Rome is located on the western-central coast of Italy. As one of the more prominent cities in the world today, it is one of the most accessible cities by land, sea, and air.

By Plane. The main airport in Rome is Leonardo da Vinci/Fiumicino International Airport, located about twenty miles from the city center of Rome. Many nonstop flights from North America fly into this airport. If you fly into Rome from within Europe, you may fly into Rome's other airport called Ciampino International Airport.

By Train. Rome is one of the easiest cities to reach from throughout Europe by train. It is the final destination for many train routes, including overnight trains. The central train station in Rome is the Stazione Termini; there is also the popular Tiburtina Station, which connects to major cities throughout Italy and Europe. When choosing which train to take (to get into or out of Rome), keep in mind that the Eurostar trains are the fastest, the Intercity trains are "kind of fast," and the local trains are the slowest. From the Leonardo da Vinci Airport, there is frequent train service to Rome's central train station.

By Boat. Cruise ships visiting Rome dock at the nearby ports of Civitavecchia or Lido di Ostia (Porto di Roma).

By Bus. Rome is easily accessible by bus from throughout Italy. Once you're in Rome, bus transportation is typically the most popular way to get around.

By Car. You do not want to drive in Rome if at all possible. If you are renting a car from elsewhere in Italy and drive in to Rome, find your hotel immediately and park. Then switch to local bus transportation, taxi, or walking to get around. (Do not worry about obtaining directions on how to get to Rome by car; as the old saying goes "all road leads to Rome.")

By Taxi. Taxis are about as plentiful in Rome as they are in New York. And, like New York, taxis are one of the best and most efficient ways to get around Rome. Just be sure to hold on to your hat—some Roman taxi drivers can get a bit crazy and don't be surprised if they drive up on the sidewalk to get around another car (I've had this happen to me more than once while in Rome). There are many illegal taxi drivers who will approach you at both the train station and airport. Do not take these taxis, no matter how tempting the drivers may sound. Instead, look for the official white taxis, which have meters. If you're at the train station or airport, just proceed to the taxi stands located outside.

What lodgings are available?

Rome has every kind of accommodation you are looking for, ranging from budget hostels to first-class hotels to ultra luxury. For those wishing to stay in a religious guesthouse, you can view a list of available places by visiting www.pnac.org/general/visiting_vatican.htm and then click on "Where can I stay in Rome."

VATICAN CITY

What should I see and do?

Be sure to visit Saint Peter's Basilica, the Vatican, the Vatican Museums, the Vatican Gardens, and the Sistine Chapel. The information below will tell you how to tour these sites.

SAINT PETER'S BASILICA

For information on guided tours of Saint Peter's Basilica, go to the web site www.stpeters-basilica.org. You have several options for a guided tour. You can rent the audio walking tour headsets and explore the basilica on your own by picking up your headsets at the bag check area located to the right of the basilica entrance. A second option is to join an actual tour with a "live" guide. If you like this idea, then proceed to the Information Desk to the left of the basilica (near the post office) and inquire about the guided tours. A third option is to join one of the companies that offer free tours of Saint Peter's Basilica. Most of these tours start at 10 AM around the obelisk. If you choose this option, know that afterward the guides will often invite you to join their paid tour of the Vatican Museums.

How can I get to Saint Peter's Basilica?

By Subway. Take Linea (red line) toward Battistini, exiting at Ottaviano-San Pietro. Then walk south on Via Ottaviano toward Saint Peter's Square and the Vatican.

By Bus. From Rome's Termini station, take bus #64 or #40.

By Foot. There are several ways to reach Saint Peter's Basilica on foot. The most direct route is from city center whereby you cross the Tiber and then walk up Via Conciliazioni. If you have a little extra time, walk under the Passetto arch near Castel Saint Angelo and continue up Pio Borgo.

What is a "Scavi" tour?

One of the most unique ways to see Saint Peter's Basilica is from underground. That's right—by walking underneath Saint Peter's Basilica through the excavations of the underground necropolis. How can you make this experience possible? You must make a reservation by contacting the Excavation Office at:

Ufficio Scavi
Fabbrica di San Pietro
00120 Citta del Vaticano
E-mail: scavi@fsp.va
Tel: (3906) 6987-3017; (3906) 6988-5318
Fax: (3906) 6988-5518; (3906) 6987-3017

When faxing, e-mailing, or phoning your request, be sure to include the following information:

- the number of visitors in your group
- your organization's name and attendee names (including yourself)
- the language requested for visit
- the date available for visit
- your contact information (e-mail, telephone, fax, mailing address, etc.)

Please note that, as there is limited availability, you must book the Scavi tour well in advance. For a full list of important and complete details about booking and joining a Scavi tour, be sure to visit the Excavations Office Web site at www.stpetersbasilica.org (and then click on the "Scavi-Necropolis" Web link).

VATICAN MUSEUM, SISTINE CHAPEL, AND GARDEN TOURS

You can visit these sites on a guided tour or alone. If you are traveling as a group, be sure to get reservations ahead of time.

What tours are available?

You have three options for your guided tour:

1. *Vatican Museums and Sistine Chapel.* If you would like an in-depth and personal experience of the Vatican Museums and Sistine Chapel, definitely consider taking this tour. This guided trip will take you to the museum's most important religious, historical, and cultural areas, including the famed Sistine Chapel. You can visit these sites on your own, but you may miss some meaningful information.

2. *Vatican Gardens.* If you would like to literally explore the backyard of the Vatican, you can take a tour of its gardens. With its exploration of the garden's botanic settings, historic artifacts, and beautiful artwork, the guided trip provides a behind-the-scenes view of the world's smallest country—the Vatican City State.

3. *Vatican Gardens and Sistine Chapel.* If you would like to combine the best of the Vatican Gardens and Sistine Chapel, then this is the tour for you. Please note that this tour does not include the Vatican Museums and is only available for groups, not individuals.

GUIDED TOURS OFFICE OF THE VATICAN

For complete information about visiting or embarking on a guided tour of Vatican sites, visit www.vatican.va and then click on the link for "Vatican Museums."

To book as an individual, contact the Vatican office via the following telephone, fax, or e-mail:

Tel: (3906) 6988-4676 or (3906) 698-84466
Fax: (3906) 6988-5100
E-mail: visiteguidate.musei@scv.va

To book as a group (advance reservations required), contact the Vatican office via the following telephone, fax, or e-mail:

Tel: (3906) 6988-3145
Fax: (3906) 6988-3578
E-mail: visiteguidate.musei@scv.va

How can I reserve a guided tour?

You must fax your request to the Vatican office (bookings are currently taken only by fax). Presuming there is availability and your booking is confirmed, you will in turn receive a fax confirmation regarding your guided tour. If you do not receive a fax confirmation, your booking is not valid. You must bring this fax confirmation with you on your trip and present it to the "Guided Tours" desk on the day of your visit.

If you're booking a guided tour as an individual, your reservation must be received one month in advance by the Vatican office. Sometimes you can book with shorter notice; however, it is subject to availability. Group tours need two months advance notice with the Vatican office; sometimes you can book with shorter notice, but it's subject to availability.

In your fax, be sure to state which guided tour you are requesting, the date, and approximate number of participants. One week prior to the tour, you must send a confirmation with the exact number of participants (if this is not received, the Office will automatically cancel your booking without warning). A group is considered twenty guests, so if the number falls below this, the tour is still responsible for paying the minimum guided tour fee for twenty guests.

What do I need to do the day of my guided tour?

On the day of your arrival, you must go to the Guided Tours desk inside the Vatican

CREDIT: ©ISTOCKPHOTO.COM/PAUL MCKEOWN

Christians gathered to worship in underground Roman cemeteries.

Museums to pay for the tickets. One of the benefits of joining a guided tour is that you do not need to wait in line. After paying, proceed to the main gate of the Vatican Museums on the Viale Vaticano (while facing the Vatican Museums Entrance door, look for the line on the right that is reserved solely for Vatican guided tours). Arrive fifteen minutes before your tour begins. Remember that proper dress is required for entrance. Identification such as passport or proper identification card (not driver's license) is required.

How can I get to the Vatican Museums?

From Saint Peter's Square, simply walk north (to the right of the Piazza) along the wall for ten to fifteen minutes. You will eventually reach the Vatican Museums entrance which will be on your left. Or, you can take bus #49 to the Vatican Museums, or take Linea to Cipro-Musei Vaticani (Vatican Museums).

GENERAL AUDIENCE WITH THE POPE

How would you like to see the Pope with eight thousand of your closest friends? Or sometimes with as many as thirty thousand of your closest friends? That is what a General Audience is all about. As few people will ever have a "private audience" with the Pope (i.e. just him, you, and your best friend), most people take advantage of the "General Audiences," which anybody can attend.

So what exactly is a General Audience? In short, it's a gathering of the Pope with the people of the world at the Vatican. It usually takes place in either Saint Peter's Square or inside the Pope Paul VI auditorium. What takes place at these events? The Pope often welcomes the crowd and specific groups in a variety of languages. This is followed by a catechesis (a teaching of the Christian faith) from the Pope. The entire event usually lasts about two hours; but be sure to allocate an entire morning for this event to allow for transportation for getting to the Vatican, getting seated, waiting for the Pope to appear, etc.

General audience information
- Time: Wednesdays at 10:30 AM
- Location: Saint Peter's Square, Saint Peter's Basilica, Paul VI Hall (Aula Nervi), or Castel Gandolfo (the Pope's summer residence located forty minutes from Rome by car)
- Cost: tickets are free of charge and available from the Pontifical Household

How can I reserve my general audience tickets?

You must have a ticket to attend the General Audience with the Pope (or other papal events such as a Mass), and you must reserve them ten days in advance. As tickets are not delivered by mail, you must pick them up in Rome in person (through whichever source you ordered them). You have several options when it comes to requesting and reserving your General Audience tickets.

Option #1

You can contact the Vatican directly at:
    Prefect of the Pontifical Household
    00120 Vatican City, Europe
    Tel: (3906) 6988-4857
    Fax: (3906) 6988-5863
You can fax your requests to the above office. After the request is made and confirmed, tickets can be picked up the afternoon before the audience between 3 PM and 8 PM at the Bronze Doors under the colonnade in Saint Peter's Square.

Option #2

You can contact the U.S. Bishops' Office for Visitors to the Vatican by e-mail at nacvisoffrome@pnac.org or fax at (3906) 690-01821 or (3906) 679-1448. Or, simply visit or write to them at:
    Casa Santa Maria
    Via dell'Umiltá, 30
    00187 Rome, Italy
The office is located one block from the Trevi Fountain; you will be required to pick up the tickets for General Audiences on Tuesday afternoons from 3 PM to 7 PM at the office.

Option #3

You can request tickets through the official American Catholic Church in Rome, which is called Church of Santa Susanna. The Web site for ticket information is: www.santasusanna.org/popeVatican/tickets.html. To request your tickets directly through the Church of Santa Susanna, you can e-mail your request to tickets@santasusanna.org or fax your request to (3906) 4201-4328.

A fourth option is simply to obtain the tickets in person at the Vatican itself. How do you do this? Just days before the Wednesday General Audience, go to Saint Peter's Square and look for the Swiss Guards located at the Bronze Doors to the Apostolic Palace. Here you can ask for the tickets. (Note: This option is usually best only for individuals, not groups.).

Special note

The General Audience is subject to availability and Pope's schedule. Before arriving in Rome, be sure to check that the Pope will be in town and that the General Audience is still scheduled as planned. As the General Audiences are always subject to the Pope's schedule and to other factors, the event can be canceled at any time.

How can I arrange a special announcement by the Pope?

If you would like to hear the Pope welcome your group by name at the General Audience, then be sure to give the name of your organization to the office above that is providing you with tickets and specifically state that you are open to your group being announced. Although it is not a guarantee that the Pope will welcome your group publicly by name, doing this increases your chances.

What are Sundays at noon with the Pope?

When the Pope is in town on Sundays, he addresses the entire crowd at Saint Peter's Basilica at noon for the Angelus. The Angelus is a short, traditional devotion prayed by Catholics to commemorate the annunciation of the angel Gabriel to Mary (Luke 1:26–38).

Traveler's tip

The best way to ensure a good seat at a General Audience or Papal event is to arrive very early. If you would like to get near the Pope, the secret is to secure an aisle seat where the pope may pass by. To learn more about the event or to request tickets for the event, you can visit one of the following Web sites:

- www.santasusanna.org/popeVatican/popeVatican.html
- www.santasusanna.org/popeVatican/tickets.html
- http://vatican.usembassy.gov/vatican/audiences.asp

How should I dress?

When visiting the Vatican, Saint Peter's Basilica, or the churches of Rome, plan on dressing modestly to conservative. In many of these places, the dress code is strictly enforced with no exceptions. In short, remember the "No" rules: no shorts, no bare shoulders, and no miniskirts (no skirts about the knees). All of the rules apply to both men and women.

EXCURSION TO ASSISI

Travel planning

Assisi is located in the Umbria region. Go to www.umbria.org.

Why should I visit?

One of the most famous and popular figures in Christian history is Saint Francis of Assisi. Born in 1181, Francis experienced a dramatic conversion as a young adult and dedicated the rest of his life to Christ. He is best known for living a life of great simplicity and poverty in imitation of the Gospel and for living in harmony with all of creation. During his time, he traveled throughout Italy preaching the love of God and sharing the Christian message to all. Many became attracted to his way of life and joined in his movement. Francis believed in living a life of humility before God. He cared for everything and everyone from the animals of earth to the poor to the lepers of society. One of his most often repeated sayings is "Preach the Gospel everywhere, and if necessary, use words."

Today, the worldwide Franciscan community (begun by Francis) continues the work of the Gospel in the spirit of Saint Francis of Assisi by ministering to all, including the alienated, abandoned, abused, poor, suffering, persecuted, mentally or physically-challenged, and the unchurched. As Francis remains one of the most inspirational Christian figures of all, many people consider a Christian pilgrimage to Italy incomplete without a visit to his hometown.

What should I see and do?

Assisi provides a very popular one- or two-day getaway from Rome (although you could easily spend a week there on retreat). The village retains much of the same unspoiled atmosphere, character, and look of the Assisi that Francis once knew and grew up in. The most common sites to visit today for the Christian pilgrim includes the Basilica of Saint Francis and the Basilica of Saint Clare, Church of Saint Damian, San

Damiano Cross, the Basilica of Saint Mary of the Angels, and the Portiuncula (located on the lower plains of Assisi). Many people also enjoy simply walking the winding medieval streets of hilltop Assisi or watching events at the main square.

What is the San Damiano Cross?

One of the most recognizable "unique" crosses in the world is the San Damiano Cross. As well as serving as the symbol of the Franciscan community today, it is from this cross that Jesus is said to have spoken to Francis the words, "Go and rebuild my church, which is in ruins."

How can I get there?

Assisi is located about 110 miles northeast of Rome and is easily accessible by road, bus, and train. Train service is frequent to Assisi from Rome, Florence, and nearby towns. From the train station in Assisi (which is located on the plains or "lower Assisi"), you will need to catch one of the frequent shuttle buses to the hilltop village of Assisi.

Why should I visit?

As the home of many prominent Christian personalities, writers, movements, and historical events, England is a wonderful destination for the Christian visitor. For example, it is here that the Venerable Bede wrote the *Ecclesiastical History of the English People*, the Wesley brothers founded the Methodist faith, and King Henry VIII broke with the Roman Catholic Church. All this combined with England's historical connection to America makes England a very popular vacation choice for the Christian traveler.

Saint Augustine of Canterbury brought the Christian faith to the Anglo-Saxon Kingdom of Kent in the sixth century. Shortly thereafter, the missionaries and monks followed. Today Christianity in England is synonymous with Thomas Becket, King Henry VIII, Thomas More, The Dissolution of the Monasteries, Edward the Sixth, Mary Tudor, the Church of England, John and Charles Wesley, Methodism, and William Carey, among others. As such, a Christian tour of England offers a little something for everyone.

When embarking on a Christian trip to England, you can choose from a variety of vacation possibilities. Some tours focus on Christian England in general while others spotlight specific denominations such as Anglicanism, Methodism, Catholicism, or the Baptist faith. Other itineraries will follow in the footsteps of prominent Christian personalities

CREDIT: ©ISTOCKPHOTO.COM/CHRISTOPHER STEER

Parliament and Big Ben are famous landmarks in England.

such as C.S. Lewis. Whichever trip you choose, you are certain to learn not only about the history of Christianity but will also about English culture, heritage, and tradition.

CONTACT INFORMATION FOR ENGLAND

Tourist Office: Visit Britain Tourist Board, www.visitbritain.com or www.visitbritain.org; Visit London Tourist Board, www.visitlondon.com; Southeast England Tourist Board, www.visitsoutheastengland.com; Southwest England Tourist Board, www.swtourism.co.uk

Embassy: www.britain-info.org

Other Helpful Web Sites: Britain Express, www.britainexpress.com; Church of England; www.cofe.anglican.org; Historic Churches, www.historicchurches.org.uk; English Heritage, www.english-heritage.org.uk

What do I need to know?

Religion. The official state religion is Christianity, specifically in the form of the Church of England (or the Anglican Church). About 65 percent of the population belongs to this particular denomination. The remaining population is Catholic (10 percent), Methodist (3 percent), Muslim (3 percent), and other faiths (less than 2 percent each). The remaining percentage of the English have no religious affiliation.

Language. English is the primarily language; however, there are a number of local dialects and accents.

Climate. "Mild and wet" is the best way to summarize the English weather. However, there are frequent periods of sun, too, so prepare for both kinds of weather in a span of several days. Keep in mind that the farther north you go, the colder (and usually rainier) it gets. Winter and fall tend to be the wettest months. The summer (May through September) can bring long periods of heat, especially in London and the south.

When to visit England. The most popular time to visit England is May through August.

The weather is pleasant, the days are long, and tourist services are widely available. July and August are the busiest months, so sites can get crowded. Spring and fall can be quite nice, and prices are typically much better than in summer. Winter (November through February) can be extremely inexpensive, especially in regards to airfare; however, not all tourist facilities are open, and the weather can be quite cold, with shorter days of light.

Clothing. More than probably anywhere else, the meaning of "dress in layers" applies in England. Expect anything from "very cool" to "very warm." And definitely bring an umbrella and rain jacket.

Transportation. England is one of the easiest places to get around. Multiple transportation venues from rail to bus to subway to even ferry are available and offer excellent and reliable service.

ENGLAND TRAVEL PLANNING

General trip planning: Transport for London, journeyplanner.tfl.gov.uk; Traveline, www.traveline.org.uk.

Airport: London Heathrow Airport, www.heathrowairport.com; London Gatwick Airport, www.gatwickairport.com.

Train: UK national rail, www.nationalrail.co.uk; BritRail, www.britrail.com; British Rail, www.britishrail.com; Eurostar (Channel Tunnel), www.eurostar.com

Bus: Metro Bus, www.metrobus.co.uk; National Express, www.nationalexpress.com; Eurolines, www.eurolines.com; Greenline, http://www.greenline.co.uk/

Boat: A number of ferry services and companies operate in Britain. For more information, visit www.calmac.co.uk, www.northlinkferries.co.uk, www.wightlink.co.uk, www.redfunnel.co.uk, www.hdferries.co.uk, www.ios-travel.co.uk.

Car (driving directions): www.viamichelin.com, www.theaa.com, www.mapquest.com.

Taxi: Taxi service, www.traintaxi.co.uk.

It Put the "Travel Bug" in Me

I returned not too long ago from a wonderful Christian trip to England—a spiritual vacation that exceeded all my expectations. I fell in love with everything from the countryside to the people to the Christian sites we visited. My favorite part of the trip was taking a C.S. Lewis tour of Oxford, which included visiting his home The Kilns. The experience inspired me to study and learn more about not just the author C.S. Lewis but also the Christian man C.S. Lewis. Other highlights included seeing Canterbury Cathedral, as well as the places related to the Wesley brothers. And I must admit: I couldn't wait to see Buckingham Palace and the changing of the guard! That's something I always wanted to see in person. As my trip to Christian England was my first journey overseas, it has put the "travel bug" in me. I now want to visit other Christian sites throughout Europe, and hopefully one day I will have an opportunity to visit the Holy Land. That would be another dream come true. —*Larry*

EXCURSIONS TO OTHER CHRISTIAN SITES IN ENGLAND

Travel planning

As England is home to many Christian sites, the list of places to visit may seem endless. If you are planning your trip either independently or with a group, you might consider these other sites:

BEDE'S WORLD (WWW.BEDESWORLD.CO.UK) If you would like to learn more about the remarkable life of the Venerable Bede (AD 673–735), you can visit Bede's World—a working museum. It also celebrates Anglo-Saxon cultural achievements. Venerable (or Saint) Bede was a Benedictine monk at the Northumbrian monastery and is best known as an author and scholar. His most famous work, The *Ecclesiastical History of the English People*, earned him the title "The Father of English History." To learn more about Bede's world visit the museum's Web site (above).

LINDISFARNE, THE HOLY ISLAND (WWW.LINDISFARNE.ORG.UK) Lindisfarne, also known as Holy Island, is a tidal island (an island with a causeway that is exposed at low tide and submerged at high tide) located in the North Sea, just off the east coast of the north of England. Lindisfarne is best known for its seventh-century monastery that served as an important cradle of Christianity in Britain and as a landing point for evangelizing the north of England. Today you can visit Lindisfarne Priory and Museum, as well as The Lindisfarne Centre.

JULIAN OF NORWICH (WWW.JULIANOFNORWICH.ORG) Although little is known about the life of fourteenth-century writer Julian of Norwich, today she is regarded as one of the great English mystics. Throughout her life, she experienced a number of visions that led to her writing The Revelations of Divine Love. She is best known for her optimistic theology and philosophy, which focuses on a God of love, joy, and compassion as opposed to a God of "rule and law." Today she is revered by many different Christian traditions, and pilgrims of different denominations travel to Norwich (located two to three hours northeast of London) to visit her cell, which is located next to Saint Julian's Church and Shrine and operated by the Julian Centre.

BRITAIN'S ABBEYS AND CATHEDRALS (BRITAINEXPRESS.COM) There are literally hundreds of abbeys and cathedrals that exist throughout England, Scotland, and Wales. Where can you find further information about these sites? Visit the UK Travel and Heritage Guide at www.britainexpress.com and click on "Abbeys" or "Cathedrals." Here you will find pertinent information about each site including location, Web site, and contact information.

LONDON

Why should I visit?

London offers the best of both Christian and English heritage. Every Christian tour should include Westminster Abbey, which is the national church of Britain and a World UNESCO Heritage Site. Owned by the royal family and located next to Parliament, this former gothic monastery has served as home to the coronation and burial sites of many English monarchs. Be sure to see the Shrine of Edward the Confessor, the tombs of Queen

CREDIT: ©ISTOCKPHOTO.COM/GRAEME PURDY

Saint Paul's Cathedral is the spiritual home for many English.

Elizabeth I and Queen Mary II, and Poet's Corner, where lies the tomb of Geoffrey Chaucer, the writer of *The Canterbury Tales*. Nearby is the Catholic Westminster Cathedral. Although these two buildings share the same name, the abbey and cathedral are not related to one another.

Saint Paul's Cathedral, seat of the Anglican Bishop of London, is the "spiritual home" for the English. The cathedral has witnessed a number of key religious and political events both religious and political in nature, ranging from the burial of Sir Winston Churchill to the wedding of Prince Charles and Lady Diana.

A tour of the Wesley Chapel and House includes the original chapel used by John Wesley (1703–1791), the founder of Methodism. You can explore his home, see his tomb, visit the memorial

Founder Chapel, and spend time inside the Museum of Methodism (which tells the story of Methodism from beginning to present day).

Other places to visit include Bunhill Fields Cemetery, which is home to the tombs of several prominent Christians including John Bunyan (the author of *The Pilgrim's Progress*) and Susana Wesley, mother of the Wesley brothers. On Aldersgate Street, near the entrance to the Museum of London in Nettleton Court, lies the memorial Methodist Flame and plaque commemorating John Wesley's Christian revelation at the site in 1738.

The renowned Metropolitan Spurgeon Tabernacle, a large Reformed Baptist Church located in the Elephant and Castle section of London, is often seen as a forerunner of today's mega-churches and has been home to a number of prominent preachers since 1650 with Charles Spurgeon, one of the most famous preachers of Metropolitan Spurgeon Tabernacle.

CONTACT INFORMATION FOR LONDON

Tourist Office: www.visitlondon.com

Bus and Trams: Transport for London, www.tfl.gov.uk; Timetables and schedules, timetables.showbus.co.uk; Metro Bus, www.metrobus.co.uk; London Big Bus "Hop-on and Hop-off Tour," www.bigbus.co.uk; Rapid Transit System (The Tube), www.tfl.gov.uk.

Taxi: Taxis are plentiful in London. The most popular are the black cabs, which can be hailed on the street, taken from designated taxi ranks, or even booked in advance. Minicabs are also popular. For more information, please visit www.tfl.gov.uk and click on "taxis and minicabs."

What should I see and do?

Without a doubt, you will want to see many of the Christian sites described above. In addition, be sure to enjoy traditional English sightseeing such as viewing "Changing the Guards" at Buckingham Palace (www.changing-the-guard.com). In preparation for your trip, listed below are the official Web sites for many of the key Christian sites in London.

- Westminster Abbey: www.westminster-abbey.org
- Westminster Cathedral: www.westminstercathedral.org.uk
- Saint Paul's Cathedral: www.stpauls.co.uk; www.explore-stpauls.net
- Wesley's House and Chapel: www.wesleyschapel.org.uk
- Spurgeon's Metropolitan Tabernacle: www.metropolitantabernacle.org

How much time should I spend?

To visit many of the key Christian sites in London, plan on a minimum of one full day. Many Christian groups will spend about two days here.

How can I get there?

Location. London is located in southeast England and is easily accessible by every major form of transportation, both locally and internationally.

By Plane. London has two major airports: Heathrow Airport (one of the world's busiest) and Gatwick. Airfare to London can be quite reasonable and much less expensive than other European cities.

By Train. London is a primary starting and ending point for many trains, so the capital city is easily accessible from anywhere throughout Great Britain (and from Paris via the Channel Tunnel operated by Eurostar). The Waterloo International station is London's main rail station, although the city features about a dozen main-line terminal stations.

By Bus. Long-distance bus service in England is excellent, and London is easily accessible from other cities including Canterbury and Oxford. Two main bus service companies include National Express and Eurolines, both of which service London's Victoria Coach Station. Once in London, the best way to see the Christian sites is on the Big Bus Company "Hop-on and Hop-off Tour."

By Car. Driving in the English countryside can be a pleasant and fun experience. Driving within London is not recommended due to congestion, parking, and its confusing ways (remember—you drive on the left!). Once inside the city, you should switch to bus or taxi for visiting Christian sites and churches.

By Taxi. Unless you plan on taking the bus and walking, taking a taxi is the best way to see the Christian sites in London. The city has two types of taxis: black cabs (which serve as traditional taxis and can be hailed anywhere) and mini-cabs (more like "private hire cars" and are pre-booked).

What lodgings are available?

London is home to hotels and lodging accommodations of every choice, budget, and taste. If you would like a monastic experience while staying in London, you can spend the night at Ealing Abbey at Charlbury Grove (www.stbenedictsealing.org.uk).

EXCURSION TO CANTERBURY

Travel planning

Canterbury Cathedral: www.canterbury-cathedral.org

Canterbury Cathedral is where Thomas Becket was murdered in 1170.

Why should I visit?

Canterbury Cathedral is a prominent Christian site for two reasons: it is the mother church of the worldwide Anglican community, and it is the site where Thomas Becket was murdered by followers of the king in 1170, making it a prominent place of pilgrimage throughout the Middle Ages.

What should I see and do?

Guided tours of the cathedral are a "must." Be sure to visit the church, cloister, and dormitory, as well as the Martyrdom Door and site of Thomas Becket's murder.

How can I get there?

Canterbury has frequent train and bus service from London and other cities. If you're driving from London, take the M2/A2 toward the city. No parking is available within the city center, but the cathedral is within short walking distance of where you can park.

Travel planning

Olney Baptist Church: www.olneybaptist.org.uk

Why should I visit?

Olney is home to the renowned nineteenth century Protestant pastor William Carey. Often referred to as the "father of modern missions," Carey took the Christian faith across the globe, including India. When not traveling, he served as the pastor of the Baptist church in Olney, which remains a functioning church to this day. In addition to assisting in translating the Bible into more than forty languages and dialects, Carey also founded the Baptist Missionary Society (www.bmsworldmission.org), which exists to this day.

What should I see and do?

You can visit the Olney Baptist Church where William Carey served. While there, most Christian groups also visit The Cowper and Newton Museum (www.mkheritage.co.uk). You might also consider a short trip to nearby Bedford, which is home to the John Bunyan Museum (www.bedfordmuseum.org/johnbunyanmuseum). Here, you can explore the life of the famed author who wrote *Pilgrim's Progress*, a masterpiece of English literature and considered the best-selling book of all time after the Bible.[1]

How can I get there?

From London, travel on the A509. Upon entering Olney, you'll find the church is on the left, opposite the Market Square.

Travel planning

Our Lady of Walsingham Shrine: www.walsingham.org.uk

Why should I visit?

Although it is not as well known today, the national shrine of Walsingham once served as the top pilgrimage destination in the Middle Ages outside of Jerusalem, Rome, and

Santiago de Compostela. Dating from the eleventh century, Our Lady of Walsingham shrine remains a popular pilgrimage destination for all faiths, especially for Catholics and Anglicans. Both of these denominations maintain a church and presence at the site, which includes offering services, activities, and events for the visiting pilgrim.

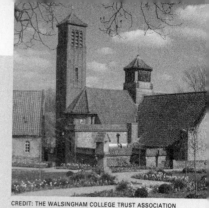

CREDIT: THE WALSINGHAM COLLEGE TRUST ASSOCIATION

Walsingham is a popular destination among Christia

What should I see and do?

The Catholic shrine and Slipper Chapel can be visited, as well as the Anglican shrine with its Holy House. Accommodation is available at the guesthouse. If traveling from London to Walsingham, you might consider stopping in Cambridge, the home of King's College and Magdalene (pronounced "maudlin") College where C.S. Lewis became a professor in 1955 (www.kings.cam.ac.uk and www.magd.cam.ac.uk).

How can I get there?

Walsingham is located about 120 miles northeast of London and just five miles from Fakenham, off of B1105. The main road from London is the M11/A11. Although train service to Walsingham does not exist, there is regular rail service to nearby King's Cross or King's Lynn. From here, there is regular bus service to Fakenham, where you can take a taxi or local bus service to Walsingham. For more information visit: www.passengertransport.norfolk.gov.uk.

OXFORD

Why should I visit?

Oxford is a city renowned for its stunning architecture and "dreaming spires." It is famous for being home to some of the world's foremost universities and colleges, and, it is where many prominent religious and historical figures taught, preached, or were educated. One of the city's most famous citizens is C.S. Lewis. Other well-known Oxford personalities include John Wesley, John Wycliffe, Lewis Carroll, and J.R.R. Tolkien.

With the blockbuster success of *The Chronicles of Narnia* movie, C.S. Lewis once again became a prominent figure not only with Christians but also with non-Christians. Known for his literary talents, C.S. Lewis earned his acclaim through his radio broadcasts and from his many writings that ranged from fiction to medieval literature to apologetic essays.

Oxford was home to prominent Christians like the Wesley brothers and C.S. Lewis.

A prominent site in Oxford is Christ Church College. Many well-known Christian figures either taught or studied here including the Wesley brothers, John Wycliffe, C.S. Lewis, and William Tyndale. To this day, many sites related to the life of C.S. Lewis and other renowned Oxford Christians can be explored, including the pub where C.S. Lewis spent many evenings with his fellow writer friends. If you are looking for a place that offers architecture and heritage grandeur combined with significant Christian personalities, consider Oxford on your next trip to England.

CONTACT INFORMATION FOR OXFORD

Tourist Office: www.visitoxford.org; Oxford City, www.oxfordcity.co.uk

Bus: "Hop-on, Hop-off" tour bus, www.citysightseeingoxford.com; Stagecoach, www.stagecoachbus.com; Oxford Tube, www.oxfordtube.com; Oxford Bus Company, www.oxfordbus.co.uk

Other Helpful Web Sites: C.S. Lewis Foundation: www.cslewis.org

What should I see and do?

Oxford is full of colleges and quadrangles, bookshops and bike paths. You definitely want to see:

- Magdalen College (www.magd.ox.ac.uk): C.S. Lewis served as a fellow here for more than thirty-five years.
- Christ Church College and Cathedral (www.chch.ox.ac.uk): This famed college played a role in the lives of many well-known Christian preachers and figures, including John and Charles Wesley. The cathedral serves as the see (seat or jurisdiction of a bishop) of the Oxford diocese.
- The Martyrs' Memorial: Located just outside Balliol College, near Magdalen and Beaumont Streets, lies the sixteenth-century Oxford Martyrs Memorial. The Martyrs' Memorial commemorates the deaths of three prominent Protestant church leaders during the reign of Queen Mary.
- Eagle and Child Pub: The pub where the "Inklings," a writing group that included C.S. Lewis and J.R.R. Tolkien, among others, met weekly. Look for the memorial plaque and portraits near the middle of the pub.
- Holy Trinity Church (www.hthq.org.uk; www.headington.org.uk): The church is located in Headington Quarry, less than five miles from Oxford, and is where C.S. Lewis is buried.

- The Kilns: This house is the former home of C.S. Lewis. Tours of the home are conducted by appointment only. To inquire about a tour of the facility visit: www.cslewis.org or contact:

  The Kilns, Headington, Oxford, OX3 8JD, UK
  Telephone (0)1865-741865
  E-mail: TheKilns@cslewis.org

How much time should I spend?

Most guided tours of Oxford last anywhere from a few hours to a full day, but you can easily spend several days here, including a trip to Blenheim Palace (the birthplace of Winston Churchill).

How can I get there?

Location. Oxford is located in southwest England, about fifty miles northwest of London. The city is easily accessible by bus, train, and road.

By Plane. The nearest major airport is London Heathrow (one and a half hours by car), followed by Gatwick (two hours by car).

By Train. Oxford's main station lies in the western section of the city and has trains from throughout England, including Birmingham in the north and London in the south (London to Oxford takes about an hour).

By Bus. Oxford is easily accessible by bus from many cities throughout England, including London's Victoria Station. A number of companies offer service between Oxford and London, as well as from London's airports to Oxford. The bus trip is about one and a half to two hours from London to Oxford. There is plenty of bus service within the city of Oxford.

By Car. Travel along M40, then exit for Oxford and follow the signs to the ring road and into the city center. Once you reach your lodgings, use other sources of transportation within the city such as taxi or bus, because the city's stringent parking and access restrictions make driving in Oxford difficult.

By Taxi. In addition to walking, taxis are one of the best ways to get around Oxford.

What lodgings are available?

Oxford is a major tourist and educational destination, so finding accommodation is very easy. A wide variety of accommodation is available, including hostels, bed and breakfast inns (B & Bs), and budget, first-class, and luxury hotels.

Travel planning

Epworth Old Rectory: www.epwortholdrectory.org.uk

Wesley Memorial Church: www.wesley-memorial.co.uk

Why should I visit?

Epworth is the birthplace of John and Charles Wesley. Built by Samuel Wesley in 1709, the Old Rectory served as the Wesley family home and is where John and Charles spent their childhood and Susanna (the mother) held her famed Sunday night gatherings. Samuel served as rector in Epworth for forty years. In the late nineteenth century, the Wesley Memorial Methodist Church was built in honor of the brothers.

What should I see and do?

The main site to visit is the childhood home of the Wesley brothers (the Old Rectory), as well as the Wesley Memorial Church. Less than one hour away from Epworth is the town of Lincoln with its castle where Samuel Wesley was imprisoned for his debt (Lincoln Castle e-mail: Lincoln_Castle@lincolnshire.gov.uk). And if you would like to visit one of the world's great cathedrals, simply head slightly north to visit the York Minster (www.yorkminster.org). The largest Gothic cathedral in northern Europe, York Minster is known for its beautiful stained glass windows, some dating from the twelfth century. Among the most famous is its Great East Window, which is the world's largest example of medieval stained glass (seventy-six feet tall).

How can I get there?

Epworth is located along the A161 road about twelve miles north of Gainsborough. Bus service is available to Epworth with a drop-off near the Old Rectory. The nearest train station is five miles away at Crowle with no tourist facilities, so bus service is recommended.

EXCURSION TO GLASTONBURY TOR

Travel planning

Glastonbury Abbey: www.glastonburyabbey.com

Glastonbury Pilgrim Reception Centre provides: www.glastonbury-pilgrim.co.uk

Why should I visit?

Glastonbury is considered the birthplace of Christianity in England and remains today a city shrouded in myths, legends, and traditions. Throughout the centuries, pilgrims traveled here to visit Glastonbury Tor (*tor* means "hill" or "peak"), a striking yet natural cone-shaped hill associated with the Holy Grail—the cup used by Jesus at the Last Supper and which served as the legendary quest of King Arthur and his knights. According to legend, Joseph of Arimathea (who, according to Scripture, gave his own tomb to Jesus; see Matthew 27:57–61) journeyed to Britain bearing the Holy Grail and settled at the Isle of Avalon (modern-day Glastonbury) on Wearyall Hill, located just below the Tor. Upon his arrival, Joseph stuck his staff into the ground, and it rooted and grew into a thorn tree—today known as the Holy Thorn. Joseph is said to have buried the Holy Grail here, and soon after, a miraculous spring (today's Chalice Well) began to flow. In addition, Joseph of Arimathea and his followers built a church in Glastonbury, making it the first Christian sanctuary in England. The church grew in size and later became a prominent abbey until it was dissolved by King Henry VIII in the sixteenth century. Today Glastonbury remains a popular pilgrimage site not only for Christians but also for others interested in heritage, history, and the stories of the Holy Grail.

What should I see and do?

Glastonbury offers much for the visiting Christian, and you can easily spend a full day there. Among the key sites to explore are:

- Glastonbury Tor: The sacred hill has been the subject of pilgrimages for centuries. At the top is Saint Michael's Tower.
- Glastonbury Abbey: The abbey and its ruins lie in a peaceful setting in the ancient market town of Glastonbury. In addition to strolling on the expansive and peaceful grounds, Christian pilgrims can explore the award-winning museum.
- Glastonbury Pilgrim Reception Centre: This center provides a wealth of information and materials about the many Christian and spiritual sites in the area.
- Wearyall Hill: This is the traditional resting place of Saint Joseph of Arimathea and the site of the original Holy Thorn.

How can I get there?

Glastonbury is located just thirty miles south of Bristol in southwestern England. The Glastonbury Tor bus operates throughout the day from May to mid-September between the abbey and Glastonbury Tor.

Why should I visit?

Germany is the land of the Reformation, the home of Martin Luther, the site of Oberammergau's famed Passion Play, and the setting for the annual and ever-popular Christmas Markets. If you are retracing the footsteps of Martin Luther, most of your time will be spent in northern and central Germany so that you can visit the sites where Luther was born, lived, preached, and died. If you wish to see the major sites of the Reformation, your trip will also encompass central and southern Germany so that you can see where the original Augsburg Confession was written, as well as where Luther defended himself at the Diet of Worms.

If you find yourself in the Bavarian region, you'll surely want to include a day trip to Oberammergau to see the illustrious town—unless you plan to be there at the turn of the decade to see the celebrated Passion Play in person! And if you visit Germany in December, you can see the famed Christmas Markets—talk about a cherished time!

CREDIT: KEVIN J. WRIGHT

All Saints Castle Church in Wittenberg holds the tomb of Martin Luther.

CONTACT INFORMATION FOR GERMANY

Tourist Office: Germany National Tourist Office: www.cometogermany.com or www.germany-tourism.de

Embassy: www.germany-info.org

Other Helpful Web Sites: Deutschland Portal: www.deutschland.de

What do I need to know?

Religion. Germany has no official state religion. About 70 percent of the population is Christian, with the numbers split evenly between Protestant (primarily northern and eastern Germany) and Catholic (primarily southern and western Germany). The country also has a large Jewish population.

Language. Not surprisingly, the official language of Germany is German. However, English is widely spoken throughout the country.

Climate. In general, Germany has warm summers and cold winters, especially the more interior or northern you go.

When to visit Germany. The ideal time for traveling through Germany is from May to October. The weather is the best, flowers are in full bloom, and most tourist facilities are open and operating with full personnel. September and October are popular for the Oktoberfest; however, if you plan to visit for "non-Oktoberfest" reasons, you might avoid Munich at this time as it can be expensive and busy. Another wonderful time to visit is December with the country's famed Christmas Markets. Not only is this a beautiful and lively time to visit Germany, but the crowds are much smaller than in the summer (as are the prices!).

Clothing. Three key pieces of advice: bring rain gear, dress in layers, and always have a sweater or jacket ready. Plan to dress warmly for the fall and spring, and dress for winter weather if you're visiting the Christmas Markets.

Transportation. Germany is home to some of Europe's finest public transportation. Rail travel is best between cities, whereas bus, tram, or underground metro transportation is best within cities, towns, and villages. Unless you really prefer to drive, there is no reason to rent a car in Germany.

Appreciate the Christian Church in a Deeper Way

A visit to Germany is always a pleasure. Combined with travel by the rail system of Europe and the sites of the Reformation, the experience is truly inspiring. We heard about Martin Luther and did not realize what he did or stood up for (in his era). He was a man dedicated to what was right and just for the church. We visited Wittenberg and saw the door where he hung the edicts. Today, in modern times, the community has a pulpit exchange program that allows ministers from the United States to come and preach for two weeks during the summer. It is a wonderful experience for pastors and their congregations. The church that we attend and the denomination that we grew up in did not stress the courage of Martin Luther, but during our tour of Germany we experienced a new appreciation for his sacrifices. A visit to the castle chambers where he was hidden, the museum, and college are well worth the visit. The Reformation Wall in Geneva (Switzerland) is also worth the visit. Visit Germany and Switzerland to enjoy the history and appreciate the Christian church of today in a deeper way.
—*Cindi and Denny*

GERMANY TRAVEL PLANNING

General Trip Planning: Martin Luther trip planning, www.routes-to-luther.com

Airport: Frankfurt airport, www.airportcity-frankfurt.com; Berlin airport, www.berlin-airport.de

Train: Germany rail, www.bahn.de

Bus: Eurolines, www.eurolines.com

Car (driving directions): www.viamichelin.com, www.theaa.com, www.mapquest.com

Why should I visit?

If you were to visit only one city related to Martin Luther, Wittenberg should top the list. It is the crème de la crème on the Luther trail through Germany. Wittenberg is not only home to where he posted his famous 95 Theses, but it is also where he spent about thirty-five years of his life. Today Wittenberg bears the name of Luther in its full official name: Lutherstadt-Wittenberg (translated as Luther City Wittenberg).

Wittenberg is a prominent city for any visiting Christian because it is the birthplace of the Protestant Reformation. When Martin Luther posted his 95 Theses on the door of All Saints Castle Church in 1517, he changed the world of Christianity forever. When you visit Wittenberg, you will experience the life of Martin Luther and learn about the events that took place during the Reformation.

Wittenberg is a charming German town with beautiful architecture and a simple way of life. As Luther both lived and served as a monk here, you can visit the house in which he lived—today called the Luther House. Inside, you can explore the largest Reformation museum in the world. You can view Luther's Bible, writings and manuscripts, pulpit, and his monk's habit. Afterward you can explore Wittenberg's many other prominent sites including the church where Luther preached. Give yourself plenty of time while visiting the town, as no other place can give you as much insight into the Reformation and its most famous figure.

CREDIT: KEVIN J. WRIGHT

See the door where Martin Luther posted his 95 Theses and forever changed Christianity.

CONTACT INFORMATION FOR WITTENBERG
   Tourist Office: Wittenberg, www.wittenberg.de
   General Information: English services at Wittenberg,
      www.wittenberg-english-ministry.com; Luther Center, www.luther-zentrum.de

What should I see and do?

The following sites of Wittenberg should be included on every Christian tour here:

- All Saints Castle Church (Schlosskirche): See the door where Martin Luther posted his 95 Theses; his tomb is inside.
- Saint Mary's Church (Stadtkirche Saint Marien): This is the church where Luther preached and served as pastor, as well as baptized his children.
- Luther Hall and Museum (Lutherhalle): Explore the Reformer's home and view many artifacts relating to his life.
- Melanchthon's House (Melanchtonhaus): Visit the home of Philip Melanchthon, a close confidant of Luther and the originator of the Augsburg Confession.
- Lucas Cranach's House (Cranachaus): Walk through the home of the famed painter who completed many of Luther's portraits.
- Luther Memorial: Visit the Luther memorial in the center of town.
- Luther's Oak: View the great oak tree where Luther is said to have burned the papal bull, which threatened him with excommunication (located at the end of Collegienstrasse).
- Luther's Wedding Festival: Every year on the second weekend in June, more than one hundred thousand people gather in Wittenberg for celebrations commemorating Martin Luther's wedding to Katharina von Bora.
- Wittenberg Tourist Office and bookstore: Many excellent materials about the life of Martin Luther can be purchased here.

How much time should I spend?

A guided tour of Wittenberg takes about two hours. If you plan on taking the local guided tour while also doing personal sightseeing, you should plan on anywhere from several hours to half a day. If you have the time and interest, you can even spend several days or longer, especially if you join any of the local conferences, festivals, or study programs.

How can I get there?

Location. Wittenberg is about sixty miles southwest of Berlin and forty miles northeast of Leipzig. The town is located along the Luther Route. The Luther Route is the collection of cities in Northern Germany that retrace the footsteps of Martin Luther. For more information, please visit www.routes-to-luther.com.

By Plane. The closest major international airport is in Berlin.

By Train. Wittenberg is easily accessible by train as it's on the major rail line "Halle-Berlin." There is frequent service from nearby towns and cities including Berlin and Leipzig (approximately one hour from each).

By Boat. Wittenberg is included on select shore excursions on cruises along the Elbe River. If you're planning a European river cruise, be sure to ask the company if Wittenberg is included.

By Bus. There is no regular bus service to Wittenberg. The train is the primary method of transportation to Wittenberg for the independent traveler.

By Car. Wittenberg is easily accessible by road via the Autobahn A9, Route B187 Torgau- Roßlau, and Highway 2. From Berlin, head south on A9, then exit at Coswig and take Route B187 to "Lutherstadt-Wittenberg."

By Taxi. Taxi service is available in Wittenberg; however, as much of the town is in walking distance of everything, you may not need the service (except maybe to the train station).

What lodgings are available?

Wittenberg offers plenty of hotels, guesthouses, private accommodations, and even youth hostels. For a list of places, visit the Wittenberg tourist office Web site www.wittenberg.de.

Traveler's tip

One of the most popular and sought after local guides in Wittenberg is Katja Kohler. Not only is she a favorite among visiting Christian groups, Katja is literally the "face of Wittenberg" as she appears on one of the town's official postcards. During festivals and "Luther's Wedding" reenactment, she plays the role of Katharina Von Bora (Martin Luther's wife). Katja is fluent in several languages including English. To inquire if she can be your guide, contact Katja directly at katjakoehler@gmx.net or call (49) 3491-437726; (49) 177-6888218. You can visit Katja's Web site at www.wittenbergtours.com or www.wittenberg1517.de.

A Warm Welcome to Wittenberg— The Town of Martin Luther

During the last seven years of being a local guide in Wittenberg I have seen and accompanied thousands of guests through our historic Renaissance town. "A warm welcome to Wittenberg— the town of Martin Luther!" is always my first sentence to the groups, but every single tour develops individually depending on age, origin, interest, and the cultural and religious background of the group members. People come to Wittenberg because of Martin Luther. He is everything and we are very proud of him. It doesn't matter if tourists see him as a rebel, somebody from the

Middle Ages, the pastor, the songwriter, or the reformer, the tourists come. And that is great. Most of our eight hundred thousand visitors per year are surprised by the variety and atmosphere that Wittenberg offers. People get more than they have expected. In my tours you will always find a mixture of facts and entertaining true stories. I believe that this is one of the best ways to keep history in mind. An increasing number of people booking theme tours—e.g. The Gossip Tour with Katharina Luther and Barbara Cranach—proves it. Next to entertainment and information, emotions and spirituality are the keys to the heart of our visitors. Where else is it possible to sing "A Mighty Fortress" at the same places where Martin Luther wrote it five hundred years before or to touch the same stones as he did or to attend a worship service in the mother church of the Reformation? As the representatives of Wittenberg we are responsible for our guests feeling comfortable and satisfied with their stay, and that they leave happy, surprised, enthused, and with the wish to come back soon! So finally, when are you coming? I would love to say again: "A warm welcome to Wittenberg!"— *Katja Kohler, Christian Tour Guide in Wittenberg*

EXCURSION TO EISLEBEN

Travel planning
www.eisleben-tourist.de; www.eisleben.eu

Why should I visit?
No trip following in the footsteps of Martin Luther is complete without a stop in Eisleben. Not only is this the city of his birth in 1483, it is also the place where he gave his last sermon and died in 1546. As with Wittenberg, the official name of the city includes Luther's name "Lutherstadt Eisleben" (Luther City Eisleben). When visiting Eisleben, plan on a minimum of two hours to see everything.

What should I see and do?
- Luthers Geburtshaus (Birth House): the house where Martin Luther was born and a UNESCO World Heritage Site
- Luthers Sterbehaus (Death House): the house where Martin Luther died while on a visit to Eisleben; also a UNESCO World Heritage Site
- Saint Peter and Paul Church: the place of Martin Luther's baptism
- Andreaskirche (Saint Andreas Church): the place of Luther's last sermon

- Lutherdenkmal (Luther Monument): popular memorial of Martin Luther in the town center

At Eisleblen go inside the birth house of Martin Luther.

How can I get there?

Eisleben is accessible by the Autobahn A9, A14, B6, B80, and B180. From Berlin to Eisleben is about two hours by car. Eisleben has frequent train service to nearby towns including Halle (there is no bus service to Eisleben).

ERFURT

Why should I visit?

Erfurt is often characterized as the "spiritual home" of Martin Luther because it is where he served as a monk inside the Augustinian monastery for about five years. Erfurt is also where he attended college prior to entering the priesthood. In fact, it was during his time at the University of Erfurt that he had a frightening encounter with a lightning storm and made a vow to enter the religious life if he survived. On July 17, 1505, Luther entered the monastery.

Today Erfurt offers the visiting Christian traveler not only the opportunity to explore sites related to the life of Luther but also the chance to see one of the best preserved medieval cities in Germany. It provides the perfect combination of faith, fun, and sightseeing.

Visit the monastery in Erfurt where Luther lived.

CONTACT INFORMATION FOR ERFURT

Tourist Office: www.erfurt.de; www.erfurt-tourist-info.de/online_en
Other Helpful Web Sites: www.routes-to-luther.com/erfurt

What should I see and do?

The most famous Martin Luther site in Erfurt is the Augustinian monastery. Today it is a Protestant monastery, and visitors can take guided tours through the cloister, church, and courtyards. For more information, visit www.augustinerkloster.de. Two other sites related to the Reformer's life include the Luther Monument and Luther Stone (in nearby Stotternheim), where Martin made a vow to enter the monastery during a frightening lightning storm. You might also consider visiting the Church of Saint Aegidius, Saint Michael's Church where Luther preached, and the famed Merchants' Bridge.

MEDIEVAL MEALS

How would you like to experience the food of Martin Luther's time? If you are traveling with a group then you can eat medieval food at various restaurants throughout Erfurt, including the Lutherkeller restaurant (at Kaisersaal, the Emperor's Hall). Meals are based on authentic recipes of the time period, as is the medieval music (upon request). Luther himself is even present sometimes and can guide you in your food selection! For more information contact the Erfurt Tourist Board and ask about "Luther's Meal" for groups.

How much time should I spend?

Half a day is typically all you need, especially if you're only focusing on Christian sites of interest.

How can I get there?

Location. Erfurt is about eighty miles southwest of Leipzig.

By Plane. Most people visiting Erfurt come from either the Frankfurt or Berlin airports. From Frankfurt, you can take the subway to Frankfurt Central (Frankfurt Hauptbahnhof) and then take the fast train to Erfurt (about two and one half hours). The trip from Berlin takes about three hours.

By Train. Erfurt is on the regular train line from Frankfurt (Main) to Dresden. If you're traveling from the south or north you will need to connect in Frankfurt or Jena. The train station is centrally located in Erfurt city center.

By Bus. There is no regular bus service to Erfurt; however, once you're inside Erfurt, there is bus and tram transportation. The primary source of transportation to Erfurt is by train for independent travelers.

By Car. Erfurt is located off A71 and A4, running east to west from Frankfurt to Dresden. Exit using either highway for Erfurt and follow the signs to the city center.

By Taxi. Taxis are fairly plentiful in Erfurt and can be a good option, especially when traveling to or from the train station to your hotel.

What lodgings are available?

Erfurt has plenty of housing options. For a unique experience, you can stay at the Augustinian monastery where Luther once lived. Many groups stay here, especially those using the facilities for Protestant seminars and conferences. Contact the monastery (www.augustinerkloster.de) for more information or to make a reservation.

EXCURSION TO EISENACH AND WARTBURG CASTLE

Travel planning

www.eisenach-tourist.de, www.wartburg-eisenach.de

Why should I visit?

If Eisenach can be summed up in one word, it's "child-hood." Eisenach is best known for being the childhood home of Martin Luther. As such you can visit the home of his schoolboy days. Other sites to see include Saint George's Church, where he preached in 1521 while on his way to and from the Diet of Worms, as well as the Luther memorial on Karlsplatz square.

CREDIT: KEVIN J. WRIGHT
Visit the childhood home of Martin Luther in Eisenach.

But that's not all. The main reason for visiting Christians is the nearby Wartburg Castle. In addition to Wittenberg, Wartburg Castle is possibly the most popular and significant site on any Luther route tour. Here he spent one year (1521) in refuge and in disguise as "Knight George" after being excommunicated. It is also where Luther translated the New Testament into German. Today it is a UNESCO World Heritage Site.

What should I see and do?

In Eisenach the main attraction is the Luther House, the youth home of Martin Luther (www.lutherhaus-eise-nach.de). Other sites to visit include Saint George's Church and the Luther Memorial. You might also visit the Bach house, a museum dedicated to Johann Sebastian Bach, as Eisenach is his birth city (www.bachhaus.de). Afterward (or before), head up the hill to visit the world-

CREDIT: KEVIN J. WRIGHT
In Wartburg Castle Luther translated the New Testament into German.

famous Wartburg Castle. You can embark on a tour that includes a visit to the same room in which Luther translated the Bible. There is an excellent lookout point that provides great views (and photo opportunities) of the castle.

How can I get there?

Eisenach lies just thirty miles west of Erfurt, and there are frequent train connections between the two cities. To reach Eisenach by car, simply take A4 (runs east-west) and follow the signs to Eisenach.

EXCURSION TO COBURG FORTRESS

Travel planning

Tourist office Web site: www.coburg-tourist.de
Official site: www.kunstsammlungen-coburg.de

Why should I visit?

The Coburg Fortress (Veste Coburg) is the site where John the Steadfast provided refuge to Martin Luther during the Diet of Augsburg in 1530. Luther spent six months here writing and continuing the translation of the Bible.

What should I see and do?

Explore Coburg Fortress. Guided tours of the fortress are available. Other sites to see include the Lutherstube (Luther Room), where Martin Luther studied and worked, and several museums located inside the castle.

How can I get there?

Coburg is accessible by car via A73, B4, B303, and B289. Coburg is also accessible by train from nearby cities and towns. Once at Coburg, take bus #8, or take the thirty-minute, steep walk up.

What lodgings are available?

A wide variety of accommodations is available including hostels, private guest houses, and hotels. For more information visit www.coburg-tourist.de and click on "Hotel–Overnight."

EXCURSION TO WORMS CATHEDRAL

Travel planning

www.worms.de

Why should I visit?

Worms Cathedral is probably best known as the site where Martin Luther presented his case before the Diet of Worms. As Luther would not recant his position or beliefs, the Holy Roman Emperor Charles V declared him an outlaw of the Holy Roman Empire. During his escape, Frederick of Saxony staged a kidnapping of Luther and brought the reformer to Wartburg Castle. Today, Worms is primarily a Protestant city, although the cathedral remains in the hands of the Catholic Church.

What should I see and do?

- Worms Cathedral (Dom Saint Peter)
- Luther Monument
- Trinity Church (Dreifaltigkeitskirch): Worms's main Evangelical church
- Magnukirche: one of the first Protestant churches established after Luther's visit in 1521
- Heylshof Garden: the spot of Luther's defense at the Diet of Worms, memorialized by a plaque

How can I get there?

Worms is located about fifty miles southwest of Frankfurt and is accessible by A5, A67, and B47. The city has frequent train service from nearby towns and lies on the Mainz-Mannheim line. The train is about one and one-half hours from Frankfurt via Mainz. Regional bus service is available through Busverkehr RheinNeckar (www.brn.de).

Travel planning
www.augsburg.de; www.regio-augsburg.de

Why should I visit?
The name of Augsburg should ring a bell for many Christians, especially Lutherans. It is here that the Augsburg Confession was written, approved, and adopted. The Confession remains the primary confession of faith for the Lutheran Church worldwide and is in the *Book of Concord*. This statement of faith was presented to the Holy Roman Emperor Charles V at the Diet of Augsburg on June 25, 1530. Although Martin Luther did not attend the presentation and instead stayed behind at Coburg Fortress, his close associate Philipp Melanchthon attended and presented the articles of faith.

What should I see and do?
- Augsburg Cathedral (Dom Saint Maria)
- Saint Anne's Church and its Luther Staircase
- Saint Ulrich Church (Protestant) and Saint Afra Church (Catholic), which are located next to each other and symbolize the Augsburg treaty

How can I get there?
Augsburg is located in southeast Germany and is easily accessible. Frequent train service to Augsburg from throughout Germany is available, with dozens of Munich-to-Augsburg arrivals daily (trip length is thirty minutes to one hour). By road, simply take the A8, which runs east to west. Once in the city, buses and trams are plentiful.

OBERAMMERGAU AND THE CHRISTIAN MARKETS

OBERAMMERGAU

Why should I visit?
Oberammergau is a name synonymous with the *Passion Play*. Ever since 1634, the

See the famed Reformation Monument.

residents of this village have hosted the great performance every ten years, fulfilling a vow to God for sparing them from the bubonic plague in 1633. Today it is world famous, and people begin purchasing tickets and making plans to attend the play several years in advance. The entire drama includes about two thousand (local resident) characters and is about eight hours long. Currently the play takes place at the turn of each decade (2010, 2020, and so on). However, Oberammergau attracts visitors every year and throughout every season. People come not only to see sites related to the play but also to visit the village's numerous woodcarving shops for which it is famous. Oberammergau is included on most Christian tours visiting southern Germany.

CONTACT INFORMATION FOR OBERAMMERGAU
www.oberammergau.de

What should I see and do?
- Passionspielhaus: The modern Passion Play theater seats almost five thousand spectators.
- Woodcarver shops and woodcarvers: See the artists at work and even purchase a woodcarving.
- Heimatmuseum: This museum features handcrafted Christmas crèches.

How much time should I spend?
If just visiting Oberammergau, about half a day is needed. If visiting Oberammergau for its every-decade *Passion Play*, then you should plan on spending two to three days.

How can I get there?

Oberammergau is located in southern Bavaria near the Austrian border. From Munich, take A95 south and follow the signs to Oberamergau (one and one-half hours). The village is easily accessible by train from Munich and even Frankfurt.

CHRISTMAS MARKETS

Why should I visit?

You might be surprised to learn that the North Pole isn't the only place to visit for Christmas gifts. If you would like to indulge in the Christmas spirit, then pack your bags and head for the Christmas Markets in Germany. The Markets are festivals held throughout the country in various town squares celebrating the Advent season with food, drink, shopping, song, and pageantry. Several million people from throughout Germany and around the world attend the events; more than 2 million visit the Dresden and Nuremburg Christmas markets. This is an ideal time to visit Germany: prices are typically less than in summer, and you get the combined experience of visiting the Christmas Markets and places of faith such as those related to Martin Luther. Many Christian travel companies offer these winter tours.

CONTACT INFORMATION FOR CHRISTMAS MARKETS

www.germany-christmas-market.org.uk, www.cometogermany.com

What should I see and do?

More than two thousand five hundred Christmas Markets take place throughout Germany in both large cities and small villages. For a list of them, visit www.germany-christmas-market.org.uk. Once you're at the Christmas Markets, you can snack on typical Christmas treats (dried plums, nuts, gingerbread, roasted almonds, etc.), buy homemade crafts, listen to choirs and orchestras, watch various Christmas programs, and simply walk around and explore the "Christmas villages" with their crèches and much more.

How much time should I spend?

Most Christian tours to the Christmas Markets are about a week in length. If traveling independently, you might consider a minimum of several days at the Christmas Markets combined.

Spend part of Advent in Germany at the famed Christmas Markets.

How can I get there?

The Christmas Markets throughout Germany (and Europe) are easily accessible by rail from other cities. Once within a city, bus or tram transportation is ideal.

What lodgings are available?

Although there is a wide choice of lodging options from budget to deluxe, it's necessary to book your hotel reservations many months in advance (six months to one year) due to the popularity of the Christmas Markets.

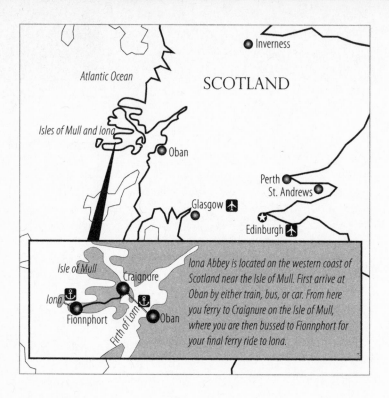

Iona Abbey is located on the western coast of Scotland near the Isle of Mull. First arrive at Oban by either train, bus, or car. From here you ferry to Craignure on the Isle of Mull, where you are then bussed to Fionnphort for your final ferry ride to Iona.

Why should I visit?

With the tremendous growth of Christian tourism around the world, Scotland is one of the countries that is welcoming religious visitors in ever greater numbers and working hard to attract even more. As a result, faith-based travel to Scotland is expected to double in the next decade with hundreds of thousands more visitors. Currently, almost 1 million people visit religious sites each year in Scotland, with Saint Giles Cathedral serving as the number one attraction.

Scotland has long been associated with Christianity. Saint Ninian brought the Christian faith to the region in AD 397, and two centuries later Saint Columba founded the famed monastery on the Isle of Iona. (Columba, by the way, wrote of seeing the Loch Ness Monster in AD 565!) In subsequent centuries, Scotland played a key role in Christian history and events including the Protestant Reformation. Today, the country is synonymous with John Knox and the Presbyterian faith (which was begun here).

CREDIT: ©ISTOCKPHOTO.COM/MICHAEL POLLOCK

Visit sites related to John Knox in Scotland.

CONTACT INFORMATION FOR SCOTLAND

Tourist Office: Scottish Tourism Board, www.toscotland.com; Scotland's National Tourism Organization, www.visitscotland.com

Embassy: www.britainusa.com

Other Helpful Web Sites: Christian Scotland, www.scottishchristian.com; Church of Scotland, www.churchofscotland.org.uk; Historic Scotland, www.historic-scotland.gov.uk; Group travel to Scotland: www.scotlandgroupsguide.com

What do I need to know?

Religion. The predominant (almost three-quarters of the population) religion in Scotland is Christianity. Almost half of the population is affiliated in one way or another with the Presbyterian Church of Scotland. The next largest category is the "unchurched" or unaffiliated at almost 25 percent. Non-Christians account for about 3 percent of the population.

Language. English is the official language. Although only a small percentage speak Gaelic, you will quickly notice its influence on Scottish English once you're there.

Climate. To use weather terms, Scotland is considered temperate and oceanic. This means that the climate in most places is fairly mild and can be quite wet in certain areas. In reality, the weather is quite unpredictable, and you need to be prepared for anything: warm or cool, wet or dry. Western Scotland tends to be warmer than the eastern side. For more information, visit www.metoffice.gov.uk (and then search for Scotland).

When to visit Scotland. The most popular time to visit Scotland is April through September. The most expensive times to visit are July and August, and due to the crowds, reservations at hotels must be made in advance. If you want the best weather months, consider traveling in May, June, or September. One of the best things about traveling in Scotland during the summer is the long periods of daylight. The winter months aren't very popular for traveling for many reasons including the very short days of light and the cold weather.

Clothing. Dress in layers and carry a light rain or wind jacket with a hood (because of frequent winds, umbrellas may not work). Bring good walking shoes, sunglasses, and insect repellent (for summer). You might consider bringing a second pair of shoes in case the first ones get very wet and need to dry out.

Transportation. Scotland is easily accessible by plane (international flights), train, or ferry. Once in Scotland, popular travel choices include rail and long-distance bus (called coaches). In cities, local buses, trams, and taxis are the most common methods of transportation. Renting a car is also a popular choice—driving here is much easier than in many other parts of Europe.

SCOTLAND TRAVEL PLANNING

General trip planning: Traveline Scotland (plan your Scotland transportation), www.travelinescotland.com; Transport Direct (public transport and car journey information), www.transportdirect.info; Scotland Travel tips and information www.scotland-inverness.co.uk/tips.htm

Airport: Edinburgh airport, www.edinburghairport.com; Glasgow airport, www.glasgowairport.com

Train: Scotland Rail: www.scotrail.co.uk, www.firstgroup.com/scotrail; UK national rail, www.nationalrail.co.uk

Boat: Caledonian MacBrayne (West Scotland ferries), www.calmac.co.uk or www.shipsofcalmac.co.uk; General ferry information, www.ferrybooker.com

Bus: Stagecoach, www.stagecoachbus.com; National Express, www.nationalexpress.com, www.nationalexpress.co.uk; Mega Bus (double-decker bus), www.megabus.com; Scottish City Link, www.citylink.co.uk

Car (driving directions): www.viamichelin.com, www.theaa.com, www.mapquest.com

Taxi: Taxi service, www.traintaxi.co.uk

IONA ABBEY

Why should I visit?

One of the more recognizable names from early Christian Europe is Iona Abbey in Scotland. Founded in AD 563 by Saint Columba (one of the most influential Celtic saints, originally from Ireland), the Celtic monastery grew to become a thriving Christian community and launched the spread of the faith throughout the country. In later years, it became a prominent place of Christian pilgrimage and today serves as Scotland's most historic and sacred site.

Iona Abbey has changed hands several times over the years. Originally a Celtic Church, it later adopted the Roman Catholic faith and joined the Benedictine order (which led to the founding of a convent around 1200). The Protestant Reformation brought the closing of Iona Abbey along with many other monasteries in Scotland, England, and Wales; however, the Church of Scotland revived the abbey in the nineteenth century. The year 1938 brought another change to Iona as the Reverend George MacLeod founded the Iona Community, an ecumenical Christian group that today still serves as the custodian of the place. Full of spiritual and historical attractions, the monastery features a number of sites to visit and explore. Today half a million people make the journey here from around the world for a taste of Celtic and historic Christianity.

The Beauty of Iona

My first visit to Iona was several years ago. My college friend and I had attended a friend's wedding and then decided to explore Scotland. We found a wonderful bed & breakfast on the Isle of Mull and were treated to homemade, fresh crab pate. Incredible! The next day we boarded the passenger ferry to take us to Iona. Founded in 563 by Saint Columba, it became a base for the evangelization of the British Isles in the sixth century, as well as a center for Christian studies. Iona was not what I expected. Of course there was the Abbey, the quaint shops, and the soft sandy beaches, but I hadn't encountered anywhere such a palpable sense of peace before. As we wandered around the Abbey, we felt as if we had stepped back in time. The modern world faded, and we were part of a centuries old tradition of worship and prayer. We were both prayerful and reflective—so much so that the last boat of the day very nearly left without us! Scotland is like that. It grips you with its intensity and encourages you to look back at your own heritage and live your life with purpose. The Iona Community (part of the Church of Scotland) welcomes visitors of all ages to spend a week at the Abbey. You'll share times of worship, join in kitchen duty, and hear teachings from special speakers. If you are looking for a place to commune with the Lord away from the distractions of the fast-paced world, head for Iona. You won't be disappointed. —*Rowena*

What should I see and do?

As you enjoy the beauty of Iona, you can visit:

- abbey church, cloisters, and museum
- the Torr and Saint Columba's writing cell
- the little shrine where Saint Columba is buried
- Saint Oran's Chapel, Saint Ronan's Church, Saint Mary's Chapel
- the twelfth century convent
- King's Walk and abbey cemetery
- Celtic crosses (throughout the Isle of Iona) and MacLean's Cross
- three remaining free-standing High Crosses including the eighth-century Saint Martin's Cross, Saint John's Cross, and Saint Matthew's Cross
- Martyr's Bay where the Vikings murdered the monks (according to tradition)

How much time should I spend?

Anywhere from a few hours to a few days could be spent at Iona Abbey. However, for most Christian groups or individuals a simple visit of a few hours should suffice. Just make sure you allow time to visit all the key sites. Longer visits are more suited for those planning to embark on a retreat.

How can I get there?

Location. Iona Abbey is located on the western coast of Scotland near the Isle of Mull. You need to first arrive at Oban by train, bus, or car. From here, you ferry to Craignure on the Isle of Mull, where you are then take a bus to Fionnphort for your final ferry ride to Iona.

By Plane. The nearest major international airport is in Glasgow. The towns of Oban and Fionnphort are about one hundred and 150 miles respectively from Glasgow.

By Train. Trains are available to Oban from the Glasgow Queen Street Station (travel

CREDIT: ©ISTOCKPHOTO.COM/STEPHEN FINN

Iona Abbey is a symbol of early Celtic Christianity that spread the Christian faith throughout Scotland.

time is under three hours); upon arrival at Oban, take the ferry to the Isle of Mull. (The train from London to Glasgow is about five hours.)

By Boat. There is a public ferry from Fionnphort, Mull, to the Isle of Iona.

By Bus. From early-March to mid-October, buses depart Glasgow Queen Street and Buchanan Street Stations for Oban. At Oban, catch the ferry to Craignure (Isle of Mull), then take the bus from Craignure to Fionnphort. From the Fionnphort, take the ferry to Iona. The entire trip from Glasgow to Iona typically takes six to seven hours. From mid-October to early-March, the Iona ferry must be booked before 4 PM the day before you ride the ferry.

By Car. You can drive to Oban or Fionnphort, Mull; however, you must leave your car at Mull as vehicles are not permitted on Iona. To bring your car onboard the Oban-Mull ferry, you must make a reservation in advance with Caledonian MacBrayne ferry service. Upon arrival at Fionnphort, you can park your car at the Columba Centre. From Glasgow, take M8 then the A82 and A85 after Loch Lomond.

By Taxi. Taxis are available twenty-four hours a day to any destination from Glasgow airport. Once you reach Oban, you will need to catch the ferry to Craignure.

What lodgings are available?

Iona Abbey Centre provides accommodations for up to fifty people who wish to partake in the daily life of the center. Another option to consider is the Bishop's House accommodation (www.a1tourism.com/uk/bishops.html); or visit www.a1tourism.com for more lodging options. For tour groups, most will stay overnight in Glasgow where there is a wide variety of hotel choices.

EXCURSION TO GLASGOW CATHEDRAL

Travel planning

www.glasgowcathedral.org.uk

Why should I visit?

As most people arrive in Glasgow (airport) before continuing to Iona Abbey, many groups and individuals first make a stop at the local cathedral. Also called the High Kirk (Church) of Scotland, the cathedral features wonderful architecture and history. Once a Roman Catholic cathedral, today it belongs to the Church of Scotland. Although it technically is not a cathedral (it is not the seat of a bishop), the church still retains this title.

What should I see and do?

From May through September, volunteer guides provide tours of the cathedral, the oldest building in Glasgow.

How much time should I spend?

Only an hour or two is needed to tour Glasgow Cathedral.

How can I get there?

The cathedral is easily accessible by bus or taxi.

EDINBURGH: HOME OF JOHN KNOX

Why should I visit?

Edinburgh and the surrounding cities are best known in the Christian world for their relationship to John Knox and Presbyterianism. Knox, a sixteenth-century Protestant reformer, led the charge in reforming the Scottish church (some call him the Martin Luther of Scotland). Preaching with Calvinist teachings and principles, John Knox spoke with

CREDIT: ©ISTOCKPHOTO.COM/STAN FAIRGRIEVE

See the home of John Knox in Edinburgh.

authority throughout Scotland in both religious and political matters.

In the spiritual realm, Knox assisted in constructing the confession of faith and constitution for the new Church of Scotland. Many things considered "Roman" were thrown out and replaced by a new Presbyterian faith of ministers and elders (not priests or bishops). Today Presbyterianism retains its church government of elders and its Calvinist theology. Located in southeast Scotland, Edinburgh is the capital of the country and the second most visited tourist city in the United Kingdom outside of London.

What should I see and do?

Edinburgh has a number of key sites related to John Knox, the Scottish Reformation, and Presbyterianism. While there, be sure to explore:

- Saint Giles Cathedral (www.stgilescathedral.org.uk) is where John Knox served as minister. Today it is known as the High Kirk of Edinburgh and serves not only as a Presbyterian church but also as the country's spiritual cathedral. In addition, Saint Giles is viewed by many as the mother church of Presbyterianism.
- The John Knox House is a historic house and museum where the reformer once lived. Owned by the Church of Scotland and operated by the Scottish Storytelling Centre (www.scottishstorytellingcentre.co.uk), the house is viewed as one of the country's most significant national heritages. It is believed that Knox died here in 1572.

How much time should I spend?

Plan to spend several hours to a full day in and around Edinburgh visiting key Christian and tourist sites.

How can I get there?

Location. Edinburgh is located in southeastern Scotland, one hour east of Glasgow.

By Plane. The Edinburgh airport is only eight miles west of the city center. It is one hour from Glasgow International Airport and offers direct flights from throughout Europe and select cities of the eastern coast of the United States.

By Train. The Edinburgh train station (Waverley) is centrally placed on Princes Street, the city's main avenue. Rail travel from London to Edinburgh is about four hours.

By Boat. For more information about ferry and boat transportation in Scotland, please see the "Boat" section for England.

By Bus. Edinburgh is easily accessible by bus from throughout Scotland and the United Kingdom.

By Car. Edinburgh is easily accessible by road with several major highways (A92, A702, M90, M8, etc.) leading into the city. Edinburgh is three hours from Inverness and less than six hours from Birmingham, England.

CREDIT: ©ISTOCKPHOTO.COM/BMPIX

Discover Saint John's Church where John Knox preached reform.

By Taxi. Taxis are plentiful around Edinburgh and are one of the most elite taxi services in the world.

What lodgings are available?

As the second largest city in Scotland and a very popular European destination, Edinburgh offers the visitor dozens of lodging options from hostels to first-class hotels to castle stays.

EXCURSION TO PERTH

Travel planning

www.st-johns-kirk.co.uk

Why should I visit?

Saint John's Church (Kirk) is where Knox preached his famed sermon against idolatry on May 11, 1559. This led to a Protestant uprising in central Scotland and instigated the destruction by some Scots of all things "idolatrous" within churches and monasteries. Knox later blamed much of this on the "rascal multitude."

What should I see and do?

Visit the very same church where John Knox preached his famed sermon on May 11, 1559.

How much time should I spend?

Only an hour or two is needed to visit Saint John's Church.

How can I get there?

Perth is accessible by the M90 from Edinburgh. It is accessible by bus and train from throughout Scotland.

Travel planning
www.saint-andrews.co.uk

Why should I visit?

Saint Andrews is named after the saint whose relics were brought here in the eighth century. The Cathedral of Saint Andrews gained its place in history when it was ransacked in 1559 by a mob after John Knox's sermon against idolatry. Saint Andrews Castle served as the headquarters and residence for bishops and archbishops and, in later years, for the Church of Scotland. It fell to ruins in the seventeenth century.

What should I see and do?

The "intact" ruins of Saint Andrews Cathedral can be visited in addition to Saint Andrews Castle, which has a spectacular location right next to the sea. You can also see the Old Course at Saint Andrews, where golf had its beginnings. Golf lovers might want to take a stroll along the perimeter of this very first golf course.

How much time should I spend?

A half day to a full day can be spent exploring Saint Andrews Cathedral and Saint Andrews Castle.

How can I get there?

Saint Andrews is less than an hour by train or car from the Edinburgh airport. The nearest train station (at Leuchars) is only five miles away. Buses to Saint Andrews connect with the train at Leuchars.

IRELAND AND NORTHERN IRELAND

Christian groups visiting England and Scotland sometimes include Ireland or Northern Ireland (which is part of the United Kingdom).

What should I see and do?

The Saint Patrick Centre (www.saintpatrickcentre.com) is an interpretative exhibition that provides the visitor with a fascinating look at the life and influence of Saint Patrick in Ireland. A number of interactive displays help guests learn about the patron saint's legacy, as well as that of the Irish missionaries and others.

What does Ireland offer the visiting Christian?

The following Web sites provide links to those places most often of interest to the visiting Christian:

- Lough Derg (ancient Christian pilgrimage site), www.loughderg.org
- Monastic Ireland, www.monasticireland.com
- Glenstal Abbey, www.glenstal.org
- Mount Melleray Abbey's, www.mountmellerayabbey.org
- The Book of Kells, www.bookofkells.com

How can I get there?

Ireland is very accessible. Between cities, rail and bus transportation are most common. Within cities, bus, tram, and walking are the most common forms of transport. However, renting a car and driving is another popular choice.

SPAIN: SANTIAGO DE COMPOSTELA AND THE WAY OF SAINT JAMES

SANTIAGO DE COMPOSTELA
The Way of St. James

Paris
Chartres
Vezelay
FRANCE
Le Puy
Santiago de Compostela
Leon
Burgos
Pamplona
Arles
PORTUGAL
Madrid
Tarragona
Lisbon
SPAIN
Valencia
Sevila

Why should I visit?

Quick trivia question: Can you name the top three Christian pilgrimage destinations of the Middle Ages? If you said Jerusalem, Rome, and Santiago de Compostela—you are right. Believe it or not, this city in northwestern Spain once ranked as one of the great shrines of Christendom.

Today, Santiago de Compostela is still one of the most famous places of pilgrimage throughout the world. Why? Historically, its popularity has been the cathedral, which, according to tradition, contains the relics of Saint James the Greater. However, these days it's the actual medieval pilgrimage route through northern Spain leading to the cathedral that draws the most attention. Known as the Way of Saint James, the path attracts more than one hundred thousand people each year who embark on its arduous journey. Four major pilgrimage routes dating back to medieval times and beginning in France have been the primary starting points. All of them converge into a single route at the Pyrenees Mountains and continue through northern Spain and finally arrive at Santiago de Compostela.

Santiago de Compostela was a great Christian shrine in the Middle Ages.

Although many people undertook the pilgrimage as a form of penance in centuries past, today many travelers embark on the trip more for vacation and adventure purposes. Some traditions of the original journey still exist, such as staying at monasteries and hospices along the way. However, with today's growing interest in active vacations, people are finding more creative ways to travel along the famed road. Today it is not uncommon to see groups or individuals not only walking or hiking its path but also biking and horseback riding it—or in some cases, combining a variety of these into a multi-sport trip. All told, today more than 2.5 million people visit the cathedral of Santiago de Compostela each year.

CONTACT INFORMATION FOR SANTIAGO DE COMPOSTELA

Tourist Office: Spain, www.okspain.org; Santiago de Compostela tourism, www.santiagodecompostela.org; www.santiagoturismo.com
Embassy: Spain Embassy www.spainemb.org; www.mae.es

What do I need to know?

Religion. About 75 percent of the Spanish population belongs to the Catholic Church. The next largest category (20 percent) is people with no religion or faith. Protestant Christians represent a very small percentage.

Language. As you would guess, Spanish is the official language of Spain. English is fairly widely spoken in key tourist areas, as well as by young people.

Climate. Spain has one of the warmest European climates. Spring and fall temperatures are quite pleasant, but summer temperatures can be quite hot. The area of Santiago de Compostela itself is known for its mild, yet rainy climate. Summer is not as hot as in southern Spain.

When to visit Spain. If you're looking for the best months to visit Spain, consider May, June, September, or October. The peak tourist season is typically May to September. Summer is the most popular time to travel, despite having the largest crowds and hottest temperatures. If you plan to embark on the pilgrimage along the Camino (Spanish for way or path), spring and fall are often the best for both temperatures and crowds.

Clothing. When visiting the cathedral of Santiago de Compostela, you will want to dress modestly with shoulders and legs covered (pants, long skirt, etc.). If you are embarking on the journey along the Camino, obviously you will want to dress accordingly. Be prepared for a variety of temperatures ranging from cold to hot, and bring very good, comfortable hiking shoes.

Transportation. Spain has excellent transportation facilities, with rail being the preferred choice of transport for long-distance travel. Bus service is especially popular for shorter commutes.

SANTIAGO DE COMPOSTELA TRAVEL PLANNING

Airport: Santiago de Compostela, www.aeropuertosantiago.cl
Train: Renfe, www.renfe.es; www.feve.es; www.seat61.com/Spain.htm
Bus: Alsa, www.alsa.es; Arriva, www.arriva.es
Car (driving directions): www.viamichelin.com, www.theaa.com, www.mapquest.com

What should I see and do?

Once you're at Santiago de Compostela, the main attraction is the cathedral itself (www.archicompostela.org/catedral/catedral.htm). Once they're inside, most people make a beeline for the altar and crypt, where the relics of Saint James are said to rest within a silver urn. Also plan on exploring or viewing the following:

- The top of the cathedral with spectacular panoramic views
- The swinging three-foot high incenser, typically used at the morning masses (According to tradition, one of the original intentions of the incenser was to eradicate any foul smells brought into the cathedral by the many Medieval pilgrims who had traveled across the Camino yet hadn't showered in days!)
- Portico de la Gloria (Door of Glory): located just inside the cathedral's main entrance
- Museo das Peregrinacións (The Pilgrimage Museum): www.mdperegrinacions.com

One of the Most Challenging
yet Rewarding Experiences of My Life

Although I'm not the most physically active person, I joined my friends two years ago to embark on an ambitious journey of walking a portion of the Camino (a nickname for the route leading to Santiago de Compostela). It was one of the most challenging yet rewarding experiences of my life. Each day brought fifteen to twenty miles of prayer, talking, laughter, and sometimes tears from bleeding blisters—the latter being the biggest problem for the Way of Saint James pilgrims. One of the great highlights was the beautiful and changing scenery from pastures to forests to rolling hills—it is these views along with prayers and the singing of hymns that kept us going on the more challenging days. I could of course share dozens of stories, but the most important thing I like to tell people is what I gained from the experience. The journey across northern Spain taught me to always persevere in whatever I do, no matter how great the joys or tough the challenges. And most importantly, the experience taught me to always persevere in my faith journey of life. As one of some one hundred thousand backpackers who signed up in 2005 with the Pilgrim Office's registry, I feel blessed that I accomplished what I did. If the opportunity ever arises again, I'd love to go back and do it again! —*Jennifer*

How much time should I spend?

There are two ways to answer this. If you are in Santiago de Compostela just to visit the cathedral and maybe a few other key attractions, you should budget just a few hours. If, however, you are embarking on the actual pilgrimage to Santiago de Compostela (by walking, hiking, cycling, or horseback riding across Spain), then you might consider spending a few days here upon arrival.

How can I get there?

Location. Santiago de Compostela is located in northwestern Spain; it is almost forty miles southwest of La Coruna and four hundred miles from Madrid.

By Plane. Santiago de Compostela does have an airport; however, most people fly into the major airports at Lisbon, Portugal, or Madrid, Spain.

By Train. Santiago de Compostela is easily accessible from throughout Spain, Portugal, France, and the rest of Europe. Trains depart daily from Madrid to Santiago de Compostela. The local train station is about a twenty-minute walk to the cathedral, or you can take the city bus to Praza de Galicia, which is near the cathedral.

By Bus. Santiago de Compostela is easily accessible by bus from throughout Spain and elsewhere. Madrid has daily bus service to Santiago de Compostela.

By Car. Santiago de Compostela is easily accessible by road; the primary highways leading into or around the city are AP-9, N-550, and N-525.

What lodgings are available?

Santiago de Compostela has a fairly wide range of hotel and accommodation options. One of the more popular lodging choices is Hesperia Peregrino (Pilgrim's Hotel). To learn more about this four-star hotel, visit www.hesperia.es/hoteles/Hesperia-Peregrino.

THE WAY OF SAINT JAMES

Traveler's tip

If you would like to embark on the authentic journey along the Way of Saint James as well as receive the official certificate of pilgrimage (often referred to as the "Pilgrim Passport" or Credential), contact an organization or association affiliated with the Camino. For general information about the Credential or to prepare for your pilgrimage visit any of the following Web sites:

- Santiago Tourism and the Camino: www.santiagoturismo.com/camino
- Santiago de Compostela Pilgrim's Office: www.archicompostela.org/Peregrinos
- Worldwide Association/Fraternity of Saint James the Apostle: www.archicompostela.org
- American Pilgrims: www.americanpilgrims.com
- Pilgrim Forum: www.santiago-today.com
- Info Camino: www.infocamino.com
- Camino de Santiago: www.santiago-compostela.net
- The Confraternity of Saint James: www.csj.org.uk

CREDIT: ©ISTOCKPHOTO.COM/SASSPHOTOS
Travel the Way of Saint James to Santiago de Compostela Cathedral.

How much time should I spend?

How long does the trip take? If you did the entire Camino beginning in France, the route is 550 miles long and takes about thirty days to walk. A more popular and shorter route begins in Leon, Spain, and takes about seven to thirteen days (about two hundred miles). Although the majority of people still walk the route, a growing number are choosing bicycling and horseback riding instead.

SWITZERLAND: JOHN CALVIN AND THE REFORMATION

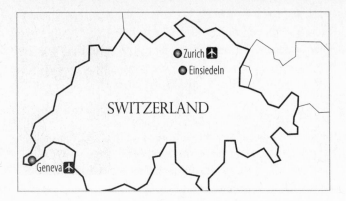

Why should I visit?

Switzerland is one of the newest popular destinations for the Christian traveler. More than just a country with fantastic chocolate, cuckoo clocks, and mountain scenery, Switzerland is also a place rich with Christian heritage.

The most prominent Christian sites are in Geneva, Zurich, and Einsiedeln. Geneva played a pivotal role in the Protestant Reformation and served as the "pulpit" of John Calvin. The Swiss Reformation was launched from Zurich under the leadership and guidance of Ulrich Zwingli. And Einsiedeln has served as a prominent place of pilgrimage for centuries with its famed monastery and shrine.

Today Switzerland is most often included on Christian tours that "follow in the footsteps of the Reformation." For this reason many Christian itineraries to this region feature a combination of Germany and Switzerland. Whatever your tour plans may be, if you include Switzerland, you will have a chance to indulge in the best of Swiss culture, heritage, and cuisine—and oh, yes, Swiss chocolate.

CONTACT INFORMATION FOR SWITZERLAND

Tourist Office: Switzerland Tourism Board, www.myswitzerland.com, www.switzerlandtourism.ch; Switzerland religious travel, www.myswitzerland.com/groups

Embassy: www.swissemb.org

Other Helpful Web Sites: Protestant, www.protestant.ch; Catholic, www.federation.ch

CREDIT: ZURICH TOURISMUS

Explore Zurich, home to the Swiss Reformation and Ulrich Zwingli.

What do I need to know?

Religion. Although Switzerland has no official state religion, Christianity is the dominant religion with more than 80 percent of the population affiliating with either the Protestant (40 percent) or Catholic (also 40 percent) faiths.

Language. Switzerland is a multilingual country with four national languages: French, German, Italian, and Romansh. Many Swiss also speak English.

Climate. As Switzerland is a fairly mountainous country, much of the weather is based on a particular region's altitude. In general, many tourist areas can be quite warm during the summer and cool in the spring. In general, think of Switzerland's climate from spring through fall as being moderate—not too hot, yet not too cold.

When to visit Switzerland. Summer from June through September offers one of the best (and most popular) times to visit Switzerland. Not only is the weather typically great at this time, but most tourist facilities are fully operational, which makes traveling and sightseeing very easy. The spring months of April and May combined with the late summer and fall months of September and October provide the best prices with the smallest crowds. As for winter in Switzerland, that's best reserved for skiing.

Clothing. Dress in layers, although lightweight clothes should be fine for summer. Be sure to pack an umbrella and raincoat.

Transportation. Switzerland has excellent transportation facilities, and its rail system is considered one of Europe's finest. Bus transportation is also very good between cities.

Airport: Geneva, www.gva.ch; Zurich, www.zurich-airport.com
Train: Swiss National Railroad, www.sbb.ch; Zurich, www.sbb.ch,
www.zvv.ch/aktuell.asp, www.bahn.de
Bus: Geneva, www.tpg.ch; Zurich, www.vbz.ch;
Car: www.viamichelin.com, www.theaa.com, www.mapquest.com

Words Can't Describe It

Words alone can't fully describe just how refreshing, encouraging, and motivating it is to take a Christian trip or tour of sites of our Christian heritage. The experience is life-changing. I know: I've done this, and it is profound. Christian travel will encourage you to live a life beyond the small, safe, and mundane. Study the lives and visit the places of our forefathers in faith, and you too will be inspired and motivated. For example, stand in John Calvin's Cathedral of Saint Peter in Geneva or Ulrich Zwingli's Grossmunster Cathedral and pray that you too will be bold to fulfill your calling. A hugely rewarding activity while on tour is meeting local Christians. Christian fellowship over a cup of tea after a church service in Switzerland, for example, is so thrilling. Cross-cultural connections with the living church while studying where God's history happened over the centuries makes for amazing travels! —*Frank*

GENEVA

Why should I visit?

When one thinks of Geneva, the United Nations often comes to mind. What doesn't always come to mind though for most people is that Geneva played a prominent role in the Protestant Reformation. Often thought of as the very embodiment of a Protestant city, Geneva is viewed by many as the "Protestant Rome." Today much of Geneva's way of life reflects the teaching of the city's most influential figure, John Calvin.

The city's relationship to Christianity dates to the fourth century when the first church was built in Geneva around AD 350 near the modern-day Saint Peter's Cathedral. About a thousand years later, Geneva played a crucial role in Christian history as John Calvin sought to reform the church while in Geneva. Second only to Martin Luther in his influence over

the Protestant Reformation, Calvin preached from Saint Peter's Cathedral and became a well-known figure. Calvin also worked closely with local authorities and sought to have much of his brand of Christian teaching integrated into Geneva's government and laws. Although this led to his eviction from the city of Geneva, it also eventually led Geneva to become one of the most prominent Protestant cities during the Reformation and thereafter.

Today you can visit Geneva and catch a glimpse of the spirit and legacy of John Calvin. In addition, you can explore the city that is arguably the most powerful political place on earth.

CREDIT: THE REFORMATION MUSEUM & LIGHTMOTIF

Tour the International Reformation Museum and Saint Peter's Cathedral in Geneva.

CONTACT INFORMATION FOR GENEVA
Tourist office: www.geneve-tourisme.ch

What should I see and do?

Not only are there many international organizations such as the United Nations and Red Cross, there are also many wonderful Christian and Reformation sites to visit:

- The International Reformation Monument: One of the most famous tourist sites in Geneva, the monument is more than three hundred feet long and features prominent Geneva reformers including John Calvin, Theodore Beza, and Guillaume Farel.
- Saint Peter's Cathedral (www.saintpierre-geneve.ch): This is the famed church from which John Calvin preached. Beneath the cathedral is a newly discovered Christian archaeological site that can be visited with audio guides.
- The International Museum of the Reformation (www.musee-reforme.ch): Located next to Saint Peter's Cathedral, the state-of-the-art museum brings to life the events of the Reformation through the many manuscripts, artifacts, rare books, artworks, and films.
- Lutheran World Federation (www.lutheranworld.org): This is the headquarters to almost 140 member churches belonging to the Lutheran tradition.
- World Council of Churches (www.oikoumene.org): An ecumenical Christian organization, the WCC's administrative office is based in Geneva and features a membership level of more than half a billion Christians.

How much time should I spend?

A visit to Geneva and its religious sites can usually be done in a half day, especially if you are on a typical group tour. A full day or more in Geneva is ideal.

How can I get there?

Location. Geneva is located on the southwestern border of Switzerland, right next to France.

By Plane. Geneva International Airport is serviced by flights from all over the world. The airport is located about twenty minutes from city center by car or bus, and a direct train connects it with the downtown rail station in just six minutes.

CREDIT: GENEVA TOURISM

The Reformation Wall in Geneva features prominent Christian personalities like John Calvin.

By Train. The Swiss National Railroad provides excellent train travel throughout Switzerland. Many international trains come to Geneva.

By Bus, Trolley, and Tram. The bus, trolley, and tram services are outstanding and can take you right up to the Christian sites in Geneva.

By Car. Geneva is literally at the crossroads of Europe and is easily accessible from France, Italy, Zurich (Switzerland), and many other cities. Driving, however, is not recommended within the center because of limited parking.

By Taxi. Like any major city, taxis are plentiful. And possibly best yet, the taxi drivers are obligated to know and speak English.

By Walking. Geneva is perfectly suited for walking and you might consider making your way on foot from your hotel to the Christian sites.

What lodgings are available?

As Geneva is a major international destination for both tourists and diplomats, you can find virtually any kind of hotel, lodging, or accommodation to fit your budget and needs.

ZURICH

Why should I visit?

Although Geneva captures most of the attention when it comes to the Reformation, Zurich is not to be missed. Much of the Swiss Reformation actually began here under the leadership of Ulrich Zwingli. Although not a household name like Martin Luther or John Calvin, Zwingli nonetheless made a big impact on the Protestant Reformation and remains one of its more prominent figures.

Christianity in Zurich dates to the third century. Like Geneva, Zurich played a pivotal role in the Christian faith a little more than a thousand years later. In the sixteenth century, Zurich gained fame for its role within the Reformation when Ulrich Zwingli implemented church reforms and even persuaded the city to become officially Protestant in 1522. Today the city is visited throughout the year by Christian groups retracing the footsteps of the European

CREDIT: ZURICH TOURISMUS

In Zurich, see Grossmunster and the Helferei.

Reformation. The visitors spend most of their time exploring key Christian sites such as Fraumünster Cathedral, Grossmünster (Great Minster) church, and the Helferei, where Zwingli lived.

When you visit Zurich, you will gain much greater insight into the pivotal events of fifteenth-century Christianity, and you will have a chance to explore one of Switzerland's more cosmopolitan cities.

CONTACT INFORMATION FOR ZURICH
Tourist office: www.zuerich.com

What should I see and do?

Among the most significant of Zurich's sites are:

- Fraumünster Cathedral (Minster of Our Lady) (www.fraumuensterchor.ch): Recognized by its graceful spire that pierces the Zurich skyline, Fraumünster Cathedral is today best known for its Marc Chagall stained glass windows.
- Grossmünster (Great Minster) (www.grossmuenster.ch): As the most recognized landmark in Zurich with its twin towers, Grossmünster was home to Zwingli's pastoral offices and the place where he preached.
- Helferei: The "Helferei" is the office located at 13 Kirchgasse where Zwingli studied, worked, and developed his sermons. The upstairs floor features his office, which has changed little since his days.

How much time should I spend?

You should budget a full morning or afternoon in Zurich to visit the key Christian sites. A full day in Zurich is ideal for exploring both Christian and regular tourist sites.

How can I get there?

Location. Zurich is located in northern Switzerland, slightly to the east. As the largest city in Switzerland and a prominent one on the world stage, it is easily accessible by many different forms of transportation.

By Plane. The Zurich International Airport is the country's largest and busiest airport; it receives flights from countries all around the world. Located about ten minutes from central Zurich by train, the airport is also very well connected with bus service.

By Train. The main Zurich train station is located at city center and provides service to and from many other Swiss and European cities.

By Boat. Zurich is located at the northern end of Lake Zurich, so it is accessible by boat from other lake towns and villages such as Rapperswil.

By Bus and Tram. Zurich has excellent bus and tram systems, making it very easy to visit the Christian sites of the city. Zurich is also very well connected by bus to and from many other Swiss and European cities.

By Car. Zurich is easily reachable by car; however, once you're in the city, you will find congestion and parking difficulties. For this reason, driving within Zurich is not recommended. To visit the Christian sites, it's best either to walk or to take a bus or taxi within the city.

By Taxi. Taxi is a great way to get around Zurich and to see the main Christian sites.

What lodgings are available?

As Zurich is a major international destination you can find virtually any kind of hotel, lodging, or accommodation that best fits your budget and desires.

Travel planning

Benedictine Monastery of Einsiedeln: www.kloster-einsiedeln.ch
Einsiedeln Tourist Office: www.einsiedeln.ch

Why should I visit?

One of the most famous monasteries in Europe is the Benedictine abbey of Einsiedeln. Dating from the nineteenth century, Einsiedeln has been a prominent place of pilgrimage for centuries because of its monastery and the renowned Lady Chapel shrine. Many Christians also visit the Diorama Bethlehem (the world's largest crèche, with more than five hundred carved wooden figures), as well as the Panorama (a giant painting of Jerusalem and the Crucifixion scene, 300 feet in length and 30 feet high). Ironically, even Ulrich Zwingli has a connection to Einsiedeln. Prior to launching his reforms, Ulrich served here as a parish priest. Today one quarter of a million people make their way to Einsiedeln each year.

What should I see and do?

Visitors can take guided tours of the monastery. The daily Liturgy of the Hours sung by the monks and the periodic orchestral services can also be attended. The Lady Chapel with its famed Black Madonna statue is a popular site. And, of course, the Diorama Bethlehem and Panorama are not to be missed.

How can I get there?

Einsiedeln is located twenty miles south of Zurich. It is easily accessible by road (A3 motorway and Highway 8) and train (direct trains from Zurich, Lucerne, etc.). It is not accessible by bus.

CHAPTER 5

MISSIONARY TRAVEL

CREDIT: ©ISTOCKPHOTO.COM/CHRISTA BRUNT

Is missionary travel right for me?

If you're looking for an experience that combines the best of travel, sharing the Christian faith, and helping those in need—missionary travel may be your calling. With thousands of opportunities to choose from, you are sure to find the mission adventure that best fits your desires, skills, and interests. The benefits gained from engaging in missionary work include personal and spiritual growth, development of lifelong friendships, and the internal joy received through sharing the Gospel and improving the lives of others. Missions range in length, destination, and type of experience. Those who embark on a missionary trip look back at such events as the most rewarding—and pivotal—times of their lives.

MISSIONS "AT A GLANCE"

TRIP SUMMARY
Typical length: 5–21 days
Average cost per day: $50 (not including transportation)
Total average cost (U.S.): $500–$1,500 (including transportation)
Total average cost (international): $1,200–$3,000 (including transportation)
Distance from home: varies from nearby to across the world
Variety of missions: many
When to go: any time of the year, depending on your destination
Why go: you feel called to missionary work
Whom to go with: your church, ministry, or missionary agency
Which mission experience to choose: one that fits your skills, talents, desires, and interests

DEMANDS AND BENEFITS
Spiritual focus: high
Fellowship opportunities: many
Physically demanding: moderately to very
Intellectually stimulating: moderately to very
Emotionally rewarding: very
Culturally enriching: moderately to very

MISSIONARY TRAVEL 101

What is the relevance of missionary travel?

Missionary travel has long been the lifeblood of Christian travel. Its very nature embraces the heart of Christianity: spreading the Gospel of Jesus Christ through faith, hope, and love. Today, Christians embark on missionary travel all over the world.

What is missionary travel at its simplest? It is a form of travel that seeks to spread the Christian faith and "plant" (establish) churches in new locations. In addition, missionary travel entails assisting with humanitarian needs through economic development, education, medical and health care, literacy, operation of orphanages, business services, and more.

Missionary travel falls into two categories: long-term and short-term. Long-term missionary travel typically consists of a two- to five-year, or longer, commitment and very often includes journeying outside one's country. Before embarking on such trips, people usually must be well-qualified spiritually, physically, emotionally, and socially. Even though the average long-term mission trip lasts anywhere from two to five years, some people dedicate their entire lives to the missions (they are often called career missionaries).

Short-term missionary travel, commonly referred to as short-term missions or STMs, typically includes a commitment of several days to two years and can take place virtually anywhere—within one's own country or outside. Although long-term missions have traditionally served as the backbone of Christian missions, today short-term missions have become the most common choice.

Short-term missionaries, like their long-term counterparts, dedicate themselves to evangelism, church development, and humanitarian assistance—just in a more limited time frame. With the recent growth of short-term missions, a wide variety of outlets, from mission travel agencies to organizations to churches, now provides these travel opportunities. Because this is currently the most popular form of missionary travel, most of this chapter deals with short-term missions.

What is the "Great Commission"?

Also known as the Great Commandment, the Great Commission is the mandate by Jesus for all believers to spread Christianity to the ends of the earth. This tenet of faith is taken from Mathew 28:18–20 where Jesus says, "All authority has been given to Me in heaven and on earth. Go therefore and make disciples of all the nations, baptizing them in the name of the Father and of the Son and of the Holy Spirit, teaching them to observe all things that I have commanded you; and lo, I am with you always, even to the end of the age."

As the last recorded personal instruction from Jesus to his disciples, this command serves as the theological foundation of all mission work and evangelism. For the past two millennia, Christians have heeded this call and embarked on mission trips all over the world, sharing the liberating message and word of Jesus Christ.

Where can I find missions in Scripture?

The concept of missions is very biblical. Although you won't find the exact words of "missions," "mobilize," or "the Great Commission" in Scripture, you will find numerous examples of each of these. For direct quotes from Scripture that provide doctrinal support of the missions, the following passages are often cited:

- "Get out of your country, From your family, And from your father's house, To a land that I will show you." (Genesis 12:1)
- "That all the peoples of the earth may know that the LORD is God." (1 Kings 8:60)
- "I will also give You as a light to the Gentiles." (Isaiah 49:6)
- The Great Commission: "All authority has been given to Me in heaven and on earth. Go therefore and make disciples of all the nations, baptizing them in the name of the Father and of the Son and of the Holy Spirit, teaching them to observe all things that I have commanded you; and lo, I am with you always, even to the end of the age." (Mathew 28:18–20)
- "And this gospel of the kingdom will be preached in all the world as a witness to all the nations, and then the end will come." (Matthew 24:14)
- "Go into all the world and preach the gospel to every creature." (Mark 16:15)
- "And you shall be witnesses to Me in Jerusalem, and in all Judea and Samaria, and to the end of the earth. (Acts 1:8)
- "For all nations shall come and worship before You." (Revelation 15:4)

And consider the following stories from the Bible:

- The Angel of the Lord commissioned Phillip the evangelist to share the Good News with the Ethiopian eunuch on a short-term mission trip (Acts 8:26–40).
- Jesus sent the apostles and disciples on mission trips (Luke 9–10).
- The Lord sent Jonah on an international mission trip to Nineveh (The Book of Jonah).
- The church community sent Barnabas to Antioch (Acts 11:22).
- And of course there are the apostle Paul's missionary journeys, which the Book of Acts covers extensively.

What is the 10/40 Window?

The "10/40 Window" refers to the portion of the world that remains the least evangelized. The term is derived from the 10th and 40th latitudes that provide a rectangular window around Africa, the Middle East, and Asia. Many missionary organizations and authorities often cite various statistics regarding this section of the world, including:

- More than half of the world's population lives in the 10/40 Window.
- Among the fifty least evangelized countries, about 95 percent of their populations live within the 10/40 Window.
- Many of the people in the 10/40 Window have never heard the Gospel message even once.
- About 80 percent of the world's poorest people live in the 10/40 Window.
- The dominant religions in the 10/40 Window are Islam, Hinduism, and Buddhism.
- Many countries inside the 10/40 Window ban or restrict the efforts of Christian missionaries.

What is the 4/14 Window?

The 4/14 Window refers not to latitudes but to the ages (four to fourteen years) when children are most receptive to faith and hearing the message of Jesus. In other words, this is the window of opportunity to evangelize children. This takes on extra significance when you consider that the majority of Christians accept their faith during this time frame and that, according to the Barna Group, what a person believes at age thirteen is most likely what he or she will die believing.

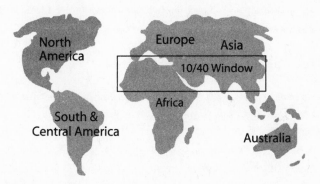

Learning missionary lingo

Church Planting. The act of establishing a network of Christian communities and/or building churches; this particularly applies to un-evangelized, indigenous, and/or mission areas.

Faith Mission. A faith mission is a mission undertaken with complete trust that "God will provide." Faith missionaries rely solely on God's provisions and not on set or guaranteed stipends. The first missionary organizations to adopt this principle were the China Inland Mission (1865), the Sudan Interior Mission (1893), and the Africa Inland Mission (1895).

Friendship Evangelism. Sharing the Christian faith and evangelizing through genuine, authentic friendships is friendship evangelism, a common form of evangelism found on mission trips.

Holistic Mission. Holistic missions are missionary efforts that not only foster evangelism and church planting but also place a strong emphasis on social responsibility and meeting all the needs (spiritual, physical, social, intellectual, and emotional) of the community and individuals.

Missiology. This is the academic study of missions, including not only theology but also history, anthropology, geography, apologetics, interdenominational relationships, and comparative religions.

Mobilizer. A mobilizer is a person who serves as the driving force behind inspiring, promoting, and organizing a church or group of people to embark on a mission trip. A mobilizer can be anyone in a leadership position such as missionary agency representative, missionary promoter, or pastor.

Tentmaking. This is the concept of participating in the workforce in order to evangelize and participate in ministry activities, especially in a cross-cultural situation. The term comes from the example of the apostle Paul, who labored in tentmaking in order to support his mission activities and spread the Gospel of Jesus Christ (Acts 18 and 21).

Unreached Peoples. This term refers to people who have no access to the Gospel. The reasons for not yet hearing the message of Jesus Christ are varied and include the prevailing conditions of a particular country, language barriers (Scripture not yet written in their language), and the minimal presence of other Christians in the area.

Who's who in Christian missions

The apostle Paul. In many ways, the apostle Paul is the missionary par excellence and was one of the first Christian missionaries. It is primarily due to Paul's missionary efforts of evangelism and church planting that the Christian faith spread throughout the Roman Empire. He traveled from Palestine to places as far away as modern-day Turkey, Greece, and Italy. Much of his travels can be read about in the Book of Acts, and Christians can even retrace his footsteps today on pilgrimage (see Greece and Turkey in the pilgrimage chapter).

Patrick. This famed fifth-century missionary to Ireland converted the local people, ordained clergy, and established monasteries. His feast day of March 17 is celebrated throughout the world as Saint Patrick's Day.

Columba. An early Irish missionary to Scotland, Columba played a pivotal role in bringing Christianity to Scotland in the sixth century (see the section on Scotland in chapter 4). He also founded the renowned Iona Abbey on the western coast of Scotland.

Augustine of Canterbury. Augustine served as first archbishop of Canterbury and helped spread the Christian faith to England in the seventh century. He is often considered the "Apostle to the English."

William Carey. Considered the father of modern missions (1761–1834), Carey was a Baptist minister and English pioneer missionary to India who founded today's BMS World Mission. He translated the Bible into the local languages of Bengali and Sanskrit and assisted with dozens of other dialects.

Hudson Taylor. One of the greatest missionaries of all time, Taylor spent more than fifty years in the missions and brought hundreds of missionaries into China, leading to the conversion of thousands of Chinese to the Christian faith. He was a pioneer missionary to China (1832–1905) and founded the China Inland Mission, today known as OMF International.

Mother Teresa. Agnes Gonxha Bojaxhiu is best known around the world as Mother Teresa (1910–1997), the Albanian-born Roman Catholic nun who founded the Missionaries of Charity. The sisters of her order can be found on five continents around the world today ministering to the "poorest of the poor."

Timeline of Christian missions through the centuries

- First century: Birth of Christian church; Paul and other apostles embark on missionary trips throughout the Roman Empire and as far away as India.
- Third century: Denis, traditionally recognized as the first bishop of Paris, is sent to Paris to spread the Christian faith.
- Fourth century: Constantine recognizes Christianity throughout the Roman Empire.
- Fifth century: Patrick converts Ireland.
- Sixth century: Columba spreads faith in Scotland.
- Seventh century: Augustine establishes Christian faith throughout England.
- Ninth century: Missionaries Cyril and Methodius, today recognized as patron saints of Europe, evangelize Moravia.
- Tenth century: Russia adopts Christianity.
- Thirteenth century: Dominican and Franciscan religious orders are launched.
- Fourteenth century: Franciscans perform missionary work in China.
- Fifteenth century: Dominicans spread faith to West Africa; Christopher Columbus brings priests on his journey, and first baptisms take place in the New World.
- Sixteenth century: Christian faith brought to Latin America; Francis Xavier embarks on missionary travels to India.
- Seventeenth century: Missionary efforts expand in Asia; Jesuits arrive in Japan.
- Eighteenth century: William Carey founds Baptist Missionary Society in 1792 and embarks on missionary travels to India; California Missions established by Junipero Serra.
- Nineteenth century: Missionary efforts expanded in Africa; numerous missionary organizations founded including China Inland Mission, in 1865, by James Hudson Taylor.

- Twentieth century: Hundreds more missionary organizations established including William Cameron Townsend's Wycliffe Bible Translators; Billy Graham begins evangelistic work; Mother Teresa founds Missionaries of Charity; short-term missions take root and founding of Short-Term Evangelical Missions reflects growing prominence; 10/40 Window concept introduced; numerous mission agencies and companies launched to assist with organized mission trips.

Who embarks on mission trips?

Church groups, ministry teams, youth groups, and individuals all embark on missionary travel. Virtually anyone from teenagers through seniors in their seventies can participate in short-term missions; however, high school and college students comprise the bulk of missionaries. In total, about 2 million people embark on mission trips a year from North America.

CHOOSING MISSIONARY TRAVEL

What can I expect to gain by embarking on a mission trip?

Many people state that a mission trip is one of the greatest experiences of their lives. Others say it served as a turning point in their life, while others find a deeper appreciation for their family, friends, and life in general. And some even decide to change their studies or career as a result of their mission trip. Above all, missionaries state that these experiences deepened their faith, enriched their lives, and gave them new friendships. Because of reasons like these, many Christian travelers embark on short-term missions again and again.

How do I know if I'm called to mission work?

How can you gauge whether you're "called" to embark on such a program? If you possess a great desire to spread the Christian faith around the world and if your heart aches to improve the lives of others, you might consider such a commitment. If this sounds like you, consider talking to your pastor, religious leader, friends, and family about your idea. Oftentimes these people can help you make a decision. Here are some questions to help you discern whether you are called to missions.

Do you have:

- a tremendous yearning to tell others about the Christian faith?
- the internal desire to make a positive impact on the lives of others?

- a willingness to engage in another's culture no matter how different from your own?
- an openness to live with greater simplicity, without all the traditional comforts of your life at home?
- the readiness to endure trials and difficulties?
- an eagerness to develop rapport with the local people?

If you discern that you are called to missions, you should take great joy in knowing that you are embarking upon one of Christianity's highest callings and one of life's most rewarding experiences.

What are the advantages and disadvantages of missionary travel?

Advantages

- spiritual growth from serving the Lord in the capacity of evangelism, church planting, and humanitarian need
- fulfillment of your call to engage in mission work
- internal reward and joy of helping others in need
- full immersion in another culture
- opportunity to meet people from around the world and develop lifelong friendships and relationships with your host community, team members, missionaries, and supporters
- break from the artificialness and commercialism often found in our regular daily life
- new perspectives on other's way of life, especially the poor and disadvantaged in other cultures
- new skills and talents related to your missionary work
- personal and often life-changing transformations that are possible only through missions
- opportunity to spread the Christian faith to others

Disadvantages

- loneliness of being away from home, family, and friends
- consuming local foods or "delicacies" that appear to border on the inedible— or the task of growing what you will eat
- living or working in unsanitary or dirty conditions
- experiencing culture shock

- working in a severe climate without heat or air-conditioning
- work that is much more challenging than expected, imagined, or were told
- ungrateful and unhappy recipients
- not enough time provided on short-term missions to feel like you "solved all the problems" or made a substantial difference
- returning home with new perspectives on life, which lead to disputes and arguments with family and friends who prefer the "old you"

What are some questions I should ask myself?

1. Why do I feel called to mission work?
2. What kind of missionary travel would I like to embark upon?
3. Where would I like to engage in mission work?
4. When shall I go and for how long?
5. Which missionary organization or group would I like to join?
6. How can I apply for a mission trip and raise the necessary funds?

What are some common questions asked by prospective missionaries? What are the answers?

Question: Who can embark on a mission trip?

Answer: Any Christian with a desire and willingness. Virtually all ages and backgrounds can participate. People under eighteen years of age (minors) will often require parent-approved supervisors. The 10/40 Window destinations are sometimes reserved for veteran missionaries or more spiritually and emotionally mature individuals.

Question: Can I join a mission trip as an individual?

Answer: Yes. Many missionary agencies accept individuals.

Question: What are the most typical groups that embark on mission trips?

Answer: Most groups are formed from churches, ministries, schools (including home-schools), youth programs, and families. Basically any Christian group is a candidate for embarking on an organized mission trip.

Question: What is the typical size of a mission team or group?

Answer: Sizes can vary from a handful of individuals to about thirty people, and sometimes even into the hundreds.

Question: Where in the world can I go on a mission?

Answer: The following are four typical geographical missionary destinations and which ones appeal to whom:

- Domestic (United States): great for first-time missionaries
- North America (U.S., Canada, and Mexico): great for first- or second-time missionaries
- International (overseas): open to either first-time or veteran missionaries
- 10/40 Window (restricted access nations): usually reserved for veteran missionaries or those with well-developed spirituality and emotional maturity

Question: What are the most typical missionary projects and activities?

Answer: If you embark on a short-term mission trip, you will most likely engage in one or more of the following three assignments and responsibilities:

- Evangelism: church planting, teaching, preaching, Bible study, theological education, door-to-door visitation, distributing pamphlets/tracts, community prayer, and friendship evangelism
- Humanitarian relief and aid (sometimes referred to as social development, social responsibility, mercy services, and project development): providing or assisting with medical care, education, food delivery, caring for orphans, visiting prisoners, providing entertainment, and other social services. Examples: youth work, teaching English, healthcare services, street ministry, prison ministry, leadership training, and business consulting services
- Construction: directing or assisting with the construction or maintenance of churches, buildings, medical/health clinics, orphanages, roads, and general infrastructure

Question: What is the typical itinerary of a two-week mission?

Answer: Although the structure of a two-week trip will vary based on the organization, destination, and mission experience, the following is a fairly typical example:

Day 1: depart for mission
Day 2: training and team bonding
Days 3–11: mission work
Day 12: sightseeing (free day)
Day 13: prepare for return home
Day 14: depart for home

Question: What is a typical day like on a mission trip?

Answer: Every trip is different, so the schedules will vary based on the type of mission, location, local culture, and other factors. The following is a fairly typical day:

6:00 AM: wake-up, get ready for the day

7:00 AM: breakfast, team meeting

7:30 AM: chapel, community prayer, devotions

8:30 AM–12:00 PM: work, mission outreach

12:00 PM–1:00 PM: lunch

1:00 PM–2:00 PM: rest or recreation

2:00 PM–5:30 PM: work, mission outreach

5:30 PM–7:00 PM: dinner

7:00 PM–8:00 PM: recreation; some evenings may have mission
    outreach activities

8:00 PM–10:00 PM: community prayer, Bible study, team meeting

10:00 PM: bedtime (personal time)

Some programs provide free time on weekends to allowing for sightseeing, shopping, exploring the local countryside, and personal time.

How much does a mission trip cost?

Costs can, of course, vary from mission trip to mission trip based on the organization, destination, and other factors. The average cost overall ranges from $500 to $3,000, and the average cost per day is about $50 (not including transportation). The following provides only estimated costs for domestic and international missionary travel:

- overall domestic average (5–10 day trips in U.S.): $600–$1,500
  - missionary organization registration fee: $300–$800
  - domestic airfare/transportation: $100–$500
  - out of pocket expenses: $200 (necessary items, gifts, soft drinks, stamps, miscellaneous items)
- overall international average (10–21 day overseas trip): $1,200–$3,300
  - missionary organization registration fee: $600–$1,700
  - international airfare: $500–$1,200
  - out of pocket expenses: $100–400 (passport, immunizations, necessary items, gifts, soft drinks, stamps, miscellaneous items)

What does the missionary trip registration fee usually include, and what doesn't it include?

Typical inclusions: lodging, food, transportation at the mission site, ministry resources, construction materials, administrative costs, training, project supplies, guides, professional staff, etc.

Typical "on your own" costs: passports, immunizations, departure tax, personal items, medical expenses, insurance (sometimes minimal amount included in registration fee), etc.

FINDING AND APPLYING FOR A MISSION TRIP

Where can I find a missionary travel agency or organization?

Because of the tremendous growth of missionary travel in the past thirty years, today there are hundreds of agencies that operate and facilitate such trips. A variety of short-term mission trips are available in regards to destination, type of work, and overall experience. For this reason, if you know what you are seeking through such a trip, chances are you will find a group, organization, or company that provides the right experience for you.

Short-term mission trip opportunities can be found almost everywhere. A search on the Internet will yield thousands of opportunities. You can also view a listing of organizations in appendix A. However, most local churches and religious organizations in your area probably offer these trips. If you belong to any ministries or Christian groups, you might first inquire as to whether they offer any short-term missionary vacations. If not, you might consider organizing one and getting your fellow church members and friends involved.

How do I apply for a mission trip?

The application process and preparatory period can be intense and lengthy, especially because your spiritual, mental, and physical health must be fully evaluated. In addition, certain skills must also be developed and refined prior to such travels, including sometimes the study or learning of the local language and culture.

What are the top ten questions I should ask a missionary agency, organization, or company?

1. What are the goals, purpose, and mission statement of your missionary agency? (Tip: Ask if they favor one type of missionary endeavor [evangelism, church planting, humanitarian need] over another.)

2. What is your denomination affiliation or Christian statement of belief? (Tip: Ask to see the official statement of belief for the organization.)

3. How long has your agency been in the business of operating mission trips? What are the history and track record of the organization? (Tip: You can review most

organizations or companies by doing some "outside" research on the Internet or by visiting the missionary resource Web sites listed at the end of the chapter.)

4. What is your organizational structure? (Tip: Ask if their headquarters or operations office[s] are based in North America or overseas [or both]. Ask about management or organization leaders and their personal experience or years in mission work.)

5. What missionary programs and experiences do you offer? (Tip: Visit their Web site and ask for their brochure or flyers; these materials and informational packets will usually answer this question.)

6. Where do you send your missionaries? (Tip: Same as above; view the organization's Web site and brochures or flyers.)

7. How does your agency expect me to pay for my mission trip (fund-raising, sponsorships, my own hard-earned money,\ etc.)? (Tip: Ask if their organization will assist with ideas or provide resources on how to increase your fund-raising or sponsorship success.)

8. Are there any policies, procedures, or regulations I should be aware of regarding joining the organization on a mission trip? (Tip: Ask if they have any rules of personal and professional conduct. What do they expect of their missionaries?)

9. Who is the "typical person" that joins your mission trips? (Tip: Don't be shy; ask about the typical person who applies and goes on their mission trips. What are their personalities like? What age[s] are they? Do they share similar backgrounds with you?)

10. Do you have a list of missionaries (former or current) whom I can contact about their experiences? (Tip: If the organization has a strong track record, they will most likely carry a list of missionaries you can call and ask about their previous experiences.)

What are the top ten questions the organization may ask me during the application or interview process?

Don't assume that signing up for a mission trip is as simple as filling out an application. In many cases, you will need to qualify and be approved. Depending on the organization, this may mean filling out multiple forms, participating in several interviews (on the phone or in person), obtaining letters of recommendation, and more.

Although applying for a short-term mission trip may not be as intense as applying for college or a job, the procedures are somewhat the same. Your goal is to convince the organization that you are spiritually, physically, emotionally, intellectually, and (sometimes) financially ready for such an endeavor. Be prepared to answer the following questions:

- Why do you wish to embark on a mission trip?
- What are your goals and vision for such an experience?

- What is your spiritual life like? Your commitment to the Christian faith? Do you belong to a particular denomination, or which tenets of the Christian faith do you subscribe to?
- What are you currently doing in life (student, job, etc.)?
- Are you in good physical and psychological health?
- Are you prepared intellectually, emotionally, and socially for mission work?
- Are you active in your church or a ministry?
- Describe your personal integrity and morals.
- Are you a team player?
- How will you be funding the trip? Are you open to seeking sponsorships?

PREPARING FOR YOUR MISSION ADVENTURE

How can I best prepare for my mission adventure?

The best way to prepare yourself for a mission trip is to develop yourself spiritually, physically, intellectually, socially, emotionally, and financially.

- *Spiritually*. Pray. Pray. And pray. Immerse yourself in Scripture, especially in relation to passages dealing with missionary activities (reading and reflecting on the missionary journeys of Paul in the Book of Acts would be ideal).
- *Physically*. Most mission work requires stamina and a healthy body. Exercise, eat right, and get into the habit of walking everywhere.
- *Intellectually*. Read about the country or place where you will be living. Study the language of the people you will be assisting (presuming they speak a language foreign to you). Learn the culture that you will be encountering.
- *Socially*. If you are traveling with a group, communicate and get to know those whom you will be joining for the mission trip. Maybe even host some "pre-missionary" get-togethers to discuss the forthcoming adventure.
- *Emotionally*. Address any fears or concerns you may have prior to departure. If you will be gone for a while, prepare your good-byes and make arrangements for how you will communicate with your loved ones while you're on the mission. In the days leading up to the trip, talk about your feelings with those closest to you.
- *Financially*. Obtain the necessary funds to make the mission happen—and then leave "financial worries" up to God.

Mission trip preparation countdown: get ready, get set, go!

One year or longer before your trip

- Pray about embarking on a mission trip.
- Research opportunities including where and when you'd like to travel.
- Contact missionary agencies and organizations about the possibilities.

One year to six months

- Choose your mission trip and apply.
- Once you're confirmed on the trip, book airline flights.
- Start language and cultural training.
- Apply for (or renew) passport, visas, and any other legal documents.
- Research necessary shots and immunizations.
- Develop a budget and begin your fund-raising campaign.

Six months to one month

- Ask others to begin praying for your mission trip.
- Begin obtaining necessary shots and immunizations as per medical recommendations.
- Make a list of all items to pack for your trip.
- Follow up with receiving your sponsorships and monies.
- Purchase or obtain any items that are still needed for your trip.
- Research and buy travel insurance.
- Receive materials from the missionary organization.
- Reconfirm all travel and flight information.

One month to one week

- Write thank-you notes to all who contributed to your mission trip campaign.
- Pack all items.
- Purchase or obtain any "last minute" necessary items for mission trip.
- Advise family and friends of your contact information while you're away, which includes providing parents and other family members with copies of your passport, travel itinerary, mission agency information, and other legal documents (i.e., birth certificate).

- Pray the night before about your mission.
- Reconfirm all your flight and travel information.
- Check the weather at your mission destination for the week ahead and dress accordingly.
- Double-check all items in luggage including passport, airplane tickets, and other required documents (including copies); this is especially important right before departing on the trip.

Checklist of "last-minute" all-important items

After you've packed all your traditional items (i.e. clothes, toiletries, etc.), just minutes before you walk out the door, be sure to double-check that you have each of the following:

- passport and other required I.D. (i.e. immunization certificate)
- copies of passport and other required I.D. (placed in separate bags/ luggage; or put one set in your wallet and the other in your luggage)
- airplane tickets and other necessary travel documents
- medicine (prescription and nonprescription)
- money
- small gift for host family
- leave all valuables (i.e. jewelry) at home
- assume that your luggage will be lost; bring two days' worth of clothes, toiletries, medicine, and other "irreplaceable" items in your carry-on bag
- a Bible that can withstand any adventure, weather, and mission, such as Thomas Nelson's *Immerse: A Water-Resistant New Testament* or *The Duct Tape Bible*

How can I successfully raise funds for my trip?

One of the most common ways to raise funds for your trip is through writing letters and asking for support. The two keys to a successful fund-raising campaign of this kind are: (1) writing an excellent fund-raising letter, and (2) sending your letter it to the "right" people and organizations. If you accomplish these two objectives, this may be all you need to secure the funds.

What's the "magic number" for a successful fund-raising campaign?

It boils down to simple math. Think of it in these terms: If you need to raise $2,500 for an overseas mission trip, you simply need one hundred people to contribute

$25. Because many Christians will be very willing to donate $25 (the cost of a Friday evening out on the town), the goal here is distributing your letter to as many people as possible. And if you think it might be easier to get only fifty people to donate, that simply equals $50 in contributions from each of them. Either way, the task of raising $2,500 is not as daunting as it usually seems at first.

What should I include in a fund-raising letter?

As I mentioned above, one of the keys to a successful fund-raising campaign is writing a good letter asking for support. Be sure to ask your mission agency or organization for a sample letter because many of them have a few on file. With or without these sample letters though, consider including the following in your letter:

- your personal relationship with God
- why you feel called to mission work
- your personal goals for the experience
- what organization you are joining and who will be joining you on the trip
- where the mission will take place (country and city)
- what project(s) you will be undertaking
- when the trip takes place
- how you are funding the trip
- what you need in regard to spiritual, physical, emotional, and financial support
- personal (background) information

To whom should I send my fund-raising letters?

Again, the goal is to distribute your letter far and wide. However, be wise with your limited time and resources and contact first those who are most likely to contribute. You can use the traditional "A, B, C" method to prioritize your contact list, with "A" being most likely to contribute. And remember, after you send the letter (or e-mail), it's best to follow up with a phone call within about seven days. Here is a sample list of proposed contacts and their priority:

A-list Contacts

- family (both immediate and extended)
- friends
- church members (ones whom you know personally)

- church ministry leaders (especially the missions committee or council)
- peers and coworkers
- local religious organizations (especially leaders)

B-list contacts

- Christian friends and family contacts
- church member acquaintances (those you know in some way)
- neighbors (both current and former)
- other churches in the area

C-list contacts

- anyone else whom you know personally, who may be interested in supporting such an endeavor (i.e. your barber, landscaper, parents' friends, doctor, dentist, insurance agent, etc.)
- alumni and administrators from schools you have attended
- members from previous churches you attended
- your Christmas card list
- your wedding guest list

What are other fund-raising ideas?

Don't forget that you can also "raise money" by saving money. Maybe skip going out to the movies and instead rent movies, make meals with friends versus going to fast-food restaurants, and hold off buying new clothes and other nonessentials. Some other ideas are:

- mow lawns, wash cars, and provide other household services
- sell cookie dough (try www.cookiehouse.com) or other "sweet products"
- host a brunch or dinner event
- have a garage sale, auction, or sell some of your belongings online
- create a gift, handiwork, or homemade craft and sell it
- ask your pastor if you can speak in front of the church (or place something in the bulletin)
- contact Christian organizations that specialize in fund-raising programs and act on one or more of their ideas (such as selling Christian t-shirts)
- obtain sponsorships from companies and organizations (secular or religious)

CREATIVE FUND-RAISING TIP:
BUILD YOUR OWN MISSION TRIP WEB PAGE!

Consider building a Web page about your upcoming mission trip. Make your Web page fun, interesting, and interactive. Start a blog. Put RSS news feeds on your Web site regarding missionary travel. Add a video of yourself speaking about your mission trip and asking for support. Post photos, your goals, and even information about the organization you're joining and the place where you will be living. You might even allow organizations to purchase "ads" on your blog. The more creative you are on your Web site with all the bells and whistles of today's technology, the easier it will be to hit your fund-raising goals in the allotted time.

Do I need missionary travel insurance?

Securing some form of missionary travel insurance is a must in all circumstances. This kind of insurance can protect you against unforeseen medical emergencies and travel-related problems. This can possibly include medical coverage and transportation, hospitalization, emergency evacuation, life, disability, death, trip-cancellation insurance, trip interruption, lost or delayed baggage, stolen property, 24/7 emergency assistance from anywhere in the world, and more.

Many travel insurance companies that specialize in mission travel can offer long- or short-term mission insurance plans. However, the best advice is to discuss the topic of insurance with the missionary organization or company you are joining. Although some of them do offer limited coverage with your registration, this is rarely enough, and many missionary organizations will require or at least strongly suggest you secure additional coverage. Just make sure you do your homework regarding whichever travel insurance company or plan you choose. Use a reputable travel insurance company with a long, strong track record and outstanding reputation. In this post-9/11 era, you should view travel insurance not as an option but as a requirement.

I Knew that I Had Received
More than I Had Ever Given

When I was eleven years old, I was given a picture of a Jesuit priest at Saint Francis Indian Mission in South Dakota. I was to write and pray for that priest and mission, which I did up to twenty-one years of age. On May 26, 1966, at twenty-one years of age, my husband of six weeks drowned. The night of the death it came to me to go to Saint Francis Indian Mission in South Dakota, which I did three weeks later by a Greyhound Bus.

That summer I did miscellaneous activities at the Indian Mission and then left for a few weeks. Upon my return I was offered the position of being a Head Start teacher for four-, five-, and six-year-old boys and girls for the upcoming school year (Head Start serves the child development needs of preschool children and their low-income families). I wasn't qualified but I accepted the position because I could be with young children, who happened to be Sioux Indians. Those children helped me get through the year following my husband's death. There was one little Sioux Indian girl that particularly caught my heart, and I took her to my home in Saint Louis over the Easter vacation. That Easter this little girl accompanied me when I went on a blind date—to the zoo. (I later married my blind date.) Near the end of that year at the Indian Mission, I knew that I had received more than I had ever given. —*Patricia*

Serving God with My Dental Skills

I was working in my dental office when I decided to go on a volunteer mission trip years ago. I decided that it was God's will that I follow his leadership, so I committed to go. I did dentistry work on hundreds of patients and they responded to hearing the Good News because we cared for their physical needs as well as their spiritual needs. I am thankful for the way God opened my eyes to the many people around the world needing Christ, and that I can serve him through my dental skills. Since my first mission trip I have traveled to twenty-six countries across the world spreading the Gospel as I serve God through my dental skills. —*Dr. William, DMD*

MISSION TRIP OPPORTUNITIES

NORTH AMERICA

Why should I go?

If you're looking to embark on a missionary trip yet hoping to remain close to home, then look no farther than North America. Although many people often think of Africa, South America, Eastern Europe, or other countries as possibilities, the reality is that thousands of charity travel opportunities exist right here in North America.

Description

North America possesses many more missionary opportunities than people realize. Most of these fall into the category of short-term missions or even volunteer vacations. Sample projects include:

- disaster areas (caused by hurricanes, tornadoes, earthquakes, floods, and man-made calamities)
- natural disaster recovery and rebuilding
- downtown areas in major cities
- rural areas
- immigrant relief and assistance
- Native Americans/First Nations
- newsmaking stories and people (i.e., remodeling the home of a ninety-seven-year-old widow after she is featured on the news as a victim of a fraud)

What are the most common mission activities?

Christian missionaries engage in a variety of tasks including house building or repairing, engineering and construction, visitation to elderly and families, friendship with children and youth, homelessness and housing, family and adult ministry, community development, emergency services and relief, evangelism, food ministry and hunger, health and medicine, orphanage, addiction and recovery, and immigrants and refugees.

AFRICA

Why should I go?

If you are looking for a full and traditional immersion experience into missionary work, you should consider Africa. Few places offer such rewarding yet challenging opportunities. It is a country with a great need for missionaries.

Description

Africa has long been a destination for missionary work. Many countries in this great continent face the everyday challenges of hunger, disease, AIDS, education, and extreme poverty. Some of the more common missionary destinations include Kenya, Ghana, Zimbabwe, Uganda, Nigeria, Ethiopia, South Africa, Swaziland, Rwanda, the Ivory Coast, and the Democratic Republic of the Congo.

What are the most common mission activities?

Missionaries to Africa spend time in a variety of activities such as: church planting, evangelism, teaching, tutoring, assisting children and youth, agriculture, community development, administration, disabilities ministry, health and medical services, women's ministry, building and operating orphanages, teaching, education and literacy, children and youth, homelessness, housing and building repairs, food/hunger ministry, Bible study, single parents, crisis pregnancy, AIDS ministry, and computers and technology.

CREDIT: ©ISTOCKPHOTO.COM/ANDYDIDYK

Africa is a top destination for missionary travel.

ASIA

Why should I go?

Although Asia is not always at the forefront of people's thoughts as a missionary destination, Asia does have needs, and it presents wonderful possibilities for those willing to travel to the Orient.

Description

Teaching English is one of the biggest areas of request. Bible education and pastoral training for the smaller Christian communities in this area of the world are two areas of great opportunity. Many long-term missionary travel opportunities exist in this part of the world. Some of the more common missionary destinations include China, Vietnam, India, Thailand, and South Korea.

What are the most common mission activities?

The majority of missionary and volunteer services provided in Asia typically include teaching, tutoring, and mentoring. This is combined with evangelism, church planting, agriculture, community development, language translation, employment training, assisting children and youth, food/hunger ministry, education and literacy, visitation to elderly and disadvantaged, delivering health and medical services, and building or running orphanages.

CHINA AS A MISSIONARY COUNTRY

Anyone considering a missionary trip to China should become familiar with the work of Hudson Taylor. A Protestant missionary, he arrived in 1854 and played a key role in church planting and spreading the Christian faith. He founded China Inland Missions. Prior to Hudson Taylor's work, the Jesuits played a key role in missionary efforts in China. Today opportunities are limited due to the Communist government; however, some options still exist, including teaching English, assisting orphanages, and providing medical services. If you are interested in China, one of the best places to start your research is Partners International (www.partnersintl.org), a global ministry that began missionary work in China in 1943.

CARIBBEAN

Why should I go?

When most of us think about the Caribbean, we imagine lying on a beach amidst a tropical paradise. However, like most countries and regions around the world, the Caribbean also has pockets of great poverty and hardship. If you would like to assist those who are facing these challenges, without traveling too far from the United States, then consider the Caribbean for your missionary trip.

Description

Missionary trips to the Caribbean feature hard work in the midst of beautiful scenery and joyous people. The need is very great because of the extreme poverty and disadvantages of some, so the rewards are often great and immediate. In a short time, you can see the results of your work, whether it's building a home for a family, providing medical services for the sick, educating children, playing with babies at an orphanage, assisting the hungry, or simply sharing the Gospel with the local population. Some of the more common missionary travel countries include Jamaica, Bahamas, Grenada, Haiti, and the Dominican Republic.

What are the most common mission activities?

Missionaries to the Caribbean find themselves engaged in evangelism, church planting, assisting children and youth, Bible studies, health and medicine, teaching, tutoring, mentoring, education and literacy, community development, health and medicine, home building and repairs, engineering and construction, and recreation.

EASTERN EUROPE AND RUSSIA

Why should I go?

If you possess a great desire to help those in need while sharing the Christian faith and if you've always dreamed of seeing Eastern Europe or Russia, then you might consider a missionary trip to this area of the world. The opportunities are vast, and the need is great for your service.

Description

Ever since the fall of the Berlin Wall in 1989, missionary travel opportunities to Eastern Europe and Russia have opened up considerably. The experiences available in this region enable you to work side-by-side with the local people in establishing church communities, teaching the faith and Scripture, and assisting with educational, health, housing, and family needs. Virtually all of Eastern Europe is open-door territory for mission work, including Romania, Bulgaria, Slovakia, Hungary, Poland, Czech Republic, Ukraine, Kazakhstan, Belarus, Estonia, Latvia, Lithuania, Georgia, and the Russian Federation.

What are the most common mission activities?

Evangelism, church planting, visiting orphanages, recreation, assisting children and youth, teaching, tutoring, mentoring, addiction and recovery, homelessness and housing, immigrants and refugees, computers and technology, visitation to elderly and disadvantaged, home building and repairs, engineering and construction, health and medicine, education, and literacy are the most common activities.

LATIN AMERICA

Why should I go?

If you would like to engage in traditional missionary work in a foreign country, Latin America might be your calling. Along with its many mission trip possibilities and opportunities, this region of the world provides a wonderful cultural experience in the midst of a vibrant people and rich history.

Description

Like Africa, Latin America is typically a place that is associated with missionary travel. According to some statistics, two-thirds of all overseas missionaries embark on trips to South America. From Mexico to the southern tip of Chile, the opportunities are numerous, and virtually every kind of missionary work can be found here. Most of

Central and South America provides missionary travel options; however, some of the more common countries include Mexico, Costa Rica, Guatemala, El Salvador, Nicaragua, Bolivia, Peru, Ecuador, Colombia, and Brazil.

What are the most common mission activities?

Missionaries typically engage in evangelism, church planting, community development, agriculture, health and medicine, teaching, tutoring, mentoring, evangelism, assisting children and youth, home building and repairing, engineering and construction, food/hunger ministry, education and literacy, and operating orphanages.

10/40 WINDOW (RESTRICTED ACCESS NATIONS)

Why should I go?

As discussed earlier in the chapter, few places in the world provide greater missionary opportunities than those countries in the 10/40 Window. Home to the least evangelized countries and the world's greatest poverty (as well as disease, lack of education, and wars in some places), the need for Christian missionaries is tremendous and vast.

Description

The 10/40 Window stretches from North Africa through the Middle East and into Southeast and Central Asia. Much of the biblical lands lie here, including the very places where Abraham, Moses, the prophets, Jesus, and the apostles lived, walked, and ministered. Yet only a small percentage of the population is Christian. Because many of the countries ban or restrict access to missionaries, the opportunities are often limited yet creative in scope. Consider that countries such as Cambodia, Thailand, Kazakhstan, India, Mongolia, Egypt, and Taiwan lie here, as well as North Korea, Iran, and Iraq. Sometimes the only opportunities available are those for professionals who teach English or provide services such as in the medical, technology, or business fields, for example. It truly is a special calling to minister here.

What are the most common mission activities?

Christian missionaries to the 10/40 Window spend their time on evangelism, church planting, discipleship, community development, agriculture, health and medicine, teaching, tutoring, mentoring, assisting children and youth, home building and repairing, engineering and construction projects, food/hunger ministry, education and literacy, operating orphanages, information technology and computers, and business services.

What is a volunteer vacation?

No Christian travel guidebook would be complete without discussing "volunteer vacations." In short, volunteer vacations are trips in which the participants dedicate their time to making a positive difference in the lives of humans, animals, or the environment. These trips are often two weeks or less in duration. Many people refer to such as experiences as "vacations with purpose" or "voluntourism." Since the events of 9/11, and especially with the more recent devastating tragedies of the Southeast Asia tsunami and Hurricane Katrina among others, interest in volunteer vacations has grown steadily.

What is the difference between mission trips and volunteer vacations?

Mission trips focus on much more than just providing for humanitarian needs or caring for animals and the environment. Missionary travel possesses at its heart the spreading and sharing of the Christian faith. Volunteer vacations primarily focus on doing something good for others through travel, with little or no focus on sharing the Christian faith.

Who embarks on volunteer vacations?

People from virtually every demographic category engage in volunteer vacations. Although mission travel remains the preferred choice of travel for most Christians, some ministries and youth groups do embark on volunteer vacations. In fact, many churches are found at the front lines of disaster recovery areas and efforts, including Hurricane Katrina. They see such opportunities as one way to carry out the Gospel message. Volunteer vacations serve as a hybrid between missions and leisure vacations.

What are some examples of volunteer vacations?

Here is a list of just some of the many volunteer vacations that take place daily around the world: assisting with natural conservation and land use management, working at an archaeological dig, building homes (Habitat for Humanity), teaching English as a second language, volunteering at children's camps, distributing pharmaceuticals in developing countries, planting trees, cleaning national parks and trails, maintaining historic sites, aiding in community and rural development, helping with forest restoration, and providing business, marketing, legal, technical, and professional services to communities in need.

How popular are volunteer vacations?

According to the Travel Industry Association of America, more than 55 million Americans have participated in these trips. And that's not all: the same study reports that 100 million more people have expressed a desire to embark on such a vacation.

MISSIONARY TRIVIA, QUOTES, AND FUN STUFF

Quotes from missionaries

"Expect great things from God. Attempt great things for God." —*Wiliam Carey*

"Let me burn out for God." —*Henry Martyn*

"Send me where workers are most needed and difficulties greatest." —*Robert Morrison*

"Preach the gospel always, and if necessary, use words." —*Saint Francis of Assisi*

"I will go anywhere provided it is forward." —*David Livingstone*

"The Great Commission is not an option to be considered; it is a command to be obeyed." —*Hudson Taylor*

"The mission of the church is missions." —*Oswald J. Smith*

"Tell the students to give up their small ambitions and come eastward to preach the gospel of Christ." —*Francis Xavier, missionary*

"Let us not be satisfied with just giving money. Money is not enough, money can be got, but they need your hearts to love them. So, spread your love everywhere you go." —*Mother Teresa*

Movies, documentaries, and television shows to watch about missionary travel

Movies

End of the Spear, Beyond the Gates of Splendor, Beyond the Next Mountain, Candle in the Dark, First Fruits, Mama Heidi, Peace Child, The Story Of Amy Carmichael and The Dohnavur Fellowship, Molokai: The Story of Father Damian

Documentaries

God at Work—Faith in Action, Jesus Film Project (www.jesusfilm.org)

Reality T.V. Series: Travel the Road—The Journey Home (www.traveltheroad.com)

What is Wycliffe Bible Translators?

Founded by Cameron Townsend in the 1930s, the Wycliffe Bible Translators remains at the forefront of missionary efforts by seeking to translate the Bible into every language of the world, thus making it possible for every person to read Scripture. Visitors can explore the work of Wycliffe by visiting its biblical interactive facility in Orlando, Florida, called WordSpring Discovery Center (see chapter 7). To learn more about the Wycliffe Bible Translators, visit http://www.wycliffe.org.

Growth of missionary travel

1979: 25,000 participants
1989: 120,000 participants
1995: 200,000 participants
1999: 500,000 participants[1]
2005: 1,600,000 participants[2]

What are some tips from the World Religious Travel Association?

If you're interested in learning more about the missions, you might consider attending a conference on the topic. Here are a few missionary travel conferences that take place annually:

- Evangelical Missiological Society: www.emsweb.org
- Fellowship of Short-term Mission Leaders: www.fstml.org
- Global Missions Health Conference: www.medicalmissions.com
- Healthcare Missions Conference: www.healthcaremissions.org
- National Short-Term Mission Conference: www.nstmc.org
- Short-Term Evangelical Missions: http://stemintl.org/training/stmlc

For more information about missionary travel conferences and to find companies and organizations that specialize in mission trips, visit www.religioustravelassociation.com.

CHAPTER 6

FELLOWSHIP VACATIONS:
LEISURE VACATIONS, CRUISES, ADVENTURE TRIPS

CREDIT: JAMAICA TOURIST BOARD

What is a fellowship vacation?

If you're ready for a vacation, then you might consider embarking on a fellowship vacation—a trip that combines the best of rest, relaxation, and play with a Christian group or within a Christian setting. Fellowship vacation options feature everything from leisure travel to cruising to adventure trips. Fellowship vacations appeal to a range of Christians—individuals, couples, churches and groups, families, youth, young adults, and senior citizens.

To make your fellowship vacation planning easier, I have divided this chapter into the following three popular travel opportunities of leisure vacations, cruises, and adventure trips. I will also discuss learning vacations as a subset of adventure trips. Along with providing inspirational stories from the faithful, each section provides the necessary information to make your trip a reality. The greatest challenge will be deciding which exciting fellowship vacation to embark upon! No matter which one you choose, you will never have to leave your faith at home again.

LEISURE VACATIONS

Is a leisure vacation right for me?

If you really want to get away, "put your feet up," and let go of all the worries and cares of life, then a Christian leisure vacation is for you. But remember, a Christian leisure vacation is meant to be enjoyed for that very purpose—leisure. It is not a pilgrimage and it is not a mission trip. A fellowship vacation of this nature is simply a time to enjoy a break from life, in the midst of Christian fellowship. That's all it is. And one thing is for sure, if you take advantage of this type of vacation, when you return home, you'll be ready to embark upon another one. Enjoy the time off . . . you deserve it!

CHRISTIAN LEISURE VACATIONS "AT A GLANCE"

TRIP SUMMARY
Typical length: 5–14 days
Average cost per day: $100–$300
Total average cost (U.S.): $250–$2,500 (including transportation)
Total average cost (international): $1,500–$5,000 (including transportation)
Distance from home: varies from nearby to across the world

Variety of leisure vacations: many
When to go: any time of the year, depending on your destination
Why go: you are ready for a leisure vacation
Whom to go with: your faith community or on a scheduled group tour
Which leisure vacation experience to choose: one that fits your desired destination, length, budget, and personal vacation objectives

DEMANDS AND BENEFITS
Spiritual focus: low to medium
Fellowship opportunities: many
Physically demanding: low to moderately
Intellectually stimulating: moderately to very
Emotionally rewarding: very
Culturally enriching: moderately to very

CHRISTIAN LEISURE VACATIONS 101

What is the relevance of a Christian leisure vacation?

You might be wondering what leisure vacations are doing in a Christian travel guidebook. Well, just like everybody else, Christians love to travel. In fact, ask almost any Christian if he or she has embarked on a vacation of any type in the past year and the answer you will almost always hear is "yes." Now ask that same person if the trip was of a leisure nature, and again, you will often hear another "yes." So, what does all this mean? It means Christians often love to travel for no other reason than leisure and fun.

Now imagine if the millions of Christians who embark on leisure vacations each year traveled with each other. Imagine the amazing fellowship opportunities there would be. Imagine the number of Christian friendships and relationships born or strengthened. And imagine the overall enrichment of the Christian community worldwide. That is the reason leisure vacations are included in this Christian travel guidebook, and that is why Christian leisure vacations should be on the palette of travel options for any person of faith.

Why should I embark on a Christian leisure vacation?

If you are one of the many millions of Christians who embark on leisure vacations each year, you might consider joining a trip of this nature with your church or faith community next time so that, in addition to experiencing the leisure vacation benefits of rest, relaxation, and play, you can also gain the added advantage of sharing fellowship while traveling.

Think of it this way: On a secular (nonreligious) leisure vacation, you may be unable to share your faith openly with others. On a Christian leisure vacation, however, not only is it possible to openly share your faith with each other, it is encouraged! For example, a day of sightseeing in the national parks can begin with praises to Jesus for creating such a beautiful destination and thanksgiving for providing your group with such a wonderful travel opportunity. You can enjoy every aspect of your leisure trip through the lens of Christian faith and fellowship.

CHOOSING CHRISTIAN LEISURE VACATIONS

What can I expect to gain by joining a Christian leisure vacation?

A Christian leisure vacation allows you, through travel and fellowship, to explore the world and all it has to offer. With other Christians, you can witness earth's most dramatic landscapes and wonders, from America's Grand Canyon to Egypt's pyramids to Peru's Machu Picchu to India's Taj Mahal. With fellow Christians, you can walk among ancient civilizations, immerse yourself in modern cultures, experiment with foreign cuisines, or relax in the sun at tropical resorts. All of these experiences will be more meaningful because of the deep joy and delight that only Christian faith and fellowship can bring.

How can I choose the right Christian leisure vacation for me?

The best way to discover which Christian leisure vacation is right for you is to take a good look at what you want from such an experience, as well as what vacation is most practical in terms of budget, time, etc. The following questions will help you develop a clearer picture of type of trip you are seeking:

- What overall leisure vacation experience am I looking for (i.e. sightseeing, relaxation, amusement, etc.)?
- Am I open to a variety of Christian leisure travel options and possibilities?
- Where would I like to travel or visit? Do I prefer to stay within North America or travel overseas?
- What is my overall budget?

- Who would I like to travel with—my church, ministry group or organization, with other Christians from a travel company, etc.?
- When am I available to travel? Am I available now, within the year, or one year from now? What season is best for me to travel—spring, summer, fall, or winter? Or can I travel anytime during the year?
- How much time do I have for such a trip? Just a few days, a full week or two, or unlimited time?

What are the advantages and disadvantages a Christian leisure vacation?

Advantages

One of the greatest advantages of a Christian leisure vacation is the ability to combine your faith with travel and fellowship. You can find churches and communities traveling the world for no other reason than leisure and fellowship. This means you can now explore national parks, major cities, and foreign cultures complete with grace before meals, sharing of personal testimonies, daily community prayer, Christian discussion, fellowship, and much more. That is the great advantage of a Christian leisure vacation.

Disadvantages

The primary disadvantage of Christian leisure vacations is that there are not many options available yet. Because so many Christians currently travel by themselves or on secular leisure tours, few opportunities exist for the faithful to travel together. For example, if you want to visit California destinations like San Francisco, Napa Valley, and Yosemite National Park on a group tour, you have dozens, if not hundreds, of secular opportunities to choose from. If you search for the same trip experience with a Christian community or travel company, you most likely not find such a vacation option—or if you do, the few options may not fit your budget or timing. Situations like this often leave Christians with one of two possibilities: travel with a secular group (and no Christian fellowship or affiliation) or choose another available Christian leisure vacation option, even if it doesn't match their original travel interests. Although this is the current situation (and disadvantage), in today's world of faith-based travel, I'm hopeful that one day the millions of Christian leisure travelers will decide to travel with each other, and this will lead to thousands of Christian leisure vacation opportunities for the faithful. It all begins with asking your faith community and Christian travel company to offer such trips.

What is the average Christian leisure trip length?

A Christian leisure trip can be as simple as your faith community traveling by personal cars to a nearby city for a day of fun, sightseeing, and exploration. Or it could include everything from hopping on a motor coach for a two-day getaway to Branson, Missouri, to flying across the country for a week-long getaway, to embarking on a three-week globetrotting vacation.

How much does a Christian leisure vacation cost?

Estimating the cost of a Christian leisure vacation is difficult because of the variety of vacations available; however, it is possible to provide some high-end estimates that you can use to prepare a preliminary budget. Here are some typical costs for group trips:

- 1 day excursion by personal cars: $50–$200 per person
- 3 to 6 day trip by motor coach: $200–$1,000
- 5 to10 day domestic (within the country) trip by plane: $500–$2,500
- 14-day overseas trip by plane: $2,000–$5,000

PREPARING FOR YOUR CHRISTIAN LEISURE VACATION

How can I arrange my Christian leisure vacation?

The best place to inquire is with your church, faith community, or any Christian organization or ministry of which you are a member. One of them probably offers some type of Christian leisure trip, whether it is a short getaway or an overseas vacation.

The second option is to look inside Christian publications for advertisements of such trips. You can also subscribe to faith-based travel publications (see appendix C). These magazines and newspapers list dozens of Christian travel opportunities.

The third option is to use the Internet. You can perform searches on the World Wide Web using terms like "Christian leisure vacations" and "Christian leisure trips." A fourth option is to refer to the section on fellowship vacations in appendix A.

Finally, keep in mind that you may need to contact multiple Christian travel companies because many Christian tour companies and agencies often specialize in only a few travel packages, such as pilgrimages or missions. It may take a few calls to find one who also offers Christian leisure trips.

Church Trip to Hawaii

We are now members of the church's Family Club. This club focuses on activities for the family, including monthly workshops where we have guest speakers that focus on family needs and activities. We also dedicate some time for family trips on weekends. A few months ago, our club decided to make our annual "big" trip to Hawaii for one week. When this decision was made, we started to call around for airfare and hotel prices and worked with many interesting people in the travel industry. Because we were not a "travel agency" per se, we looked for the most comfortable price for this trip so that many could go. We announced this trip at our church, and within two weeks, we had forty people registered. By the third week we totaled sixty-three people. For our surprise, we noticed that 70 percent of the group wasn't church members—they were family and friends of church members. Many more wanted to go, but we decided to limit the number so as not to take too big of a group. In coordinating this event, we added a few items that we felt that were important for the group, which many travel agencies do not include. Along with the anticipation of the trip, we have scheduled a "Hawaiian Night" in which we will include basic information for those who have not visited this island before.—*Alan & Lili*

STUDENT AND YOUTH LEISURE VACATIONS: EDUCATING THROUGH TOURISM

Today, more Christian schools, universities, and youths embark on leisure tours and vacations than ever before—most of which are primarily educational in nature. On any given day of the year, Christian students can be found in groups visiting historical sites here in America (such as a sightseeing tour of Washington D.C.) or exploring Christian heritage sites in Europe. This trend is expected to continue because each year more of the nearly ten thousand Christian and private schools in the United States make the decision to embark on a group trip.

The primary difference between a Christian school trip and a non-Christian school trip is that the former integrates Christian history and faith into the tour. Everything is seen through the lens of our Christian faith. In addition, Christian school groups often incorporate praise and worship into these trips. Such tours take place in a Christian atmosphere and context and make for an ideal Christian learning environment for youth and young adults.

CREDIT: ©ISTOCKPHOTO.COM/ FREDRIK LARSSON

Student vacations are becoming very popular.

How can I make the most of my Christian leisure vacation?

Although it may be tempting to choose any Christian leisure vacation that comes along or one that your church or faith organization offers, make sure it is one that you truly wish to embark upon. Any trip of this nature is an investment of money and time, so choose wisely.

With that said, once you select a trip of interest, how can you make the most of it? The number one tip is to make the most of the "rest, relaxation, and fellowship" opportunities it affords. That is, truly take a break from life and engage in the trip fully, reaping all of its re-energizing and revitalizing benefits. And be sure to make the most of the social interaction—many trips lead to new or enriched friendships and relationships.

LEISURE VACATION OPPORTUNITIES

Although virtually any place in the world qualifies as a leisure vacation destination, what are some of the more popular or interesting leisure destinations for the Christian community? In the United States, Branson (Missouri), Eureka Springs (Arkansas), Lancaster (Pennsylvania), and Orlando (Florida) are several of the more engaging destinations for Christian travel groups. Appealing overseas destinations include the Bahamas, China, and India. The remainder of this section on Christian leisure vacations provides more information on how to make leisure trips to these destinations possible.

UNITED STATES

BRANSON, MISSOURI AND EUREKA SPRINGS, ARKANSAS

Why should I visit?

If you are looking for a great getaway to one of America's top entertainment cities, but one that is also Christian and family-friendly, then look no farther than Branson, Missouri and nearby Eureka Springs, Arkansas.

Description

Branson is not only one of the top vacation destinations in the United States, but it is also one of the top Christian travel destinations. A city rich in traditional values and "good old country" hospitality, Branson offers more than one hundred live entertainment shows complete with family-friendly attractions, theme parks, and outdoor activities in spectacular natural surroundings. In addition, Branson hosts numerous Christian concerts and Gospel music performances throughout the year. Add the nearby city of Eureka Springs (located about an hour from Branson) and you have the ideal twin city destination for people of faith.

With nearby mountains and lakes featuring scenic and natural wonders, the entire region between Branson and Eureka Springs is very popular with Christians for retreats, youth camps, schools, conferences, and rallies. Each of these groups can choose virtually any style of lodging, from camping to economy lodgings to grand hotels.

Branson and Eureka Springs have garnered a reputation for their very family-friendly environment. Unlike Las Vegas, virtually all of Branson and Eureka Springs entertainment and recreational venues gear themselves to families and people of all ages. Many of the venues do not allow alcohol on their premises. Branson and Eureka Springs proudly advertise wholesome family entertainment and atmosphere.

Branson is considered a very affordable destination, and as a small city of about five thousand people, there is not the hustle and bustle found in other popular tourist destinations. Many churches and religious groups travel from all over the United States to vacation in southern Missouri and the land of the Ozarks.

Activities available

Branson features a number of Christian attractions and shows including:

- Sight & Sound Theatre biblical performances
- The Promise Theatre—award-winning musical production based on the life of Christ
- The Shepherd of the Hills—a drama featuring strong Christian themes
- Christian concerts and gospel music shows at various outlets throughout the year
- Special Sunday services and shows hosted by churches and theaters
- Living Word National Bible Museum, which the *Dallas Morning News* called "World Class"

In Eureka Springs, Christian groups will find multiple faith-based attractions including the very popular *The Great Passion Play* (for more information, see the chapter on Christian Attractions).

In Branson and Eureka Springs, you can take your pick of what you'd like to do with your Christian group or family. Located in the midst of rolling hills and lakes, both cities feature a range of activities:

- award-winning theme parks like Silver Dollar City

- boat rides including the showboat Branson Belle
- children's activities such as live animal farms, mini-golf, and go-carts

Special features and notes

If you would like to organize or lead a group trip to Branson, you can contact the Branson Convention and Visitors Bureau and ask for the Group Sales Kit, which includes a Branson Vacation Guide, Show and Attraction Guide, and Group Tour Planner.

Branson . . . Calling all Christians

As a native of the Ozarks, I've been fortunate to experience the phenomenal growth of the travel industry. At its roots are Christian values and an appreciation of gospel music. My first visit to Silver Dollar City, which has been a beacon of tourism in these hills for over forty years, was in 1964. It's always been taken for granted that this is a family entertainment park. Silver Dollar City is an alcohol-free environment with plenty of gospel music. It is no coincidence that the first theaters in Branson were opened by the Presley and Mabe families, who had often entertained at area attractions including the City. These shows were composed of native folk or country music, comedy, patriotic country music, and a healthy dose of gospel music. Well, the area has gone from a couple of music shows to over one hundred, but the recipe is still the same. In fact, the Branson area actually receives credit for putting Eureka Springs, Arkansas on the map. The first music show was opened by a daughter and son-in-law of the Presleys, and Silver Dollar City's success was a wonderful blueprint for the founders of the Great Passion Play. Branson's newest crown jewel is the Sight & Sound Theatre featuring Bible-based productions including the classic Noah as their opener. The company mission statement says it all: "Our purpose is to present the Gospel of Jesus Christ and sow the Word of God into the lives of our customers, guests, and fellow workers through inspirational productions." I honestly believe the Ozark mountain region is this country's top Christian travel destination and that the next couple of years will produce another "Gold Rush"—a gold that symbolizes better people, families, and a better country. —Tim

ORLANDO, FLORIDA

In addition to Branson and Eureka Springs, several other places in America have developed into top Christian travel leisure destinations. One of these is Orlando, Florida—but not necessarily for the reasons you would think. Yes, there is Disney, SeaWorld, and Gatorland, but the city is also home to three Christian attractions: the Holy Land Experience, WordSpring Discovery Center, and the JESUS Film Project Master Studio Tours. For more information visit the Web sites of Orlando Convention and Visitor Bureau (www .orlandoinfo.com) and Kissimmee Convention and Visitor Bureau (www.floridakiss.com).

LANCASTER, PENNSYLVANIA

Mention the name of Lancaster to virtually anyone and immediately images of the Amish community come to mind. Because of the Amish presence, many Christian groups travel here on leisure trips, primarily seeking to learn more about the centuries-old "plain lifestyle" in America's oldest Amish settlement. While enjoying a slower, more contemplative way of life, Christian visitors can participate in and enjoy the best of Amish hospitality, events, crafts, and cuisine. The more popular activities include touring the Amish countryside, shopping at the Amish Farmer's market, learning about the Amish lifestyle at the Amish Experience Theater, exploring the charming Amish Farm and House, enjoying meals at places such as Plain & Fancy and Good n' Plenty, and visiting the Mennonite Information Center. One event not to be missed, however, is riding through the countryside on an authentic Amish buggy ride. This is the highlight for many Christian visitors to Amish country. To learn more about all these possibilities, visit the Lancaster County Web site at www.padutchcountry.com. And don't forget, the popular Christian attraction of Sight & Sound Theatre is located in Lancaster (see chapter 7).

THE ISLANDS OF THE BAHAMAS

Why should I visit?

If there is one international leisure destination that ranks above all others for the Christian community, it is the islands of the Bahamas. A country rich in Christian heritage, hospitality, and traditions, the Bahamas serve as an ideal leisure vacation, spiritual getaway, or convention host site for the faithful.

Description

Christian faith-based groups from around the world find enlightenment and spiritual reawakening among the Bahamas. As one of the most popular destinations for worship gatherings, the islands have played host to some of the most influential spiritual leaders in the Christian faith: T. D. Jakes, Benny Hinn, Rod Parsley, Promise Keepers International, Tony Evans, and Paula White. These islands also helped inspire one of the greatest Christian leaders in American history, Dr. Martin Luther King Jr. King drafted his Noble Peace Prize acceptance speech here and said how the serene, pristine, and tranquil environment gave him the feeling of being close to God.

The Bahamas is one of the most Christian-enriched nations, as is evident in the history and culture of the Bahamian people since 1629 when the Eleutheran Adventurers migrated to these islands seeking religious freedom. They solidified the presence of the Christian faith among the islands through The Preamble of the Bahamas Constitution. Today, there are more than twenty different denominations in the islands, with the Anglicans, Baptists, and Catholics having the largest groups.

The Bahamas have produced many devoted spiritual leaders and contributors to the spiritual culture. One such leader is Dr. Myles Monroe, who was recently honored for

CREDIT: ©ISTOCKPHOTO.COM/TAMMY PELUSO
The Bahamas are rich in Christian heritage.

his best-selling book *Rediscovering the Kingdom*. Dr. Monroe has sold over 1 million copies of his books to date.

The islands offer a place to become centered in one's faith to those seeking spiritual reawakening. Inspirational retreats, conferences, and weddings are held here. The seven hundred islands and 2,500 cays that comprise The Bahamas rest fifty miles east of the coast of south Florida in the Atlantic Ocean, adjacent to the Caribbean area. Travel to the islands is a fifteen-minute flight from southern Florida to the closest Bahamian island. Travelers revel in the miles of white and pink sandy beaches, lined by the clearest waters in the world.

Though they share similarities, each island has its own special diversity. Leisure vacation experiences range from custom-made packages at plush resorts able to accommodate groups seeking a facility for their faith-driven gatherings, to secluded boutique hotels that offer an intimate atmosphere for worship and retreats.

The Bahamas establishes the foundation for a spiritually enriched life by providing travelers with a balance of experiences that enrich the mind, body, and soul.

FOCUS ON FAITH TOURISM

The Bahamas government recognized a few years ago the growing importance of Christian and faith-based tourism, and now the country has become one of the very few destinations in the world to have an entire department (the Bahamas Tourist Office) that caters specifically to religious travelers. As a result, Linville J. Johnson, was appointed director of religious tourism for the Bahamas, with the primary mission of raising the visibility of the Bahamas as a getaway destination or convention site among Christians and the faith-based community. Since then, the Bahamas Tourist Office has taken a leading role in religious tourism, and these islands have become a "first choice" destination for many churches, groups, schools, and Christian families seeking a wholesome vacation—whether it be for leisure, adventure, religious, cruise, conference, fellowship, or missionary purposes.

Special features and notes

Among all the islands, the Grand Bahama Island is one of the most dedicated to attracting Christian travelers, groups, and churches. The island has a number of wonderful resorts and hotels, perfect for Christian conventions or leisure travel. For more information, visit www.grand-bahama.com.

The Bahamas Minister of Tourism and Christian Travel

I have been blessed to participate with the Bahamas Tourist Office in several conferences designed to raise world awareness of this country's position as a top Christian travel destination. In the summer of 2007, while on a Christian cruise to the Bahamas, I personally met with the Bahamas Minister of Tourism, Neko C. Grant, on behalf of the World Religious Travel Association. The Minister

> reaffirmed his country's commitment to promoting Christian travel, and along with the popular Christian preacher Dr. Myles Monroe, both of them remain at the forefront of inviting and welcoming Christian groups to the Bahamas for leisure travel, faith meetings, conferences, rallies, crusades, conventions, and retreats. —*Author*

GENERAL INFORMATION

To learn more about Christian travel and tourism in the Bahamas, visit www.worship.bahamas.com.

The Bahamas Ministry of Tourism
P.O. Box N-3701
Nassau, Bahamas
Tel: (242) 302-2000
Fax: (242) 302-2098
E-mail: tourism@bahamas.com
Toll Free: (800) Bahamas
Religious Tourism Department
Linville Johnson, Director - Religious Market
1200 Pine Island Road, Suite 770
Plantation, FL 33324
Tel: (954) 236-9292; (954) 888-1094; (800) 327-7678
E-mail: ljohnson@bahamas.com

JAMAICA

Another Caribbean country attracting Christian travel groups and conferences is Jamaica. A spirit of faith pervades the island, which is believed to be home to some six hundred Christian denominations[2] and is said to feature more churches per square mile than almost anywhere else. In recent years, the country has become very popular with Christians for its annual Fun in the Son gospel festival. Serving as one of the Caribbean's premier Christian events, "Fun in the Son" takes place every March in Montego Bay, Ocho Rios, and Kingston. Activities include sunrise services, starlight devotionals, street evangelism, and a gospel party. To learn more, visit www.funinthesonjm.com. Similar to the Bahamas, Jamaica also serves as a popular destination where Christian groups host their conventions, with many organizations holding their events at the waterfront Jamaica Conference Center. For more information, visit the Jamaica Tourist Board Web site at www.visitjamaica.com.

Why should I visit?

If your church or Christian group is looking for an exotic vacation to an intriguing travel destination with a fast-growing Christian community, then you've found your next leisure destination in China.

Description

Although Asia is filled with many great options for the Christian traveler, China is one of the countries that stands out for three primary reasons: (1) China offers a very rich culture and heritage for the visiting tourist; (2) China is major force economically and politically; and (3) Christianity is the fastest growing religion in this country of one billion people, and many are watching closely to see how this growth of Christianity manifests itself within the communist country.

Christianity in China dates back to the seventh century (to the fifth century, by some accounts). The Chinese government says there are 16 million Christians in the country, but unofficial reports put that number closer to 30 to 40 million Christians or even higher (still comprising just a few percentage points of the entire population). Although there currently are not many options for Christian trips to China, several travel companies do specialize in such trips.

Activities available

The following sites are sometimes included on Christian leisure vacations to China; however, it's best to discuss your planned trip with a knowledgeable China travel specialist.

Tourist sites:

- Great Wall of China
- Tiananmen Square
- Qin Army Vault Museum (two-thousand-year-old terra-cotta soldiers)
- Yangtze River cruise
- Chinese gardens

Christian sites:

- Nestorian Christian Monument (635): Carved in the eighth-century, this monument is the oldest archaeological artifact of Christian activities in China.

The carvings refer to early Christian missionary activities in China. (Note: Nestorianism was an early Christian sect, considered to be the first Christian entry into China.)

- Taiping Kingdom History Museum: The museum features artifacts from the quasi-Christian Taiping uprising in the mid-nineteenth century.
- Nanjing Union Theological Seminary: This is the national Christian seminary in China.
- Macao: The city became a cultural and religious center during the sixteenth century and features one of China's oldest churches.
- South Beijing Church: The oldest Catholic church in Beijing, it was built in 1605 by the Jesuit priest Matteo Ricci.
- Tomb of Matteo Ricci: The resting place of the famed Jesuit missionary priest to China, on the tomb lie the words: "1610, Pioneer of Christian Missionary." The Communist government holds the tomb in high regard due to Matteo Ricci's contributions to the country.

Special features and notes

If possible, set up a visit to a local Christian Chinese community, fellowship group, or church. The fellowship shared could serve as one of the trip's top highlights. Ask your travel organizer how to do this.

GENERAL INFORMATION
China National Tourist Office: www.cnto.org
China National Tourist Office, New York
350 Fifth Avenue, Suite 6413,
Empire State Building,
New York, NY 10118 USA
Toll Free: (888) 760-8218
Fax: (212) 760-8809

China National Tourist Office, Los Angeles
550 North Brand Boulevard, Suite 910
Glendale, CA 91203 USA
Toll Free: (800) 670-2228
Tel: (818) 545-7507
Fax: (818) 545-7506

Why should I visit?

If your church or organization is looking for a fascinating leisure destination that has ties to ancient Christianity, then India is your place.

Description

Christianity in India dates back to the very beginning of the Christian faith. According to one tradition, the apostle Thomas sailed to the East and spread the Gospel of Jesus Christ here. The next major influx of Christian mission activity in the area took place in the fifteenth century. Shortly thereafter, the construction of India's great colonial Christian churches began. Today many of these Christian historical sites and churches can be visited, along with other shrines and places related to the apostle Thomas.

Activities available

If you are planning a Christian leisure trip to India, you might consider these top tourist and Christian sites and cities:

- Taj Mahal
- Agra Fort
- Fatehpur Sikri (architecture)
- Lotus Temples
- India Gate
- Khajuraho Temples
- Khajuraho
- Red Fort (Lal Qila)
- Agra
- New Delhi
- Mumbai
- Goa
- Jaipur

- Goa's famed colonial-style churches, including Se Cathedral
- Goa's Basilica of Born Jesus with the tomb of Saint Francis Xavier
- Rachol Museum of Christian Art; Madras (Chennai), the first place where Christian missionaries arrived almost two thousand years ago
- sites related to the apostle Thomas (see the apostle Thomas box below)
- Calcutta with Mother Teresa's resting place and her religious order the Missionaries of Charity

THE APOSTLE THOMAS

A number of Christian sites related to the apostle Thomas can be visited in India. Kerala is considered the cradle of Christianity in India (and even the cradle of Christianity in Asia). Here the apostle is said to have founded the Seven and a Half Churches (popularly known as Ezharappallikal), which can be visited at the following sites:

1. Cranganore or Maliankara (Kodungallore)
2. Palur or Palayur (located near Thrissur)
3. Paraur or Kottukavu (located near Cochin)

4. Kokkamangalam (located between Allappy and Kottayam)
5. Niranam (located near Tiruvalla)
6. Chayal or Nilakkal (located near Sabarimala)
7. Quilon or Kollam

Today, many Indian Christian denominations refer to themselves as "Thomas Christians" because of their Christian lineage dating back to the apostle Thomas's missionary work in the area. For this reason alone, many Christians travel from throughout India, from Asia, and from around the globe to visit these ancient communities. Christian travelers can also visit the Malayatoor Church itself where the apostle is said to have prayed. Christian tours to India will often include Madras on their itineraries, as the city features two prominent faith sites: (1) Cathedral of San Thome, which is home to the apostle's tomb and where Thomas is said to have preached; and (2) Saint Thomas Mount, where according to tradition Saint Thomas was martyred in AD 72.

SPECIAL FEATURES AND NOTES

Because Christian tours to India are not as common as other faith journeys such as to the Holy Land or Europe, be sure to discuss or design such a trip with a knowledgeable travel company or agent. If you plan to conduct research on the Internet for your Christian trip to India, some of the best terms to use in your search are "Christian India tours," "Kerala," "Apostle Thomas India," "Goa Christian," and "Madras India Christian."

GENERAL INFORMATION

India Ministry of Tourism: www.incredibleindia.org
Regional Director Govt. of India Regional Tourist Office (New York)
1270, Avenues of Americas Suite 1808
New York City, NY 10020-1700
Tel: (212) 586-4901
Fax: (212) 582-3274

Director India Tourism (Los Angeles)
3550, Wilshire Boulevard Suite 204
Los Angeles, CA 90010-2485
Tel: (213) 380-8855
Fax: (213) 380-6111

CHRISTIAN CRUISE VACATIONS "AT A GLANCE"

TRIP SUMMARY
Typical length: 4–8 days
Average cost per day: $100–$300
Total average cost (Caribbean): $300–$1,500
Total average cost (All other cruises): $1,000–$4,000
Distance from home: varies from nearby to across the world
Variety of cruise vacations: many
When to go: any time of the year, depending on your destination
Why go: you are ready for a cruise vacation
Whom to go with: by yourself to join a Christian cruise or with your faith community
Which cruise vacation experience to choose: one that attracts your interests, including destination, and fits within your budget and calendar

DEMANDS AND BENEFITS
Spiritual focus: medium
Fellowship opportunities: many
Physically demanding: low
Intellectually stimulating: medium
Emotionally rewarding: high
Culturally enriching: low to medium

CHRISTIAN CRUISE VACATIONS 101

What is the relevance of a Christian cruise vacation?

One trend that is growing faster than any other within Christian travel is Christian cruising. Cruise vacations in general have evolved into one of tourism's most popular travel choices; so, it was only a matter of time before this popular vacation option "reached the shores" of Christianity.

Interestingly, the term "sail" appears in one form or another about twenty times in Scripture. References include everything from Jonah setting sail on the open ocean to Jesus sailing across the Sea of Galilee to the apostle Paul sailing throughout the Roman Empire spreading the Christian faith.

Although today's modern style of cruising differs from that found in the Bible, the purpose still remains the same. Christians set sail to share and spread the Christian faith, just as Paul did some two thousand years ago. The biggest difference is that Paul never experienced what it was like to sail with three thousand other Christians all heading for the dinner buffet at once!

Why should I embark on a Christian cruise vacation?

No vacation better exemplifies the benefits of rest, relaxation, and revitalization than cruising. And virtually no vacation can match the economic value and convenience of a cruise. To begin with, almost everything is included in your price, and you do not need to deal with the hassles of a land-based vacation. Cruising is also a year-round vacation that can include anyone of any age. You can also rest as much as you like or be as active as you like. Add to all this that the sea has always served as a source of romance, exploration, excitement, wonder, and awe and you have an ideal vacation.

A Christian cruise vacation has all these benefits plus one more: spiritual rejuvenation and replenishment. Few vacations can bring such peace, solace, and refreshment to the soul as sailing within a Christian atmosphere complete with Christian fellowship, entertainment, activities, inspirational talks, and the like. Because of this, Christian cruising truly provides an experience found nowhere else. Once you embark on your first Christian cruise, you will want to return for more.

CHOOSING CHRISTIAN CRUISE VACATIONS

What can I expect to gain by joining a Christian cruise vacation?

The best way to think about what you will gain through a Christian cruise is to think in terms of "re"—you will return home from such an experience reenergized, rejuvenated, revitalized, recuperated, reinvigorated, refreshed, and recharged. And all of this renewal will take place spiritually, emotionally, socially, intellectually, and physically. That is why few vacations can match the benefits of a Christian cruise.

How can I choose the right Christian cruise vacation for me?

Within the world of Christian cruising there are three questions to address in order to discover which Christian cruise vacation is right for you:

- What type of cruise experience do I desire?
- What cruise destination appeals most to me?
- What type of onboard Christian cruise activities am I seeking?

The first question refers to whether you prefer big-ship cruising, small-ship cruising, river cruising, or another form of cruising. The second question refers to which destination you desire to visit the most. For example, do you wish to explore the Caribbean, Alaska, Europe, or elsewhere? The third question helps you discern what type of Christian experience you wish to participate in. Do you prefer a biblical study cruise, a Christian music cruise, a Christian inspirational speaker cruise, a Christian youth cruise, or are you seeking another Christian experience or form of entertainment? Once you are able to answer all three of these questions, you will know what Christian cruise vacation is calling your name.

CREDIT: ©ISTOCKPHOTO.COM/RAMESH KUMAR

More than a dozen full-ship Christian charters occur annually.

Isn't cruising just for "old people"?

Absolutely not. The average first-time passenger is under forty years old. On a typical Christian cruise, you will find every age group, from babies to those in their nineties. And you will meet everyone from students to singles to couples to families to retirees.

What are the advantages and disadvantages of embarking on a Christian cruise vacation?

Advantages

A cruise is one of the most affordable, all-inclusive, and entertainment-filled vacation experiences for any Christian traveler or group. Almost everything you could want or need is included in the price including transportation, lodging, activities, entertainment, and variety of cuisine. And imagine, you get to enjoy traveling to some of the world's most exotic and spectacular destinations.

Furthermore, you can choose to do what you want, when you want. If you prefer to relax in the sun, you can do just that. If you wish to remain physically active and take advantage of everything the cruise has to offer (and there's plenty!), you can do just that. Everything is your choice and at your pace. This means that your entire vacation is simplified regarding travel logistics (you only have to unpack once!), enabling you to focus on your trip experience at hand. You can set aside all the worries of life and breathe in the fresh ocean air.

The "heart" of a Christian cruise is often experienced through its onboard faith events ranging from Bible studies to Christian speakers and music artists to inspirational speakers. If you're not out enjoying the Christian entertainment, you're probably off the ship exploring a port city or maybe even snorkeling in crystal clear waters. Best yet, all of this takes place within the context of Christian fellowship, sometimes with as many as three thousand fellow travelers. Countless friendships are born or enriched on such vacations.

But the advantages don't stop there. Christian cruises are perfect for people of any age, making it great for families, children, youth, young adults, couples, singles, or seniors. Christian cruises often attract not only Christians but also non-Christians (or nonchurch members), making for a wonderful opportunity to share the Gospel. If the advantages of a Christian cruise had to be summarized into one sentence, it would be this: Christian cruises provide one of the least expensive yet most spiritually uplifting vacations of all.

Disadvantages

Some disadvantages include crowded ships, small rooms, little seclusion from others, limited time to visit each destination (most port visits last only one-half to one day), poor weather can change an itinerary (which means you miss a visit to a city, usually with no refund), and your vacation is "fixed"—the flexibility of changing your vacation midstream is gone. One other disadvantage to consider is that, although cruises are often "all-inclusive," the extra costs can sometimes add up. Expenses often not included in the cruise price are tips and gratuities (to ship staff), certain beverage purchases (even Coca-Cola sometimes), and most shore excursions.

What is the average Christian cruise length?

The most common length for most cruises is seven days. However, in the world of Christian vacations, cruises last, on average, anywhere from four to seven days.

How much does a Christian cruise vacation cost?

The cost of a Christian cruise depends on the destination and style of ship chosen, as well as the type of accommodations you choose on board (whether budget or luxury). With this in mind, here is a breakdown of estimated average costs:

- Total average cost (Caribbean): $300–$1,500
- Total average cost (Alaska cruise): $1,000–$3,000
- Total average cost (American river cruise): $1,000–$4,000
- Total average cost (European river cruise): $2,000–$3,000

What types of Christian cruise experiences and themes exist?

One of the most appealing and engaging aspects about Christian cruises is that many revolve around a particular Christian theme or experience; in other words, many Christian cruises sail with a particular mission or focus in mind. What are some examples?

Christian cruise themes and experiences can range from "Bible seminars at sea" to "Christian singles gatherings" to "Christian cruise retreats" to "Christian entertainment cruises"—the latter featuring prominent onboard Christian entertainers, music bands, and speakers. Other Christian cruises feature a missionary element complete with shore excursions such as street witness ministry or evangelism, prison ministry, prayer and healing ministry, or school ministry at port cities. Still other Christian cruises feature a crusade or rally at a particular destination. Because so many Christian theme cruises exist, be sure to search for the one that most fits your desires. Fortunately, with the tremendous growth of Christian cruising in recent years, there are plenty of options.

What cruise destinations and styles can I choose from?

Cruising is a very broad term. Although the word often evokes images of sailing through the Caribbean or Alaska, this is really the tip of the iceberg. Cruising today takes place throughout the world at different destinations. Furthermore, cruising in the modern sense doesn't always mean "big ship" cruises (ships carrying one thousand to three thousand people); it also refers to "small ship" cruises (ships carrying several hundred people) as well as "river cruises" (boats that navigate rivers and waterways only).

To help you choose the right Christian cruise trip, below is a list of the more popular cruise destinations for many Christian groups, complete with their greatest appeal factors, as well as the cruising styles chosen most often.

Alaska

- This type of cruise attracts primarily adult Christian groups.
- The journey provides spectacular scenery and wildlife viewing.
- Most Alaskan cruises take place May through September, which is when the

weather is quite mild to warm. And don't forget, in the height of summer, Alaska enjoys virtually twenty-four hours of daylight.

American Rivers and Lakes

- American river and lake cruising offers one of the most romantic and nostalgic ways to explore North America.
- Much of this cruising takes place on steamboats, paddleboats, yachts, and small ships, making for much more "intimate" settings for Christian groups.
- The rivers and lakes are typically located near your hometown or within the continental United States. The most common routes include the Northern Rivers (e.g., Hudson, Great Lakes, Saint Lawrence), the Mississippi River, the Pacific Northwest Rivers, and intracoastal waterway cruises between New Orleans and Texas. Many of the lakes lie in or near national parks or recreational sites.

Canada and New England

- Although this destination is not as popular as the Caribbean or Alaska for cruising, it is growing in popularity with Christian groups.
- The best time to go is in the fall for the autumn leaf colors.
- These types of cruises combine the best of American and Canadian big cities with visits to small coastal villages and historic sites. Whale sightings are often common.

Caribbean and Mexico

- These destinations are the most popular for Christian cruise groups.
- They rank as the least expensive of all big-ship cruises.
- These cruises offer the greatest variety of choices in terms of itinerary, trip length, and services (i.e., from budget to luxury cruises).

European River Cruising

- One of the newest forms of cruising for Christian groups is European river cruising.
- These trips combine easily with excursions to Europe's many cathedrals and

CREDIT: GENEVA TOURISM

European river cruising combines traditional European sightseeing with visits to cathedrals and churches.

churches, which can be viewed or visited while en route.

- With boats typically limited to a capacity of fifty to two hundred people, these cruises make for small, intimate settings. Similar to the American river cruising, this also makes it much easier to charter.

Mediterranean and the Holy Land

- Mediterranean and Holy Land cruises sail in the same waters as Paul and other biblical figures did some two thousand to three thousand years ago, providing a unique insight into the New and Old Testament.
- Many of the ports and cities cited in Scripture are included on a Holy Land cruise including Rome in Italy; Athens and Patmos in Greece; Kusadasi/Ephesus in Turkey; Haifa, Nazareth, Galilee, Jerusalem, and Ashdod in Israel; and Port Said, Cairo/Giza, and Alexandria in Egypt.
- These cruises provide a fascinating and unique way to explore the biblical lands, cities, and seas versus traditional land touring.

PREPARING FOR YOUR CHRISTIAN CRUISE VACATION

How can I arrange my Christian cruise vacation?

In addition to inquiring with your faith community about such trips, the ideal starting place to plan or join a Christian cruise is with a company that specializes in these faith vacations. Today, a number of Christian cruise companies and agencies exist across North America (see the fellowship vacations section in appendix A). Many of these feature cruise vacations designed and catered specifically to Christians.

Once you contact an agency, ask the company about its credentials. Is it affiliated with any major organizations such as CLIA (Cruise Lines International Association) or WRTA (World Religious Travel Association)? Does the agent possess the credentials of ACC (Accredited Cruise Counselor) or MCC (Master Cruise Counselor)? Also, does the company work with other high-profile Christian cruises? What is its track record of working with cruises in general? The answers to these questions will help you determine whether it's the right company to work with or not—or whether they are at least qualified.

Once you find the right cruise agent, let that person guide you in every way possible. The company or agency should become your "best friend" in assisting, designing, and choosing the right Christian cruise for you, your family, church, ministry group, or organization. With your cruise agent's guidance, you are sure to increase your chances for the experience of a lifetime.

What questions should I ask a company that provides Christian cruise vacations?

- What types of cruises do you offer (big ship, small ship, European river cruising, American river cruising, etc.)?
- Which destinations do you feature (Caribbean, Alaska, Hawaii, America, Europe, Mediterranean, etc.)?
- When do the cruises take place?
- What Christian entertainment will take place onboard?
- What is included in the cruise price, and how much should I budget overall?
- What kind of accommodation would you suggest for my budget and preferences?
- If our Christian organization wishes to embark on a full-ship charter, how can we make this possible? What is the process, and what are the requirements?
- If our Christian organization will not be on a full-ship charter, are there any other groups of people onboard this particular departure that may conflict with our Christian values and overall vacation experience?

The Dream Was Crazy Enough

"Twenty years from now you will be more disappointed by the things that you didn't do than by the ones you did do. So throw off the bowlines. Sail away from the safe harbor. Catch the trade winds in your sails. Explore. Dream. Discover." —Mark Twain

Those words ran through my mind as I contemplated taking a group of young adults on a tall ship ministry cruise over a decade ago. The dream was crazy enough that it captivated my imagination. We sailed to remote islands accessible only by ship in the southern Caribbean. Some of them had more animals than humans. Imagine their surprise as we came ashore like missionaries of old on a small tethered boat, ship anchored at bay, delivering the good news of the Gospel. We carried only the sword of God's Word. We planted no flag, only eternal seeds in the hearts of curious listeners. Tiny, thatch-roofed churches and schools were packed to see our Gospel presentations. Our ministry spilled over onto the ship where crew members and passengers were drawn to our worship under the stars at night. Sails billowing in the warm evening breeze over the rhythmic motion of the ship sailing through the moonlit ocean created a unique worship experience I will not soon forget. Our captain as a man of faith even allowed our presentation to be performed onboard.

> Perhaps the greatest ministry of all was to our fellow passengers. It's amazing what one can discover when we have the courage to lose sight of the shore. Now I encourage others to expand their Christian worldview and chart their next church event at sea. It's easy, just add water. —*Author*

What are some tips for making the most of my Christian cruise vacation?

The number one tip I hear from Christians who embark on faith-based cruises is this: Be sure to "soak up" everything the cruise vacation has to offer. If Christian speakers, comedians, or entertainers are part of the trip, take time to attend the events and performances. You will come away inspired, laughing, and filled with joy. If street ministry is offered on the trip, take advantage of it. Nothing is more fulfilling than sharing the Gospel with those who need it most. If onboard group activities are offered, make a point to participate in such events. There's often no better way to share fellowship and meet new people, some of whom blossom into wonderful new friends. By taking advantage of all that the Christian cruise has to offer, you will have one of the greatest vacation experiences of your life.

CHRISTIAN CRUISE VACATION OPPORTUNITIES

One of the most important factors to consider is the cruise line itself. It is imperative that you do your research before embarking on a cruise. As there is no such thing (yet) as a Christian cruise line, all Christians will find themselves on ships and boats owned by secular companies. The closest you can get to an "all-Christian cruise" is by joining (or arranging) a full-ship Christian charter (where you lease the boat exclusively for your use and services). In instances such as this, the majority of the cruise environment is dictated by the Christian organization responsible for the charter. For example, many Christian full-ship charters close down the casinos and do not permit alcohol on board these trips.

With this in mind, whether you plan to join or to arrange a Christian cruise, you should know the basic attributes of various cruise lines before making any commitments. For example, if a particular cruise line is known for attracting mostly older and affluent clientele, then you are wise to learn this information before you organize a national Christian youth cruise on it. It is also helpful to learn which cruise lines currently attract the most Christian and faith-based groups, as well as which ones are most conducive to receiving them. And last, remember to do your homework about each cruise line's "personality," as this will impact everything including price, level of service and comfort, style of cruise, entertainment, shore excursions, and overall experience.

If you are wondering which cruise lines are the most popular or frequently used by Christian groups, the answer is Carnival Cruise Lines, Holland America, and Princess Cruises (all of which belong to the prominent cruise network World's Leading Cruise Lines [www.worldsleadingcruiselines.com]). In general, each of these three cruise lines features the greatest appeal in terms of prices, itineraries, and clientele. They are also recognized as being among the most faith- and family-friendly. Royal Caribbean is also a popular choice. For a full list of cruise lines, see below.

Amadeus Waterways: www.amadeuswaterways.com

American Canadian Caribbean Line: www.accl-smallships.com

American Cruise Lines: www.americancruiselines.com

Avalon Waterways: www.avalonwaterways.com

Carnival Cruise Lines: www.carnival.com

Celebrity Cruises: www.celebrity.com

Costa Cruises: www.costacruises.com

Crystal Cruises: www.crystalcruises.com

Cunard Line: www.cunard.com

Discovery World Cruises: www.discoveryworldcruises.com

Disney Cruise Line: www.disneycruise.com

Fred Olsen Cruise Lines: www.fredolsencruises.com

Holland America Line: www.hollandamerica.com

Imperial River Cruises: www.cruisebyriver.com

Louis Cruise Lines: www.louiscruises.com

Majestic America Line: www.majesticamerica.com

MSC Cruises: www.msccruises.com

Norwegian Coastal Voyage: www.norwegiancoastalvoyage.us

Norwegian Cruise Line: www.ncl.com

Oceania Cruises: www.oceaniacruises.com

Orient Lines: www.orientlines.com

Orion Expedition: www.orioncruises.com.au

Princess Cruises: www.princess.com

Radisson Seven Seas Cruises: www.rssc.com

River Barge Excursions: www.riverbarge.com

Royal Caribbean International: www.royalcaribbean.com

SeaCloud: www.seacloud.com

SeaDream Yacht Club: www.seadreamyachtclub.com

Silversea Cruise Line: www.silversea.com

Star Clippers: www.starclippers.com

The Yachts of Seabourn: www.seabourn.com

Uniworld: www.uniworld.com

Viking River Cruises: www.vikingrivers.com
Windstar Cruises: www.windstarcruises.com

CHRISTIAN ADVENTURE VACATIONS

Is a Christian adventure vacation right for me?

Are you interested in an adventure vacation with a spiritual component? If you are, then a Christian adventure vacation may be ideal for you. There is no difference between the physical activities that take place on a Christian adventure versus a non-Christian adventure vacation. What makes the difference is the Christian context or environment of the vacation. First and foremost, a Christian adventure trip is conducted under the banner of Christ. Second, Christian adventures will often include the sharing of biblical stories, personal testimonies, prayer, and worship. Third, Christian adventures will view all challenges and activities of the trip through the lens of the Christian spiritual life. And last, Christian adventures are facilitated with the intent to share and deepen Christian fellowship. What an adventure!

CREDIT: JAMAICA TOURIST BOARD

Christian adventure travel has climbed to new heights.

CHRISTIAN ADVENTURE VACATIONS "AT A GLANCE"

TRIP SUMMARY
Typical length: 1–8 days
Average cost per day (U.S.): $0–$200
Average cost per day (international): $200–$500
Total average cost (U.S.): $100–$2,000 (including transportation)
Total average cost (international): $1,500–$5,000 (including transportation)
Distance from home: varies from nearby to across the world
Variety of adventure vacations: many
When to go: any time of the year, depending on your activity
Why go: you are ready for a physically active vacation or getaway
Whom to go with: by yourself (and join a scheduled Christian adventure tour) or with your faith community
Which adventure vacation experience to choose: one that fits your interests and physical abilities

CHRISTIAN ADVENTURE VACATIONS 101

What is the relevance of a Christian adventure vacation?

Scripture is full of adventure stories. Think of Noah and his ark, Jonah and his encounter with the whale, David and his slingshot, Moses and his climb up Mount Sinai (not to mention his forty years of walking and hiking through hot desert sands), Jesus and his trials in the wilderness, Paul and his untimely shipwrecks. In every one of these situations, God tested the person's faith through physical and emotional challenges. And in every case, the individual emerged with a deeper and richer faith.

Today is no different. Christians embark on journeys and adventures to test their body, mind, and spirit. They seek the same goals—spiritual and emotional strength and renewal. The result? Christians return home from such experiences with a faith "purified in gold" and an emotional outlook on life filled with great joy, hope, and inspiration.

Why should I embark on a Christian adventure vacation?

Physically active challenges can enrich and test one's faith, body, mind, and soul unlike any other experience. When such a journey is undertaken with other Christians, another benefit is gained—fellowship. In many ways, a Christian adventure trip is a microcosm of the Israelites' adventure in the desert. Joys, tears, sweat, laughter, and heartache often fill such experiences. And like the Israelites, you walk away from such adventures with a stronger faith, greater identity, larger purpose, and enriched relationships. Those are just some of the reasons to embark on a Christian adventure or active trip.

What can I expect to gain by joining a Christian adventure vacation?

Most people who embark on a Christian adventure of one kind or another say that they return home feeling refreshed and renewed, ready to "tackle" life—challenges and all. You can also expect to return home with a "bigger picture" and vision for your life, a bigger vision for your spiritual life, and a bigger vision for your dreams and goals— including a plan of how to accomplish them. Not bad for just a few days to a week away from home!

How can I choose the right Christian adventure vacation for me?

A Christian adventure can be as simple as a day's hike with your fellow church members to a three-day rafting trip to a challenging international multisport trip that combines rafting with horseback riding and rock climbing. With the wide variety of options, how can you choose the right journey or activity for you? You should conduct an honest evaluation of where you are in life spiritually, physically, and emotionally.

For example, do you need just a simple getaway? If so, maybe just a day or weekend active trip is all you need. Or, maybe you need a full one to two weeks away that challenges you not only spiritually, but also physically and emotionally. If so, then your calling might be to a more extensive and arduous Christian adventure trip and environment. Whichever experience seems to call your name, let that be your guide to which adventure might be right for you.

What are the Christian adventure vacations I can choose from—or organize for my church or faith community?

Adventure cruises and expeditions	Horse breeding/horseracing
Agriculture tours	Horseback trips and trail rides
Archaeological tours	Hot air ballooning
ATV tours	Ice and igloo hotels
Back-country skiing	Ice climbing
Ballooning	Ice fishing
Bicycle tours and mountain biking	Jungle expeditions
Camel safaris	Kayaking
Camping	Motorcycle tours
Canoeing	Mountain and rock climbing
Canyoning	Multisport adventures

Cattle drives and working ranches
Caving
Covered wagon vacations
Cross-country skiing
Culinary vacations
Cultural tours
Desert expeditions
Dolphin research/swim with dolphins
Dog sledding vacations
Dude and guest ranches
Eco- and jungle lodges
Ecotourism excursions
Elephant rides
Equestrian tours
Fishing charters, guides, lodges
Glacier tours
Gold-panning tours
Golf vacations
Gorilla viewing
Heli-adventures, Heli-skiing
Hiking

Paragliding tours
Photography tours in remote areas
Private yacht charters
Railway and train tours
Rainforest hikes
Research expeditions
Rock climbing, mountaineering
Safaris (African safaris)
Sailing lessons
Scuba diving vacations
Skiing
Snorkeling vacations
Snowshoeing
Snowmobiling
Surfing vacations and camps
Trekking tours
Walking tours
Whale watching tours
Whitewater rafting
Wildlife viewing tours
Wilderness vacations/expeditions

What are the advantages and disadvantages of embarking on a Christian adventure vacation?

Advantages

- discovering new ways of exploring God's creation (i.e. safaris, rappelling, snorkeling, etc.)
- gaining greater self-confidence
- experiencing spiritual rejuvenation
- enjoying emotional renewal and excitement in life
- testing your limits physically
- participating in adventures with others that you would never try on your own
- learning about new geographies and cultures
- developing deep fellowship with others through challenging adventure experiences

- risk of injury
- different levels of participants' skills on adventure trip
- uncomfortable "accommodations" (i.e. having to "rough it")
- increased opportunity for getting sick (due to extreme outdoor weather conditions)
- embarrassment in front of others if you cannot perform a challenge or perform it well when others can

What is the average trip length for a Christian adventure vacation?

Although some adventure trips can be as short as one day or as long as one or two weeks, the average adventure trip is about four days.

How much does a Christian adventure vacation cost?

In order to get a more precise idea of average estimated adventure travel costs, I have divided such experiences into four trip lengths complete with examples.

- 1 day trip: $0–$100
- 3–5 day trip: $300–$1,000
- 5–10 day trip: $500–$2,500
- 11–14 day overseas trip: $2,000–$5,000

PREPARING FOR YOUR CHRISTIAN ADVENTURE VACATION

How can I arrange my Christian adventure vacation?

As always, the first place to look is with your church or any faith community you belong to (ministry group, organization, etc.). Second, you can contact the Christian travel companies that exist for the sole purpose of hosting Christian adventure trips. Although there are not many of them (to learn more, please see adventure vacations in appendix A), they are specialists in such trips and offer a variety of options. Third, you can always contact a travel agent who may be willing to help you put such an experience together.

What questions should I ask a company that provides Christian adventure vacations?

Be sure to ask all the traditional questions such as "What adventure trips to you offer?" and "Can you send me a brochure?" The following are the next most important questions to ask:

- How many years has your company been in business? What is your company's safety record? What happens if I get injured?
- Is your company associated with an adventure travel organization—or at least with another travel association?
- How do I know if I'm qualified physically for such a trip?
- How can I best prepare myself for such an adventure spiritually, emotionally, and physically?
- What Christian activities, events, and fellowship opportunities are integrated into the adventure trip?

What are some tips for making the most of my Christian adventure vacation?

CREDIT: TURKISH CULTURE AND TOURISM OFFICE, NEW YORK

Nothing builds Christian fellowship like adventure vacations.

First, be sure you know what you are getting yourself into. Make sure you understand the full scope and nature of the trip's physical and emotional challenges. Second, make sure you are prepared for these challenges and the trip itself. This includes preparing yourself spiritually, emotionally, and physically. For example, if you will be embarking on a multi-day Christian biking trip, be sure to start biking weeks in advance. Don't just show up and expect to bike ten to twenty miles a day with no consequences! By properly preparing yourself, you will not only maximize the joys of your experience, but you will also deepen the benefits gained from such a trip.

The Night Hike

As each man turned on his headlamp, the darkness stepped aside as the march of the Cyclops began. The parked cars vanished in the darkness below, and our L.E.D. lights illuminated the trail above us. It would take approximately forty-five minutes of hiking before we would reach our midnight destination, the Pinnacle. The Pinnacle was an old fire lookout tower atop of one of the tallest hills in the area. It's been known to be host of many teenage parties over the years, but on this particular midnight clear there would be no rowdy drinking binges at this old and dilapidated structure. Sweat dripped profusely from my brow. The breeze was refreshingly cool and the midnight acoustics were perfect. After catching our breath and downing a few liters of H_2O, we began. The opening prayer echoed in the darkness and the men were no longer illuminated by the lights on their heads, but by the lighted embrace of the full moon, which was now directly overhead. It only took a few moments and I knew right away that this would be no ordinary night; however, little did I realize how this night would affect the rest of my life. A few months prior to this evening's trek, I had finished a very rugged and physically challenging rim to rim hike through the Grand Canyon. It was on this trip that God lit the spark in me to combine outdoor adventure with Christian ministry. After participating in the Grand Canyon trip combined with witnessing the benefits of men connecting with each other and with God out in His creation, is when God fanned my spark and it grew into a hot flame. He revealed to me this night the awesome power of using His creation to get men to worship, connect and draw closer to Christ. When you experience God's awesome power and His creation's ability to draw you closer to Him, you have no choice but to step out in faith and do the unimaginable. A midnight hike, a group of men, an environment that demands reverence to God is what finally sealed the deal for me, and started me on my quest to leave the corporate world behind and to start an outdoor adventure ministry.—*Michael*

CHRISTIAN AFRICAN SAFARI

Is there such a thing as a Christian African safari? Yes, there is! And in fact, several companies offer trips that are conducted in a Christian environment and atmosphere. Here are six great reasons to consider a Christian African safari:

- Safaris appeal to all ages.
- Christian guides accompany the safari.
- It enables you to experience God "in the bushes of Africa."
- You can enjoy prayer, worship, singing, and religious services while on safari.
- You will learn about early Christianity in Africa.
- You can provide witness ministry to local African villages and/or meet Christian leaders of African villages.

Because of the limited number of a high quality, Christian-based safari companies operating in Africa, each of these organizations strives to provide the greatest possible Christian experience in the midst of the African bush. They will customize the adventures, whether it be hosting a morning service or daily devotional, taking time out for prayer before a game drive, or sharing an evening of personal testimonies around a campfire while listening to sounds of the African wild. In the words of one safari operator, "We are passionate about the extension of God's Kingdom on the continent of Africa."[3] And in the words of another Christian African organization, "My safaris are for people who want to take God on vacation with them."[4] If you're wondering what an African safari is like and whether it's the equivalent of a youth camping trip, you might think again. In today's world, African safaris often feature very comfortable accommodations, fabulous dining, hot showers, professional guides, and much more. You can choose anything from an economical (budget) safari to a luxury one. No matter what you or your faith community decides, one thing is certain: few vacations will ever match the unforgettable fellowship memories and experiences of an Christian African safari. To learn more about companies offering these experiences, visit the appendices.

LEARNING VACATIONS

Is it possible to combine your hobby or passion with your Christian faith and travel? In many cases, yes! The expansion of Christian adventure travel in recent years has given birth to a new type of travel called learning vacations.

Learning vacations are a type of vacation in which people travel for the primary purpose of sharing mutual interests. A Christian learning vacation is simply the combination of the Christian faith with travel and mutual interests. Though still in its infancy, Christian learning vacations are growing in popularity. One of the driving forces behind this growth is the increased number of Christian affinity groups traveling together.

One example of a Christian learning vacation is a Christian culinary tour in France. This Christian learning vacation combines the best of fellowship with travel and common culinary interests. Other examples include mystery tours, sporting event tours, and flower show getaways.

So what are your interests? Golf? Photography? Quilting? Ecology? Good chocolate? Whatever your interests might be, there might be a corresponding Christian learning vacation for you. Or you can work with a travel agent to design your own. How can you learn more about these travel options and ideas? Below is a sample of learning vacations that can be adapted to Christian travel groups. If you embark on a Christian learning vacation, you will find that not only do you enjoy the benefits of faith, fun, and fellowship, but you also gain the added joy of sharing your passions, interests, and hobbies with fellow Christians. Now that truly is an ideal vacation!

Sample of Christian learning vacations

SPECIAL INTEREST	SAMPLE TRIPS
Archaeology	Christian archaeology tours of Israel or Egypt led by expert archaeologist

Architecture	Architecture tours through Christian Europe
Art	Art tours through galleries, museums, and exhibits in Paris, Rome, and Venice led by Christian university art professor
Astronomy	Astronomy vacations to see total solar eclipses and visit observatories
Biblical history	Guided tours through biblical lands with a Scripture expert
Bird-watching	Birding tours to Central and South America to observe exotic birds with a local guide
Botany	Botany tours around the world to explore the planet's diverse flora
Bears	Observe grizzles in Alaska or Polar Bears in northern Canada
Chocolate	Gourmet chocolate tours to Belgium's world famous chocolate makers; or even simply to Hershey, Pennsylvania
Coffee	Guided tours to the coffee fields of Kona (Hawaii), Costa Rica, or Colombia
Culinary and cooking	Culinary vacations led by chefs with cooking lessons, vineyard tours, visits to local food producers and gourmet dinners; focus could include biblical foods
Crafts	Carpet weaving tours in Turkey
Films	Trips to film festivals around the globe
Foliage	Fall foliage tours through New England
Gardens	Bulbs and blooms of Belgium and Holland
Genealogy	Ancestral tours to Europe while meeting local genealogy experts
History	History tours around the world with expert historians; Christian history can be integrate as well
Horses	Visit Lexington, Kentucky, on a horse breeding tour
Languages	Study a language (or the roots of language) while on a trip
Literary	Christian literary and author tours of C.S. Lewis and J.R.R. Tolkien through England
Military history	World War II tours to Normandy, France, and Europe; Civil War tours
Music	Tours to classic American music cities such as Nashville or even music festivals
Natural foods	Private tours and workshops of sustainable farms by local growers

Northern Lights	Trips to Alaska and northern Canada to view the Aurora Borealis
Opera	Opera tours to Europe including Salzburg Festival
Photography	Photography tours to Alaska with professional photographer and teaching lessons
Polar bears and penguins	Tours to Arctic to view polar bears and tours to Antarctica to view penguins
Sailing	Sailing lesson tours in New England
Trains	Ride aboard the world's top trains including traveling across Canada
Veterans	Veterans tours to places of American history and wars including Vietnam
Volcanoes	Tours to Hawaii's Volcanoes National Park

Make this the year of Christian adventure for you!

If you're ready to embark on a challenge unlike ever before, make this the year you embark on a Christian adventure trip. Whether you join your faith community or a Christian travel company, you are sure to experience an adventure that will challenge and strengthen you in mind, body, and spirit. The result? Life will take on a whole new meaning as you will see any obstacles—whether spiritual, physical, or emotional—merely as walls to climb over. Best yet, you have many vacation options to choose from, whether it be a one-day hike, week-long multisport trip, or even an African safari. Of course, you can choose to embark on a Christian learning vacation with fellow Christians who share your same interests. No matter what you choose though, wait no longer—make that phone call today to a Christian adventure travel specialist. Your life will be changed!

CHAPTER 7

CHRISTIAN EVENTS, RETREATS, CAMPS, MONASTIC GUEST-STAYS

CREDIT: ©ISTOCKPHOTO.COM/ CHRISTOPH RIDDLE

What is a Christian event, retreat, camp, or monastic guest-stay vacation?

In many ways, Christian gatherings and spiritual getaways such as conferences, crusades, retreats, and camps are the most common of all faith-based vacations. Christians are often attracted to these vacations for their convenience, affordability, and engaging characteristics; however, the primary reason for such popularity may just be that Christian events and retreats can often provide a quick "jolt" of Christian renewal and enthusiasm. There's nothing like standing amidst thousands of other Christians in a packed stadium sharing fellowship, praise, and worship; or spending quality time on a retreat, whether at a conference center or monastery; or sharing fellowship and good times at a Christian camp. Each of these vacation experiences and Christian gatherings serves as much-needed refreshment for the soul and can often lead to life-changing decisions.

To help you decide which vacation or getaway option might be right for you, I have divided this chapter into four segments: Christian events, Christian retreats, Christian camps, and monastic guest-stays. Each section comes complete with its own unique travel information and inspirational story so you can make vacation plans right away. Just imagine, rather than sitting behind a desk, in a few months you could be attending a Christian rally or retreat of your choice . . . or even joining monks for dinner!

CHRISTIAN EVENTS

Is a Christian event experience right for me?

We all need a spiritual pick-me-up from time to time. If you are in need of one of these, then consider attending a Christian conference, crusade, or rally of your choice this year. These events can often serve as the perfect wake-up call to our spiritual lives, and there's nothing like experiencing Christian solidarity with others who share the same goal of developing a closer relationship with Jesus. When we attend a Christian event, we realize that others are making the same journey. We realize that we have others to lean on, as well as others who can lean on us. If it has been a while since you've participated in a Christian gathering outside of church or your ministry organization, start looking for an event that matches your interests. If you make the decision to do this, you'll be giving your spiritual life a double espresso.

CHRISTIAN EVENT VACATIONS "AT A GLANCE"

TRIP SUMMARY
   Typical length: 1–4 Days

Average cost per day: free admission for many events, otherwise $20–$80 (not including transportation)

Distance from home: varies from nearby to across the world

Variety of leisure vacations: many

When to go: any time of the year

Why go: you're looking for a "jolt of enthusiasm" in your spiritual life and/or seeking an experience of great Christian fellowship

Whom to go with: join an event individually or with your church or ministry group

Which Christian event experience to choose: one that fits your current state in life or meets your present needs and desires

DEMANDS AND BENEFITS

Spiritual focus: high

Fellowship opportunities: many

Physically demanding: low

Intellectually stimulating: moderately to very

Emotionally rewarding: very

Culturally enriching: low to moderately

CHRISTIAN EVENT VACATIONS 101

What is the relevance of a Christian event vacation?

Every year, millions of people attend Christian conventions, crusades, and rallies in North America and elsewhere. Christian gatherings range from crusades to teen rallies to denomination conventions to music festivals and the like. Some of these events are small and attract several hundred attendees while others are large enough to "take over cities" with more than one hundred thousand participants. When many of us think of Christian gatherings, the name Billy Graham often comes to mind. Probably best known for his fifty years of preaching, Billy Graham hosted dozens of crusades around North America and throughout the world. Many of these colossal-sized events took place in professional sport stadiums, large parks, and throughout whole sections of cities. Another Christian leader, Pope John Paul II, hosted one of the world's largest gatherings in history in 1995 with World Youth Day. This Christian youth event which, included several days of Christian teaching, preaching, and entertainment, attracted an estimated 5 million attendees.

Christians gathering together is as old as the faith itself. Scripture speaks of the apostles gathering together with Jesus. The New Testament talks about the apostle Paul preaching to the gathered crowds. The catacombs in Rome are also a visible reminder of Christians congregating together (while risking their safety) in the first few centuries after Jesus's death.

After Constantine recognized Christianity as a religion in the fourth century, the faithful began gathering openly, and the era of large churches and cathedrals commenced in earnest. History is filled with stories of Christians gathering together for one purpose or another. Today, Christians can be found congregating anywhere from open-air fields to mammoth-sized convention centers; however, the purpose of Christians coming together remains the same as it did when the apostles met: to proclaim that Jesus Christ is Lord.

Although there are hundreds of types of Christian events, most of them find their roots in one of five categories: denominational or Christian organizational conventions; crusades, rallies, and Christian entertainment events; youth and young adult rallies; Christian marketplace conventions; and affinity-based conferences.

Why should I embark on a Christian event vacation?

If you're looking to light a fire in your spiritual life, there's no better way to make this happen than by attending a Christian crusade, rally, or conference. These gatherings often provide a wonderful opportunity for opening your heart, mind, and soul to the Holy Spirit while in the midst of Christian fellowship and solidarity. For "nonbelievers," these experiences can often serve as a way to accept Jesus Christ. One person who attended a Billy Graham crusade years ago explained that the experience was the most powerful moment of his life and that the events of that day changed not only who he was, but also what he lived for. That is the reason to embark on a Christian event vacation.

CHOOSING CHRISTIAN EVENT VACATIONS

What can I gain from attending a Christian convention, crusade, or rally?

Many of the benefits of attending a Christian convention, crusade, or rally are similar to those gained by Christian travel in general: deepening of faith, enrichment of life, enhanced fellowship, new or strengthened friendships, witnessing the faith to the world, greater insight and understanding of Christianity, and networking with fellow Christians. Although there are many benefits gained by attending such an event, none outweighs the ultimate goal of such a cause: the opportunity to share, experience, and support one another in the Christian journey of life.

How can I choose the right Christian event vacation for me?

No matter who you are or what your interests are, there is a Christian event that's right for you. Some programs are designed for youth and young adults while others target singles, couples, or families. Still others cater directly to professionals, families, or retirees. There is no age group or demographic untouched by Christian events.

You can also choose a Christian gathering based on a particular topic or issue. The list of these Christian event options is expansive. Some focus on music, education, or apologetics, while others highlight evangelism, (Christian) business, or missions. With thousands of Christian meetings taking place annually, you are sure to find one that fits your interests and preferences.

What are the advantages and disadvantages of embarking on a Christian event vacation?

Advantages

- inspirational speakers and testimonies
- often intensely emotional
- energy-filled environment
- short in duration/trip length
- affordable, often free admission
- can attend either individually or with group
- serves as wonderful venue to accept Christ or to deepen one's relationship with Christ
- provides sense of Christian fellowship and solidarity
- brings Christians from all different backgrounds, and sometimes denominations, together

Disadvantages

- sometimes too short in duration
- too many people, too crowded
- positive emotions can fade quickly after the event
- if long-distance travel required, can become too expensive
- event can feel intimidating or uncomfortable if it is hosted or sponsored by a different Christian denomination than yours

How much does a Christian event vacation cost?

Most Christian events such as crusades and rallies are free to attend. On the other hand, Christian conferences and seminars that do charge an admission fee range often range from $20 to $80 (with $25 to $50 being a typical cost). Some events may cost more, but these are typically highly specialized functions such as Christian business networking venues. Some Christian marriage conferences that have materials and resources can climb into the hundreds of dollars.

PREPARING FOR YOUR CHRISTIAN EVENT VACATION

Should I travel independently or with a group?

The answer to this varies, depending on the event you choose. (1) For conventions, many local churches will travel as a group to the major conventions of their respective denominations. These national (or even international) events are often advertised well in advance, providing plenty of time for planning such a group trip. If your church or ministry is not traveling as a group to a convention or conference, you're always welcome to attend the events as an individual. (2) Many Christian crusades, rallies, and entertainment and music festivals are attended equally by both groups and individuals, so you can come with others or alone. (3) Many of the larger youth rallies are attended primarily by youth groups, complete with chaperones and sometimes parents. (4) As a general rule, Christian marketplace conventions are geared more towards receiving individuals versus groups. (5) Depending on the type of affinity-based conference, sometimes people travel in whole groups to an event. On other occasions, it is primarily individuals traveling to a particular conference.

How can I arrange my Christian event vacation?

The four best ways to learn about Christian events are (1) through your church, ministry group, or faith community; (2) through Christian friends or contacts; (3) from advertisements (inside publications, posted flyers, etc.); and (4) from the Internet. Generally, you'll find all the information you need from one of those four sources. If you need more information, you can usually contact the event organization directly.

What questions should I consider before choosing or embarking on a Christian event vacation?

- What does the event entail? What will I experience?
- Why do I want to attend? What am I seeking?

- Will I have the time (or time off from work or school) to attend?
- Who else can join me?
- Are there any similar events closer to my home or area (versus traveling long-distance)?
- How can I arrange my attendance or registration?
- Can I afford the cost including transportation, meals, and lodging (if applicable)?

How can I make the most of my Christian event vacation?

The key word is "openness." When you attend a Christian event of any kind, you should remain open to any and all experiences that God may bring you—whether it is in the form of people, activities, testimonies, speakers, tears, challenges, or even altar call invitations to accept (or recommit yourself to) Jesus Christ as your personal Lord and Savior.

Many of Our Students Have Made Life-Changing Decisions

As a youth minister for the past seven years, one of the highlights of my ministry is taking our youth to a summer event called Christ in Youth. This week-long conference challenges young people to grow deeper in their faith. This opportunity allows the students to leave behind the distractions of day-to-day life and refocus their life on Christ. As our youth group shares in this unique experience, their bonds between each other grow stronger. As a result of these trips, many of our students have made life-changing decisions. As I think about the benefits of these types of trips, one student's story comes to mind. I worked with this young lady for months, ministering to her in our home church. It was not until she had an opportunity to attend a summer conference and be away from the pressures of her life that she made the decision to accept and follow Christ. She is now attending Bible College to get her degree in Christian counseling, and she is also working in a children's ministry. Giving students the opportunity to go on various trips, whether they are missions, conferences, or excursions, is giving them the opportunity to grow in their faith. It enables them to build lasting friendships that create a sense of community for teenagers. This is one of the major benefits of taking such trips. —*Steve*

CONVENTIONS FOR DENOMINATIONS AND CHRISTIAN ORGANIZATIONS

Why should I attend?

If you belong to a denomination or branch of Christianity that gathers together for a major convention, you might consider attending such an event. Not only do these programs provide a wonderful opportunity to learn more about your faith, but they also help strengthen bonds with fellow church members and leaders.

Description

Some of the largest meetings in North America include the major Christian denomination conventions. Although conducting "business" is one of the primary purposes of such gatherings (defining or declaring beliefs and positions on key issues, electing new leaders, etc.), other purposes include hosting seminars about teaching the faith and providing social opportunities for members to meet one other. The following section discusses four major annual gatherings.

Conventions available

The National Baptist Convention, USA—Annual Session (www.nationalbaptist.com)

Each year the National Baptist Convention, USA, hosts its Annual Session, the official gathering of its members. Attracting approximately forty thousand attendees each year, the event features everything from board meetings to convention exhibitors to general sessions to individual workshops and meetings for various delegates (youth, women, musicians, ministers' wives, laymen, nurses, etc.) to worship services to foreign mission fellowship dinners, and much more.[1]

United Pentecostal Church International—General Conference (www.upci.org)

The United Pentecostal Church International hosts each year its General Conference with about twenty thousand attendees.[2] The events includes such scheduled topics as Ministers Business Session, Pentecostal Music Association Expo, Ladies Day, Youth Division Service, Deaf Evangelism Service, Media Missions, Home and Foreign Missions Services, and the closing Crusade Service.

The Southern Baptist Convention (SBC) hosts its Annual Meeting which attracts ten thousand to fifteen thousand attendees.[3] The schedule features such programs as Pastors' Conference, Pastors' Wives' Conference, Ministers' Wives' Conference, Wellness Walk/Run, pastors and chaplain meetings, and fellowship luncheons of the various SBC theological seminaries.

The North American Christian Convention is an annual gathering of about ten thousand to fifteen thousand Christians.[4] Representing the six thousand five hundred churches in North America that identify themselves as part of the fellowship of "Christian churches and churches of Christ," the event features workshops, Bible studies, worship, preaching, teaching, networking, Christian entertainment, day trips, speakers, and general sessions complete with an exhibit hall during this four-day summer gathering of vocational and nonvocational Christian leaders and their families.

Special features and notes

To learn if your denomination or branch of Christianity hosts conventions, simply ask your pastor or church leader. You can also conduct a quick search on the Internet for a particular Christian denomination Web site. Keep in mind that many Christian bodies also offer smaller conferences or seminars throughout the year geared toward specific ministries such as youth, families, men, women, or missions. As these may be of interest to you as well, be sure to inquire about these.

CRUSADES, RALLIES, AND CHRISTIAN ENTERTAINMENT EVENTS

Why should I attend?

If you're looking to experience the best of Christian faith, fun, and fellowship through a conference experience or setting, you might consider attending a crusade, rally, or event that features top Christian speakers and entertainment including music artists, comedians, or the like. Many of these events are highly energized, inspirational, and spirited, providing a wonderful jolt of enthusiasm and joy for your life.

Description

The very term "Christian crusade" conjures up images of Billy Graham speaking to thousands of people in one setting complete with prayer, worship, and invitations to commit (or recommit) one's life to Jesus. Today, similar Christian crusades and Christian entertainment venues and rallies are carried out around North America and the world virtually every day of the year. These events come in all sizes from small gatherings of several hundred people to mega gatherings in the tens of thousands. In fact, taken together every year 22 million Christians attend Christian music festivals and performances alone.[5] As the list of Christian gathering opportunities is vast, here are just some of the ones you can choose to attend:

- Christian crusades
- Christian festivals (or music festivals)
- Christian concerts
- Christian comedian acts
- Christian conferences with inspirational/motivational speakers
- Christian drama or theatrical performances
- Christian mega-church presentations

The Christian Festival Association represents about twenty-five major Christian music festivals that are held in North America featuring more than 1 million attendees.[6] Many of the events take place between April and September.

Festivals available

One of the largest and most popular Christian music festivals is Spirit West Coast (SWC), an annual gathering of church groups, youth groups, and Christian individuals from around the world seeking fun and entertainment. The primary focus of the festival is the musical performances by top Christian artists (which has included Michael W. Smith, Jars of Clay, Rebecca Saint James, Chris Tomlin, The Newsboys, Audio Adrenaline, Jeremy Camp, Skillet, Delirious, and others). Other attractions at the festival include seminars, workshops, youth events, Christian comedians, and even petting zoos. The festival is usually three to four days long and both Christians and non-Christians attend (baptisms take place at the festival).

Another of North America's largest and longest-running Christian music festivals is the Kingdom Bound Festival (www.kingdombound.org). Drawing sixty-five thousand people annually, the four-day event occurs every August and features more than sixty-five popular recording artists and fifteen inspirational speakers from around the world.[7] Hosted at the Darien Lake Amusement Park in Darien, New York (Buffalo-Niagara region), the festival attracts some of the biggest names in Christian music (from Christian pop to rock to rap) including MercyMe, Dave Crowder Band, Audio Adrenaline, Casting Crowns, Third Day, Lenny LeBlanc, Chris Tomlin, Rebecca Saint James, and Newsboys. Each year the festival seeks about five hundred Christian volunteers to assist with various needs including security, transportation, ministry, ushering and so forth.

Special features and notes

Some Christian festivals are beginning to take their entertainment "on the road," such as onboard cruises. Spirit of West Coast is just one of the entertainment venues that have done this. So if you're looking for a vacation with Christian entertainment, you might consider embarking on one of the Christian music festival cruises.

YOUTH AND YOUNG ADULT RALLIES

Why should I attend?

For anyone from elementary through high school and college age, there is no better way to experience the best of Christian faith and fellowship than by attending a youth rally. Nobody knows these benefits and advantages better than Christian churches and organizations themselves, and that is why each year they host thousands of Christian youth rallies across North America and around the world, with many attracting tens of thousands of participants and attendees.

Description

Youth and young adult rallies have become integral to the mission of the church today. These events not only teach the young about Jesus and the Gospel but also inspire and encourage youth and young adults to live the Christian faith with passion and integrity. Many of these rallies feature top Christian speakers, music artists, and celebrities. Here are a handful of North America's larger youth rallies:

- United Pentecostal Church International—Youth Congress
- Church of the Nazarene—Youth Quadrennial
- Evangelical Lutheran Church—America Youth Gathering
- World Youth Day—Hosted around the globe by the Catholic Church and the Pope
- National Federation for Catholic Youth Ministry—National convention for Catholic youth and ministers.

Rallies available

The Evangelical Lutheran Church of America (ELCA) hosts one of the largest gatherings of youth every three years. Known as ELCA Youth Gathering, the event is attended by about forty thousand people, many of whom are teenagers and students.[8]

The national convention features activities such as Bible study, education and learning, prayer and worship, reflection, Christian entertainment (including inspirational speakers and musicians), fellowship and celebrations, and community service projects.

Special features and notes

Youth rallies are typically promoted well in churches and through youth programs, so if you're interested in learning about any youth rallies that are being hosted locally or nationally, you can usually just ask someone involved in youth ministry about these events.

CHRISTIAN MARKETPLACE CONVENTIONS (PROFIT AND NON-PROFIT)

Why should I attend?

If you are a Christian and work in the marketplace, there is a good chance that you attend some type of conference or convention related to your job, especially if you are in sales, marketing, or act as the leader of your organization. Attending these events provides numerous benefits including meeting key peers and colleagues in your industry, increasing visibility of yourself and organization, and learning the latest about your field.

Description

Today most areas of Christian business will host conventions and conferences related to their mission. Such gatherings are critical for networking and for setting a vision for a particular trade. Industries represented include every profit and nonprofit Christian sector (education, medical/hospital, broadcasting, business and retail, travel, and much more). There are hundreds of Christian marketplace conventions and conferences in existence; here is a list of the largest or better-known shows:

- International Christian Retail Show: www.christianretailshow.com
- National Religious Broadcaster's Convention and Exposition: www.nrbconvention.org
- Gospel Music Association Convention: www.gospelmusic.org
- Evangelical Press Association Convention: www.epassoc.org
- Christian Management Association Conference: www.cmaonline.org
- National Catholic Education Association Convention: www.ncea.org
- Association of Gospel Rescue Missions Convention: www.agrm.org
- Christian Medical & Dental Associations—multiple conferences: www.cmdahome.org
- Council for Christian Colleges and Universities—multiple conferences: www.cccu.org

Marketplace conventions available

The World Religious Travel Expo & Educational Conference (www.religioustravelexpo.com) is the world's largest international convention on Christian and faith-based travel, tourism, and hospitality. The Expo features two segments: The Educational Conference, which includes top learning seminars on Christian travel ministry and faith vacation opportunities, and The International Tradeshow, which serves as a venue for Christian group travel planners to meet with companies and organizations specializing in faith-based travel. The World Religious Travel Expo & Educational Conference serves as the ideal meeting place for any church or ministry organization interested in beginning or enriching your Christian travel ministry program. For descriptions of other marketplace conventions available, log onto any of the Web sites listed above.

CREDIT: ©ISTOCKPHOTO.COM/OLEG PRIKHODKO

Many Christians attend faith-based conventions.

Special features and notes

If you've never been to a conference or convention related to your field of work, you should strongly consider it for all the benefits it brings. Ask your manager or employer about the opportunity of attending such an event in order to increase your skills, networking contacts, and visibility of your organization.

AFFINITY-BASED CONFERENCES

Why should I attend?

If you are passionate about a particular subject or belong to a certain ministry, you might consider attending a convention of related interest. Or, if you are a big fan or close follower of a particular well-known Christian preacher, speaker, author, or figure—again, you might consider going to their respective crusades or gatherings (these events can also fall under the "Entertainment and Music Festivals" category). Experiencing fellowship, developing new friendships, reigniting or enriching your faith, and gaining new insights into your passion or area of ministry are just a few of the benefits you can receive by attending these events.

Description

One of the most popular types of Christian gatherings is affinity-group events (affinity groups are individuals who share similar interests). No matter what Christian topic or subject you are interested in, there is most likely a corresponding gathering or conference for it. Examples of possible Christian affinity group or interest-related events include those that involve ethnic heritages, charities, biblical study programs, Christian authors, and so forth. The following provides a list of actual affinity-based organizations that host Christian conventions, gatherings, and rallies:

- Pro Athletes Outreach: www.pao.org
- Christian Motorcyclists Association: www.cmausa.org
- National Hispanic Christian Leadership Conference: www.nhclc.org
- National Catholic Committee on Scouting: www.nccs-bsa.org
- Christian Writers Guild www.christianwritersguild.com
- Christian singles conferences (multiple organizations)
- The National Black Catholic Congress: www.nbccongress.org

Affinity groups available

One of the most prominent Christian affinity groups and conferences is Women of Faith (www.womenoffaith.com). A faith-based organization, Women of Faith encourages women of all ages and stages in life to grow in faith and spiritual maturity through a relationship with Jesus Christ and an understanding of God's love and grace.[9] Since its inception in 1996, Women of Faith has hosted nondenominational conferences throughout North America with more than one hundred and fifty thousand women making decisions to start or renew their relationship with God.[10] Special guests have include Avalon, Nicole C. Jullen, Max Lucado, Kathy Troccoli, Robin McGraw, and Natalie Grant. Women of Faith is a ministry division of Thomas Nelson, Inc. (www.thomasnelson.com).

For descriptions of other available affinity-based groups, log onto any of the Web sites listed above.

Special features and notes

Major affinity-based associations and organizations often look for volunteers to assist with their conventions. If you're looking for ways to get more involved in a particular group, you might inquire about volunteer opportunities.

CHRISTIAN RETREATS

Is a Christian retreat right for me?

In this age of constant on-the-go, we can all use a retreat, a spiritual timeout. If it's been a while since you last took advantage of participating in a little spiritual rest and relaxation, maybe it's time to do just that. As the Christian retreat opportunities are vast, you can choose one that fits your budget, time, and interests. If you do take advantage of engaging in such an experience, you can count on one thing happening: everybody will much prefer the more "relaxed you" than the "stressed-out you."

CHRISTIAN RETREATS "AT A GLANCE"

TRIP SUMMARY
Typical length: 3–7 days
Average cost per day: $30–$300 per day (includes lodging and meals)
Average total cost: $100–$700 (includes lodging and meals)
Distance from home: varies from nearby to throughout North America; some worldwide opportunities
Variety of Christian retreats: many
When to go: any time of the year
Why go: need time for personal or communal prayer and reflection
Whom to go with: by yourself, friends, or family
Which Christian retreat experience to choose: one that fits your current personal and spiritual needs

DEMANDS AND BENEFITS
Spiritual focus: high
Fellowship opportunities: low to high (whether individual or group retreat)
Physically demanding: low
Intellectually stimulating: moderately
Emotionally rewarding: very
Culturally enriching: low

CHRISTIAN RETREATS 101

What is the relevance of a Christian retreat?

A Christian retreat is often a time set aside for "evaluation," that is, a time set aside to evaluate your personal relationship with Jesus, others, and even yourself. In addition, Christian retreats are a time to evaluate your life as a whole including the direction from which you have come, where you are now, and where you are going.

Another word often used to describe a Christian retreat experience is "withdrawal." A Christian retreat is in many ways a withdrawal from daily life for a short period in order to connect deeply and personally with God. We know from Scripture that Jesus and other biblical figures often withdrew and set time aside for prayer and reflection. Mark 1:35 speaks about Jesus's doing just this: "Now in the morning, having risen a long while before daylight, He went out and departed to a solitary place; and there He prayed." And of course there is the story in Luke 4:1 of Jesus withdrawing into the desert for prayer and fasting before he began his public ministry: "Then Jesus, being filled with the Holy Spirit, returned from the Jordan and was led by the Spirit into the wilderness." And even the Old Testament refers to biblical men and women embarking on retreats. In Exodus 24:18, we read about Moses taking time alone to commune with God: "So Moses went into the midst of the cloud and went up into the mountain. And Moses was on the mountain forty days and forty nights."

Today is no different. As Christians, we are called to imitate Jesus in all we do, and that includes setting aside periods of our life exclusively for prayer, reflection, and conversing with God. In short, taking a time-out retreat should be a part of every Christian's spiritual life.

Why should I embark on a Christian retreat?

If you're looking to develop a more personal relationship with Jesus while also reflecting on your own life and purpose, then a Christian retreat is for you. Or, if you're finding it difficult to develop a healthy, strong spiritual life, then you are also a good candidate for a Christian retreat. But still, why should you embark on a retreat rather than just take some "personal time" while at home? The number one reason for Christian retreats is that they help take you out of your element, away from your daily routine and life so that you can focus on your relationship with God and your life as a Christian. Christian retreats help change not only your pace of life but also your frame of mind.

Best yet, when you do embark on a retreat, it does not need to be for forty days like Jesus or Moses. A retreat can be as simple as a one-day retreat or a weekend retreat. If you can afford to, you can even embark on a retreat lasting one to two weeks. No matter what you decide, as the Nike slogan says: Just do it. ™ By embarking on a Christian retreat, you are sure to gain not only spiritually refreshment but also greater insight into what your purpose in life is. Isn't that worth a few days of your time?

CHOOSING CHRISTIAN RETREAT

What can I gain from attending a Christian retreat?

Many of us have embarked on a retreat at one time or another and have experienced its fruitful benefits. It provides us with a renewed outlook on life as well as a refreshed mind, body, and soul, and it can deepen our relationship with God and others. Retreats can teach us to love ourselves or help us get through a very difficult time in our life; however, the number one benefit of embarking on a Christian retreat is "renewal."

Through Christian retreats, we can experience renewal in our personal relationship with Jesus, with ourselves, and in our relationship with others whether it be family, friends, or church members. The renewal can be one of a personal nature, as well as renewal of your purpose and direction in life. Jesus says it best in Matthew 11:28: "Come to Me, all you who labor and are heavy laden, and I will give you rest."

How can I choose the right Christian retreat for me?

In the world of Christian retreats, you typically have one of five opportunities from which to choose: personal growth retreats; marriage, family, and couples retreats; youth and young adult retreats; faith community retreats; and affinity group retreats. Once you discern what you are hoping to gain from participating in a Christian retreat, you are ready to choose your Christian retreat experiences. As each of these retreat themes focus on a different subject with different interests, you'll want to make sure you choose the right opportunity for you.

Christian retreat and conference centers come in all shapes and sizes. Some are located in remote areas such as the mountains or countryside, while others are situated in the heart of large cities. Some places are small and can handle only a few visitors, while others are enormous and can handle dozens of large groups. Some retreat and conference centers belong to a particular Christian denomination while others do not.

For these reasons and more, it's imperative that you know exactly what you hope to experience and what you hope to gain by embarking on a retreat. Once you've done this and identified the reasons and purpose of your retreat, you can then begin your search for the right Christian retreat that matches your goals and current state in life. Fortunately the options are plentiful, and you will have many Christian retreats to choose from.

What are the advantages and disadvantages of embarking on a Christian retreat vacation?

Advantages

- experience spiritual renewal or deepened relationship with God
- new or clearer perspective in life
- greater optimism
- strengthened and restored relationships with family and friends
- healing (spiritually, emotionally, spiritually)
- inspiration, motivation, and encouragement

- receive a new calling in employment or career
- gain a greater understanding about yourself
- stronger marriages and families

Disadvantages

- timing of the retreat doesn't work with your schedule
- attending a retreat with a spouse or family member who doesn't want to be there
- retreat experience differs from what you researched about it
- desired retreat site is located far from your home, making transportation expensive
- retreat is of another denomination and some of the teachings conflict with your beliefs

How much does a Christian retreat vacation cost?

The cost of attending a Christian retreat can range from donation-based to the hundreds of dollars (even more than $1,000 for select retreats). The costs will vary based on duration, quality of facility including lodging, and the type of retreat. With this in mind, you should consider budgeting anywhere from $50 to $150 (or more) per day.

PREPARING FOR YOUR CHRISTIAN RETREAT

How can I arrange my Christian retreat?

First, you will need to research various Christian retreat opportunities before making a decision. Once you've found a few Christian retreat centers or experiences that pique your interest, you're ready to begin calling each of them and finding more information. Once you've chosen your desired Christian retreat, how do you make arrangements? It's typically quite similar to booking a hotel reservation. First, you need to ask if space is still available. If so, you are ready to begin making your reservation.

What questions should I consider before choosing a Christian retreat vacation?

- What types of Christian retreats do you offer?
- What are the lodging facilities like?
- Are all ages welcome or are there any restrictions?

- Do you accept groups, and if so, what sizes?
- What is the spiritual atmosphere or environment like?
- Who are the retreat leaders or counselors?
- How far in advance do I need to book my retreat reservation?

What are some tips for making the most of my Christian retreat?

The best tip for making the most of your Christian retreat is choosing the right retreat format. If you are seeking a time of silence and solitude, then be sure to choose a retreat site that can match this experience. On the other hand, you may wish to embark upon a group retreat that includes attending seminars and preaching. These types of retreats tend to be more interactive and much more scheduled than the personal private retreat. For example, the retreat leader will conduct daily conferences while often being available for counseling.

Another option that many people choose is a "directed retreat." This type of retreat is essentially a hybrid between a private retreat and a preaching/teaching retreat. In this instance, much of the retreat is spent in personal reflection and prayer; however, the retreat is conducted under the guidance of a retreat or spiritual leader. For example, the spiritual director may suggest certain Scripture passages to reflect on and pray about, while also being available for personal counseling.

As you can see, choosing the right retreat experience is the key to making the most of your experience, so be sure to research various retreat centers and what they have to offer before making that commitment.

What is a typical Christian retreat schedule?

As every Christian retreat program and center is different, there is no one set schedule; however, there are some similarities. The following provides an example of a typical daily retreat schedule:

7:00 AM	Wake up
8:00 AM	Chapel or devotions
8:30 AM	Breakfast
9:00 AM	Workshop or spiritual direction/counseling
12:00 PM	Lunch
1:00 PM	Rest
2:30 PM	Workshop or personal time
5:30 PM	Dinner
7:00 PM	Personal time/Scripture reading

Note: Breaks included throughout the above schedule.

PERSONAL GROWTH RETREATS

Why should I attend?

Are you feeling stressed out? Are you feeling like your life is going nowhere or has plateaued? Do you need spiritual rejuvenation or renewal? Or, do you feel like you have no time for a retreat? If you answered "yes" to any of these questions, you are ripe for attending a "personal growth retreat."

Description

A personal growth retreat focuses primarily on you and your relationship with God, with others, and with yourself. The goal of this retreat is to deepen each of these relationships, while also discovering what your purpose or role in life is—and then acting upon it. Personal growth retreats can range from silent retreats to communal and preaching retreats. Much of your time will be spent in prayer, reflection, Scripture reading, taking walks, journal writing, and possibly attending seminars and receiving spiritual direction or counseling. Personal growth retreats can take place at any phase in life, whether you are "riding high on life" or facing tremendous challenges.

MARRIAGE, FAMILY, AND COUPLES

Why should I attend?

Marriage, couples, and families should participate in retreats together at least once every few years. As family relationships often lie at the very core of our lives, they are in need of our attention and nurturing, especially because few things in life are as important as caring for and fostering these intimate relationships.

Description

Retreats that involve marriages, couples, and families often share the same two underlying themes and goals: (1) growing closer to God, and (2) growing closer to each other. What can you expect by attending a family retreat? Your family will have an opportunity to participate in indoor or outdoor activities, prayer and song, special programs for children, music performances and skits, meals together, and much more. Above all, retreats of this nature often provide opportunities for open sharing, reflection, and communication. Marriage and couples retreats spend less time on the various activities found

CREDIT: ©ISTOCKPHOTO.COM/
ANDREW F. KAZMIERSKI

Christians can choose from a variety of retreats.

on family retreats and much more time on one-on-one communication, workshops, and personal counseling (or guidance from a spiritual leader). In the end though, the goals of both family and couple retreats remain the same and include:

- developing greater love and charity for each other
- increasing good communication
- facing conflict
- dealing with finances
- setting a vision for our lives

YOUTH AND YOUNG ADULT RETREATS

Why should I attend?

Many youth and young adults enjoy attending retreats designed specifically for them because many of them find such experiences very inspirational, fun, and energizing. Furthermore, they discover that these retreats are wonderful places to meet new people and find new friends.

Description

What is the difference between a Christian youth retreat and a Christian camp? In many ways, there are few differences. In fact, many organizations that conduct Christian youth retreats also conduct Christian camps, or even combine the two. However, Christian youth retreats do carry a slightly different "tune" than camps. Retreats of this nature often provide Christian youth with a more "reflective" atmosphere. What can you expect when you attend a retreat of this nature? A heavy emphasis is placed on exploring your current relationship with God, your family, your friends, and yourself—and discovering how you can enrich it. What activities will you experience? The following provides a sample list:

- inspirational talks
- group prayer and worship, oftentimes combined with singing
- Bible study
- skits (with Christian teaching elements)
- group sharing
- time for individual/personal reflection
- watch Christian movies, videos, or documentaries
- outdoor activities (swimming, hiking, etc.)
- retreat booklets distributed and completed by participants

Why should I attend?

An affinity-group retreat is right for you if you want to attend a Christian retreat with others who share a similar interest or background as you. Retreats are often hosted by a variety of Christian groups and organizations, so there is most likely a retreat geared specifically to your personal hobbies, passions, or even heritage.

Description

As an affinity group is nothing more than a group of people with shared interests or commonalities; essentially everyone belongs to an affinity group of one kind or another. Within the context of Christian ministry, a men's ministry group is an affinity group, as is a women's ministry group. A Hispanic ministry group is also an affinity group. What does this has to do with Christian retreats? Some of the most popular retreats are those that revolve around affinity groups—for example, men's ministry retreats or women's ministry retreats. As many organizations and conference centers host retreat programs for affinity groups (that is, for people of similar interests or background), you might consider attending such a Christian retreat that involves your interest or background. Many people are drawn to affinity group retreats not only for their potential for friendship and fellowship but also for their focus on shared challenges in life. For example, a Christian business retreat can include workshops, seminars, discussions, and personal reflection regarding common challenges and issues faced by people of faith within the business world. Such retreats provide for very unique and special experiences. What are other affinity group retreats? The following provides a small sampling:

- men's or women's retreats
- Christian singles
- heritage retreats: Hispanic, African-American, Asian, etc.
- people with disabilities
- golfing or other sports
- divorced individuals
- substance abuse
- military, police officers, etc.

Is a Christian camp right for me?

Would you like to do something this year that can change your life? Would you like to do something that will provide you with cherished memories for the rest of your life, while also helping you develop some new friendships along the way? If that sounds appealing then you might make this the year you embark on a Christian camp vacation. The most common types of Christian camps are day or residential camps, special needs camps, travel camps, wilderness or outdoor camps, and work camps. With so many options to choose from, you are sure to find one that is just right for you. Best yet, the experience is one that can provide you with the personal and spiritual growth you are looking for in life.

CHRISTIAN CAMPS "AT A GLANCE"

TRIP SUMMARY
Typical length: 1–7 days
Average cost per day: $15–$80 per day (includes lodging and meals)
Average total cost: $15–$500 (includes lodging and meals)
Distance from home: varies from nearby to throughout North America; some worldwide opportunities
Variety of Christian camps: many
When to go: summer is most popular
Why go: great opportunity for youth to experience Christian faith and fellowship within the context of an environment designed for personal and spiritual growth
Whom to go with: by yourself, friends, or your church youth
Which Christian camp experience to choose: one that fits your beliefs, interests, and goals

DEMANDS AND BENEFITS
Spiritual focus: medium to high
Fellowship opportunities: high
Physically demanding: medium to high
Intellectually stimulating: moderately to high
Emotionally rewarding: very
Culturally enriching: low to moderately

CHRISTIAN CAMPS 101

What is the relevance of a Christian camp vacation?

Embarking on a Christian camp trip or vacation is almost a rite of passage for most Christian youth. Millions of teenagers and children can count themselves among these new inductees every year. But despite the large numbers and great interest, what role or contribution do Christian camps provide the church? More than any other venue, service, or experience, Christian camps offer young people an opportunity to grow not only spiritually but also emotionally, physically, socially, and intellectually. For this reason alone, Christian camps play a vital role in shaping the youth of today. Virtually every Christian denomination hosts or provides camps for its young people. In short, Christian camping is today not only a key mission of the church but is also a mainstay of Christian youth development.

Why should I embark on a Christian camp vacation?

For youth and young adults, these camp experiences often serve as the first real taste of Christian faith, fun, and fellowship. Furthermore, they often act as a bridge from "childhood faith" into a more personal relationship with Jesus. Above all, Christian camps provide youth with an opportunity to experience Christian community, learn independence, develop a spirit of gratitude, work within a team, commit to a lifestyle rooted in Scripture, and develop a habit of devotions and prayer.

CHOOSING CHRISTIAN CAMP VACATIONS

What can I gain from embarking on a Christian camp?

The key word regarding benefits is "maturity." Christian camps provide one of the best venues for developing personal, spiritual, emotional, and even social maturity among its participants. Through Christian camp experiences, education, and activities, youth learn the virtues of service, charity, and leadership. Other virtues developed include fortitude, courage, courtesy, determination, fidelity, forgiveness, generosity, graciousness, gratitude, and integrity. As such, many young people walk from such experiences more passionate not only about their faith but also about life in general.

How can I choose the right Christian camp vacation for me?

The list of Christian camps is extensive. Most of them fall under the category of day camps, resident camps, travel camps, wilderness camps, or work camps. The programs also vary among age groups ranging from children, youth, teenagers, to young adults. There are even some Christian camps designed for families and people of all ages. Furthermore, some camps are designed for those with special or serious issues including abuse (physical and substance), disorders (emotional, eating, behavioral), and physical or mental challenges, as well as those with hearing, speech, and visual impairments.

CREDIT: ©ISTOCKPHOTO.COM/ NANCY LOUIE

Eight million Christians go to camps each year.

So how can you choose the right one for you? Choose the Christian camp that is geared toward your age, matches your interests, and fits within your budget and timing. With thousands of camps to choose from, you are sure to find one just right for you.

What are the advantages and disadvantages of embarking on a Christian camp vacation?

Advantages

- wholesome and caring environment
- engaging atmosphere for hearing the Christian message
- socially interactive
- opportunity to challenge yourself physically
- emotionally rewarding
- time for reflection—past, present, and future
- opportunity to develop an appreciation of God's creation
- affordable compared to other vacations

Disadvantages

- desired Christian camp may be too far from your hometown
- limited timeframe to permanently impact a youth's life
- chance for injury, especially with more physical Christian camps
- homesickness
- child doesn't want to attend a Christian camp, but the parent does

How much does a Christian camp vacation cost?

Christian camps as a whole are quite affordable, especially when compared to traditional or secular vacations. When planning a budget for a Christian camp, keep in mind that camps have differences in the quality of services, accommodations, and amenities, as well as other factors such as staff to participant ratio. As such, prices can differ considerably as well. With this in mind, here is a sample of average estimated costs of a Christian camp including meals and lodging:

- Daily cost: $15–$80 (with a median cost ranging from $35 to $50)
- 2–4 day camp cost: $50–200
- 4–7 day camp cost: $200–500

PREPARING FOR YOUR CHRISTIAN CAMP VACATION

How can I arrange my Christian camp vacation?

One of the best places to look for a Christian camp is by visiting the Web site of the Christian Camp and Conference Association at www.ccca.org. As the most recognized Christian camp organization of its kind, you will find hundreds of opportunities throughout North America representing virtually every Christian denomination and a wide variety of Christian camp experiences. You can research and select your ideal Christian camp vacation from the Christian Camp and Conference Association, and then simply contact the Christian camp of your choice to register.

What questions should I ask a Christian camp?

- What type of Christian camp do you operate?
- What is the history of your Christian camp?
- What are your goals for each Christian camp participant?
- What ages do you work with?
- Where are you located and do all events take place on site?
- What are typical activities that youth participate in?
- What happens if my child gets sick, lonely, or injured?
- What is your organization's Christian denomination or statement of belief?

How can I make the most of my Christian camp vacation?

The best tip is preparation. Any youth planning to attend a Christian camp should properly prepare themselves for such an experience. This means the youth (or parent) should learn all they can about the upcoming Christian camp experience in advance and plan accordingly. This especially includes planning and preparing what you will bring on the trip. Make sure you not only bring the right clothing but also any necessary medications and the like. In addition, be sure to bring whatever the camp requires, such as a Bible or a daily journal. By being properly prepared before the first day camp and by having all the essentials, you are sure to enjoy one of the most memorable experiences of your life.

What is a typical Christian camp schedule?

Although every camp has a different schedule, here is a look at a typical day's activities:

7:00 AM	Wake up/Cabin cleanup	2:30 PM	Recreation
		5:30 PM	Dinner
8:00 AM	Breakfast	7:30 PM	Evening worship,
9:00 AM	Chapel, singing		personal testimonies
9:30 AM	Classes or Bible study	8:30 PM	Games, skits, camp
11:30 AM	Free time		store open
12:00 PM	Lunch	10:00 PM	Bedtime and
1:00 PM	Rest and relaxation		lights out!

CHRISTIAN CAMP OPPORTUNITIES

DAY AND RESIDENTIAL CAMPS

Why should I attend?

The most common Christian camp is a day or residential camp. These types of experiences often provide a wonderful break in life, especially for students during the summer. At these camps, participants can deepen their relationship with God, with themselves, and with others. For many, the memories and experiences from day or residential Christian camp sessions often last a lifetime.

Description

There are literally hundreds of Christian day and residential camps to choose from. Whatever type of Christian camp experience you are looking for, it probably exists. Here are some key attributes to look for and discuss with the camp's management or staff when you're choosing a camp:

- Camp style or type: Christian denomination, teaching philosophy and principles, camp atmosphere, goals and mission
- Participants: age group of participants, typical demographic/attendee

- Facilities: type of lodging, camp capacity (group sizes), location, facilities or equipment for special needs
- Types of programs: outdoor activities, indoor activities
- Staff: credentials of camp management/staff, safety record, staff to attendee ratio
- General information: costs, operating season (spring, summer, fall, or winter), history and experience of camp
- Programs: types of programs offered, length or duration (one week programs, etc.)

SPECIAL NEEDS CAMPS

Why should I attend?

A number of Christian camps are designed to receive individuals with special needs. These programs can often serve as much-needed places where attendees can meet with others struggling with similar issues. Unlike other special needs places, at a Christian camp, everything takes place within a Christian atmosphere of faith, hope, and love. For these reasons and more, the programs often serve as very uplifting and inspirational times for the participants.

Description

Many Christian camps specialize in and assist individuals with special needs or conditions, so it's imperative to find those that offer the exact services you are looking for. Services should be provided by a trained staff that understand and know the emotional, physical, social, intellectual, and spiritual needs of its attendees who are challenged by impairments, disorders, or other medical conditions. You can also expect to find facilities and programs geared exclusively for these individuals. Four common types of programs provided by special needs Christian camps are: disorders (behavioral, eating, emotional), impairments (hearing, speech, visual), challenges (mental, physical, emotional), and abuse (physical, substance).

TRAVEL CAMPS

Why should I attend?

If you want to combine a Christian camp experience with travel, look no further than a Christian travel camp. You can travel the world and enjoy exotic destinations while

enjoying the traditional benefits and experiences provided by a typical Christian camp.

Description

Christian camps are a tradition of youth.

Travel camps are similar to Christian youth trips, but they focus primarily on delivering the "camp" experience. The primary motive of Christian travel camps is to spend time in some of God's most beautiful creations, while experiencing companionship, recreation, and spiritual enrichment. These camps teach Christian youth how to cultivate a proper sense of independence and how to move outside their comfort zone. Christian travel camps can take place in your hometown, in a national park, as far away as Hawaii, or even internationally.

WILDERNESS (OUTDOOR) CAMPS

Why should I attend?

Christian wilderness camps (sometimes referred to as Christian outdoor camps) are primarily geared to those youths who want to combine a physical challenge with their faith. With a focus on adventure and fitness, these camps test the mind, body, and soul. Each wilderness or outdoor experience is viewed through the lens of the Christian faith, and the youth are taught lessons about how the lifelong journey to God is often be accompanied by joys, sorrows, accomplishments, and trials, but ultimately with triumph.

Description

Many wilderness or outdoor camps are often situated in very scenic, rustic spots. They provide a natural removal from all worldly things and engender the feeling of being in the midst of God's country. It's not uncommon to enjoy a Bible seminar near a breathtaking waterfall or panoramic vista, for example. Wilderness camps are designed not only to teach the Christian faith but also to encourage participants to develop self-confidence and self-esteem and to learn how to fulfill their potential. Although each outdoor camp features different adventure and physical activities based on their locations, philosophies, and styles of teaching, you will find some of the following opportunities at many of them:

* camping
* land activities: hiking, backpacking, horseback riding, rock climbing, repelling, mountain biking, canyoneering, caving, paintball, general sports such as softball

- water activities: swimming, paddling, canoeing, kayaking, whitewater rafting, fly fishing
- challenging activities: obstacle (challenge) course, teams course, ropes course

WORK CAMPS

Why should I attend?

If you're looking for an opportunity to vacation while at the same time putting your faith into action by serving others, consider a Christian work camp. In many ways, these camps are quite similar to or even synonymous with short-term missions. If you're looking for Christian faith, fun, and fellowship while getting your hands dirty by helping others, consider a Christian work camp for your summer or travel plans.

Description

Christian work camps come in many varieties, but most of them center on construction, repair, or cleaning of some kind. Most work camps do not require a certain set of skills by its participants; however, any qualified or professional skills are often considered a bonus. Many work camps are designed to help the elderly, disabled, disadvantaged, poor, or those who recently suffered a traumatic loss of property, health, or family through a natural or man-made disaster.

CREDIT: ©ISTOCKPHOTO.COM/CHRISTIAN WEIBELL
Your choices of Christian camps are many.

What is the experience of a work camp like? The primary focus is accomplishing the major project or task(s) at hand, while filling the remaining time with fun and faith-filled activities. In terms of the daily work, crew members often take on specific roles in accomplishing the project at hand. Some activities found at a typical Christian work camp include building or repairing homes, painting (interior or exterior), making repairs to a home or facility, landscaping, and general clean up.

MONASTIC GUEST-STAYS

Is a monastic guest-stay right for me?

Are you looking for something very different in your life? Maybe even something very different in your spiritual life? If so, then you might choose to become "a monk for a day" and spend time either visiting or on retreat at a monastery. Few places offer such solitude, peace, and an atmosphere that breathes contemplation and reflection. Regardless of their denomination or faith belief, nearly all guests find the experience of visiting or staying overnight at a monastery enlightening, engaging, and rewarding. To make your trip happen, simply contact the monastery of your choice and let them know you want to embark on a retreat within a monastic setting. Of all the Christian vacation opportunities, monastic getaways offer the most unique experience of all.

MONASTIC GUEST-STAYS "AT A GLANCE"

TRIP SUMMARY
Typical length: 2–7 days
Average cost per day: donation or $15–$50 per day (includes lodging and meals)
Distance from home: varies from nearby to across the world
Variety of monastic guest-stays: many
When to go: any time of the year
Why go: you're looking for one of the most unique experiences in the Christian faith
Whom to go with: by yourself or with a friend
Which monastic guest-stay experience to choose: one that fits your interests
and intrigues you

DEMANDS AND BENEFITS
Spiritual focus: high
Fellowship opportunities: low
Physically demanding: low
Intellectually stimulating: moderately
Emotionally rewarding: very
Culturally enriching: low to moderately

MONASTIC GUEST-STAYS 101

What is the relevance of a monastic guest-stay?

Why do monasteries and abbeys open their doors to guests? The answer lies in the Bible, specifically in Matthew 25:35: "For I was hungry and you gave Me food, I was thirsty and you gave Me drink; I was a stranger and you took Me in." Other biblical passages have also influenced the monastic way of life and hospitality, including Genesis 18:1,

The Abbey of Saint Peter in Solesmes, France offers a genuine monastic experience.

2 Kings 4:8, Hebrews 13:2, 1 Peter 4:9–10, and Revelation 3:20 which says, "Behold! I stand at the door and knock. If anyone hears My voice and opens the door, I will come in and dine with him, and he with Me."

Saint Benedict, the founder of Western monastic life, is probably most responsible for implementing the above biblical passages into monasticism's focus on hospitality. He wrote in his Rule (spiritual and living guidelines for monasteries) that monks should welcome and receive guests at their door, just as they would welcome and receive Christ. Today the practice continues, so if you are looking for a place that can provide a spiritual atmosphere and environment conducive to deep contemplation and reflection, consider a monastery for your setting.

Why should I embark on a monastic guest-stay?

Have you ever wondered what life as a monk must be like? Well, if you would like to experience that very same feeling and "be a monk for a day," I have good news for you—it is possible. As many monasteries and abbeys in North America and around the world feature guesthouses, many people are welcome to stay overnight at one of these places and participate in the daily lives of the monks.

Depending on the type of monastery, you may be able to embark on a scheduled retreat, private retreat, or directed retreat. A scheduled retreat is one that is hosted by the monastery and typically available and advertised publicly to groups or individuals. A private retreat is primarily a self-directed retreat that you conduct within the atmosphere of a monastery. A monastic directed retreat is often self-directed retreat but includes a daily visit or meeting with a monk for spiritual counseling or guidance.

If you're like most people, you're probably thinking, "Do I have to be Catholic to do this?" Or, "Do I have to be a Christian?" The simple answer to both questions is no. Anyone is welcome to stay at monastic guesthouses, presuming of course, the guest is respectful of the monastery's traditions.

CHOOSING A MONASTIC GUEST-STAY

What can I gain from embarking on a monastic guest-stay?

First and foremost, you truly are treated and welcomed as a visitor of Christ, regardless of your religious affiliation. Second, you are provided a wonderful spiritual atmosphere for reflecting, contemplating, and praying. Third, in many cases you are invited to join in and personally experience the life of the monks. This can include everything from partici-pating in prayers to sharing meals to walking the grounds. Fourth, you often can speak with the monks in order to seek spiritual counsel, discuss your life, or simply talk about God.

Above all, by visiting or staying at a monastic guesthouse, you experience a much-needed oasis of peace. In today's world, that can often be the best possible escape or hol-iday. And it's the one kind of travel that when you come home from it, you won't feel like you "need a vacation from a vacation."

What are the advantages and disadvantages of embarking on a monastic guest-stay?

Advantages

- contemplative and peaceful environment
- get away from it all
- experience an ancient tradition
- conducive atmosphere for reflection
- life slows down
- simple homegrown foods/meals
- engaging conversations with monks

Disadvantages

- possibility of feeling uncomfortable if you're not Catholic or even Christian
- rituals seem intimidating
- not the place to be (for select monasteries) if you don't like to chant
- in some places, silence is required for certain hours of the day (although this could be viewed as an advantage by others)
- simplicity of life—no cell phone, e-mail, etc., (though this could be seen as an advantage by some)

How much does a monastic guest-stay cost?

Many monasteries operate on a "donation only" basis, so there is no set fee for your lodging or retreat; you donate the amount that you are willing or can afford. In other cases, monasteries will charge a designated amount similar to a hotel or other places of lodging. Although prices can vary from monastery to monastery, you can expect to pay anywhere from $15 to $50 on average per day, which includes your meals. Again though, this amount can vary depending on which part of the world you are in, the type of monastery, and the overall facilities.

How can I arrange a visit or guest-stay at a monastery?

Contact the monastery you are interested in, just as you would a museum or a hotel. If you're planning to visit a monastery during the day for a few hours only, keep in mind that there is typically no need to advise the monks in advance (presuming it's a monastery that normally receives visitors). However, if you are hoping to join or arrange a guided tour of the monastery for yourself or a group, you will often need to give advance notice (not always, but often especially if it's a group). Similarly, staying at a monastery's guesthouse for one or more nights usually requires advance reservations.

How do you contact a monastery? Typically it is by whatever forms of communication the monks use (and you use). Today many monastic places have telephones, faxes, web sites, and even e-mail addresses, all of which can serve as ways of receiving reservations and correspondence. And, of course, there's the old form of communication, the postal service. When contacting the monasteries, simply advise them of the following:

- your name and contact information (and group/organization name, if applicable)
- your desired request (guided tour, overnight stay at the guesthouse, etc.)
- dates and times of arrival and departure
- number of people in your group (or if it's just yourself)
- purpose of your visit (to see the monastery, to experience monastic life, need a retreat, etc.)

The monastery will act similarly to a hotel and typically confirm your reservation by e-mail, fax, or (postal) letter. Most monasteries will often reply with a confirmation (or not) within a week or two. If you do not hear from them within fourteen days or so, it would be appropriate to follow up. Upon receiving your confirmation, you will usually receive at that time any further details you need (when to arrive at the monastery, the time of "checkout," the cost or donation, etc.).

What questions should I ask a monastery before visiting?

- Do you have a guest house, and if so, can anyone make reservations for a retreat?
- What is the cost?
- How long can I stay?
- When is a good time of the year to visit?
- Are there various types of retreats offered (i.e. private, directed, etc.)?

- Do you accept groups on retreat?
- Is it possible to get spiritual counseling from a monk?
- What rules or guidelines must one follow while at the monastery?

How can I make the most of my monastic retreat?

The best way to make the most of your monastic retreat is to fully engage yourself. Take advantage of everything the monastery and surrounding environment has to offer, including solitude, contemplation, prayer, worship, spiritual reading, and Scripture study. Take an active role in the life of a monk by attending worship services, participating in the periods of silence, and following the general rhythm of the day (that is, synchronizing your activities with that of the monastery). And lastly, if the opportunity arises, be sure to spend time visiting with a monk—these conversations often become some of the most enlightening or memorable of all monastic experiences.

What is a typical monastic guest-stay schedule?

The following is an example of a schedule for a monastic retreat or guest-stay (Monday–Friday). Depending on the monastery, some activities may be required (or strongly encouraged) for attendance while others are not.

5:30–6:15 AM	Office of Vigils (early morning prayers of the monks in the church).
7:00–7:30 AM	Office of Lauds (morning prayers of the monks in the church)
7:30–8:00 AM	Breakfast
8:00–11:00 AM	Retreat workshops or personal retreat/reflection time including Scripture reading
11:00–12:00 PM	Morning Mass
12:00 PM	Lunch
12:45 PM	Office of Sext (afternoon prayers of the monks)
1:00 PM	Retreat workshops or personal retreat/reflection time including Scripture reading
5:00–5:30 PM	Office of Vespers; followed by private prayer or reading in silence until supper
6:00 PM	Dinner
6:45 PM	Personal time or recreation
8:00–8:20 PM	Office of Compline
8:20 PM	the "Grand Silence" (no conversation) begins following the Office of Compline and continues until morning

Note: Depending on the monastery, some meals may be taken in silence. Most meals last thirty to forty-five minutes.

Simplicity and Sacredness

Of all my travels in life, few compare to my time at the renowned Solesmes Monastery in western France. With an authentic monastic environment and atmosphere reminiscent of the Middle Ages, Solesmes provides an experience unlike any other. How can I describe my visit and retreat there? I can summarize it in two words: simplicity and sacredness. What I mean is that everything during my visit seemed to take on an air of "simplicity and sacredness." This includes everything from time itself to meals (with the monks) to walks on the grounds to personal reflection to Bible reading to chapel visits and to personal and communal prayers. I found that being in such an environment really fosters contemplation about one's life. However, for me personally, my favorite part of Solesmes is listening to the monks sing Gregorian chant "live" in the chapel. Like the three million other Americans who paid $16 in the mid-1990s for one of Santo Domingo de Silos Gregorian chant CDs (which reached the mainstream pop charts), I also bought one (see their story in this section). I must admit, it was at that time I first listened to the music and fell in love with it. I found it very beautiful and enriching (yet I'm the same person who also loves music bands ranging from Jars of Clay to Creed to Lifehouse!). Shortly after buying the CD I set a goal to one day visit Solesmes, which I did accomplish several years later. Today, I still carry with me my wonderful memories of that first visit to Solesmes. I can't wait to return again. —*Author*

MONASTIC GUEST-STAY OPPORTUNITIES

UNITED STATES

THE MONASTERY OF CHRIST IN THE DESERT

Why should I visit?

If you are looking for a genuine getaway to an authentic monastic environment, right here in the United States, the Monastery of Christ in the Desert is a great choice. It offers a natural surrounding and an atmosphere of silence, solitude, privacy, reflection, and prayer.

Description

Founded in 1964, the Roman Catholic Benedictine Monastery of Christ in the Desert is located in a very picturesque canyon of northwestern New Mexico. Surrounded by miles of undeveloped wilderness, the abbey's life revolves around its daily liturgy and duties of agriculture, crafts, gift shop, and guesthouse. In addition, the community runs a mail-order business of books and religious items. Men and women who desire a genuine monastic retreat and are willing to participate in and live the Benedictine way of life (charity, prayer, spiritual reading, and manual labor) are welcome visitors to the guesthouse.

CREDIT: JEFF PAGE; JCPAGE.COM

The Monastery of Christ in the Desert in New Mexico is tranquil.

The Learning Channel (TLC) provides a wonderful overview of the monastery, based on its experience of filming a reality show in 2006 at The Monastery of Christ in the Desert. The program offered this description, "The Monastery offers unprecedented access into the lives and rituals of thirty Benedictine monks [and] a rare glimpse into a closed community that follows an ancient discipline."[11] To learn more about the show visit http://tlc.discovery.com/fansites/monastery/monastery.html. The TLC Web site also features an excellent section on "Visiting the Monastery," complete with in-depth information on spending time at the monastery on retreat. To learn more visit http://tlc.discovery.com/fansites/monastery/visit/visit.html.

Special features and notes

The monastery is located at an altitude of six thousand five hundred feet high (about a mile high). The nearest public telephone is fifteen miles away. Personal cell phones do not work at the monastery. Most meals are taken in the refectory (the monastery dining room). Breakfast is taken in the guest dining room. Meals are held in silence, except for spiritual reading or music. The minimum stay is two days and two nights, and the maximum stay is a month. Day visitors to the monastery are welcome.

Groups

- Accommodations are limited to adults coming as individuals, couples, or very small groups.
- The monastery features two guest residence areas, the main Guesthouse (thirteen rooms) and the Ranch House (three rooms).

Location

The monastery is about 135 miles from the closest major airport in Albuquerque, New Mexico, seventy-five miles north of Santa Fe, over fifty miles south of Chama, and just thirteen miles off of U.S. Route 84.

MONASTERY AND GUESTHOUSE INFORMATION
MONASTERY INFORMATION
Web site: www.christdesert.org

E-mail for all inquiries: guests@christdesert.us, guestmaster@christdesert.us, or cidguestmaster@christdesert.org.

Tel: (801) 564-8567 or (801) 545-8567

Fax: (419) 831-9113

MONASTERY MAILING ADDRESS
Monastery of Christ in the Desert
Attn: Guestmaster
P.O. Box 270
Abiquiu, NM 87510-0270

THE ABBEY OF GETHSEMANI

Why should I visit?

If you want to embark on a contemplative retreat in the midst of a truly monastic environment, the Abbey of Gethsemani is waiting for you. Home to the well-known American monk and author Thomas Merton (1915–1968), the monastery today receives visitors from throughout the United States and around the world.

Description

The name Thomas Merton is almost synonymous with monasticism in America. Here at Gethsemani, the famed Trappist monk and author spent his life and wrote influential books on the monastic and spiritual life including the best-seller *The Seven Storey Mountain*. The abbey has received visitors since its founding in 1848 and continues the tradition to this day. What draws people of different faiths here is the opportunity to experience the heart of authentic monastic life, culture, and hospitality, all while seeking God on a personal and intimate level. As Thomas Merton himself said about the monastic milieu, it offers a place apart "to entertain silence in the heart and listen for the voice of God—to pray for your own discovery."[15] In addition to a daily life of prayer and sacred reading, the monks carry out various duties including the making and selling of fruitcake, cheese, and bourbon fudge. The fudge is sold throughout the world and is quite famous in its own right.

Special features and notes

As silence, solitude, and prayer govern the atmosphere of the monastery, speaking is restricted and limited. Although retreats are neither guided nor directed, private consultations with a monk can be arranged. Donations as a guesthouse visitor are made in lieu of set prices.

Groups

- As the retreat house is suited to individuals, groups are normally not accommodated.
- Individual reservations are required during the four-month period prior to your desired stay.
- The monastery features both a retreat house (open to men and women), as well as rooms within the monastic enclosure (for men only).

Location

Louisville International Airport is located fifty miles north of the abbey. The nearest town is Bardstown, Kentucky, located about twelve miles north of the abbey. From Bardstown, drive south on 31-E and then briefly head east on 52, arriving at the Abbey of Gethsemani.

MONASTERY AND GUESTHOUSE INFORMATION
ABBEY INFORMATION
Web site: www.monks.org
E-mail: To e-mail the Abbey of Gethsemani, visit www.monks.org and then click on "Contact Us." From this Web page you can contact the abbey via the e-mail form (or visit www.monks.org/contact.asp)
Tel: 502-549-3117
Retreat reservations (made only by telephone): (502) 549-4133
Fax: 502-549-4124
ABBEY MAILING ADDRESS
Abbey of Gethsemani
3642 Monks Rd.
Trappist, KY 40051

ABBEYS OF SAINT PETER AND SAINT CECELIA

Why should I visit?

If you're looking for an authentic monastic experience complete with chanting, then pack your Bible and head at once to France for the Abbeys of Saint Peter and Saint Cecelia. Recognized as leaders in Gregorian chant, the Benedictine Congregation of Solesmes provides a monastic setting and atmosphere reminiscent of the Middle Ages.

Description

About 150 miles west of Paris are the Abbeys of Saint Peter (men's) and Saint Cecelia (women's). Serving as the heart of Gregorian chant spirituality, song, and research, the Benedictine Congregation of Solesmes is home to about eighty monks and sixty nuns. Recognized as one of the world's most prominent monasteries, Solesmes is considered a leader in recordings and publications of sacred liturgical music. As contemplative communities, the abbeys provide an atmosphere of prayer, silence, and solitude not often found elsewhere. The men's abbey and the women's abbey are located within a block of each other, making it very accessible for the traveler to visit both sites.

Special features and notes

Many Solesmes chant recordings can be purchased not only from the abbey itself but also from the Internet or from many Christian or music gift-stores throughout North America and elsewhere. One of the best times to visit is during the high holy days of Easter and Christmas.

Groups

- Groups that wish to visit Solesmes should contact the guestmaster well in advance by e-mailing abbaye@solesmes.com.
- The following accommodations are available: Men can stay at the Abbey of Saint Peter's guesthouse (located within the monastic enclosure). All guesthouse visitors are expected to participate in the daily liturgical life of the monastery. Youth groups can stay at the Old Factory Marble, located just outside the monastic grounds (operated by the Abbey of Saint Peter). Women and family can stay at the Abbey of Saint Cecelia guesthouse. It is open from Palm Sunday to the end of September; however, groups of twelve or more can possibly be accommodated at other times with previous arrangements.

Location

Situated 150 miles west of Paris, the abbey is about five miles from the city of Sablé sur Sarthe (which is about halfway between Le Mans and Angers).

MONASTERY AND GUESTHOUSE INFORMATION
ABBEY OF SAINT PETER (GUESTHOUSE)
Abbaye Saint-Pierre
1 Place Dom Gueranger
72300 Solesmes (France)
Abbey Web site: www.solesmes.com
Abbey e-mail: abbaye@solesmes.com
Guesthouse e-mail: hospes@solesmes.com
Tel: (0243) 95-03-08
Fax: (0243) 95-03-28
ABBEY OF SAINT CECELIA (GUESTHOUSE)
Soeur Hoteliere
21, rue Jules Alain
72300 Solesmes, France
Tel: (0243) 95-45-05
Fax: (0243) 95-52-01

SANTO DOMINGO DE SILOS MONASTERY

Why should I visit?

Does the name Santo Domingo de Silos "ring a bell"? If you're a fan of pop music from the 1990s, it should. You may remember a group of European monks from this monastery hit number three on the Billboard 200 charts with their CD of Gregorian chant. You can now hear them in person at their abbey located near the center of Spain.

Description

Dating back almost a millennium, the Monastery of Santo Domingo de Silos is located in north-central Spain and is a branch of the Benedictine Congregation of Solesmes (France). The monks gained popularity due to the worldwide release of their Gregorian chant recordings more than a decade ago. Their first album, *Chant*, sold 3 million copies[13] in the U.S. alone, and the monks appeared on *Good Morning America* and *The Tonight Show*.[14] Guests can attend the daily liturgical services and listen to the chants firsthand, as well as enjoy tours of the cloister and library. Visitors can stay overnight at the nearby monastery hotel.

Special features and notes

The monks' popular CDs of *Chant*, *Chant II*, and *Chant III* are available at most music stores.

Several hotels are located near the monastery; guesthouse accommodations are provided for men at the monastery (located within the monastic enclosure).

Groups

Groups with twenty or more people are asked to contact the guestmaster in advance by e-mailing abadia@abadiadesilos.es.

Location

Located about one hundred miles north of Madrid, the monastery is accessible only by road or bus (not train). From Burgos, drive south on N1 toward Madrid, exiting at Lerma; then head east on the local road to Santo Domingo de Silos.

MONASTERY AND GUESTHOUSE INFORMATION
Web site: www.abadiadesilos.es
Abbey e-mail: abadia@abadiadesilos.es
Telephone: (947) 39-00-49 or (947) 39-00-68
Fax: (947) 39-00-33
MONASTERY MAILING ADDRESS
Abadía Benedictina de Santo Domingo de Silos
C/Santo Domingo, 1
09610 Santo Domingo de Silos (Spain)

BUCKFAST ABBEY

Why should I visit?

If you're looking for an all-inclusive visit to a monastery, you might consider Buckfast Abbey in England. Featuring an authentic monastic daily life, the monastery also provides the individual traveler and groups with much to see and do including visiting the abbey church, Medieval Guest Hall, farm, monastic produce shop, gardens, gift and bookstore, video presentations, conference facilities, and much more.

Description

The history of Buckfast Abbey dates back almost one thousand years to 1018, the year it was founded. In 1882, it was refounded by the Benedictine order and today remains one of England's most prominent monasteries. A self-supporting and very active abbey today, Buckfast operates a farm that includes growing vegetables, beekeeping, and raising pigs and cattle. With its conference and seminar facilities, fully-functioning restaurant, and guesthouse facilities, Buckfast Abbey is one of the few monasteries suited to receive groups. More than five hundred thousand people visit the abbey each year.

Special features and notes

The monastery features a restaurant (Grange Restaurant), a monastic produce shop, and a gift shop and bookstore. Conference and group seminar facilities are available at the abbey's Saint Cuthbert's Conference Center.

Groups

- Groups, couples, or individuals (men or women) can be accommodated in Southgate, the monastic retreat house.
- Men can stay at the guesthouse within the enclosure and partake in meals with the monks.

Location

Buckfast Abbey is located centrally in South Devon. Buckfast is half a mile from the A38 dual carriageway and halfway between Exeter and Plymouth. Buckfastleigh is accessible by bus and train from throughout England. From Buckfastleigh station, you can take the Buckfast Heritage Bus to Buckfast Abbey.

ABBEY AND GUESTHOUSE INFORMATION
ABBEY INFORMATION
Web site: www.buckfast.org.uk
E-mail: You must visit the Web site to send an e-mail.
Tel: (01364) 645-550; Fax (01364) 643-891
Retreats and Southgate: (01364) 645-521
ABBEY MAILING ADDRESS
Buckfast Abbey
Buckfastleigh, Devon
TQ11 0EE (England)

ABBEY OF MONTE CASSINO (ITALY)

Why should I visit?

Have you ever wondered where western monasticism got its start and by whom? If you travel to the Abbey of Monte Cassino in central Italy, you will find your answer. Here, in the fifth century, Saint Benedict wrote his Rule, the principles of communal living later adopted by many monasteries in the West. The guidelines are today known as the Rule of Saint Benedict.

Description

No book about monastic sites would be complete without Monte Cassino, the first monastery established by Saint Benedict—founder of western Monasticism. Although the abbey does not offer a guesthouse, it is a working abbey and a popular tourist site today. Monte Cassino is visited by thousands of pilgrims and tourists each year. Many come not only to experience Benedictine life but also to see the historically important monastic buildings (which were rebuilt after their destruction in World War II). The most visited sites include the abbey's museum and church. Many tour groups, both Christian and secular, include a visit to Monte Cassino while traveling through central Italy.

Special features and notes

Shorts, sleeveless shirts, and short skirts are not permitted inside the abbey or museum. Be sure to eat before arriving at Monte Cassino as there are no restaurants or places to purchase snacks or drinks.

Groups

Many tour groups, both Christian and secular, traveling through central Italy often include a visit to the abbey on their itineraries.

Location

Monte Cassino is located above the town of Cassino. The abbey is located about seventy-five miles southeast of Rome and is easily reached by train or bus. If you're traveling by car from Rome or Naples, take the A1 and exit at Cassino.

ABBEY INFORMATION
Abbey Web site: www.montecassino.it
E-mail: info@montecassino.it
TO ARRANGE A GUIDED TOUR OF THE ABBEY CONTACT:
Tel: (0776) 311-529
Fax: (0776) 312-393
ABBEY MAILING ADDRESS
Montecassino Abbey
03043 Cassino FR (Italy)

CHAPTER 8

CHRISTIAN ATTRACTIONS

CREDIT: WYCLIFFE BIBLE TRANSLATORS, INC

Is a Christian attraction right for me?

If you're looking for an experience that combines the best of faith, fun, education, and entertainment—then visiting a Christian attraction might be right up your alley. You can choose from multiple venues including biblical parks, museums, missions, theatres, visitor centers, and much more. Today the most popular Christian attractions include those with first-class facilities, experiences, and services. Many individuals, families, and Christian groups are choosing venues that are more wholesome in entertainment than secular venues are. With this growing popularity comes an increase in the number of Christian attractions and sites built each year, many of which are perfectly suited for all ages. Best yet, it only takes one visit to a Christian attraction for you to leave refreshed, inspired, and enriched in your faith.

CHRISTIAN ATTRACTIONS "AT A GLANCE"

TRIP SUMMARY
Typical length: 1 day
Average admission cost: $5–$50 (some admissions, however, are free or based on donation)
Distance from home: close to moderately close, depending on where you live
Variety of attractions: many
When to go? any time of the year
Why go? wholesome or faith-based fun and entertainment
Whom to go with? by yourself or with family, friends, church, or ministry group
Which Christian attraction to choose? one that appeals to your interests; also consider one located near your residence or vacation destination

DEMANDS AND BENEFITS
Spiritual focus: high
Fellowship opportunities: few to many (individual or group visit)
Physically demanding: low
Intellectually stimulating: moderately to very
Emotionally rewarding: moderately to very
Culturally Enriching: low

What is the relevance of faith-based attractions?

The concept of seeking entertainment, amusement, and knowledge is as old as the human race. Virtually every generation since Biblical times has built museums, theatres, and other attractions to inspire, educate, and entertain its people. Think of the Roman Coliseum, Ephesus Theatre and Library, and the ancient stadium of Olympia. Each of these venues existed during its day to fulfill the purpose of entertainment.

Things are no different today. People still seek social, emotional, and intellectual fulfillment and enrichment through leisure venues, outlets, and attractions. In fact, in the twenty-first century the entertainment industry serves as one of the major driving forces behind the world's economy and acts as the backbone for many people's daily lives. Think of the economic and social clout of *American Idol*, as well as how many people's schedules revolve around the show's airing. For these reasons and more, much of today's culture, beliefs, and views result directly from the leisure pursuits and interests that people choose and experience.

This is why Christian attractions are relevant. Only Christian facilities seek to serve a higher purpose and integrate faith into their overall missions. While other recreational venues seek primarily to inspire, educate, and entertain, Christian leisure and entertainment venues accomplish all of this and more. They also evangelize the culture and people. In other words, Christian attractions fulfill Jesus's mandate to spread the Gospel to the ends of the earth. And what better way to share the Christian faith than through the two popular venues of entertainment and leisure?

Why should I visit a Christian attraction?

Imagine for a moment a world of no religious entertainment venues, only secular ones. Imagine a world of no Christian museums, theaters, destinations, or welcome centers. Imagine a world where the Christian story cannot be told by more than just words.

Although this scenario hasn't exactly happened, there is no denying that non-Christian attractions and venues by far outnumber faith-based ones. In fact, if we are honest with ourselves, the few Christian entertainment facilities that have existed over the years have often suffered from a reputation of low quality. For these reasons and more, many Christians have instead opted for top quality nonreligious attractions when making vacation plans.

I have great news for you. Times are changing. Christians are now building and debuting new, top quality, faith-based attractions and facilities each year. The result? We now have our own first-class venues that can inspire, educate, entertain, and evangelize. And best yet, Christians are turning to these new venues in droves! Some of the more prominent Christian entertainment places today attract anywhere from several hundred thousand visitors to almost a million.

CHOOSING CHRISTIAN ATTRACTIONS

What can I expect to gain by visiting a Christian attraction?

If you visit a Christian theatre and watch a performance, you can expect to be moved, maybe even to tears, about your faith. If you visit a Christian Welcome Center of a nationally known organization, you can expect to learn about a key ministry of the church. If you visit a Christian theme park, you can expect to enjoy fun and amusement as you interact one-on-one and even shake hands with biblical figures. And above all, if you visit any Christian attraction, you can expect to share in the liberating gospel message of Jesus Christ.

How can I choose the right Christian attraction for me?

Here are the top questions to ask yourself when deciding which Christian attraction might be right for you:

- What is my budget?
- Which Christian attractions are close to my home or within driving distance?
- Am I open to traveling a long-distance even by plane or train?
- What are my interests? What experience am I seeking: theatre, museum, welcome center, theme park?
- How much time do I have for visiting the Christian attraction (a few hours, a full day, more than one day)?
- When am I able to visit: spring, summer, fall, or winter? What time of day am I able to visit?
- Where would I like to take my next vacation? Can I incorporate a Christian attraction into it?
- Who might be able to join me for the trip? Family, friends, church or ministry group members?
- If I lead a group, which Christian attraction will appeal to the most people?

What are the advantages and disadvantages of visiting a Christian attraction?

Advantages

Admission fees are fairly inexpensive, especially when compared to their secular counterparts. Another advantage is that Christian attractions are very conducive to families and you never need to worry about the atmosphere or "message" of a particular place. Best yet, it is a place that you can experience and share the Christian faith with family and friends in a fun and entertaining format.

Disadvantages

You may have to drive a long distance or even fly to visit a popular Christian attraction. If so, this means the price of your trip will increase dramatically, as you now must consider other costs such as transportation, lodging, and food. Now, that $20 admission cost may turn into a $200 trip or more.

How much does a Christian attraction cost?

It depends on the place you will be visiting. Aside from a few places that provide free or donation-based admission, a typical entrance fee to a top quality Christian museum, interactive center, or similar facility will usually range from $5 to $20. First-class theaters and theme parks will often cost $20 to $50 for one person. Of course, keep in mind that many Christian attractions and venues offer discounts for groups, seniors, children, and the like. So be sure to ask about these when purchasing your tickets. When planning a budget for your family or group, remember that there might be other costs such as the purchase of food or souvenirs while at the site. Include these in your planned expenses.

PREPARING FOR YOUR CHRISTIAN ATTRACTION VISIT

How can I arrange my visit to a Christian attraction?

First, contact the Christian attraction and obtain all pertinent information (costs, hours of opening and closing, etc.). Second, if your visit will require travel plans such as booking a flight or lodging, you might consider contacting a travel agent that specializes in trips such as these.

What are some tips for making the most of my Christian attraction visit?

- Choose the right attraction for you, your family, or group.
- Dress appropriately (expect to get rained on).
- Wear comfortable shoes.
- Time your visit wisely (time your arrival when the attraction is less crowded, etc.).
- Plan your day in advance (or at the beginning of your visit).
- Find out if any special events are taking place during your visit.
- If allowed, bring your own food and "brown-bag it."
- Carry the mental attitude that "you don't have to see everything."
- Honor all Christian attraction rules and guidelines.

What questions should I ask a Christian attraction prior to my visit?

- What are your most popular shows, attractions, or sites?
- When is the best time to visit?
- What are all the discounts you offer?
- Are there any special upcoming performances, guest visitors, exhibits, tours, etc.?
- How can I purchase tickets? Can I purchase them in advance?
- How can I make the most of my visit?
- Where are you located, and how do I get there?
- Is there anything else I should know?

Above all, have fun!

As the Book of Ecclesiastes says, there is a time and season for everything. And that includes fun. If you have never visited a first-rate Christian attraction before, you are in for a treat. Today's most popular faith-based entertainment venues feature top performers, cutting-edge technology, and excellent customer service. And many of these facilities have only arisen in the past few years, including the Holy Land Experience, Creation Museum, Billy Graham Library, and WordSpring Discovery Center. We have entered into a new era of Christian attractions in recent years. Whether your interests lie in theater, museums, or good old-fashioned fun and entertainment, you should consider making this the year of Christian attractions for you, your family, church, or ministry organization.

BIBLICAL PARKS AND INTERACTIVE CENTERS

WORDSPRING DISCOVERY CENTER

Why should I visit?

If you've ever wanted a real, hands-on experience of the Bible, you've found your source: WordSpring Discovery Center in Orlando, Florida. Serving as the only first-class biblical facility of its kind in the world, the Discovery Center provides a fascinating, intimate, and educational interactive encounter with Scripture. After one visit here, the Bible and history will take on a whole new (and fun) meaning.

Description

WordSpring Discovery Center is the first center in the world that brings to life the Bible through interactive state-of-the-art technology. With five thousand square feet of high-tech equipment, the center appeals to all ages from five to seventy-five. Here is the official description:

See the world in a day. Visit Africa. Gaze at the exquisitely-carved image of a FareFare man from Ghana and examine the authentic clothing he is wearing, as you listen to a recording of John 3:16 in their own language. Then take a trek across Europe. Explore the stories of heroes from the past—people like Franzisco de Enzinas of Spain, who believed that no sacrifice was too great for spreading God's Word. Track the lives of those who often sacrificed so much to make the Bible available in our own language. Next, set sail for the Orient. Interact with the unique sounds and symbols of complex languages that challenge linguists and computer software developers. Pause in the shade of the language tree and visualize the millions of people who do not have a Bible in the language they understand best. Gain a renewed appreciation for God's Word in your own language. For the first time, visitors to Orlando can be immersed in the exotic and often dangerous world of the Bible translator and explore cultures many have never even heard of, much less actually seen. Experience all this and more at the WordSpring Discovery Center, a presentation of Wycliffe Bible Translators.

Activities available

Among the many activities, visitors can:

- experience the unique sounds of John 3:16 spoken in twelve minority languages from around the world,
- penetrate the darkness of the "Life without the Bible" tower to hear about what life was like for a cross-section of peoples from around the world before they received God's Word—and what a difference a translated Bible has made in their lives,
- add your own voice by writing about what the Bible means to you on the "graffiti scroll,"
- immerse your imagination in audio dramas about the history of early Bible translations around the world,
- test your knowledge with the Bible Trivia Game,
- create rubbings of the Ten Commandments in Hebrew and John 3:16 in the very first English translation,
- enjoy the award-winning film *The Power of the Word* in the Townsend Theatre,
- try your hand at Bible translation for the Tzeltal language of Mexico,
- print your name in twelve different ancient, modern, and fantasy alphabets (including Klingon!) to take home, and
- play the Translation Daze simulation game to experience life in another culture.

Special features and notes

A behind-the-scenes building tour offered weekdays at 10:00 AM takes visitors inside the U.S. headquarters of Wycliffe Bible Translators, where you can learn more of the fascinating story of modern day Bible translation. The daily "Face to Face" presentation offered weekdays at 1:00 PM features Wycliffe translators, literacy workers, teachers, and other special guests talking about their experiences.

When you're hungry, the Café Karibuni serves a delicious variety of lunch choices, each day from 11:30 AM to 1:00 PM, and the Village Shop features exotic and unique gifts from around the world, books, and mission resources.

Group tours and special events

- Admission discounts to WordSpring are available for groups of ten or more.
- Two half-day student programs are offered: A–Z Adventure (1st–6th grade) and Mission:Encounter (7–12th grade). Reservations are required.
- WordSpring is available for hire for your special event—such as a seniors luncheon, formal banquet, or wedding ceremony and reception. Choose from

an extensive banqueting menu. Guests can enjoy complimentary admission to WordSpring during the event.

* Conference and meeting facilities are also available.

WordSpring Made a Profound Impact upon My Heart

Thank you for providing such a wonderful place as the WordSpring Discovery Center. It meant so much to me to discover so many important facts about Bible translation and all that is entailed in bringing the word of God to a people group. What I saw and heard at WordSpring made a profound impact upon my heart. What I have brought back from this visit includes pencil rubbings of God's word in Hebrew and English, and the names of my sons and several friends in other languages that has sparked further interest in Bible translation, as well as brochures about WordSpring and Wycliffe. I am hopeful that some in my circle of acquaintance will be spurred toward involvement with Bible Translation as God directs them.
—*Individual from Santa Clara, CA*

Location

WordSpring Discovery Center is located fifteen minutes from Orlando International Airport. From Interstate 4, take Route 528 (Beachline) east. Exit at Narcoossee Road (Exit #13, Route 15). Turn right onto Narcoossee Road and go two and a half miles south to Moss Park Road. Turn left onto Moss Park Road and go two miles. Turn left at the WordSpring sign. Look for the WordSpring entrance on your left.

VACATION INFORMATION
Web site: www.wordspringdiscoverycenter.com
E-mail: wordspring@wycliffe.org
Tel: (407) 852-3626
Group sales: Ask for special group rates

PHYSICAL ADDRESS
WordSpring Discovery Center
11221 John Wycliffe Boulevard.
Orlando, FL 32832

MAILING ADDRESS
WordSpring Discovery Center
P.O. Box 620483
Orlando, FL 32862-0483

THE HOLY LAND EXPERIENCE

Why should I visit?

If you're looking for a vacation that combines faith, family, and fun, look no further than the Holy Land Experience in Orlando, Florida. With two hundred thousand visitors annually, the Holy Land Experience is North America's number one Christian biblical attraction. This should be a must for any family vacation.

Description

The Holy Land Experience is situated on fifteen acres in Orlando, Florida. A not-for-profit organization founded in 2001, the Christian attraction is educational, inspirational, theatrical, and historical. The following is the park's description:

The Holy Land Experience brings together the sights and sounds of the world of the Bible in a unique and interactive way unlike anywhere else. It is a living, biblical attraction that transports its guests seven thousand miles away and two thousand years back in time to the land of the Bible. Its combination of sights, sounds, and tastes stimulate the senses and blend together to create a spectacular new experience. Beyond the fun and excitement, it is the heartfelt desire of everyone associated with this wonderful ministry that God and His Word is exalted and that visitors are encouraged in their search for enduring truth and the ultimate meaning of life.

Attractions available

Here is a sampling of sites and shows you can visit:

- Live shows bring the Gospel to life in song and drama.
- Jerusalem Street Market looks like an ancient Middle Eastern marketplace.
- Dead Sea Qumran Caves are a replica of the desert caves with Dead Sea Scrolls.
- Wilderness Tabernacle gives an overview of an Old Testament ritual of worship.
- Calvary's Garden Tomb is the stage for the Passion Drama, which occurs daily.
- Plaza of the Nations and The Temple of the Great King contains a replica of the Temple of the Great King, called the Herodian Temple in its day.
- The Scriptorium Center for Biblical Antiquities houses one of the world's finest private collections of biblical artifacts.
- The Seed of Promise theater shows a film from the Garden of Eden to the final judgment.

- Oasis Palms Café features Mediterranean and American lunch platters and gourmet desserts.
- Jerusalem Model AD 66 is the largest indoor model of Jerusalem in the world.
- KidVenture houses a kid-friendly rock-climbing wall, a misting station, and interactive live presentations for children.

Special features and notes

Twenty-minute guided tours of the park occur once daily Monday through Friday, weather permitting, and are led by one of The Holy Land Experience's ministry team scholars. If you plan to visit several times, be sure to purchase the Jerusalem Gold Pass which provides unlimited admissions for a full year. Don't forget to visit the Ex Libris Book Shoppe and also experience the exhibit entitled *A Day in the Life of a Monk*.

Group tours and special events

- Discounts are provided for groups of fifteen or more people.
- Wedding ceremonies and receptions can be hosted at the Holy Land Experience, with the Temple or Shofar Auditorium as your backdrop.
- Conference and seminar facilities are available.

One of the Most Awesome Days I Spent in Florida

My wife and I visited The Holy Land Experience this past May. It was one of the most awesome days I have spent in Florida. The live performances were second to none! It was great to see sections of God's Holy Word come alive right before our eyes! The movie about the Lamb was great as well, and so were the performances about art and music. What an incredible day we had. It truly was a memorable experience. —*Michael*

Location

The Holy Land Experience is located in Orlando alongside Interstate 4, Exit 78, at the corner of Conroy and Vineland Roads, immediately off the I-4 exit ramp. From the airport, take the Beachline (formerly the Beeline) Expressway 528 West to I-4 East. Take I-4 East to Exit 78. Turn left onto Conroy Road, going west. Go to Vineland Road. Turn right, and the entrance to The Holy Land Experience is on the right.

MEGA-CHURCHES

CRYSTAL CATHEDRAL

Why should I visit?

If you have never visited one of the more than 1,200 mega-churches in the United States, you are in for a treat with the wide variety of ministries, activities, and professional performances available. If you plan to visit one, put Crystal Cathedral near the top of your list. Few churches in America are as well known, especially as almost everyone has viewed Pastor Robert Schuller's *Hour of Power* on television.

Description

Since its dedication in 1980, the architecturally renowned Crystal Cathedral has grown into a mega-church with ten thousand members. Known around the world for its weekly televised *Hour of Power* church service, people come from around the United States and the world to visit the cathedral.

Activities available

Two of the most significant events attended by visitors each year are: *The Glory of Easter*, a dazzling reenactment of Jesus's Passion by one hundred-plus cast members using drama, song, and pageantry (details at www.crystalcathedral.org/glory_easter) and *The Glory of Christmas*, a spectacular rendition of Jesus's birth in Bethlehem, complete with not only an orchestral accompaniment prerecorded by the London Symphony Orchestra but also with live animals, flying angels, special effects, and much more (details at www.crystalcathedral.org/glory_christmas).

Special features and notes

Crystal Cathedral operates one of the best travel ministry programs in the country. You can learn more about their events by visiting www.crystalcathedral.org/travel.ministry.

One Can Walk the Campus and Read Scriptures Underfoot

One can visit a church as a place of spirituality and intimacy with God. The Crystal Cathedral has that too, but includes so much more for the visitor. This campus in the midst of a thriving city is an oasis of serenity and quietude, of inspiration and excitement. Innovative ministry over some fifty years is reflected in the award-winning architecture of its buildings, in the biblical sculptures by noted artists set throughout the campus, in the use of flowing waters and beautiful landscaping. But talk with the staff and volunteers, and if you're lucky, Dr. Schuller himself, and you'll sense the warmth of the people and the urgency of the worldwide ministry of this congregation. For it is first a congregation that reaches out to members' needs and observances. Built on that foundation the Crystal Cathedral has used its facilities to serve the needs of many people throughout the world—and throughout its community. It is a local church with a universal mission. One can walk the campus and read Scriptures underfoot, each dedicated to an individual or couple or family. For me there was a unique feeling of being blessed for having been there, and to have taken part in this ministry in a small way. Visit the Crystal Cathedral and attend one of its services, and the world feels just a little more sane and the possibilities of life and service all the more real.—*Ronald E. Keener, Editor of* Church Executive

Group tours and special events

Group tours are also available through special accommodations. For more information call (714) 971-4013.

Location

Four major airports are within one hour of Crystal Cathedral. From I-5 North into North Orange County, continue past the 22 Freeway for approximately one mile. Exit at Chapman Avenue/State College Boulevard. Stay in the far left lane and turn left onto West Chapman Avenue. Pass under the freeway and continue for one mile. Turn left onto South Lewis Street. The Crystal Cathedral entrance is the first driveway on the right.

PHOTOGRAPH BY JOHN CONNELL
COURTESY CRYSTAL CATHEDRAL MINISTRIES

Mega-churches, such as Crystal Cathedral, attract hundreds of thousands of visitors each year.

MISSIONS

THE CALIFORNIA MISSIONS

Why should I visit?

One of the best ways to experience California's history and heritage is through a visit to the California Missions. The twenty-one missions are located up and down the coast of the Golden State and near other popular sites and attractions, so you can easily integrate a mission visit into virtually any California vacation.

Description

The California Missions, also known as the Spanish Missions, lie at the root of California's founding. So important are they to its history that the state's fourth-grade students study the missions as part of their curriculum. Established in California by Father Junipero Serra, the Franciscans built the missions between 1769 and 1869. Today many of the missions remain intact and function primarily as either fully active churches or museums.

Attractions available

* *Mission San Carlos Borromeo* (headquarters of Father Serra). Founded in 1770 as the second mission, San Carlos Borromeo grew to become one of the most prominent of the missions and served as the residence of Father Serra. Today it offers the visitor much to see and do. Among the most popular sites to explore include the Junipero Serra Convento Museum, which includes Father

Serra's bedroom, kitchen, library, guest dining room, and refectory. You can also visit the Mora Chapel (which houses the tomb of Father Serra), Sir Harry Downie Museum (dedicated to the renowned restorer of the California Missions), Munras Memorial Museum (featuring artifacts and artworks of the period), the basilica, and more.

- *Mission San Luis Obispo de Tolosa* (Prince of the Missions). Founded in 1772 as the fifth of the California Missions, San Luis Obispo de Tolosa Mission still plays a key role in the life of the city. In fact, the local people fondly refer to their city as "The City with a Mission." Among the highlights is the spectacular mission museum that features early photographs and artifacts, providing a wonderful glimpse into the life of California at the turn of the twentieth century. It, too, remains an active parish at the center of its town.

- *San Juan Capistrano* (Jewel of the Missions). Built in 1776, this is the seventh mission founded by Father Serra. San Juan Capistrano lies almost halfway between Los Angeles and San Diego and is considered the birthplace of Orange County. The mission church is best known for its annual "miraculous" return of the swallows each year on March 19, the feast day of Saint Joseph. Along with its ten acres of serene gardens and adobe walls, San Juan Capistrano features the Serra Chapel (where Father Serra celebrated Mass), Padres Quarters, Industrial Area, Soldiers Barracks, Cemetery, and The Great Stone Church. You can also view the welcome video which provides an overview of the mission's history.

- *Mission Santa Barbara* (Queen of the Missions). Sitting high on a hill overlooking the city of Santa Barbara and the Pacific Ocean, this mission church is considered one of the loveliest and most popular of the California Missions. As the tenth mission founded (two years after Father Serra died, in 1786), it is unique in that it is the only one that has remained under the control of the Franciscan community without interruption since its founding. Today it remains an active parish, and along with visiting the church and rose garden, you can view the Chumash Indian art room and one of the original missionary's bedrooms.

- *Mission San Juan Bautista* (largest of the missions). Founded in 1797 as the fifteenth mission, it became known as the largest of the missions, serving more than one thousand Indians. Among the "must see" sites are the church, Guadalupe Chapel, museum, gardens, cemetery (with burial grounds of Christian Native Americans of the era), and much more. Two interesting facts surround the mission: it is built on the San Andreas Fault, and it was featured in Alfred Hitchcock's *Vertigo*. Although it is a part of a State Historic Park, the mission remains an active parish and is said to have celebrated Mass every day since its founding more than two hundred years ago.

- *Mission of San Luis Rey de Francia* (King of the Missions). Considered a "jewel" of the California Missions, San Luis Rey de Francia is the eighteenth of the missions (founded in 1798) and became the most populous and wealthiest of them all. It is also believed to have had the largest number of Native American converts. With its spectacular setting near the Pacific Ocean (in Oceanside to be exact), the mission today offers self-guided tours of its church, sunken gardens, museum, and cemetery. A Franciscan Retreat Center is also available for those who wish to use its services.

- *Mission Santa Ines* (also called Mission Santa Ynes). As the nineteenth mission founded, in 1804, Santa Ines was established for the Franciscans to minister to the Indians of the coastal mountains. In the early 1900s, the Danish town of Solvang was built up around Mission Santa Ines and today the mission still remains a focal point of the city. Self-guided tours of the museums and garden take place daily. Home to an active parish, the mission church features spectacular views of the Santa Ynez River Valley and the Santa Ynez and San Rafael mountain ranges.

No Visit Is Complete
without a Stop at the Missions

I have been to many of the California Missions. Each one is unique in character, design, atmosphere, and spirit. What I love about the missions is how they clearly demonstrate faith as being at the root of California's history. I often tell my friends that no visit to California is complete without a stop at the missions! —*Author*

Special features and notes

As it's fairly impractical to see all twenty-one missions on one trip, most people integrate only one or a handful of mission visits into their regular vacation to California.

Group tours and special events

Some of the active missions do offer group tours. Contact each mission individually for specific information (see Web sites on the following page).

Location

As the missions stretch along the coast of California and vary from each other (some are active, some are not), contact each mission individually for specific information, including hours of operation.

CALIFORNIA MISSIONS INFORMATION

There is no single official Web site for the California Missions. However, any search on the Internet for "California Missions" will yield a number of Web sites and organizations closely affiliated with the missions.

The following are official mission Web sites (in geographical order, north to south):

Mission San Francisco Solano, in Sonoma: visit www.parks.ca.gov; search for "Sonoma SHP)

Mission San Rafael Arcangel, in San Rafael: www.saintraphael.com

Mission San Francisco de Asis (Mission Dolores), in San Francisco: www.missiondolores.org

Mission San Jose, in Fremont: no official Web site

Mission Santa Clara de Asis, in Santa Clara: www.scu.edu/mission

Mission Santa Cruz, in Santa Cruz: www.santacruzstateparks.com

Mission San Juan Bautista, in San Juan Bautista: www.oldmissionsjb.org

Mission San Carlos Borromeo del Rio Carmelo, south of Carmel: www.carmelmission.org

Mission Nuestra Senora de la Soledad, south of Soledad: no official Web site

Mission San Antonio de Padua, northwest of Jolon: www.sanantoniomission.org

Mission San Miguel Arcangel, north of Paso Robles: www.missionsanmiguel.org

Mission San Luis Obispo de Tolosa, in San Luis Obispo: www.missionsanluisobispo.org

Mission La Purisima Concepcion, northeast of Lompoc: www.lapurisima.org or www.lapurisimamission.org

Mission Santa Ines, in Solvang: www.missionsantaines.org

Mission Santa Barbara, in Santa Barbara: www.sbmission.org

Mission San Buenaventura, in Ventura: www.sanbuenaventuramission.org

Mission San Fernando Rey de Espana, in Mission Hills, Los Angeles: no official Web site

Mission San Gabriel Arcangel, in San Gabriel: www.sangabrielmission.org

Mission San Juan Capistrano, in San Juan Capistrano: www.missionsjc.com

Mission San Luis Rey de Francia, in Oceanside: www.sanluisrey.org

Mission San Diego de Alcala, in San Diego: www.missionsandiego.com

BILLY GRAHAM LIBRARY

Why should I visit?

You probably have heard the name Billy Graham. You've most likely listened to him speak in person or on the air. Now, you can get to know this great evangelist and his message, ministry, and mission on a more personal basis at the newly launched Billy Graham Library in Charlotte, North Carolina. Only here can you relive his life, crusades, travels, sermons, and experiences from the past fifty years.

Description

On May 31, 2007, the three former U.S. Presidents George H.W. Bush, Bill Clinton, and Jimmy Carter came to North Carolina to participate in the dedication ceremony of the Billy Graham Library. Virtually every major U.S. media outlet covered the historic event. The Library is an extension of the ongoing outreach of the Billy Graham Evangelistic Association (BGEA) and is designed to inspire visitors to carry on the message of John 3:16, which Billy Graham preached to the "ends of the earth."

Attractions available

Whether you spend just a few hours or a full day visiting the Billy Graham Library, one thing is certain—you will walk away inspired and enriched. Located on the grounds of the organization's international headquarters, the Billy Graham Library features six exhibits, four galleries, and two theatres. It is also home to personal papers, correspondence, and sermon manuscripts of this great crusader. The self-guided tour of the Library takes about ninety minutes and includes multimedia displays, films, and several hundred photographs. You can also visit the original Graham family home place, where Billy Graham grew up as a teenager (see story below).

A restaurant and bookstore are also located on the premises, as is an exhibit on the Billy Graham Evangelistic Association—providing an insider's look at what the ministry is doing in today's world. Among the main attractions is the state-of-the-art multimedia exhibit entitled *One Man's Journey*. Here you can engage yourself in the life of Billy Graham from his modest beginnings as a child of a dairy farmer to the day he founded the Billy Graham Evangelistic Association in 1950. You can then travel through each subsequent decade of his life experiencing the crusades, radio and television broadcasts, and his meetings with kings, queens, celebrities, and everyday men, women, and children.

Another main attraction is the reconstructed Colonial house that Billy Graham grew up in with his family. Inside are original furnishings along with authentic appliances and furniture of the time. The home itself is located on the campus of the Billy Graham Library, just four miles from the original Graham homestead.

Special features and notes

There is no cost for admission. Free parking is also available, including auto, bus, RV, and disabled spaces. Hours of operation are Monday-Saturday, 9:30 AM–5:00 PM. The Library is closed on Sundays. Hours are tentative and subject to change. Food and beverages are available for purchase in the Graham Brothers Dairy Bar.

You can get involved in different ways with the Billy Graham Evangelistic Association, including volunteering at the Library. For more information, contact the Billy Graham Library (see contact information below).

Group tours and special events

Groups of fifteen or more will require a reservation. E-mail BGEA at librarytours@ bgea.org or call 704-401-3200 to book your group tour.

Location

The Library is conveniently located off Billy Graham Parkway, near the Charlotte Douglas International Airport, I-77, and I-85 in Charlotte, North Carolina. From I-85: Take exit 33—Billy Graham Parkway and follow Billy Graham Parkway/ US-521 approximately four miles. Turn left at the traffic light onto Westmont Drive. Follow Westmont Drive around to the left into BGEA.

VACATION INFORMATION
Web site: www.bgea.org or www.bgea.org/BGLibrary_Index.asp
Reservations: For six or fewer tickets, you can book online at www.bgea.org/ BGLibrary_Reservations.asp. Groups of fifteen or more require a reservation. To arrange these visits, you must e-mail BGEA at librarytours@bgea.org or call (704) 401-3200.

PHYSICAL ADDRESS
Billy Graham Evangelistic Association
4330 Westmont Drive
Charlotte, NC 28217

MAILING ADDRESS
Billy Graham Library
1 Billy Graham Parkway
Charlotte, NC 28201

THE CREATION MUSEUM

Why should I visit?

The Creation Museum presents a unique and unparalleled experience—a walk through time that portrays significant, life-altering events from the past, illuminating the effects of biblical history on our present and future world. Be prepared to experience history in a completely unprecedented way. This state-of-the-art museum brings the pages of the Bible to life, casting its characters and animals in dynamic form through the use of animatronics and placing them in familiar settings.

Description

The Creation Museum is an outreach of Answers in Genesis, the world's largest apologetics (Christianity-defending) ministry. At its location on forty-nine beautifully manicured gardens just outside Cincinnati (but in northern Kentucky), this $27 million

CREDIT: ANSWERS IN GENESIS

An animatronic 40-foot-long sauropod dinosaur overlooks the Creation Museum's large main hall. Other dinosaurs that move realistically can be found placed here.

"walk through history" museum counters evolutionary natural history museums. The museum's animatronics displays (especially its impressive, moving dinosaurs), its theaters that show fifty striking videos, a state-of-the-art planetarium, and the Special Effects Theater are spread out over sixty-five thousand square feet, incorporating up to forty-foot ceilings to contain some of its massive exhibits.

The museum goes beyond telling the compelling story of the creation of life on this planet—it proclaims that the Bible is the supreme authority in all matters it addresses, from Genesis to Revelation. At the same time, the ministry's Ph.D. scientists have taken great care to maintain the highest standards of scientific accuracy. The museum is the brainchild of Ken Ham, AiG president, best-selling author, speaker, and the host of the daily "Answers" radio program.

Attractions available

As the museum presents its walk through the history of the Bible, visitors experience a facility that rivals a first-class natural history museum.

- The museum's striking exhibits demonstrate to guests that the Scriptures are the "true history book of the universe" as they take a time journey through a visual presentation of the Seven Cs of History according to the Bible: Creation, Corruption (the fall into sin), Catastrophe (Noah's Flood), Confusion (Tower of Babel), Christ, Cross, and Consummation (restoration of a new earth one day).

- The museum also features a high-tech, $500,000 planetarium and is a fully engaging, sensory experience for guests.
- It includes huge murals and realistic scenery, computer-generated visual effects, exotic animals, life-sized people and dinosaur animatronics, and a Special Effects Theater complete with misty sea breezes and rumbling seats.
- A superb fossil of dinosaur bones and a mineral collection are also on display.

Spectacular!

The Creation Museum is spectacular! I've been a Christian for many years, but this museum has strengthened my faith. Visitors won't leave untouched after touring this museum.—*Zig Ziglar, motivational speaker and author*

Special features and notes

Reserve some time to visit the museum's exquisite gardens and trails, and enjoy a picnic lunch with your family under the shade of spacious pavilions overlooking a three-acre lake. The arching bridges, lakeside dock, and waterfalls are joined to a five-foot-wide paved walkway, just under a mile long, suitable for strollers and wheelchairs. Or eat at Noah's Café, which seats three hundred inside and out and is a perfect stopping place for guests. Have a hot lunch, sandwich and salad, or a snack with a beverage.

The strikingly designed Dragon Hall Bookstore offers a wealth of Bible-affirming science, world view, and family resources in a dramatic setting. You should allow three to four hours to explore all of the exhibits, attend the Special Effects Theater, and peruse the bookstore—and longer if you watch all the fifty-plus videos. Should you choose to enjoy the Stargazers Planetarium and wander through the gardens, add an extra hour of entertainment and discovery.

Group tours and special events

- Discounts are provided for groups of fifteen or more people (fourteen-day advance reservations are required for discount).
- The Creation Museum is open seven days per week between Memorial Day and Labor Day and is open Monday–Saturday the rest of the year.

- Planetarium programs change every few months.
- Rotating exhibits are also featured, along with special lectures on such topics as astronomy, biology, and geology that are held in the museum's lecture rooms.

Location

The Creation Museum is conveniently located in Greater Cincinnati off I-275 (exit 11), just minutes west of the Cincinnati/Northern Kentucky International Airport.

VACATION INFORMATION

Web site: www.creationmuseum.org
E-mail: tlaughlin@answersingenesis.org
Tel: (888) 582-4253
Group sales: (888) 582-4253, ext. 355 (Monday–Friday, 9 AM–5 PM EST), or e-mail reservations@creationmuseum.org. All events must be scheduled at least fourteen days in advance to quality for group pricing and benefits.

PHYSICAL ADDRESS
The Creation Museum
2800 Bullittsburg Church Road
Petersburg, KY 41080

MAILING ADDRESS
The Creation Museum
P.O. Box 510
Hebron, Kentucky 41048

POPE JOHN PAUL II CULTURAL CENTER

Why should I visit?

Karol Wojtyla, also known as Pope John Paul II, grew up in Poland during the Communist era, was ordained a priest in 1946, and became the first non-Italian Pope in almost five hundred years. During his twenty-five-year pontificate (the second longest one in modern times), Pope John Paul II became one of the most recognizable Christians in history and one of the few people to be named to *TIME* magazine's top one hundred most influential people in two different centuries. Pope John Paul II emphasized a "universal call to holiness" for all Christians. Few people influenced and inspired the world last century as Pope John Paul II did. If you are traveling to Washington D.C., for vacation or business, there's no better opportunity to explore the life of the late pontiff than with a visit to the award-winning Pope John Paul II Cultural Center.

Description

Located near The Catholic University of America and Basilica of the National Shrine of the Immaculate Conception (in northeastern Washington D.C.), the Pope John Paul II Cultural Center features interactive and multimedia technologies regarding faith, culture, and the world. Its chapel is graced with a number of artworks including a rare portrait of Saint Teresa, a popular Catholic saint and Carmelite nun from 1873–1879, which was painted by her sister, Celine.

Attractions available

The Five Galleries

Gallery of Church and Papal History. This gallery provides an opportunity to learn about the popes throughout history from the first century through today. Interactive stations provide a fun and user-friendly way to learn about the Catholic Church. Listen to some of Pope John Paul II's most memorable speeches.

Gallery of Faith. Discover your and others' faith in more depth. You can even create a Testimonial of Faith through any of the following methods: audio or video recordings, written statement, or even a computer drawing.

Gallery of Community. Catholic social and community services is the premise of this gallery. Read about organizations that "put faith into action" and best exemplify Pope John Paul II's commitment to community service and assisting others in need.

Gallery of Wonder. Explore the intersection of faith and science, as well as the relationship between religion and technology, in this "wonder-filled" gallery. Interactive tools allow you to answer some of life's most pressing questions, and you can also leave behind a written record of your vision and hope for the world.

Gallery of Imagination. This interactive exhibit allows you to combine your faith with the best of your creativity. Hands-on opportunities include such activities as "Ring the Bells!" (where your group can discover melody selections from hymnals), or spend time creating dynamic works of art such as an electronic stained-glass window.

Activities for Children. No matter their age, all children have something to do at the Pope John Paul II Cultural Center, including ringing bells, creating art rubbings of saints and angels, watching Bible stories under a tent, building blocks, and participating in a scavenger hunt.

Special features and notes

Admission to the Cultural Center is by donation, and the Center is handicap accessible. While in Washington D.C., you may wish to visit other Christian sites such as the Washington National Cathedral (www.cathedral.org), the Basilica of the National Shrine of the Immaculate Conception (www.nationalshrine.com), and the Franciscan Monastery & Holy Land (www.myfranciscan.org).

Group tours and special events

To book a group visit, fill out the Group Reservation Form; to obtain either, call or visit their Web site (www.jp2cc.org).

Wonderful and Refreshing Excursion

The Pope John Paul II Cultural Center is one of the finest faith-based museums in North America. It reminds me of the other first-class Christian interactive museums and attractions such as WordSpring Discovery Center. Many hands-on opportunities here make faith "come alive," and it's entertaining as well. One of my favorite memories is seeing the actual skis of Pope John Paul II! Whether you are Catholic or not, the Pope John Paul II Cultural Center provides a wonderful and refreshing excursion while visiting the nation's capital. —*Author*

Location

From I-95, I-495 and I-295: Take Route 50 West and exit onto South Dakota Avenue, NE. Follow South Dakota and turn left onto Monroe Street, NE and follow it to Michigan Avenue. Turn right onto Harewood Road, NE just past the entrance to the Basilica of the National Shrine of the Immaculate Conception. The Cultural Center is on the left about half a mile down the road.

VACATION INFORMATION

Web site: www.jp2cc.org
Tel: (202) 635-5400
Fax: (202) 635-5411; info@jp2cc.org
Group Sales: Telephone (202) 635-5475 or e-mail GroupSales@jpcc.org

PHYSICAL ADDRESS

Pope John Paul II Cultural Center
3900 Harewood Road, NE
Washington, D.C. 20017

SIGHT & SOUND THEATRES®

Why should I visit?

If you're looking for a Broadway style performance yet within a Christian setting, then look no further than Sight & Sound Theatres. With theatres in Pennsylvania and Missouri, you can choose from a wide variety of first-class biblical theatrical and musical performances.

Description

With more than eight hundred thousand guests per year, Sight & Sound Theatres are arguably the most visited Christian entertainment attraction in North America. Founded more than thirty years ago, the site is today honored with the title "the Christian Broadway" and is categorized as "one of the top three theatre destinations on the East Coast."[1] With more than two thousand seats, the theatres feature state-of-the-art sound and lighting and a full cast of biblical characters and animals.

Attractions available

With a spectacular dramatization of the Bible, the following provide Sight & Sound's official show descriptions:

- *Noah, the Musical* (this is the trademark show). "A show of unbelievable proportions! Relive an amazing time in history when God told a man to build a huge floating vessel and fill it with every kind of animal. Experience the enduring faith of Noah and his family as they believe God and rise above the tests, trials, and flood of destruction, to receive a promise from God to go forth and fulfill His plans on earth."[2]
- *In the Beginning.* "This new epic musical brings Creation to life! Be there as God creates the heavens and the earth and all the extraordinary animals. Witness the fall of Adam and Eve, and their glorious restoration. With spectacular special effects, *In the Beginning* promises to be an experience beyond your imagination!"[3]
- *The Miracle of Christmas* (played during Christmas season). "Follow the extraordinary journey of Mary and Joseph, and witness the miraculous birth of Jesus, the Savior. Arrive early and enjoy our holiday festivities with live animals and shepherds, delicious seasonal treats, elaborate lights, decorations, and a thirty-foot high 'angel' tree!"[4]
- *Daniel and the Lion's Den.* "Experience Daniel's harrowing condemnation to the

lions' den. Discover the fate of the Hebrews and their beloved Jerusalem. And, with Daniel, witness the fleeting nature of the kingdoms of earth, and the enduring power of the kingdom of God."[5]

Special features and notes

Reservations are strongly recommended to ensure your choice of show dates, times, and seats.

Group tours and special events

- Group rates and children's prices are available, as are packages combining show tickets, dining, attractions, and lodging.
- A behind-the-scenes tour is offered on selected dates.

As impressive as the Theatre is, it pales in comparison to what we saw on the stage. To have a story from the Bible presented as was the story of "Noah" has left a lasting impression on me. The realism was outstanding; I felt as if I were experiencing the entire event first hand, as it happened. The images will stay with me forever. —*Cindy*

I have seen many Broadway shows in New York, but none of them compare to the shows at Sight & Sound. The shows truly do honor to our Lord and Savior. They bring to life the stories in the Bible. —*Lynda*

Our youth group leaders have been taking us to the Sight & Sound shows for the past couple of years. All of us love this trip the best of all. Bowling, ski trips, and ice cream parties do not even come close to watching these performances. —*Brittney*

Location

Both the Millennium Theatre® and the Living Waters Theatre are located approximately six miles east of the city of Lancaster, Pennsylvania, along PA Route 896 south between US Route 30 and Strasburg. The Branson theater is located less than ten minutes from city center.

VACATION INFORMATION

Web site: www.sight-sound.com
E-mail: customerservice@sight-sound.com
Telephone: (800) 377-1277 or (717) 687-7800
Fax: (877) 662-4849

PHYSICAL ADDRESSES (TWO LOCATIONS IN PENNSYLVANIA)

Millennium Theatre   Living Waters Theatre
300 Hartman Bridge Road   202 Hartman Bridge Road
Ronks, PA 17572   Ronks, PA 17572

NOAH'S LANDING® (NOTE: THIS IS THE RETAIL LOCATION/GIFT SHOP IN A NEARBY OUTLET MALL)

35 S Willow Dale Drive, Suite 112
Lancaster, PA 17602

PHYSICAL ADDRESS (BRANSON, MISSOURI)

Sight & Sound Theatres
1001 Shepherd of the Hills Expressway
Branson, Missouri 65616

MAILING ADDRESS (FOR ALL THEATRES)

Sight & Sound Theatres
P.O. Box 310
Strasburg, PA 17579-0310

THE GREAT PASSION PLAY

Why should I visit?

Ask almost any Christian what film or theatrical performances comes to mind when you mention the "Passion of Jesus Christ," and most will respond with either Mel Gibson's blockbuster movie (*The Passion of the Christ*) or the *Passion Play* in Oberammergau, Germany—which takes place every ten years. However, few know that America's most attended outdoor drama is *The Great Passion Play* in Eureka Springs, Arkansas. If you're looking to experience the epic drama of The Greatest Story Ever Told right here in America, head for the hills of Arkansas!

Description

With forty years under its belt, *The Great Passion Play* has been viewed by more than seven million people from every state and around the world. Each year from April through October, people fill the 4,100-seat outdoor amphitheater to witness the two-hour, spectacular drama of Jesus's last week and Passion. With state-of-the-art sound and lighting, as well as a 250-plus person cast, first-century Jerusalem comes alive with vivid colors, smells, historically accurate stage settings, Roman soldiers, and the hustle and bustle of the crowds and Roman soldiers of the time.

Attractions available

In addition to *The Great Passion Play*, other attractions include:

- *The New Holy Land Tour.* This living history experience, featuring thirty eight exhibits of the Holy Land, allows guests explore and interact with the biblical people, culture, and history of the ancient Middle East. Take the tram to meet characters from the time of Moses to Christ as they explain their significance and experiences. Highlights include speaking with a "Levitical Priest," exploring a replica of the inn where Mary and Joseph asked for shelter, stepping inside a first-century stable that is typical of where Jesus was born, walking along the "Sea of Galilee" and listening to Saint Peter, and seeing the "Upper Room" where the Last Supper took place.
- *Sacred Arts Center.* Depicting the life of Christ, the Sacred Arts Center includes more than one thousand works of religious and inspirational art.
- *Bible Museum.* As one of the largest Bible museums in the United States, this museum helps guests trace the history of Scripture via a collection of six thousand Bibles, manuscripts, and artifacts in 625 languages. View the Gutenberg Exhibit, the Greek New Testament published by Erasmus in 1516, the original 1611 King James Version, and much more.
- *Other Attractions.* Other sites to visit at the Great Passion Play include the Christ of the Ozarks statue, Parables of the Potter, The Tabernacle Tour, Smith Memorial Chapel, Wedding Chapel, Berlin Wall, and Museum of Earth History.

Special features and notes

Seating is reserved for *The Great Passion Play* performance, and reservations are recommended for the best seating available. The New Holy Land Tour requires reservation in advance. Military, veterans, and ministerial discounts are available, but they do require ID.

Group tours and special events

*   Special rates are offered for groups of fifteen or more.
*   For the best all-inclusive visit (and price) to *The Great Passion Play*, you can purchase the Premier Package. This package offers a price savings for all the activities including: *The Great Passion Play* performance, New Holy Land Tour, Museum of Earth History, Sacred Arts Center, Bible Museum, special features at *The Great Passion Play*, and dinner.

Location

The Great Passion Play is located in Eureka Springs, Arkansas, almost fifty miles south of Branson, Missouri, and just minutes west of downtown Eureka Springs on Passion Play Road, North of Highway 62.

VACATION INFORMATION
Web site: www.thegreatpassionplay.com, www.greatppassionplay.com
E-mail: info@greatpassionplay.com
Tel: (866) 566-3565
GROUP AND PROFESSIONAL TRAVEL SALES
E-mail: sales@greatpassionplay.com
Tel: (866) 566-3565

PHYSICAL ADDRESS	MAILING ADDRESS
The Great Passion Play	The Great Passion Play
935 Passion Play Road	P.O. Box 471
Eureka Springs, Arkansas 72632	Eureka Springs, Arkansas 72632

THE MIRACLE THEATER

Why should I visit?

If your family is planning a road trip to Nashville, the Smoky Mountains, or anywhere near Tennessee, you'll want to include The Miracle Theatre in your itinerary.

Recognized as one of the top faith-based theatrical productions in America, it is a spectacle not to be missed.

Description

Referred to as a "lavish, biblically accurate, full-scale Broadway-style musical that retells many miraculous events from Creation to Christ's ascension," the production was launched on Good Friday 2006. The Miracle Theater itself states:

> The Miracle attraction in Pigeon Forge, TN is a stunning musical recreation of the life of Christ told in epic proportion. Featuring an enormous cast of actors, singers, dancers, technicians, and live animals, you will be awed by the magnificence of this performance. From centurion soldiers on horseback to majestic kings on camels, the huge scope of the production is amazing. The curtains will rise with the dawning of creation, as the fingerprint of Christ is illustrated throughout the Old Testament. See angels flying overhead proclaiming His Birth. Feel the wind and the rain as Jesus calms the sea. Witness the glory of His spectacular ascension. You'll be inspired and renewed as you witness the glory of The Miracle in Pigeon Forge, TN.[6]

Special features and notes

The Miracle Theater is open year-round (except January and February), and shows take place everyday except Sunday. Depending on the day of the week, shows are offered in the afternoons and/or evenings. Season passes are available, and so are soundtracks of the performance. You can view clips of the shows at www.miracletheater.com. The Fee/Hedrick Family Entertainment Group is an East Tennessee entertainment conglomerate dedicated to family, faith, and fun. To learn more about their other theaters and shows including the Southern Gospel sounds of The Blackwoods visit www.feehedrick.com.

Group tours and special events

- A minimum of twenty paying adults is required for group rates; anything less reverts to regular rates. For group pricing call (888) 568-4253.
- Groups can ask for the Bible study program materials designed for those planning to visit The Miracle Theater; post-viewing devotional materials are also available. Call 1-866-492-6972.
- Cast members lead backstage tours before each performance while the theater is in pre-show mode. The "Producer's Pass" allows you access to all the action beyond the stage to see for yourself what truly makes The Miracle miraculous (including visiting the stables where the animals are kept).

- Camel rides are available one hour before each show at the Noah's Ark Animal Rides complex, located right in front of The Miracle Theater.

Location

The Miracle Theater is located near the heart of Pigeon Forge on Parkway/US-441 South.

VACATION INFORMATION
Web site: www.miracletheater.com
E-mail: info@miracletheater.com
Tel: (865) 428-7469; (800) 768-1170

MAILING ADDRESS
The Miracle Theater
2046 Parkway
Pigeon Forge, TN 37863

WELCOME CENTERS

FOCUS ON THE FAMILY

Why should I visit?

If you've never been to Colorado before, there are now two good reasons to visit: Not only can you explore the Rocky Mountains, but you can also visit one of North America's best known Christian organizations and one of the top tourist attractions in Colorado Springs, Focus on the Family. More than two hundred and fifty thousand people come to Colorado each year to share in this opportunity.

Description

If there's one word that sums up the essence of Focus on the Family, it's relationships. Using time-tested Christian principles and common sense, founder Dr. James Dobson opened the doors of Focus on the Family to build relationships with families worldwide in a variety of ways. Focus on the Family offers a multitude of resources (books, CDs, films, radio broadcasts, radio theater, magazines, programs) for whatever your role is in the family—as a mother or father, husband or wife, son or daughter. The people at Focus on the Family are committed to understanding your needs and doing all they can to meet them. They are ready to help when you need them.

More than a decade ago (in 1994), Focus on the Family opened its doors with its Welcome Center. To date, more than 2.5 million guests have toured its facilities. As one of the top four tourist attractions in Colorado Springs, visitors come from all over the world. Focus on the Family offers free forty-five-minute tours of the Administration Building and Operations Building. On recording days, visitors can sit in and watch a taping of the Daily Broadcast hosted by either Dr. James Dobson or Dr. Bill Maier.

It is Simply Astonishing

My first visit to the headquarters included a guided tour of the building. What I remember most is listening to the breadth of activities and initiatives that Focus on the Family has undertaken over the years, as well as what it currently oversees. It is simply astonishing. I also remember the many smiling faces and hellos I received from Focus on the Family employees while our tour group made its way through the building. Afterwards I spent time browsing the immense bookstore and the kid's area (the three-story slide looked very tempting). Fortunately, as Focus on the Family is located not far from where I live in Colorado, I am able to return there anytime I want. And you can't beat its location—-it's situated right there under beautiful Pikes Peak Mountain.—*Author*

Activities available

The Welcome Center features a display gallery, G. Harvey art gallery, and a fabulous seven-thousand-square-foot bookstore.

Downstairs in the kid's play areas is Whit's End, a turn-of-the-century soda shoppe inspired by the popular radio drama series *Adventures in Odyssey*—now celebrating twenty years of production. The play area has been voted as Best Play Area in Colorado Springs—and it's free!

Just a few things you will see in the play area are two Birthday Party Rooms, a three-story slide, puppets, costumes, Toddler Room, Narnia room, and KYDS' Radio where the kids' voices are recorded into a special take-home CD Adventures in Odyssey! There is also a 170-seat theater featuring Christian films such as *Welcome Home* and *Last Chance Detectives*.

Special features and notes

Free tours of the main administration and operations buildings are provided. Administration building tours last about forty five minutes, and operations tours are about fifteen minutes.

Group tours and special events

To reserve a free birthday party for your child at Whit's End, please call (719) 531-3400 ext. 1906.

Personal invitation

Dear Friends,

On behalf of Dr. Dobson and the entire ministry staff, welcome to Colorado Springs—one of America's most spectacular vacation playgrounds and the home of Focus on the Family! While you're here, please come visit our campus. Whether you have a couple of hours or an entire day, you'll be glad you included Focus in your family plans. For more than a quarter-century, we've focused on nurturing and defending families around the world. And we'd love to help you create some wonderful family memories!"

Sincerely,
Jim Daly, President and CEO

Location

Focus on the Family is located in Colorado Springs; take I-25 and exit at Briargate (Exit 151); travel east for about two miles, and then Focus on the Family will be on the right-hand side, located off of Explorer Drive. The welcome center and bookstore are on the north side, the main administration building is on the south side.

VACATION INFORMATION
Web site: www.focusonthefamily.com/visitus
Guest Relations Hotline: (719) 531-3328
Tel: (800) 232-6459 or (719) 531-5181

PHYSICAL ADDRESS
Focus on the Family Welcome Center and Bookstore
8685 Explorer Drive
Colorado Springs, CO 80920

MAILING ADDRESS
Focus on the Family
(street address not required)
Colorado Springs, CO 80995

THE JESUS FILM PROJECT™—
MASTER STUDIO TOURS AT LAKE HART

Why should I visit?

Whether or not you have participated in one of the 6 billion viewings of The JESUS Film Project since 1979, there is no better place to learn about its remarkable history than in person with a Master Studio Tour at the World Headquarters of Campus Crusade for Christ, an international, interdenominational Christian ministry committed to taking the Gospel of Jesus Christ to all nations.

Description

What is the JESUS film? It is a two-hour docudrama about the life of Christ based on the Gospel of Luke. Created and distributed by Campus Crusade for Christ, the film has been viewed in every country around the world since 1979 and translated into more than a thousand languages. The mission of The JESUS Film Project® is to help share Jesus Christ with everyone in his her own language using media tools and movement-building strategies. The film and project is considered one of Christianity's greatest evangelistic success stories of all time.

Activities available

* Hear how God is changing lives around the world.
* "Experience" a Third World film showing.
* Record your voice in a simulated translation.
* See how the latest technology accelerates translation.
* Learn how you can help give every person one chance to see Jesus.

Special features and notes

Tours offered daily, Monday through Friday, at 10:00 AM, 11:00 AM, 1:00 PM, 2:00 PM, and 3:00 PM.

Personal invitation

We want to extend an invitation to come and visit us in person and witness firsthand what our Lord has done and is doing through this ministry around the world. Lake Hart plays a significant role in giving every person everywhere an opportunity to say "yes" to Jesus Christ. Our headquarters serves our staff ministering worldwide in more than 190 countries, representing 99.7 percent of the world's population. God has blessed our movement with invaluable laborers.

Yours in Christ,
Steve & Judy Douglass

Location

Located at the World Headquarters of Campus Crusade for Christ (just twelve minutes from Orlando International Airport). From the airport, travel east on the 528 Tollway (also called the Beach Line Expressway). Take Exit 13 at Narcoossee Road (Route 15). Turn right onto Narcoossee and travel south two miles to Moss Park Road. Turn left onto Moss Park and travel three miles. The entrance to Campus Crusade for Christ will be on the left.

CONTACT INFORMATION

Web site: www.jesusfilm.org ; www.jesusfilm.org/aboutus/tours.html
E-mail: Tour@JESUSfilm.org
Tel: 1-888-2CJESUS (1-888-225-3787); (407) 826-2300

PHYSICAL ADDRESS

Master Studio Tour
The JESUS Film Project
100 Lake Hart Drive
Orlando, FL 32832

PART THREE

CHRISTIAN TRAVEL MINISTRY

CHAPTER 9

EVERY CHURCH SHOULD HAVE
A CHRISTIAN TRAVEL MINISTRY

CREDIT: JORDAN TOURISM BOARD NORTH AMERICA

For the first time ever, Christians are beginning to see travel not only as vacation but also as *ministry*. This is a major breakthrough. As the biblical concept of ministry is "service rendered to God and people," *travel* ministry is exactly that—rendering ministry through travel and vacation to God and His people.

Today, churches and religious organizations are finally giving travel ministry its rightful place within their communities, and many have launched programs to provide their members with Christian travel opportunities. Because so many Christians are looking for ways to integrate faith into their leisure and vacation time, now is the time to begin (or enrich) a travel ministry.

Have you ever stopped to think how many of your church members travel or vacation each year? *Consider the following:* More than half of the adults from your faith community take an average of three trips per year, spending $1500 and traveling one thousand two hundred miles from each home each time.[1] About 10 percent of your members traveled overseas last year,[2] and 15 percent have taken at least one cruise in their life.[3] With these statistics in mind, every church and Christian organization should ask itself:

- Are we providing our members with Christian travel opportunities?
- If not, then who is providing our members with travel choices?
- Where are our members receiving their trip and vacation ideas?
- Do they know Christian travel opportunities exist?
- By not offering Christian trips, are we missing opportunities for evangelization and building fellowship with our members when they vacation?

TOP FIFTEEN REASONS FOR A TRAVEL MINISTRY

Travel ministry offers so many wonderful benefits and advantages. Through travel and shared vacation experiences such as Christian pilgrimages, missions, cruises, leisure vacations, and retreat getaways, faith communities become much more vibrant and grow closer together. If your church or organization doesn't yet have a travel ministry (or a very large one), consider these fifteen reasons to build or enrich one.

1. Travel ministry deepens our faith in God.
2. It enriches personal relationships with Jesus Christ.
3. It builds fellowship and enlivens a community.
4. It enables members to experience the Christian faith and sites firsthand.

5. Travel ministry develops greater insight into and knowledge of the Bible.
6. It makes Christian history, heritage, and culture come alive.
7. Christian travel touches Christian travelers physically, intellectually, emotionally, socially, physically, and spiritually.
8. It provides a Christian vacation option.
9. It appeals to all ages including retirees, families, couples, singles, and youth.
10. Christian travel offers outreach opportunities to inactive or nonmembers.
11. It fills travel participants with inspiration, purpose, or healing in life.
12. It presents a chance to see the world and God's creation.
13. It gives the opportunity to learn about world history, events, cultures, politics, and peoples.
14. It creates a closer bond between church/organization leaders and members.
15. Finally, it can provide free travel or possibly serve as a fund-raiser.

As Christian travel embraces so many of the initiatives set forth by our faith, Christian travel ministry is in many ways the zenith of all ministries. Only Christian travel embraces and combines the many outreach ministries of a church or organization into one setting. On any given Christian trip, you can find a combination of adult ministry, youth ministry, family ministry, evangelism, faith education, biblical studies, hospitality, small groups, and more.

CHRISTIAN TRAVEL MINISTRY FUND-RAISING 101

One of the greatest benefits of a Christian travel ministry is its ability to possibly act as a fund-raiser. Hosting Christian travel events such as crusades, rallies, music festivals, concerts, or conferences can serve as a venue for acquiring necessary funds. Even leisure vacations or getaways trips sponsored by your church or organization can sometimes accomplish the same objective. No matter what the trip or vacation, your faith community can possibly turn such experiences into excellent and exciting fund-raisers.

How can the dollars received be used? Many churches and organizations will channel the money raised by travel ministry programs (or group trips) to assist with building funds, missionary work endeavors, and community projects such as feeding and clothing the homeless. And of course, the fund-raising dollars can be used to support the church and its many ministries in general.

One example of a cruise line that currently donates and gives back is Carnival Cruise Lines' Cruising for Charity program (see following box).[4]

NONPROFITS AND CHURCHES RAISE MUCH-NEEDED CASH WHILE CRUISING THE HIGH SEAS

Special to the *American-Statesman*
By Cheryl Coggins Frink
Sunday, May 20, 2007

To the casual observer, the crowd certainly appeared to be partying. After all, there was the mandatory noshing on the foie gras and lobster tails, the sunning on the tropical beaches, the day-tripping to exotic locales. Yes, these people were exhibiting in remarkable style all the appropriate behaviors associated with a luxury cruise. But they were really paying off their church's heating and air-conditioning unit. Oh, and finishing off the church's last payments for a very nice sound system. And, though it might sound too good to be true, they were retiring all that fine church debt while working on their tans and ordering room service 24/7.

If you want to get a grip on a seemingly impossible combination of activities—taking a cruise to pay off church debt—talk to members of the Metropolitan Community Church of Austin. Over the past four years, Metropolitan members, along with their friends and relatives, have taken three cruises through Carnival Cruise Line's Cruising for Charity program and, in the process, raised about $65,000 for the church. The playing/praying/paying down debt approach to vacationing has proved to be an attractive combination for the church participants. "I'd never been on a cruise before, and I thought it was wonderful," says the Reverend Karen Thompson, interim executive director and a pastor at Metropolitan Community Church. "It was great just knowing so many people and going to so many different things. You could go to variety shows or karaoke or anywhere on the ship and feel like you were at a party where you know most of the people," says Thompson, who traveled with her church on its first fund-raising cruise in 2003.

But perhaps the best part? "We were able to retire a lot of church debt," she says of the money raised through the three cruises. Through its Cruising for Charity program, Carnival has donated an estimated $1 million in matching funds to various nonprofit entities and other groups with fund-raising programs benefiting children and educational purposes, says Cherie Weinstein, vice president of group sales and administration for Carnival. The program, which now involves about two thousand Carnival cruises annually and is available with some limitations wherever the company has ships, was launched ten years ago in an effort to combine the company's commitment to charitable causes and its interest in boosting group cruises. This approach to fund-raising—and group bonding—has attracted churches, fraternal organizations, children's advocacy groups, lobbying entities, and rescue organizations. "We've done cruises with the Make-A-Wish Foundation, the Red Cross, and with fraternal organizations like the American Legion and Rotary," she says. Yet, smaller groups also work well with this sort of fund-raiser, Weinstein says. "We're working with a lady in Buffalo on something for a pug rescue shelter."

To qualify as a group, an organization must reserve at least eight cabins, with two people assigned to each room. "Some groups may end up with only twenty people, but the larger groups usually have anywhere from one hundred to three hundred people participating," Weinstein says. Carnival's program provides matching funds of $5 per night per passenger, Weinstein says. The participating group must also add at least $5 per person per night to the cost of the trip to earn the matching funds, but most groups add more—some as much as $100 per person. That surcharge, along with Carnival's matching funds, is returned to the group's cause, says Austin travel planner Amy Ford, who now works almost exclusively putting the fund-raising cruises together with Carnival.

Even with the extra trip charges that go into the fund-raiser kitty, Ford says she works with Carnival to keep costs low. For example, the first Metropolitan Community Church trip with Carnival—a five-day cruise out of Galveston to Cozumel and Cancún in Mexico—cost each participant $450, and that price included the surcharge that was donated to the church as well as taxes, says Ford, who helped organize that cruise. That kind of pricing is not unusual, says Ford, who is working on a five-day fund-raising cruise out of New Orleans to Mexico that will cost $500 per person. The program also tends to generate a good return for organizations because people outside the core group—friends, neighbors, relatives, coworkers—frequently join the trip because it serves up a planned, reasonably priced vacation that also supports a worthy cause, she says.

Such was the case with Ford's first fund-raising cruise effort, the trip Metropolitan Community Church took in 2003. "I started with my own church, which was trying to get out of debt. And it was just after 9/11, and I was trying to drum up business," she says. "I convinced the board of directors to give this a try, although they were really skeptical. We'd hoped thirty people would participate, but we ended up with three hundred. And this is in a church with four hundred members. "But we had church members, friends, neighbors, coworkers, and families of church members involved, and we raised $33,000 for the church that first year." Though a wide variety of organizations have been part of the Cruising for Charity program, Ford works extensively with churches interested in group vacations that raise money. "I'm working with about dozen churches around the country right now that are planning these cruises, churches that are willing to think outside the box, churches that are interested in trying something other than bake sales or raffles to raise money," says Ford, who owns Signature Journeys in Round Rock, Texas. "I wish I could write my church a check for $65,000. I can't. But I can help the church raise that money through these cruises."

The Cruising for Charity program also addresses another problem nonprofits often face: fund-raising fatigue. "The other thing that is so beautiful about this program is that the nonprofit doesn't have to do any of the work in executing the program," says Shannon Lipscomb, Carnival's business development manager for South Central Texas. "We formulate a plan based on a timeline and how much money the group wants to raise. The travel agent with my support works on getting out flyers and creating marketing material that the nonprofit can give to its members," she says. "You are basically handing them this planned vacation with great group pricing, and, hey, it's for a good cause."

In addition to traditional cruise activities, Metropolitan Community Church held a service the Sunday of the trip. "We brought our worship bulletins with us, we had music, and we took a special offering for the children's Sunday school program," Thompson says. Though raising money is an important goal for these cruises, some churches are especially attracted by the opportunity for members to grow closer through a shared vacation experience. That is one of the reasons First United Methodist Church of Round Rock is looking into the Cruising for Charity program. "We're hoping to get more church involvement," church member Todd Hunt says. "When you get people to play together and work together, it builds a stronger community, a stronger church."

Like Carnival, other cruise lines also offer group cruises with fund-raising angles. Holland America Line has worked with the Seattle affiliate of Susan G. Komen for the Cure and the Hospice of the Treasure Coast in Stuart, Florida, on fund-raising cruises, says Ellen Stearns, who is in corporate community relations for the cruise line. Holland America's Charity Group Program is available to nonprofit organizations that support environmental, health-related, cultural arts, educational, or maritime causes. Through the program, participating groups receive donations of $50 to $100 per stateroom depending on the length of the cruise. And Royal Caribbean Cruise Lines has fund-raising cruises with United Way when the company launches new ships, says Lynn Martenstein, vice president of corporate communications.

Although Ford is proud of the $100,000 she's helped generate for churches and other groups in the past four years, she sees great potential for growth in this cruising niche. "I've yet to hear of a church or a nonprofit say, 'We don't need money,'" Ford says. "This is a win-win situation," she adds. "You're indulging yourself while benefiting someone else."

What are some obstacles I might face when building a travel ministry program?

There are *many* reasons for your faith community to host a Christian travel ministry. Not only can such a program build fellowship, enrich lives, and deepen faith, but it can also sometimes assist the church financially through stewardship. It might not be easy, however, to implement a travel ministry program. Below is a list of the top five obstacles you might encounter from others. To help you explain the benefits and highlights of Christian travel ministry to your church or organization, I have provided a response to each concern.

1. Vacations are a luxury; we should only focus on "real ministries."

First of all, let's keep in mind that people travel—period. Whether your church hosts a travel ministry or not, the majority of people in the congregation will spend money on vacations and trips each year. In this day and age, most people do not view vacations and trips as a luxury, but rather as a right. If you do not offer Christian travel opportunities to church members, then who will minister to them while they are on vacation? Christian travel provides a service that bridges people with God, which is why it is a ministry.

2. We should not promote vacations that only some people can afford.

Whoever said that your travel ministry must promote vacations that people can't afford? To begin with, keep in mind that not everyone will be interested in or able to participate in this particular ministry of Christian travel. However, this is definitely not a reason not to offer a travel ministry program. If this were the case, most church ministries would need to be dissolved. The more important point here is this: offer a variety of faith-based travel opportunities ranging from overseas trips to local getaways so that the majority of your members can get involved in one way or another. And in many cases you will find that those who were never previously involved in other ministries will take advantage of community trips.

3. We don't have the people or resources for another ministry.

If you get the pastor to announce your new travel ministry and ask the congregation for a volunteer to lead the program, you will probably have several leaders from whom you may choose. As faith and travel are two very popular topics in almost any church setting, finding a travel ministry organizer will be much easier than you think. As for financial resources, you do not need to worry for two reasons: (1) travel ministry members pay for their own trips and activities, and (2) travel agents and tour operators often provide the resources to promote your trips. So don't let the idea of "we don't have the people or resources" stop you from starting this important ministry.

4. We have too many ministries.

So, are you saying that your members should be left without Christian travel options? Will you not provide your people with the opportunity to touch the ground where Jesus walked? Will you not provide a missionary travel option to plant new churches, spread the Christian faith, and assist those in need around the world? Will you not provide the possibility of a Christian retreat getaway? Will you not provide the chance to watch a biblical theater performance? I think you get the point. If you don't offer a Christian travel option, your members will be off on vacations that don't always build community or faith—or worse yet, where they "take a vacation from their faith."

5. We are too small a community to support a travel ministry.

Of all the five objections to a travel ministry, this one might be the most accurate, and truest, obstacle of them all. However, there is hope. Remember, travel ministry is not only about hosting long, overseas trips. Travel ministry is much more than that. Enjoying a dinner with international foods while hearing a missionary speak is travel ministry. Watching a movie or documentary together about the Holy Land or historical religious events is travel ministry. Inviting a Christian travel agent to serve as a guest speaker is travel ministry. Sharing your own previous Christian trip experiences in a group setting is travel ministry. So whether you are from a large church or not, there are ample opportunities to carry out a travel ministry.

There is no simpler way to put it—*every church should have a travel ministry*. Other Christian organizations and para-churches should also consider hosting a travel ministry or offering an annual group trip. Imagine the lives that could be changed through exploring the Holy Land, performing missionary travel, studying the Bible on a cruise, or simply traveling together on a leisure vacation and sharing fellowship. Few activities can have such immediate, powerful, and long-lasting effects as these types of experiences. By adopting such a program, this area of your members' lives will never remain "unchurched" again.

Touched Their Lives and Changed Them

The Crystal Cathedral Travel Ministry started in the 1980s with day trips to various places in Southern California and extended trips around the world. These trips were originally designed for the seniors of our ministry, since they are the ones who were not working and had the time and money to travel. Since then, our travel ministry has expanded to all ages. The people who went on our trips often brought other people from outside our ministry, and after the trips, relationships deepened and people got more involved in our ministry. Many joined our church due to the fellowship they encountered through our trips. Many people brought children and families on these trips, and because of the bonding and fellowships that took place, they started attending our Children's Ministry and school. It brought people to our church as volunteers to serve other parts of our ministry and productions of The Glory of Christmas and The Glory of Easter. Thousands of people have attended these productions every year for the past twenty-six years, and it has touched their lives and changed them to be open to the word of God! We have visited places like Branson (Missouri), San Antonio (Texas), Yosemite National Park (California), Alaska, England, Ireland, Scotland, Russia, Holland, Canadian Rockies, Panama Canal, Tahiti, Australia, New Zealand, China, Oberammergau for the Passion Play, Israel, and many more interesting cities in the United States and countries around the world. It has been my pleasure and joy to work for this ministry for the past twenty-six years in the Reservation Center and travel ministry to bring people from all over the world to visit and travel with Crystal Cathedral Ministry. I have met many people from around the world, and we have remained friends throughout the years. We have united couples in marriage after meeting on one of our travel tours. This is an awesome feeling when we can use our gifts with the Lord and bring such joy and happiness to others on our tours.

—*Sharon Hunter, Crystal Cathedral Travel Ministry*

CHAPTER 10

HOW TO BUILD A THRIVING
TRAVEL MINISTRY

CREDIT: TURKISH CULTURE AND TOURISM OFFICE, NEW YORK

O nce you've made the decision to launch a Christian travel ministry at your church or organization, how can you build it from just an idea into a thriving program? This chapter will teach you the necessary building blocks, from presenting your travel ministry idea and receiving approval to naming your program to polling your congregation on their travel interests to finding the right travel provider to obtaining a quote for a tour to promoting your very first trip—and each one thereafter. To make this easier for you, I have outlined eleven steps for you to follow. When you implement these steps, your travel ministry will be well on its way to becoming a vibrant new outreach ministry within your faith community.

STEP 1: ASK FOR AND OBTAIN YOUR PASTOR OR FAITH COMMUNITY LEADER'S APPROVAL

First, seek your pastor or organization leader's approval and blessing. Tell him or her about your planned Christian travel ministry. Describe your vision for the program along with its many benefits and advantages, as well as sharing the biblical and Christian relevance of a travel ministry. This should include highlighting outreach opportunities that your program will open up for the community. It is also a good idea to put your travel ministry idea on paper and present it in written form (see the sample letter in the box below).

When you have the chance to talk with your pastor or organization leader in person, be sure to emphasize your enthusiasm and commitment for taking on a travel ministry program. Outline your responsibilities verbally (even if you have them written out) and reaffirm your pledge and dedication to fulfilling them. You should also be ready to respond to any initial objections or hesitations about a travel ministry (see the top five most common obstacles in the previous chapter). In the midst of your discussions, you might point out other churches with similar programs or tell stories of members who have recently returned from Christian trips and how their lives were changed. Most important, ask for your pastor or leader's support, approval, and blessing. Once he or she welcomes you and the new program onboard as an official ministry of the church or organization, it's relatively smooth sailing from here on out.

(Sample Travel Ministry Letter/Proposal for Your Pastor or Leader)
TRAVEL MINISTRY—A NEW OUTREACH OF OUR COMMUNITY

Dear Pastor Jones,

I would like to present you with the idea of our church starting a travel ministry. With many of our members each year embarking on trips and vacations of all kinds, such a program would provide our brothers and sisters in Christ the option of traveling or vacationing in a Christian environment.

Imagine the opportunities for fellowship and deepening of faith. We can offer Christian pilgrimages, mission trips, cruises, leisure vacations, retreat getaways, and much more. With a travel ministry in place, our members would now have an option to travel together in community versus on their own and without the support and joy of Christian fellowship. Imagine the outreach ministry opportunities for both members and nonmembers alike. And imagine the possibilities of sharing the Gospel with others while they vacation.

If our church received your approval and blessing for a travel ministry, what would such a program look like? Below is a "Who, What, Where, When, Why, and How" of my vision for a travel ministry.

Who would be responsible for the travel ministry?

I would serve as the primary leader and group trip(s) organizer. I also plan to seek a group of volunteers to assist me.

What trips or activities would be offered?

A variety of Christian trips would be offered to members including pilgrimages, mission trips, leisure vacations, retreat getaways, as well as visits to faith attractions, Christian events, and more. We will also offer a variety of in-house Christian travel activities such as hosting international potluck dinners, watching Christian travel documentaries, inviting Christian travel agent guest speakers, forming biblical lands study and discussion groups, as well as hosting evenings of sharing travel experiences. By offering both trips and in-house activities, any church member can get involved with travel ministry.

Where will the travel ministry trips go?

We will design our travel ministry to appeal to all church members, so we will offer a variety of trips and destinations based on feedback we receive from our members. Some trips will be one-day excursions, while others will be weekend getaways. Still others will be longer trips (one to two weeks) that take place in North America or overseas.

When would the trips or activities take place?

In the beginning, we will offer one travel ministry event or activity each month. As the ministry grows, we may increase those offerings.

Why offer a travel ministry?

This will open up a new outreach ministry for our church. Many of our members embark on trips each year, but travel remains one area of their lives that is "unchurched."

Not only will a travel ministry provide an opportunity to share fellowship and deepen faith among our members, it will also open the doors for inactive and nonmembers.

How will the travel ministry operate? How will the trips and activities be promoted?
This ministry will be run by volunteers, and I will serve as the travel ministry leader and main contact person. A few of our church members are travel agents, so we'll use one or more of them as our official travel providers. If approved as an official ministry of the church, the travel ministry and its trips/activities will be promoted through the normal channels such as the bulletin, announcements, flyers, posters in the church, and word of mouth.

I hope I have provided you, Pastor Jones, with a clear vision of the proposed church travel ministry program—as well as the many benefits and blessings it will bring our community. If I serve as the travel ministry leader and organizer, you will have a very dedicated and passionate volunteer in me.

I've also spoken with others in the church community recently about the idea, and they are very excited about a possible travel ministry. If you provide me with your approval and blessing for the new travel program, I can assure you that it will become a vibrant ministry within our church and one that greatly enriches our community fellowship.

For all these reasons and more, I very much look forward to hearing from you and discussing the travel ministry in person. You can reach me any time at (your phone number).

Blessings in Christ,

(Your name)

P.S. I'd also love to invite you to join us as the spiritual leader on some of our trips!

STEP 2: NAME YOUR TRAVEL MINISTRY

Once you receive approval for your travel ministry, what do you do next? Your first job lies in choosing a title for the travel ministry. Although this is a fun step in the creation process, it is also a very important and pivotal decision to make. Whatever name you choose, that will become the travel ministry's identity to all church members—so choose wisely.

To assist you in the ministry naming process, keep in mind that you typically have three choices when deciding on a title. The first option is simply to add the name of your church or faith community before the words "Travel Ministry." For example, if your church is Bethany Baptist Church, you can choose the simple and straightforward title of "Bethany Baptist Church Travel Ministry" or "Bethany Baptist Church Outreach Travel Ministry." Or, you can use a slight variation and title your program "Bethany Baptist Church Travelers."

The second option is to pick a more creative title, yet one that still has a direct connection with the Christian faith and travel. Examples I've seen include Blessed Byways

Travelers, Holy Rollers, Travel with Angels, Paul's Travel Companions, and God's Travelers.

A third choice is to choose a fun and vibrant ministry name that is "catchy" yet still carries a direct connection to travel. Here are some sample titles of this kind: Cruisin' Creekers, Happy Wanderers, Let's Go Too, Roadrunner Travelers, and Travel with Us.

The only word of advice is to not get so cute, clever, or fancy with a program name that when someone hears it they have no idea what it is or means. Whether it includes an element of fun or not, the ideal name is one that appropriately describes the nature of the program.

Some churches and faith communities call their travel programs a "club." This is okay too. In the example of Bethany Baptist Church above, you could title your ministry "Bethany Baptist Church Travel Club." Although ministry is the primary motivator behind any Christian travel program, if the word "club" fits better for your faith community, then by all means use that word.

STEP 3: CHOOSE YOUR TRAVEL MINISTRY'S "HOME BASE"

The next question for you or the faith community to answer is this: what will be the "home base" of travel ministry operations? You need to decide if you will operate the travel ministry at the church or from your home and whether the contact information for the travel ministry will be the church itself or your own personal contact information (home address and phone number, etc.).

You should choose whatever "home base" is most practical. A small travel ministry with just a few small activities or events probably doesn't require office space at the church, especially if your position is part-time volunteer. In this type of situation, you can serve as the main point of contact with your own personal information.

On the other hand, if your travel ministry grows to a healthy size, then you may want to consider the use of church resources. This is especially true if the travel ministry becomes large enough to support full-time personnel (whether volunteer or paid). In this event, you may also want to have a phone number dedicated to the travel ministry itself.

STEP 4: FIND VOLUNTEERS

Unless you plan to take on the travel ministry by yourself, you will need to find some volunteers who can help you. Along with inviting church friends or members, you might also ask the pastor or organization director to make an announcement about the new ministry to the community and invite volunteers to step forward. Ideally you should look for volunteers who share a similar passion for the Christian faith, travel, and people. And if you can find others who either have embarked on Christian trips or have experience in the travel industry that would be an added bonus.

Once you've gotten to this point, you are ready to conduct a travel survey with your church or organization members. Poll your congregation and find out which trips, destinations, and activities they prefer. Whatever their choices, design your travel ministry calendar around their interests.

What is the best way to poll your members? For churches, the most effective way is either to insert a travel survey flyer into the weekly bulletin or to ask the pastor to provide members with five minutes during a Sunday service to fill out the form. Although not everyone may fill out and return the survey, those who do will often be those with the most interest in a travel ministry program. So this type of written survey will provide you with the clearest indication of your members' travel interests.

What should your survey look like? How many questions should you include? (See the box below for an example of a travel ministry survey.)

TRAVEL MINISTRY SURVEY

Hello! As we are planning to launch a new travel ministry at (your church or organization name), we are taking a short survey to find out the travel interests of our members. We hope to offer you a variety of vacation and travel opportunities that you can take with our Christian family. In addition, we plan to provide a number of in-house travel ministry activities and events. You can fill out this survey either individually or on behalf of your family. Your feedback will help us match your interests with our travel ministry offerings—so thank you in advance!

1. Would you be interested in taking trips with our church? Yes_____ No_____
2. Have you taken one or more vacations or trips in the past two years? Yes_____ No_____. If so, please list the type of vacation(s) and destination(s).

   _____

3. Which of the following trips would be of most interest to you? Please place the number 1, 2, or 3 next to each activity below representing your level of interest, with 1 representing high interest and 3 representing low interest.
   ___ Pilgrimage trip to the biblical lands (Israel, Jordan, Egypt, Turkey, or Greece)
   ___ Pilgrimage trip to Europe (visit Christian heritage sites)
   ___ Mission trip
   ___ Christian cruise
   ___ Leisure vacation—North America
   ___ Leisure vacation—International
   ___ Retreat getaway
   ___ Christian camp

___ Monastery visit or guest-stay

___ Adventure trip (i.e. hiking, biking, rafting trips)

___ Christian event, rally, or concert

4. Which of the following travel ministry activities would be of most interest to you? Please place the number 1, 2, or 3 next to each activity below representing your level of interest, with 1 representing high interest and 3 representing low interest.

___ Host international potluck dinners

___ Watch Christian travel documentaries

___ See travel slideshows and presentations

___ Attend Christian travel guest-speaker nights

___ Share travel stories and experiences

___ Join a travel study or discussion group (i.e. biblical lands study or discussion group)

___ Other (please list below)

_____

_____

_____

5. What is your ideal trip length? Please place the number 1, 2, or 3 next to each trip below, again with 1 representing high interest and 3 representing low interest.

___ One-day excursion (no overnight)

___ Weekend getaway

___ 3–5 day trip

___ 6–10 day trip

___ 11–15 day trip

6. What time of year would be best? Please place the number 1, 2, or 3 next to each one, with 1 representing high interest and 3 representing low interest.

___ Summer

___ Fall

___ Winter

___ Spring

7. Would you be interested in taking a vacation or trip with the church in the next year? Yes_____ No_____

8. How many people in your family would be interested in joining a church trip? _____.

9. Would you be interested in volunteering in organizing or putting together a trip? Yes_____ No_____

10. Would you be interested in volunteering for the travel ministry in an ongoing basis? Yes___ No___

STEP 6: DESIGN YOUR CALENDAR OF TRIPS AND ACTIVITIES

Once you have received and reviewed the completed surveys by members, you should be ready to develop a year-long calendar of trips and activities based on their interests. You will most likely find that many members share similar interests in types of vacations and activities desired, yet they will differ sometimes in such things as time available or time of season desired. It is wise to offer a variety of travel activities and events that cover the spectrum in regard to vacation style, trip (or activity) duration, travel distance, in-house options, budget, and so forth.

You might also consider providing your faith community with a list of major trips planned over the next three years. By doing so, you provide ample time for members to plan and prepare accordingly, both time-wise and financially. Furthermore, it gives people plenty of time to invite their nonmember family and friends on the trip.

The following is a sample calendar of travel ministry events and opportunities. Keep in mind that it isn't necessary to have trips and activities scheduled for every month of the year.

TRAVEL MINISTRY CALENDAR
- January: Watch a documentary about the Holy Land.
- February: Arrange a weekend retreat at a guest-house.
- March: Invite a Christian travel agent to be a guest speaker.
- April: Offer a one-day hiking trip and sunrise service.
- May: Host an international potluck dinner.
- June: Embark on a Holy Land trip.
- July: Visit a Christian attraction.
- August: Engage in a short-term mission.
- September: Host a travel show after Sunday services.
- October: Take a one-day regional excursion to view fall colors.
- November: Treat families to a three-day getaway in the mountains.
- December: Offer a church ski trip.
- Future trips: We also plan to host a Christian Caribbean cruise next year and an overseas leisure vacation to Australia/New Zealand in the third year. For more information and details, just ask us!

Another popular travel ministry activity that you can add to your calendar is hosting pre-trip study and discussion groups. For example, if your ministry will be hosting a missionary trip to South America, the travelers can meet monthly to study the local culture, history, and language. The same applies for any group planning to visit the Holy Land or Christian sites in Europe. Study or discussion groups do not need to end once a trip is completed. Travelers can still continue to meet on a regular basis after a trip, whether for further study purposes or to share post-trip stories and experiences.

STEP 7: FIND A TRAVEL PROVIDER

Once you've developed your calendar of trips and events, you are ready to find a qualified travel provider who can help your group. First, ask within your community if any members are travel agents or employees of a travel company. Another option is to ask church members for recommendations of travel professionals who could serve as your travel ministry provider.

In choosing a travel company, you have several options including travel agency, tour operator/cruise line, or you can book your travel arrangements directly. Below is a summary of each option along with advantages and disadvantages.

TRAVEL AGENCY

One of your best allies in developing a thriving travel ministry is finding a good travel agent (or travel agency). The benefits of finding and using a qualified travel agent are numerous, especially as these agents can often meet virtually all of your program's travel needs. You can rely on travel agents for virtually everything from travel research to providing "insider's knowledge" of destinations and tours to booking and making travel arrangements and reservations. In short, they are truly a one-stop shop. Whether you plan to offer a pilgrimage, cruise, mission trip, leisure vacation, or short getaway for your church members, a travel agent can handle planning each of these trips and reservations. (It's also important to point out here that many cruise agencies also exist. Cruise agencies are quite similar to travel agents but tend to feature a slightly stronger focus on cruising. However, many of them can also serve as a one-stop shop for most other types of vacations and trips—especially for group tours.)

Travel agents provide a personal connection you can't find elsewhere because your travel agent will usually live and work in your same area. That means you can meet with your travel agent in person on a continual basis. Best yet, as being a travel agent is a fairly common profession, you will most likely find that one or more of your church members are travel agents. There is often a no more ideal situation than a fellow church member serving as your travel ministry provider.

TOUR OPERATOR/CRUISE LINE/CONVENTION PLANNER

Another option is for you and your travel ministry to work directly with a tour operator, cruise line, mission agency, or convention planner. In many cases tour operators, cruise lines, mission agencies, and convention planners can provide all-inclusive packages and can serve as a one-stop shop for your trip or event. Another great advantage is that your church or organization can sometimes earn higher fund-raising dollars by working directly with these travel suppliers.

A disadvantage, however, is that more work falls on your shoulders. While a travel agent can usually take on all travel planning responsibilities and operations, including accepting phone calls and reservations, when you work directly with a tour operator or cruise line, you sometimes become the person responsible for collecting payments and answering phone calls from fellow members and travelers. Another disadvantage is that a tour operator or cruise line is limited to offering only their own products. A travel agent can book virtually any vacation or trip for you, such as cruises, missions, adventure travel, retreats, Christian camps, and the like.

BOOK TRAVEL ARRANGEMENTS DIRECTLY

The third option is to book all travel arrangements directly. In other words, you are responsible for acting as a "travel agent" or "convention planner" yourself by contacting and making all reservations directly with hotels, transportation (airlines, motor coaches, airport transfers, rail, etc.), restaurants, sightseeing excursions, attractions, museums, tour guides, and so forth. As this is obviously the most time consuming and absorbs the greatest risk in multiple ways, booking travel arrangements directly is recommmended in only two circumstances:

1. You and/or others on your travel ministry staff are seasoned travel agents or qualified travel planners.

2. You only need to make reservations directly with two or three venues and the trip is localized (no air transportation) and fairly risk-free. For example, a nearby retreat getaway may only need travel arrangements for bus transportation and the retreat facility itself.

Advantages of booking travel arrangements directly are that it provides the great potential for fund-raising while keeping the cost the lowest for fellow member travelers. The greatest disadvantage is the time involved and the increased risk that you and the church take on (you are directly responsible for any travel problems, mishaps, misquotes, etc.).

SUMMARY CHART FOR CHOOSING THE RIGHT TRAVEL PROVIDER

Types of Travel Providers	Advantages	Disadvantages	Overall Recommendation
Travel Agency	One-stop shop for all travel needs; personal connection; travel agent can be a member.	Possibly fewer fund-raising dollars	Working with a travel agent is ideal for your travel ministry if (1) your travel ministry is limited in personnel or time, (2) your ministry offers a variety of vacations and trips, or (3) one-stop shopping.
Tour operator/ Cruise line	Possibly higher fund-raising dollars; working directly with actual supplier of trip	More work and responsibilities fall back on you and the travel ministry; the company is restricted in its travel product offerings.	Working directly with a tour operator or cruise line is ideal for your travel ministry if (1) your ministry wants to earn the highest possible fund-raising dollars or (2) you prefer to work directly with the supplier for the purpose of customized tours, etc.
Book all travel arrangements directly	Highest possible fund-raising dollars while maintaining lowest price for member travelers	The workload and absorption of risk is the highest by booking all travel arrangements directly.	Booking all travel arrangements directly is ideal for your travel ministry if (1) a seasoned or qualified travel professional is on your travel ministry staff or (2) your ministry needs are simple and fairly risk-free.

STEP 8: EVALUATING A TRAVEL PROVIDER'S SERVICES

While you're still in the decision-making process for choosing a travel provider, what other criteria should you look for in a travel provider? If one of the goals is to reduce both your workload and any potential costs absorbed by the ministry, you will want to make sure you fully evaluate the services provided by each travel company before hiring anyone. As you want the best value, choose a travel provider that can possibly provide the following services for your travel ministry program:

Travel planning and reservations. The provider researches tours and companies for you, handles deposits, makes reservations, takes the payments, and produces travel documents.

Marketing and sales services. The travel provider gives your travel ministry promotional materials such as professionally designed brochures, flyers, postcards, and maybe even posters and other collateral materials. Some companies will even provide your ministry with Web pages that not only advertise your tour but also come complete with online registration forms, booking capability, and the ability to forward notices about the trip to family, friends, and other church members by e-mail.

OTHER POSSIBLE SERVICES TO LOOK FOR IN A TRAVEL PROVIDER

- Takes care of travel planning and research
- Offers analysis and recommendations of hotels and tour operators
- Arranges group transportation including air, rail, motor coach, car rental
- Assists in locating unique travel activities, excursions, entertainment, restaurants
- Delivers variety of travel options with comparative analysis
- Recommends trips and destinations
- Provides brochure or customized tours
- Can add pre- and post-trip extensions to scheduled tours
- Acts as travel supplier liaison and performs contract negotiations
- Secures group discounts
- Develops/provides group travel promotional materials
- Hosts travel shows and distributes travel documents
- Takes phone calls, bookings, and reservations from group participants
- Handles financial collections and disbursements
- Takes registrations by phone, fax, e-mail, or Internet
- Designs group Web page on your Web site
- Advises visa/passport requirements; health updates; insurance reccomendations; and other pertinent information

STEP 9: DECIDING ON A TRAVEL PROVIDER AND EVALUATING THEIR CREDENTIALS

Now it's time to decide which travel company is right for your travel ministry. But how can you make the right decision out of thousands of companies? The first step begins with researching and reviewing those travel companies and organizations that specialize in Christian and faith-based travel and events. Where can you look? Appendix A provides a full list of resources and Web sites. Once you've found a few possible travel providers whom you are interested in, the next step is to review their credentials.

Since you are dealing with people's dreams and money, you want to make sure that your travel ministry is working with the most reputable companies. One of the most effective and efficient ways to evaluate a travel provider's credentials is to review their organization and/or individual professional travel affiliations and accreditations. You can do this either by asking the travel provider directly or by reviewing their Web site, brochure, and other collateral materials. The following provides a list of the most prominent travel organizations and affiliations in North America. If a company belongs to two or three of the associations below, you can usually trust that the organization is a qualified travel provider or planner.

CRUISE INDUSTRY

- Cruise Lines International Association (CLIA) www.cruising.org: an organization sponsored by the cruise industry that provides training and support to approximately twenty thousand affiliated travel agencies

LODGING INDUSTRY

- American Hotel and Lodging Association (AHLA) www.ahla.com: the largest national trade association for the U.S. hotel and lodging industry

CONVENTION PLANNING INDUSTRY

- Meeting Planners International (MPI) www.mpiweb.org: a trade association for individuals and professionals who organize meetings and conventions
- Religious Conference Management Association (RCMA): www.rcmaweb.org: an international, multifaith association exclusively for religious meeting planners
- Christian Meetings and Conventions Association (CMP) www.christianmeeting.org: an organization of meeting planners who are Christians and the various suppliers who service their meetings

MOTOR COACH/TRANSPORTATION INDUSTRY

- American Automobile Association (AAA) www.aaa.com: the most prominent organization in North America that provides services and assistance for motorists
- American Bus Association (ABA) www.buses.org: the oldest and most recognized bus association in North America

RELIGIOUS TOURISM INDUSTRY

- World Religious Travel Association (WRTA)
  www.religioustravelassociation.com: the leading global network for the faith
  tourism industry; WRTA's primary purpose is to shape, enrich, and expand
  religious tourism while also connecting the travel trade with the faith consumer

STUDENT TRAVEL INDUSTRY

- Student and Youth Travel Association (SYTA) www.syta.com: an association
  that promotes and encourages student travel while safeguarding the integrity
  of its providers

ADVENTURE TRAVEL INDUSTRY

- Adventure Travel Trade Association (ATTA) www.adventuretravel.biz:
  represents the adventure and active travel industry and seeks to unify and
  promote its growth

TRAVEL AGENCY INDUSTRY

- The Airlines Reporting Corporation (ARC) www.arccorp.com: administers
  the accreditation of travel agencies
- American Society of Travel Agents (ASTA) www.astanet.com: the world's
  largest association of travel professionals with more than twenty thousand
  members, many of whom are travel agents, tour operators, cruise companies, and other tourism-related companies
- The Travel Institute www.thetravelinstitute.com: an international
  organization that administers the credentials of Certified Travel Counselor
  (CTC), Certified Travel Associate (CTA), and Destination Specialist (DS)
  programs
- National Association of Commissioned Travel Agents (NACTA)
  www.nacta.com: an association representing independent travel agents
- International Air Transport Association (IATA) www.iata.org: an association
  founded by a consortium of international airlines that certifies travel
  agencies and issues an identification card (www.iatan.org) for accredited
  travel agents

- National Tour Association (NTA) www.ntaonline.com: a travel trade association of tour operators, as well as travel agents, travel suppliers, tourist boards, and convention and visitor bureaus; offers a Consumer Protection Plan that protects travelers in the case of a tour operator's bankruptcy
- United States Tour Operator Association (USTOA) www.ustoa.com: one of the most respected and recognized trade associations in the world representing the tour operator industry
- Travel Industry Association of America (TIA) www.tia.org: a nonprofit trade association that represents the U.S. travel industry

STEP 10: REQUESTING A GROUP PROPOSAL QUOTE

Once your travel ministry is up and running and you've chosen a travel provider to work with, it's time to begin planning your first major trip. Where to begin? Let's imagine after reading through this guidebook that you decide Jordan will be the first major trip for your travel ministry. Your initial move should be to ask your travel provider for a brochure or a list of tours available for Jordan, as well as to ask if it's possible to customize a trip to Jordan.

After reviewing the itineraries provided, you will be ready to decide whether you wish for your group to embark on a predesigned itinerary or on a customized itinerary. In either case, you will need to ask your travel provider for a group tour proposal request form. This document needs to be filled out by you as a travel ministry leader in order for your travel provider to develop a price quote for you and your group.

The following *Group Proposal Request* form is a typical example of what you will receive from a travel provider (the form will, however, vary based on whether it comes from a travel agency, tour operator, cruise line or cruise agency, missionary agency, convention planner, and so forth). To assist you in learning what kind of information you will need to know in order to fill out such a form, I have provided sample answers below based on an imaginary customized trip by my organization to Jordan.

GROUP TOUR PROPOSAL REQUEST
CONTACT INFORMATION
Organization Name: World Religious Travel Association
Group Leader: Kevin J. Wright
Title/Position: Travel Ministry Leader
Address: 8156-E South Wadsworth Blvd., #338

Home or Work Phone: (800) 657-1288
Cell Phone: n/a
Fax: 294-0937
E-mail: info@religioustravelassociation.com
Web site: www.religioustravelassociation.com
What is your preferred method of contact? E-mail
What is the best time to contact you? 9AM-5PM MST (Mon-Fri)

GROUP INFORMATION

Group type/profile Association/Organization
What is the size of your group? About 45 people
What is your desired tour budget—land only (price per person; double occupancy)? $2,000
What is your desired tour budget—land and air (price per person; double occupancy)? $3,000
Preferred airline? No preference

TOUR INFORMATION

Where do you want to travel? Jordan
When do you want to travel? Spring
What is your desired tour length? 10-12 days
What are your desired travel dates? March of next year
Do you have flexibility of dates? Yes—but only plus or minus a few weeks
What is your nearest major city and airport? Denver International Airport (Colorado)
What is your preferred departure city? Denver, Colorado
What would you like to be the focus of your tour? Christian tour through Jordan
What attractions and sites would you like to visit/see? All main Christian sites and especially Mount Nebo and Bethany Beyond the Jordan (baptism site of Jesus)
What other sightseeing excursions do you request? Important nonreligious historical sites such as Jerash
Do you wish the tour to be accompanied by an escort (tour director) throughout the trip? Yes
Do you have a desired day-by-day itinerary planned (if so, please describe it here)? Here is our preliminary itinerary; however, we are open to your suggestions, ideas, and recommendations.
Day 1 Depart USA
Day 2 Arrive in Amman, Jordan
Day 3 City tour of Amman
Day 4 Jerash, Ajlun, Pella, Umm Qays
Day 5 Madaba, Mount Nebo, Karak

Day 6 Petra
Day 7 Wadi Rum
Day 8 Aqaba
Day 9 Lot's Cave, The Dead Sea
Day 10 Bethany Beyond the Jordan
Day 11 Depart for USA

HOTEL & MEALS

What hotel quality level do you prefer (budget, first-class, deluxe)? First-class

What type of hotel location do you prefer (downtown/city center, suburb, outside the city/country)? Downtown/city center

What type of lodging do you prefer (hotel, resort, boutique, other/explain)? Hotel

What hotel rooms do you request (doubles, triples, singles, quad)? Doubles

Do you prefer smoking or nonsmoking rooms? Nonsmoking

Other specific room requests? None

Which meals would you like included in the price of the tour (breakfast, lunch, dinner)? How many meals in total would you like included? Breakfast daily and dinner daily

Would you like a Welcome Reception and/or Farewell Dinner? Yes—both

OTHER INFORMATION

How many free land trips are you requesting (note: we normally provide 1 free for every 15 paying passengers)? 2 free—one for the group leader and one for the pastor

Do you want the number of free land trips adjusted in the price of the tour (i.e. 1 free for every 10 paying passengers)? No, we want the normal 1 for every 15 passengers.

Are you obtaining price quotes from any other travel companies or competitors? No, we are only requesting a quote from your company.

Is there anyone with special needs (handicap, dietary, etc.)? Not that I am aware of yet.

Would you like all entrance fees and standard admission costs included in the tour? Yes

Would you like tips and gratuities included in the price quote? If so, please advise whether to include the tips/gratuities for tour director, motor coach driver(s), local guides, and other/miscellaneous. No, please keep tips and gratuities separate from the price quote.

Which taxes would you like included in the price quote (airport, hotel, port)? Please include hotel and airport taxes in the quote.

Unless you are a seasoned professional in sales or advertising, the task of promoting a trip (or Christian travel ministry as a whole) to your fellow members can seem quite daunting at first. No need to worry though. First, as travel is a popular conversation topic in many circles, you will find that many people are very receptive to hearing about a church-sponsored trip. Second, I have provided ten ideas for promoting your Christian trip. By following these strategies, you will greatly increase your chances of hosting a very successful trip.

1. *Word of mouth.* Nothing works better for promoting a trip to your fellow members than word of mouth, especially in a church or ministry group setting. Best yet, it costs nothing.
2. *Invite nonmembers.* Encourage the community to invite nonmember family and friends. Trips are one of the best ways to attract people currently not involved in their Christian faith.
3. *Flyers and posters* (please see the following pages for sample). After receiving approval from your pastor or organization leaders, take your Christian trip flyers and put them in the church bulletin, hand them out to people after services, and place them in the church rack. Also be sure to hang Christian travel (or trip) posters around the church.
4. *Phone calls.* Conduct a calling campaign to church members and prospective travelers.
5. *Pastor or leader joins the trip.* Everyone loves a celebrity. Get your pastor or organization leader to serve as spiritual director. On trips to the Holy Land, get a Bible professor or scholar to join the trip.
6. *Pastor or leader makes the announcement.* Whether the pastor or leader can make the trip or not, be sure to obtain his or her support for the Christian travel event. This includes asking him or her to make an announcement about the trip to the congregation.
7. *Letter or e-mail* (please see the following pages for sample). Send out letters or a blast e-mail to church members about the trip.
8. *Web page.* Design a Web page about the trip and place it on the "Travel Ministry" section of the church's or organization's Web site. Your Web page can feature an "About Us" description of the travel ministry, details about the upcoming trip(s), a photo gallery of previous group trips, and travel planning tools and resources for church members (including providing information about the official church travel agency or provider, if applicable). You can also promote your trip at www.religioustravelnetwork.com.
9. *Travel show and social events.* Host a travel social event any day of the week or evening at the church and invite members to come and learn about the trip. Another popular option is to host a Christian travel show after Sunday services and provide information about the trip. This could include playing a video or PowerPoint presentation

about the planned trip. Be sure to also consider providing food and drink for attendees and turning it into a fun event!

10. *Special groups, committees, or events.* Advise fellow ministry leaders about the trip and ask them to promote the event among their members.

By implementing these ten steps, you will not only garner enough interest for the trip, but you will also generate even further excitement and interest in your travel ministry program as a whole. You can take these same promotion tips and apply them to all future trips, as well as to the overall promotion of your travel ministry itself. By doing this, you will be well on your way to hosting a thriving and vibrant travel ministry for your community.

CREDIT: JORDAN TOURISM BOARD NORTH AMERICA & RON STERN

Christian travel combines the best of faith, fellowship, and vacation.

(Sample Flyer or Poster)

OUR SAVIOR'S CHURCH TRAVEL MINISTRY
BIBLICAL JOURNEY TO ISRAEL & JORDAN

May 1-12

$2,800 (plus taxes & tips)

Join us and Pastor Fitzmorris on a life-changing trip to the heart of the Holy Land!

We will visit the land "flowing with milk and honey" and spend time in biblical cities and sites such as Jerusalem, Nazareth, Bethlehem, Sea of Galilee, Mount Nebo, and much more. We will see and touch the places where Jesus walked and ministered.

It is truly the trip of a lifetime!

How can you learn more or sign up?

Call Katherine at *Angels Among Us Travel Agency* at 933-8705.

Space is limited to fifty people. Reserve your spot today!

OUR SAVIOR'S CHURCH
FROM THE DESK OF PASTOR JOSEPH FITZMORRIS
BIBLICAL JOURNEY TO ISRAEL & JORDAN (MAY 1–12)

Dear Family and Friends in Christ,

I would like to invite you to join our church on a memorable twelve-day pilgrimage to the biblical lands of Israel and Jordan. I've chosen this trip because, over the years, many of our members have shared their dreams of seeing and touching the very places where Jesus walked. The time has finally arrived, and we will be making our journey next spring, May 1–12.

What can you experience? You will have an opportunity to explore the land "flowing with milk and honey." We will spend time in such biblical cities and sites as Jerusalem (where our Savior taught and was crucified, died, and rose), Nazareth (Jesus's hometown), Bethlehem (Jesus's birthplace), Sea of Galilee (where Jesus preached), Mount Nebo (where Moses viewed the Promised Land), and much more. And there will be plenty of time to enjoy the local culture, geography, and cuisine—all in the midst of Christian fellowship. It truly will be the trip of a lifetime!

Also, beginning next month I plan to host a monthly biblical study series in preparation for the trip. Stay tuned—I will be sharing more details about this at next Sunday's religious service, as well as in the church bulletin.

The biblical lands tour includes round-trip airfare from our hometown to Israel/Jordan. Once in the Holy Land, we'll enjoy deluxe air-conditioned motor coaches, daily breakfast and dinner, first-class accommodations, and a professional tour director and local guides. Our travel ministry director, Pat, will also be accompanying us and has some exciting fellowship activities and events planned!

How can you reserve your spot today? Call Katherine at Angels Among Us Travel Agency at 933-8705.

I encourage you to invite your family and friends—both church members and non-members alike. All are invited to explore the land of the Bible with us.

I'm very much looking forward to you joining us on this unforgettable journey of faith, fun, and fellowship.

Sincerely yours in Christ,
Pastor Joseph Fitzmorris

P.S. Remember . . . space is limited with only fifty seats!

CHAPTER 11

FULFILLING THE GREAT COMMISSION AS A GROUP TRAVEL LEADER

CREDIT: © ISTOCKPHOTO.COM/LAWRENCE SAWYER

T here is no more fitting way to complete this guidebook than by discussing the subject of fulfilling the Great Commission as a group travel leader. Up until now, we've covered the venerable tradition of Christian travel (part one), the many Christian travel opportunities available (part two), and the importance of every church or faith community hosting a travel ministry (part three). The only thing missing at this point is the discussion of _you_ and your role as a group travel leader, changing lives and spreading the Gospel through travel.

Should I become a group travel leader?

Have you ever thought about organizing trips on behalf of your church, organization, or faith community? As you have learned by now, the benefits are truly priceless, and the travel possibilities and experiences are virtually endless. You can take your members to the Holy Land and experience the Bible personally. You can lead them to Europe where they can witness Christian history firsthand. You can embark on a short-term mission in South America and assist with housing and medical needs while teaching the local population about Jesus Christ. You can host a biblical seminar cruise on the high seas of the Caribbean or a Christian crusade in a professional sports stadium. All of these opportunities begin with one person saying "yes" to the call of a group travel leader. Can that person be you?

How can I discover if travel ministry is my calling?

The key word here is "passion." If you are passionate about your Christian faith, travel, and people, then you might be called to the ministry of group travel planning or leadership. The following will help you determine the level of your passion and commitment to travel ministry.

Passionate about your Christian faith. If you plan to encourage others to embark on Christian trips or even lead them yourself, it goes without saying that you must be personally excited and passionate about your faith. Since the primary purpose of Christian travel is to deepen not only your faith but also that of others, you must be someone who is eager and passionate to share and spread the Christian faith (the Great Commission); furthermore, you should be a person who faithfully witnesses to the Christian message in word and deed.

Passionate about travel. This is probably the most obvious qualification for a group travel leader. Since "travel" lies at the heart of any travel ministry program, it is imperative that you possess a great love of travel. Your desire and passion for travel will be one of your vital assets in developing your ministry as well as getting others to sign up for a trip. Enthusiasm is often the driving force behind hosting a vibrant Christian travel ministry in your faith community.

Passionate about people. Because people are the heart of group travel, you must be a person who is passionate about people. This qualification takes on greater significance when you consider that group travel is a time to build fellowship and enrich relationships. As such, it takes a skilled "people person" who can encourage and motivate others to sign up for a trip. It also demands a capable "people person" who can carry out a journey's day-to-day operations, including answering traveler questions, ensuring the enjoyment and happiness of the travelers while they're on tour, spending time with the participants, and watching out for their safety. In short, a qualified group travel leader is one who is willing to take a genuine active interest in the travel ministry participants.

What other attributes or characteristics should a group travel planner or organizer have?

A travel ministry leader should be someone who (1) possesses attention to detail, (2) is comfortable with promoting trips, (3) enjoys being creative with travel ideas and activities, and (4) is open to inviting others on an ongoing basis to join the travel ministry or a particular trip.

First, regardless of how involved you become with the planning of a trip, your ability to be meticulous with details will enrich a vacation from beginning to end. Second, if you enjoy the thought (and challenge) of promoting Christian trips and spreading the word about them, this will help you recruit enough people to join your trip or ministry. Third, if you are creative, your creativity will be very helpful in planning a versatile travel ministry that features a variety of activities, events, and trips. And fourth, the more open and willing you are to invite others (whether church members or not) to join your travel ministry or trips, the more successful your travel ministry endeavors will be.

So, if you are passionate about your Christian faith, travel, and people and if you possess the other necessary qualities such as attention to detail and creativity, then you might be called to travel ministry leadership or group travel planning. If this sounds like you, read on!

Once I take on the role of serving as a group travel leader or organizer, what is expected of me?

The best analogy is that you become the Pied Piper. Your job is to educate and excite those around you about the joys and benefits of Christian travel while also encouraging their participation in a group trip (or travel ministry in general). You can accomplish this goal by giving presentations, hosting travel shows, distributing flyers, hanging up travel posters, sending e-mails, being available for discussion and questions, as well as possibly maintaining a Web page about Christian travel and your upcoming group trip(s).

With all the work involved in organizing or leading a trip, what is one of the perks you receive as a group travel planner? *Free travel.* That's right. As discussed earlier, many travel providers include a free trip(s) for the group leader. Most tour operators, cruise lines, and travel agencies offer special incentives for individuals who arrange group trips.

What does it typically take to earn a free trip? Although the benefits vary from one company to another, many organizations offer one free trip (not including air transportation) for every ten to twenty paid travelers. If you wish to receive a free trip plus free airfare, typically you need about twenty-five paid passengers in your group.

COMMON QUESTIONS BY GROUP TRAVEL LEADERS

What is the "magic number" we need in order to have our own customized or charter group tour?

Fifteen to twenty passengers is typically the smallest number of passengers required to charter your own group trip (that is, to include your own private transportation, personal tour director, etc.). However, because a "sole-use" group trip of twenty people can be quite pricey, the usual number for a more economically priced charter trip is thirty to thirty-five passengers. Of course, if you are able to secure more passengers than this, you can bring the price down even further.

Will others in my group know that I'm traveling for free?

That is for you to decide. Most travel companies will honor the confidentiality of your trip arrangements. However, as organizing a group trip often takes an enormous amount of work and commitment, it is only right that you earn free travel as "compensation" for your dozens, if not hundreds, of hours involved in putting together a vacation for your group or community. Your fellow members will be thankful that you have provided such a wonderful travel opportunity for them.

Do travel companies assist me in promoting our trip?

Yes. Most travel companies will print flyers and other promotional materials for your trip at no cost (or at least give you a certain amount of free materials). Some will also assist you by providing a Web site (or Web page) for your trip or travel ministry program. Still others may print posters that you can hang around your church facility. Above all, as travel companies are just as eager as you are to see your trip succeed, don't be shy to ask for help and assistance on how to promote your trip or vacation to your faith community.

And although free travel is one of the great perks and enjoyments of organizing group trips, for many Christian group planners the impetus of participating in travel ministry lies in other much greater rewards. Among these is the internal satisfaction and joy of assisting and working with the travel dreams of fellow Christians. As a group travel planner, you become the lever that enables others to fulfill their desire of visiting such places as the Holy Land, participating in mission trips, or joining an event hosted by a prominent Christian figure or ministry organization.

Many group travel planners literally see people's lives changed before their eyes. They watch people become baptized for the first time. They witness people asking God or others for forgiveness. They observe others renewing their lives. And they experience firsthand people reclaiming the passion, purpose, and inspiration they once possessed in life. For these reasons and more, many Christian group travel planners testify that these are the great rewards of travel ministry and leadership.

However, the greatest reason to participate in travel ministry and become a group travel leader is to partake in the fulfilling of the Great Commission. Because the Great Commission is the spreading of the Good News to the ends of the earth, it is a personal instruction to all followers of Jesus:

And Jesus came and spoke to them, saying, "All authority has been given to Me in heaven and on earth. Go therefore and make disciples of all the nations, baptizing them in the name of the Father and of the Son and of the Holy Spirit, teaching them to observe all things that I have commanded you; and lo, I am with you always, even to the end of the age." Matthew 28:18–20

To serve as a Christian travel group leader is one of the best ways to fulfill the Great Commission. Travel knows no boundaries and can take the Good News anywhere. In fact, it is through the travels of Paul, the apostles, and other disciples that the Gospel originally spread throughout the Roman Empire after Jesus's death. In later centuries, Christians traveled to the shores of Asia, Africa, and the New World with the same purpose in mind, to share the Good News.

Today the purpose of Christian travel remains the same: to fulfill the Great Commission. This is true whether it is a mission trip, pilgrimage, cruise, retreat, or visit to a Christian attraction. Each of these trips or vacations can and should be embarked upon with the purpose of "making disciples of all the nations, baptizing them in the name of the Father and of the Son and of the Holy Spirit, and teaching them to observe all things that Jesus has commanded." For this reason, it is common to see baptisms taking place on Christian cruises, at Christian crusades, or in the Jordan River on a Holy Land pilgrimage.

As a group travel leader, how and where can I fulfill the Great Commission?

First and foremost, you can witness to the participants on your trip. Not only can you witness to your fellow church members, but you can also witness to the nonbelievers who often go on Christian trips with their family or friends. And just how many people can you witness to as a group travel leader? If you're on a Christian pilgrimage, you can often witness to a group size of about thirty to fifty travelers. On cruises you can witness to as many as several hundred to several thousand. And if you're leading a Christian event, rally, or crusade, you can often witness to anywhere from a few hundred to tens of thousands.

Second, as a group leader you can witness to the local population that you visit on your travels. This can include people you meet the street, at the hotels or hostels, at the religious sites, in mission territories, at attractions, at a bakery, and so forth. And again, this witnessing can take place on any kind of trip or vacation that you organize or lead, ranging from a pilgrimage to a leisure vacation or even an adventure trip. When you add up the number of people you meet from a local population on a single trip, it can often range in the dozens to sometimes several hundred. And it's very common that, in situations like this, you might become the only person who ever tells someone in a local population about Jesus Christ, especially if it's in a non-Christian setting or country.

Thirdly, you can witness to travel personnel. As a group travel leader of a Christian trip, you create opportunities of witnessing to flight attendants on a plane trip, to porters who carry your bags, to hotel staff who check you in, to clerks who rent you a car, and even to your trip's professional tour director and local guides. I have seen and heard many stories of Christian travelers witnessing to tourism and hospitality personnel that resulted in amazing conversion stories. For example, I've heard numerous times of Christian cruise charters where some of the ship's personnel made the decision to get baptized while on the cruise, in the pool, and in front of everyone—and while on the job!

Above all, as a group travel leader you are given opportunities to witness and to fulfill the Great Commission in ways that are not available with other ministries. If you ever talk with a Christian who has served as a group travel leader for many years, he or she will most likely have more stories to share with you of conversions and lives changed than anyone else. In fact, the apostle Paul is a prime example of this. With all his travels through modern-day Greece, Turkey, Syria, and Rome, Paul probably witnessed more conversions and changed more lives than any other Christian of his time, all because he set out and traveled in the name of the One who issued the Great Commission.

If you accept this same call to fulfill the Great Commission through travel ministry and as a group travel leader, you are embarking on one of the great new callings of the modern era. Few areas of ministry within the Christian church provide such wonderful *and* much-needed opportunities for evangelization. This is especially poignant when you consider that the majority of North American Christians embark on vacations each year, yet only a small percentage of them travel with each other. Think of the opportunities lost in fellowship and community building. Think of the opportunities lost in taking

Christians to the Holy Land or to the roots of our faith in Europe. Think of the opportunities lost in spending time on retreat or gathering together en masse at a Christian event. Think of the opportunities lost in enjoying biblically-based plays or entertainment. And think of the opportunities lost of engaging in missionary work in those areas of the world with the most need.

When you accept your calling to travel ministry and to being a group travel leader, all these opportunities lost become opportunities realized. And who will thank you most? Your fellow Christians and church members. Because of you, they will now have an option to choose travel that enriches their life, builds fellowship, and deepens faith. Just imagine how these fruits of Christian travel will affect your faith community. Imagine the renewed vibrancy and liveliness in your church. And imagine if every Christian church globally could experience this same dynamism and robust vitality.

It all begins with saying "yes" to faith travel, just as Abraham did several thousand years ago. And it all begins with saying "yes" to serving as a group travel leader, just as Moses did before guiding his people to the Promised Land. By embarking on Christian travel today, you are saying "yes" to a venerable tradition of our faith, and you are saying "yes" to fulfilling the Great Commission of Jesus Christ. To participate in Christian travel ministry today is to participate in one of the great callings of our time.

CHRISTIAN TRAVEL WEB SITES AND RESOURCES

What is the most important decision you will ever make when planning a trip or vacation? Choosing your travel provider. When you travel with a company or organization, you are placing your (and your family's, friends', or group's) personal money, health, safety, and security into the hands of another. *The importance of this cannot be underestimated.* A poor decision here can place your finances, health, safety, and security in jeopardy. Almost every year, travel providers in North America go out of business "overnight," leaving customers without access to their several-thousand-dollar payments and, in some cases, stranded in foreign destinations.

For these reasons and more, it is imperative that you thoroughly research a travel provider prior to making a decision to travel with them and before delivering any type of payment (even a small deposit). How can you be sure that a travel provider is reputable? The following is a checklist that will help you determine an organization's credibility, financial stability, recognition (in the industry), and overall qualifications.

CREDIT: ©ISTOCKPHOTO.COM/DANE WIRTZFELD

TOP TEN QUALIFICATIONS CHECKLIST FOR TRAVEL PROVIDERS

1. What is the status of the travel provider with the Better Business Bureau? Visit www.bbb.org for more information.
2. Is the travel provider a member of any travel trade associations? Do the travel provider and its employees possess any travel professional affiliation(s) or certifications? Do the association and professional affiliations require that the travel provider or individuals maintain a standard of ethical conduct, integrity, and professional

responsibility? See a sample list of these associations in chapter 10. You can also visit www.tia.org for a list of key travel trade associations.

3. Does the travel provider carry a consumer protection plan, appropriate liability coverage for the client's protection, an escrow account, and/or appropriate professional liability insurance? Do any of these coverages and/or protection plans require that the travel provider provide financial stability, as well as additional liability coverage from suppliers? To verify if the travel provider possesses any of these consumer protection plans/programs, you can ask the organization directly for written verification. You can also review their Web site, brochure, and collateral (accompanying) materials. If a travel provider does not list any consumer protection plans on its Web site or collateral materials and cannot provide you verification in written form, then you must assume an organization does not possess any plans (regardless of what you are told verbally). Sometimes you can also get confirmation from independent sources (such as a consumer protection plan) regarding the travel provider's affiliation with any particular programs.

4. How many years has the travel provider been incorporated and operating as a travel business? Has the travel provider remained in business the entire time without interruption? Has the travel provider ever been the subject of any scandals or associated with any unscrupulous public dealings? You can usually find the answers to each of these questions independently with a little research on the Internet or by contacting a regulating body such as the Better Business Bureau. You can also visit your local library to perform research on various companies.

5. Who are the executives and/or owners of the travel provider? What is their professional background and experience? What are their credentials in travel and tourism? Most reputable organizations will list executives and/or owner profiles on their Web sites, brochures, or collateral materials. You can also ask the travel provider for the written information directly (do not accept verbal confirmation). Another option is to conduct a search on the Internet or contact independent sources, such as other organizations or personnel who possess a working relationship with the travel provider (i.e., supplier, public relations firm, etc.).

6. How professional are the travel provider's Web site, brochure, and collateral materials? Do these materials detail the company's history, trade association memberships, professional affiliations, listing of personnel, and so forth? Do the Web site and promotional materials convey a sense of a reputable travel provider, or the opposite? If it's almost impossible to learn about a company and its history, association memberships, professional affiliations, personnel, years of operation, and accomplishments through their brochure and collateral materials, this is often a sign that the company may be questionable and should be avoided until you learn more about it through an independent source.

7. How accessible and knowledgeable is the travel provider? Does the travel provider answer the phone quickly and directly—or do you always get their voicemail even

during work hours? Does the travel provider offer personal, knowledgeable, and professional service? In regard to faith-based vacations, has the travel provider worked with Christian and religious groups before?

8. Does the travel provider offer a list of testimonies and endorsements from high profile/recognizable organizations and individuals? You should be able to obtain from the travel provider a list of current or former clients to call for references.

9. What is the size of the travel provider's office? Is it a large office or a small one in terms of personnel? If it is a smaller office, does the travel provider work hand-in-hand with reputable and financially stable travel wholesalers, tour operators, and other travel groups? Does the organization truly care about you as a customer and seek to develop a lasting relationship with you (versus "just making the sale")?

10. Is the travel provider a recognized company or organization in the industry or at least locally? Make sure that independent sources (clients, industry professionals, Web site reviews, Better Business Bureau, travel trade associations, etc.) all validate the organization's years of experience, excellence, qualifications, and reliability.

TRAVEL WEB SITES AND RESOURCES

The following is a list of travel providers, contacts, and other resources for all of the travel discussed in this book. Thousands of companies and organizations are involved in Christian travel, so please note that this section is not an exhaustive list but rather a starting point for your research and travel planning. Many other qualified companies, organizations, events, and destinations exist that are not included in this appendix directory. For this reason, I encourage you to conduct further research by using the listed resource Web sites, contacting your ministry organization or denomination headquarters, discussing Christian travel options with your family, friends, church members, pastor, and religious leaders, as well as speaking with an independent travel professional such as your personal travel agent or travel provider. If you do not have a travel agent, you might begin by visiting the ASTA directory (www.astanet.com), which provides a listing of accredited travel agents throughout North America.

Because the list of companies, organizations, Christian events, and so forth continues to expand and grow each year, if you wish to stay abreast of the "latest and greatest" in Christian travel, you can always refer to the directory at the World Religious Travel Association Web site www.religioustravelassociation.com. The WRTA serves as the world's most comprehensive Christian and faith-based travel directory, and the registry is continuously updated and new entries added almost daily.

Above all, the final decision and responsibility of choosing a travel provider rests solely with you. All companies and organizations listed in this book are provided for listing purposes only, not as recommendations; therefore, it is imperative that you conduct thorough research of any travel provider before selecting one. It is also imperative that you perform due diligence in selecting a travel provider that meets the *Top Ten Qualifications Checklist for Travel Providers* criteria and that also possesses the necessary credentials, consumer protection plans, professional liability insurance, and so forth. And it is your responsibility to purchase travel insurance at the time of making a trip reservation or booking, regardless of the travel provider you choose.

PILGRIMAGES AND TOURS

- Visit the Web site for the World Religious Travel Association (WRTA) at www.religioustravelassociation.com. You can search here for tour operators, travel agents, and other travel providers of Christian and faith-based travel.
- Visit the Web site for the United States Tour Operator Association (USTOA) at www.ustoa.com. You can search here for tour operators, and you can even search by topics such as "religious."
- Visit the Web site for the National Tour Association (NTA) at www.ntaonline.com. You can search here by clicking on "Find an NTA Tour Operator" and then refine your search by clicking on "religious."

TRAVEL AGENTS

One of the best recommendations is to work closely with a travel agent whether for individual or group travel. Most travel agencies work with a variety of tour operators, cruise lines, and suppliers. To learn more about finding a qualified travel agent, visit www.religioustravelassociation.com or visit the Web site for the American Society of Travel Agents (ASTA) at www.astanet.com. You can search for an ASTA-affiliated travel agent near you by inserting your zip code (for a larger list of agents in your region, enter only the first number or two in your zip code). You can also perform an "advanced search" by refining your search to the specialty category of "religious."

TOUR OPERATOR AND TRAVEL PROVIDER LINKS

7Tur: www.7tur.com
Alpha Christian Tours: www.alphatours.com
Altura Tours: www.alturatours.com

America Israel: www.americaisrael.us
Ancient Adventures: www.ancientadventures.com
Art to Heart: www.arttoheartweb.com
Arza World: www.arzaworld.com
Avia Tours: www.aviatours.net
Bell Wholesale Travel: www.bwti.com
Best Catholic Pilgrimages: www.bestcatholic.com
Bob Neff Tours: www.bobnefftours.com
Brennan Vacations: www.brennanvacations.com
Burke Christian Tours: www.burkechristiantours.com
Canadian Gateway: www.canadiangateway.com
China Christian Travel Service: www.chinachristiantour.com
Christian Travel Finder: www.christiantravelfinder.com
Christian World Travel: www.christianworldtravel.com
Collette Vacations: www.collettevacations.com
Consolidated Tours: www.ctoinc.com
Coral Travel and Tours: www.coraltours.org
Covenant Tours: www.covenant-tours.com
Craig Travel: www.craigtravel.com
Creative Travel Partners: www.creativetravelpartners.com
Dehoney Travel: www.dehoneytravel.com
Discovery Ministries: www.discoveryministries.com
Ed Hill Tours: www.edhilltours.com
Educational Opportunities Tours: www.eo.travelwithus.com
Egypt Tours and Travel: www.egypttours.com
Fellowship Travel: www.fellowship.com
Friendly Planet Travel: www.friendlyplanet.com
Friendship Tours: www.friendshiptours.com
Gama Tours: www.gamatours.com
Gate 1 Travel/Classic Pilgrimages: www.gate1travel.com
George's International Tours: www.georgesintl.com
Gil Travel: www.giltravel.com
Globus: www.globusjourneys.com; www.globusfaith.com
Glory Tours: www.glory-tours.com
GM Tours: www.gmtours.com
Group IST: www.groupist.com
Heavenly International Tours: www.heavenlytours.com
Holy Lands Sun Tours: www.holylandssuntours.com
IGM Tours: www.igmtours.com
Insight Vacations: www.insightvacations.com
Israel Tour Connection: www.israeltour.com

Israel Vision Tours: www.israelvisiontours.com
Isram World: www.isram.com
JeriCo Christian Journeys: www.jericojourneys.com
Jerusalem Tours: www.jerusalemtours.com
Journeys Unlimited: www.journeys-unlimited.com
LeSea Tours: www.leseatours.com
Luther Tours: www.luthertours.com
Lynott Tours: www.lynotttours.com
Maranatha Tours: www.maranathatours.com
Margaret Morse Tours: www.margaretmorsetours.com
Maupintour: www.maupintour.com
Mayflower Tours: www.mayflowertours.com
Meander Travel: www.meandertravel.com
Morning Star Tours: www.morningstartours.com
MTS Travel: www.mtstravel.com
Nawas International: www.nawas.com
Omega Travel: www.omegatravelusa.com
Pacific Delight Tours: www.pacificdelighttours.com
Peter's Way Tours: www.petersway.com
Pilgrim Tours: www.pilgrimtours.com
Priority Travel and Tours: www.prioritytravelandtours.com
Quest Travel Group, The: www.questtravelgroup.com
Rainbow Tour Turkey: www.rainbowtourturkey.com
Raptim Travel: www.raptimusa.com
Regina Tours: www.regina-tours.com
Reformation Tours: www.reformationtours.com
Rostad Tours: www.rostad.com
St. Francis Pilgrimages: www.stfrancispilgrimages.com
Sunny Land Tours: www.sunnylandtours.com
Sweet Magnolia Tours (Branson): www.sweetmagnoliatours.com
Tours 206: www.206tours.com
Tours thru the Book: www.toursthruthebook.com
Trafalgar Tours: www.trafalgartours.com
Trinity World Tours: www.gotrinitytours.com
Ultimate Journeys: www.ultimatejourneystravel.com
Unitours: www.unitours.com
Wilcox World Travel and Tours: www.holylandtours.com
World Express Travel: www.worldexpresstravel.com
World Mission Tours: www.womito.com
Worldwide Christian Tours: www.worldwidechristiantours.com
Ya'lla Tours: www.yallatours.com

YMT Vacations: www.ymtvacations.com
Zealandier Tours: www.zealandier.co.nz

MISSIONARY TRAVEL

BOOKS

Mission Handbook: U.S. and Canadian Ministries Overseas by Brant L. Myers provides more than six hundred pages of information on North American ministries that serve overseas.

NEWS, RESEARCH, AND MISSIONARY TRAVEL LINKS

Association of Gospel Rescue Missions: www.agrm.org
Finishers: www.finishers.org
Mission Finder: www.missionfinder.org
Mission Groups links: www.mnnonline.org/groups
Mis-Links: www.mislinks.org
Mission Next: www.missionnext.com
Mission Network News: www.missionnetworknews.org
NVision: www.thebodybuilders.net
Perspectives on the World Christian Movement: www.perspectives.org
Preparing to Go: www.preparingtogo.com
Right Now: www.rightnow.org
Short-term Missions: www.shorttermmissions.com
Standards of Excellence in Short-term Missions: www.stmstandards.org
The Center for the Study of Global Christianity: www.globalchristianity.org
The Journey Deepens: www.thejourneydeepens.com
The Network for Strategic Missions: www.strategicnetwork.org
The Next Step: www.thenextstep.org
Urbana: www.urbana.org
Wycliffe: www.wycliffe.org

DENOMINATIONS

Nazarene: www.nazareneworldmission.org
Baptist: www.imb.org (International Mission Board)
Lutheran Service Corps: www.lscomaha.org

Mennonite Mission Work: www.mennonitemission.net
Presbyterian Church of America: www.mtw.org (Mission to the World)
Salvation Army: www.salvationarmy.com
United Methodist: www.umvim.org (United Methodist Volunteers in Mission)
Catholic: www.uscatholicmission.org (United States Catholic Mission Association) and
www.worldmissions-catholicchurch.org (The Pontifical Mission Societies in the
    United States)

MISSIONARY TRAVEL OPPORTUNITIES

Adventures in Missions: www.adventures.org
Africa Inland Mission International: www.aimint.org
Association of Baptists for World Evangelization: www.abwe.org
Avant Ministries: www.avantministries.org
Baptist Mid-Missions: www.bmm.org
Bethany Fellowship: www.bethanyinternational.org
Caleb Project: www.calebproject.org
CAM International: www.caminternational.org
Casas por Cristo: www.casasporcristo.org
Catholic Medical Mission Board: www.cmmb.org
Child Evangelism Fellowship: www.cefinc.org
Christ in Youth: www.ciy.com
Christian Appalachian Project: www.christianapp.org
Dawn Ministries: www.dawnministries.org
Evangelical Foreign Missions Association: http://efma.gospelcom.net
Foreign Missions Conference of North America: http://foreignmissions.com
Glenmary Home Missionaries: www.glenmary.org
Global Frontier Missions: www.globalfrontiermissions.com
Global Opportunities: www.globalopps.org
Global Outreach International: www.globaloutreach.org
Golden Rule Travel: www.goldenruletravel.com
In His Image: www.inhisimage.org
Interdenominational Foreign Missions Association of North America:
    www.ifmamissions.org (For an excellent list of mission agencies, visit
    www.ifmamissions.org and then click on "member missions.")
InterServe: www.interserve.org
InterVarsity Christian Fellowship: www.intervarsity.org
Jesus Film Mission Trips: www.jesusfilmmissiontrips.org
Joshua Project: www.joshuaproject.net
Life Connections International: www.lifeconnectionsintl.com
Medical Ambassadors International: www.lifewind.org

Medical Ministry International: www.mmint.org
Medical Missions: www.medmissions.org
Mercy Ships: www.mercyships.org
Mission Alive: www.missionalive.org
Missionary Aviation Fellowship: www.maf.org
Mission Year: www.missionyear.org
Northwest Medical Teams: www.nwmti.org
Operation Mobilization: www.om.org
Overseas Express: www.ovex.com
Overseas Ministries Study Center: www.omsc.org
Overseas Missionary Fellowship: www.omf.org
Partners International: www.partnersintl.org
Raptim Travel: www.raptimusa.com
Serving in Mission: www.sim.org
Short-Term Evangelical Missions: www.stemintl.org
Student Volunteer Movement 2: www.svm2.net
The Evangelical Alliance Mission (TEAM): www.teamworld.org
TEAR Fund: www.tearfund.org
The Jesus Film Project: www.jesusfilm.org
The World Race: www.theworldrace.org
United States Center for World Missions: www.uscwm.org
World Servants: www.worldservants.org
World Vision: www.worldvision.org
World Wide Youth Camps: www.wwyc.org
Youth Group Mission: www.groupworkcamps.com
Youth with a Mission: www.ywam.org
Youth Works: www.youthworks.com

TIPS FOR SEARCHING THE INTERNET

When searching the Internet for missionary travel opportunities or information, try these search terms: missionary travel, missionary trips, short-term missions, Christian missions, and missionary travel insurance.

VOLUNTEER VACATIONS

Catholic Network of Volunteer Service: www.cnvs.org/volunteers
Christian Voluntouring: www.christianvolunteering.org
Crisis Recovery International: www.crisisrecoveryinternational.com

Global Volunteers: www.globalvolunteers.org
Habitat for Humanity: www.habitat.org
The Volunteer Family: www.thevolunteerfamily.org
Tourism Cares for America: www.tourismcares.org

FELLOWSHIP VACATIONS

Leisure vacations

To find a travel provider for your leisure vacations, you can use the same search recommendations found in the Pilgrimages and Tours section of this appendix. For example, you can visit the Web sites and directories of www.religioustravelassociation.com, www.astanet.com, www.ustoa.com, and www.ntaonline.com. However, instead of refining your searches with "religious," you can leave your search open and unrestricted.

LEISURE VACATION LINKS

African Travel and Tourism Association: www.atta.co.uk
America's Byways: www.byways.org
Arab World Travel and Tourism Association (AWTTA): www.awtta.com
Branson Church Groups: www.bransonchurchgroups.com
Canada: www.canada.travel
Caribbean Tourism Organization: www.doitcaribbean.com
Convention and Visitor Bureaus: www.tia.org/pressmedia/cvb_directory.asp
Latin American Travel Association: www.lata.org
National Park Service, U.S. Department of the Interior: www.cr.nps.gov
National Register of Historic Places, U.S. Department of the Interior:
    www.cr.nps.gov/nr
National Register of Travel Itineraries, U.S. Department of the Interior:
    www.cr.nps.gov/nr/travel
See America: www.seeamerica.org
South Africa Tourism (SAT): www.southafrica.net
South and Central American Travel Association: www.sata-usa.com
South Pacific Tourism Organization (SPTO): www.spto.org; www.south-pacific.travel
Southeast Asia Tourism (ASEAN): www.asean-tourism.com
State Tourism offices: www.tia.org/pressmedia/sto_directory.asp
Tourist Information Directory: www.touristinformationdirectory.com
Tours.com: www.tours.com

USA Tourist: www.usatourist.com
Visit Central Europe: www.visitcentraleurope.com
Visit Europe: www.visiteurope.com

Christian cruising

To find a CLIA certified cruise counselor (agent), you can visit the Cruise Lines International Association (CLIA) Web site www.cruising.org. You can search for agents in your area by inserting your zip code (for a larger list of agents in your region, enter only the first two or three numbers in your zip code). The CLIA Web site www.cruising.org also provides a listing of cruise lines and educational information for anyone interested in or planning a cruise.

CRUISE AGENCIES AND OTHER LINKS

Christian Travel Finder: www.christiantravelfinder.com
Group IST/Waterways: www.worldwaterways.com
Inspiration Cruises: www.inspirationcruises.com
JRI Cruises: www.christiancruises.com
Louis Cruise Lines: www.louiscruises.com
Monarch Classic Cruises: www.mccruises.gr
Premier Christian Cruises: www.premierchristiancruises.com
Steps of Paul Coastal Cruises: www.stepsofpaul.gr; www.stepsofpaul.com
Templeton Tours: www.templetontours.com

Adventure vacations

To search for tour operators and travel providers specializing in adventure travel, you can visit the Adventure Travel Trade Association (ATTA) Web site www.adventuretravel.biz.

ADVENTURE VACATION LINKS

African Christian Tours and Safaris (ACTS): www.actsoverland.com
Challenge Point: www.challengepoint.org
Christian Adventure Association: www.caainfo.org
Christian Adventure Camps: www.christianadventurecamps.org
Christian Adventures: www.christianadventures.org
Christian Adventures Fellowship: www.itsanadventure.org
Christian Mission Tours and Safaris: www.christianmissiontours.com

Christian Outdoor Guide: www.christianoutdoorguide.com
Cross-country Overland Missions: www.crosscountrymissions.com
Footstep Safaris: www.footstepsafaris.com
Gofan Safaris and Travel Africa: www.gofansafaris.com
Going the Distance Adventure Ministry: www.goingthedistance.org
Gordon's Guide: www.gordonsguide.com
His 2 Overcome Adventure Ministries: www.his2overcome.org
Leadership Treks: www.leadertreks.com
Looking for Adventures: www.lookingforadventure.com
The Adventure Guild: www.theadventureguild.com
Wilderness Trail: www.wtrail.com

Student and youth vacations

To search for tour operators and travel providers specializing in student travel, you can visit the Student Youth Travel Association Web site www.syta.org.

STUDENT AND YOUTH VACATION LINKS

American Christian Tours: www.acts-tours.com
Christian Discoveries: www.christiandiscoveries.com
Youth Group Travel: www.youthgrouptravel.com

CHRISTIAN EVENTS, RETREATS, CAMPS, AND MONASTIC GUEST-STAYS

In addition to the links below, you can perform searches on the Internet with terms such as "Christian events," "Christian crusades," "Christian concerts," "Christian theatre (or theater)," "Christian performances," and so forth. If you will be planning a Christian event, conference, retreat, seminar, workshop, or the like, you might consider the book *The Christian Conference Planner* by Angela Yee.

CHRISTIAN EVENTS LINKS

Christian Comedy Association: www.christiancomedyassociation.com
Christian Concert Search Engine: www.ccauthority.com

Christian Concerts: www.christianconcerts.com
Christian Happenings: www.christianhappenings.com
iTickets: www.itickets.com
Ticket Servant: www.ticketservant.com

CHRISTIAN FESTIVAL LINKS

Agape Festival: www.agapefest.com
Alive Festival: www.alive.org
Atlanta Fest: www.atlantafest.com
Collide Festival: www.collidefestival.com www.collidefest.com
Cornerstone California: www.cornerstonecalifornia.com
Cornerstone Festival: www.cornerstonefestival.com
Cornerstone Florida: www.cornerstoneflorida.com
Creation Festival: www.creationfest.com
Ichthus: www.ichthus.org
Kingdom Bound: www.kingdombound.org
King's Fest: www.kingsfest.com
LifeLight Festival: www.lifelight.org
Lifest: www.lifest.com
Purple Door Festival: www.purpledoor.com
Rock the Coast: www.rockthecoast.net
Rock the Desert: www.rockthedesert.com
Rock the Light: www.rockthelight.com
Rock the Universe: www.rocktheuniverse.com
Sonshine Festival: www.sonshinefestival.com
SoulFest: www.thesoulfest.com
Spirit Song: www.spiritsongfestival.com
Sprit West Coast: www.spiritwestcoast.org
Unity Christian Music Festival: www.unitymusicfestival.com

DENOMINATIONAL CONVENTION LINKS

To learn about conventions hosted by various denominations, you can visit their respective Web sites by visiting www.usachurch.com (or www.usachurch.com/christian_denominations.htm), www.usachurches.org (and click on "Christian denominations"), www.religiousresources.org (click on Traditions and Denominations), or www.religionfacts.com/christianity/denominations.htm.

CHRISTIAN RETREAT LINKS

The Christian Camp and Conference Association (www.ccca.org) is an excellent resource for researching and finding Christian conference and retreats. Another good Web site is www.christianconferencecenters.com. You can also conduct a search on the Internet with terms such as "Christian retreats," "Christian retreats listing," and "Christian retreats directory."

CHRISTIAN CAMP LINKS

The Christian Camp and Conference Association (www.ccca.org) is the number one resource for researching and finding a Christian camp. You can also visit the Christian Camp Leaders Web site www.cclcamps.org and Christian Adventure Camps www.christianadventurecamps.org. If you conduct research on the Internet, a few excellent search terms to use include "Christian camp, "Christian day camp," "Christian work camp," "Christian wilderness camp," "Christian special needs camp," and "Christian travel camp."

MONASTIC GUEST-STAYS LINKS

For an extensive listing of monasteries including those with guesthouses, visit www.religioustravelassociation.com and then click on "Directory." Here you will find listings for monasteries, convents, monastic guesthouses, and places of retreat. If searching on the Internet, the best search terms to use include "monastic guesthouse," "monastery guest stays," "monastery guesthouse directory," and "monastery retreats."

MONASTIC AND RELIGIOUS ORDERS LINKS

Augustinian Order: www.osanet.org
Benedictine Order: www.osb.org
Carmelite Order: www.ocarm.org
Carthusian Order: www.chartreux.org
Cistercian Order of the Strict Observance (Trappists): www.ocso.org
Discalced Carmelite Order: www.ocd.pcn.net
Dominican Order: www.op.org
Franciscan Order: www.ofm.org
Franciscan Order, Capuchins: www.capuchins.org
Franciscan Order, Conventual: www.ofmconv.org
Orthodox Monasteries: www.orthodox-monasteries.com

CHRISTIAN ATTRACTIONS

If you are conducting a search on the Internet for Christian attractions, you might consider search terms such as "Christian attractions," "Christian theaters (or theatres)," "Christian theme parks," "Christian biblical parks," "Christian museums," "Christian welcome centers," and "Christian performances." You can also visit the following Web sites, although they primarily feature non-faith-based attractions: www.themeparkcity.com, www.museumsusa.org, www.aam-us.org, www.touristinformationdirectory.com (then click on amusement parks and theme parks), and Travel Industry Association www.tia.org/pressmedia/attr_directory.asp (then click on Attractions).

TRIP PLANNING TOOLS AND WEB SITES

GENERAL TRIP PLANNING

Airline (group booking specialists): www.objectix.com

Airline complaints (delays, baggage): http://airconsumer.ost.dot.gov

Airline delays: www.fly.faa.gov/flyfaa/plaintext.html

Airline flight status: www.flightstats.com

Airline seats: www.seatguru.com

Airline tickets: www.kayak.com; www.sidestep.com

Airline toll free numbers: www.tollfreeairline.com

Airline tracker: www.flightarrivals.com

Airport security wait times: http://waittime.tsa.dhs.gov

Airports (information, maps): www.airports.com

Bus and subway directions: www.hopstop.com

Calendar and holidays: www.timeanddate.com/calendar

Calling codes: www.countrycallingcodes.com

Country facts: www.cia.gov/library/publications/the-world-factbook/index.html

Currency converter/foreign exchange data: www.oanda.com; www.xe.com

Customs (USA): www.customs.ustreas.gov

Department of Homeland Security: www.dhs.gov

Driving directions: www.mapquest.com; www.randmcnally.com;
    www.viamichelin.com; www.theaa.com; www.maps.google.com

Electric Guide: www.kropla.com

Embassies: www.embassyworld.com; www.tripresource.com/embassy.htm

Emergency/disaster information: www.redcross.org; www.disasternews.net;
    www.fema.gov

FAA Air Traffic Control: www.faa.gov

Farecast: www.farecast.com

Flight delay information: www.fly.faa.gov/flyfaa/usmap.jsp

Flight tracker: www.flightview.com

Frequent flyer programs: www.webflyer.com

Group travel planners: www.grouptour.com; www.goexperience.com;
www.glamer.com

Health (travel health info): www.cdc.gov; www.who.int; www.who.org;
www.passporthealthusa.com; www.tripprep.com

Hostels: www.hostels.com; www.hostelworld.com

Internet access/hotspots: www.wi-fihotspotlist.com; www.wififreespot.com

Language translation (learning phrases): http://babelfish.altavista.com/tr

Last-minute travel planning: www.dontforgetyourtoothbrush.com

Lodging (Christian lodging): www.christianhospitalitynetwork.org,
ACH Hotels: www.christian-hotel.com

Passports and visas: www.embassy.com; www.projectvisa.com;
http://travel.state.gov; http://travel.state.gov/passport; www.travisa.com

Physical disabilities and special needs travel: www.access-able.com

Time around the world: www.timeanddate.com/worldclock;
www.worldtimezone.com; www.time.gov

Tipping guide: www.tipping.org

Tourist offices and embassies (worldwide): www.towd.com;
www.embassyworld.com;
www.tripresource.com/embassy.htm

Traffic advisories: http://traffic.tann.net

Trains: www.cwrr.com; www.railagent.com; www.amtrak.com;
www.railpass.com; www.eurail.com; www.raileurope.com

Transportation Security Administration (TSA): www.tsa.gov

Transportation Security Administration Traveler's Tips:
www.tsa.gov/travelers/index.shtm

Travel planning: www.worldtravelguide.net

Travel planning (religious sites): www.sacred-destinations.com;
www.bibleplaces.com

Travel planning (USA): www.homeandabroad.com; www.planetware.com

Travel planning (worldwide): www.homeandabroad.com;
www.worldtravelguide.net

Trip planning tools and resources: www.religioustravelassociation.com

U.S. State Department and Travel Warnings: http://travel.state.gov

Visas (see Passport and Visa Information)

Weather around the world: www.weather.com; www.accuweather.com;
www.intellicast.com

World Health Organization: www.who.int/eha/disasters

TRAVEL AND TOURISM ASSOCIATION AND ORGANIZATIONS

Travel and Tourism Research Association (TTRA): www.ttra.com
World Tourism Organization (WTO): www.world-tourism.org

SPECIAL TRIP PLANNING NOTES

Health

If you plan to travel outside of the country, you should contact a travel health provider immediately after booking your trip so that you can discuss what you must do to prepare and protect yourself for each destination you plan to visit. Your health should not be taken lightly when you are embarking on a trip for multiple reasons, ranging from the unpleasantness of being sick to missing out on your vacation (or mission trip) due to the enormous costs of visiting hospitals and doctors overseas for medical or emergency purposes. For more information about travel health protection and requirements, visit the Web sites of www.cdc.gov; www.who.int; www.who.org; www.passporthealthusa.com; and www.tripprep.com.

Passport and Visa Information

Passports and visa rules can change often, so it is imperative that you learn the travel requirements of the foreign countries you plan to visit before making a trip reservation or booking. Obtaining a passport and/or visa (as well as knowing whether you need one or not, and if so, to which countries) *is the responsibility of the traveler* and not the travel provider. Regarding passports, it is typically required that at least two blank pages are available and that your passport is valid for at least six months beyond the conclusion of your trip. Regarding visas, it is the traveler's responsibility to contact the respective consulates or visa agencies to determine whether any visas are required. You should begin checking into passport and visa requirements about a year before a trip (or immediately upon booking a trip if you are within one year of departure). As with traveler health requirements, obtaining the necessary travel documentation for your trip is not to be taken lightly. Don't procrastinate. Without proper documentation, you risk forfeiting your entire trip with no recourse to reimbursement or, worse yet, being advised while traveling outside the United States that you are not allowed entry into another country due to missing or inaccurate documentation. For more information about passports, visas, and travel documentation requirements, visit www.embassy.com; www.projectvisa.com; http://travel.state.gov; www.travisa.com.

Travel Insurance

No matter how well you plan your trip or vacation, things can go wrong. Trips can turn from life's most memorable moments into life's most challenging or even disastrous moments due to illness, medical emergencies, severe weather, missing or lost luggage, delayed flights, stolen passports or visas (or belongings of any kind), identity theft, security risks, change in political conditions, terrorism, and simply any other form of travel disruption. When such events happen, it's not uncommon if you are forced to alter, interrupt, or simply cancel your trip altogether. Not only can you risk losing your entire vacation investment, but you may even be forced to incur additional and potentially very large unplanned expenses. For these reasons and more, every traveler should consider purchasing travel insurance. If you will be traveling with a group (such as your church or faith community), travel insurance should be mandatory for all, especially if it's an international trip or vacation. To learn more about travel insurance, contact your travel provider or a travel insurance company and specialist. To find a travel insurance provider visit www.religioustravelassociation.com (and then click on the travel insurance section in the directory). You can also research travel insurance providers on the Internet by searching for "travel insurance," "travel insurance directory," or "travel insurance providers."

TRAVEL MINISTRY RESOURCES AND MATERIALS

WORLD RELIGIOUS TRAVEL ASSOCIATION

Global network and community of the religious travel industry
www.religioustravelassociation.com

The World Religious Travel Association (WRTA) is the leading organization dedicated to shaping, enriching, and expanding faith travel around the world. As a global network and community, WRTA's membership includes Christian travelers, group planners, churches, pastors and clergy, ministry organizations, travel companies and suppliers, tourist boards, and convention and visitor bureaus. Anyone can join for free. The World Religious Travel Association serves as a one-stop shop for Christian travel group planners and travelers. You can view and research vacation opportunities, travel companies, and travel agencies from throughout North America and around the world. In addition, as a free member you can access the association's many planning tools and resources specific to group planners and individual travelers.

WORLD RELIGIOUS TRAVEL EXPO
AND EDUCATIONAL CONFERENCE

International tradeshow and educational conference for faith tourism
www.religioustravelexpo.com

Join hundreds of Christian group planners, churches, travel agencies, tour operators, tourist boards, and travel companies at the annual World Religious Travel Expo and Educational

Conference. Learn how to develop or enrich your travel ministry by attending the educational seminars, while also meeting other leaders involved in Christian travel ministry. At the tradeshow event, you can interact with hundreds of travel providers specializing in faith tourism by visiting their booths and exhibits. Top entertainment and local sightseeing excursions for the faith travel planner round out the event. It is the single most important event of the year to attend for any church, organization, group planner, or individual involved in Christian and faith-based travel.

WRTA SOCIAL NETWORK

A social network for Christian and faith-based travelers
www.religioustravelnetwork.com

Whether you are an individual traveler or group planner, you can join the world's first-ever social network and community for Christian and faith-based travel at www.religioustravelnetwork.com. You can post videos, photos, music, and blogs of your Christian trips while meeting other travelers with similar interests. You can also join groups or create your own. Possibly best yet, you can host your church or organization's travel ministry program on the network for free. Along with chatting and communicating with others on the network, you can research travel destinations, companies, agencies, and vacation options from around the world, including viewing other Christian travelers' photos and videos. Once you sign up with the WRTA Social Network, be sure to join *The Christian Travel Planner* group on the network. This is a group designed specifically for readers of this guidebook.

RELIGIOUS TRAVEL BUZZ

Keeping you abreast of faith tourism news, announcements, and press releases
www.religioustravelassociation.com

As the official e-newsletter publication of the World Religious Travel Association, *Religious Travel Buzz* keeps you abreast of the latest in Christian and faith travel news, events, and announcements. Each issue comes complete with stories of travel destinations, breaking news, company profiles, travel ministry tips, faith tourism conferences and events, and much more. To receive your free subscription, visit www.religioustravelassociation.com or send an e-mail to info@religioustravelassociation.com and ask to receive *Religious Travel Buzz.*

GOING ON FAITH

National newspaper for religious travel groups
www.goingonfaith.com

Going on Faith is the national newspaper for Christian and faith-based travel groups. The publication also serves as the official newspaper and host of the *Going on Faith Conference* (www.gofconference.com), an annual gathering of its readers and subscribers. As the only national publication written exclusively for the church group travel planner, *Going on Faith* includes destination features, travel industry news, trip advice columns, and other tourism information, including a section dedicated to youth group travel ideas. The publication was founded in 1997 by publishers Mac Lacy and Charlie Presley. The six print issues published each year are read by more than five thousand five hundred subscribers; this is in addition to a growing online readership.

CHRISTIAN TRAVEL AND CRUISE GUIDE

Church Executive's publication for church group planners and travelers
www.christiantravelandcruiseguide.com

The *Christian Travel and Cruise Guide* is the latest publication from Power Trade Media, publishers of *Church Executive* magazine. Through ongoing readership surveys and industry research, *Church Executive* focuses on the pulse of large church and mega-church issues that include the growing importance of religious group travel. From interviews to travel tips, the *Christian Travel and Cruise Guide* is specifically written for the pastor, the church group travel planner, and the leisure traveler. Each issue of the *Christian Travel and Cruise Guide* contains critical and informative articles, including interviews, regional trip planners, theme trips, "how to" planning, and editorial features for the religious group travel planner.

LEISURE GROUP TRAVEL

The largest and oldest publication for group travel
www.leisuregrouptravel.com

Since 1994, group travel leaders, religious travel groups, tour operators, travel agents, and other group travel organizers have relied on *Leisure Group Travel*, and now www.LeisureGroupTravel.com, to provide destination knowledge and how-to advice to help them plan better group trips. Each edition features a domestic city focus, state feature, cruise section, international destination, regular news brief columns, and a reference guide. *Leisure Group Travel* is distributed in print six times per year with a special bonus issue each November. Web site content is updated weekly. Subscriptions to the magazine and InSite (a bi-weekly e-newsletter) are free to qualified group travel organizers. You can also visit www.grouptraveldirectory.com, a search engine for the group travel industry. It represents over thirty thousand group-friendly suppliers and special group offers.

RELIGIOUS MARKET CONSULTING GROUP

Assisting companies and organizations in faith tourism
www.religiousmarketconsulting.com

The Religious Market Consulting Group (RMCG) is a team of independent consulting professionals who specialize in assisting companies, organizations, and travel agencies in developing a vision and plan for entering or expanding their presence in Christian and faith tourism. Founded by the author, RMCG specializes in seminars and workshops, providing business plan templates and resources, market lists, recruiting, consulting opportunities, and much more. The Religious Market Consulting Group's collective experience and clientele list features virtually every segment of the travel, tourism, and hospitality industry including tour operators, tourist attractions, amusement parks, cruise lines, travel agencies, tourist boards, restaurants, and much more.

NOTES

Foreword

1. World Religious Travel Association, "$18 Billion Dollar Religious Travel Industry Gives Birth to International Association, " Press Release, January 29, 2007, http://www.religioustravelassociation.com/wrta_release_012907.pdf (accessed September 18, 2007).

Introduction

1. BBC News, "Vatican plans flights to shrines," August 21, 2007, http://news.bbc.co.uk/2/hi/europe/6956715.stm (accessed September 14, 2007).
2. Kevin Donovan, "Christian Festival Association Opens," *Christian Today*, October 2, 2006, http://www.christiantoday.com/article/christian.festival.association.opens/7836.htm (accessed September 18, 2007).
3. Christian Camp and Conference Association, "About Us Webpage," http://www.ccca.org/public/about/aboutus.asp (accessed September 14, 2007).
4. Christian Camp and Conference Association, "About Us Webpage," http://www.ccca.org/public/about/aboutus.asp (accessed September 14, 2007).
5. Quoteworld.org, "Saint Augustine Quote," quote attributed to *City of God*, http://www.quoteworld.org/quotes/719 (accessed September 14, 2007).

Chapter 1

1. World Tourism Organization, "Statement by World Tourism Organization at the United Nations Conference on Trade and Development – 11th Season," June 15, 2004, http://www.unctadxi.org/sections/u11/docs/GeneralDebate/15wto_eng.pdf (accessed September 18, 2007).

Chapter 2

1. News from the World Tourism Organization, "Millenium Tourism Boom in 2000," January 30, 2001, http://72.14.253.104/search?q=cache:lMtIpwW9vmUJ:www.wto.org/English/tratop_e/serv_e/results_e.doc+israel+2.8+record+2000+visitors&hl=en&ct=clnk&cd=2&gl=us (accessed September 18, 2007).
2. News from the World Tourism Organization, "Millenium Tourism Boom in 2000," January 30, 2001, http://72.14.253.104/search?q=cache:lMtIpwW9vmUJ:www.wto.org/English/tratop_e/serv_e/results_e.doc+israel+2.8+record+2000+visitors&hl=en&ct=clnk&cd=2&gl=us (accessed September 18, 2007).
3. Hotel Online (Special Report), "Middle East Hotels Leap Forward with Double-digit Growth / Deloitte," December 2004, http://www.hotel-online.com/News/PR2004_4th/Dec04_MiddleEastHotels.html (accessed by September 18, 2007).
4. Travel Industry Association, "TIA Travel Tidbits," November 21, 2006, http://www.tia.org/pressmedia/pressrec.asp?Item=736 (accessed September 14, 2007).
5. The JESUS Film Project, "Website—About Us Web page," http://www.jesusfilm.org/aboutus/index.html (accessed September 18, 2007).
6. Stephen J. Binz, *Pilgrimage in the Footsteps of Jesus* (New London, CT: Twenty-Third Publications, 2004), 4.
7. Jennifer, Riley, United Methodists report 455% increase in Mission Volunteers," *The Christian Post*, May 15, 2007, http://www.christianpost.com/article/20070515/27426_United_Methodists_Report_455%25_Increase_in_Mission_Volunteers.htm (accessed September 14, 2007).
8. William J. Holstein, "Casting off the myths of cruise," interview with Richard D. Fein, *New York Times*, July 21, 2007, http://travel.nytimes.com/2007/07/21/business/21interview.html?pagewanted=print (accessed September 14, 2007).

9. Sight & Sound Theatres, "About Us Webpage," http://www.sight-sound.com/WebSiteSS/getaboutus.do (accessed September 14, 2007).

Chapter 4

1. Orion's Gate, "Books—Pilgrim's Progress," http://www.orionsgate.org/books.html (accessed September 22, 2007).

Chapter 5

1. Leon H. Greene, M.D., *A Guide to Short Term Missions*. (Waynesboro, GA: Gabriel Publishing, 2003), 18.
2. G. Jeffrey MacDonald, "On a Mission—A Short-Term Mission," *USA Today*, June 18, 2006, http://www.usatoday.com/news/religion/2006-06-18-mission-vacations_x.htm (accessed September 14, 2007).

Chapter 6

1. Leonard John, *The Novalis Guide to Canadian Shrines*. (Ottawa, Canada: Novalis, 2002).
2. Julia Duin, "Religion New Jamaican Tourism Lure," *WorldWide Religious News*, April 25, 2006, http://www.wwrn.org/article.php?idd=21287&sec=41&con=3 (accessed September 19, 2007).
3. African Christian Tours & Safaris, "Affiliations," http://www.actsoverland.com/affiliations/index.php (accessed September 14, 2007).
4. Miles Bredin, "Go with God," interview with Chris Foot, *New York Times*, March 19, 2006, http://travel.nytimes.com/2006/03/19/travel/tmagazine/19ts-safari.html (accessed September 14, 2007).

Chapter 7

1. Visit Houston, "June Convention Brings $15.3 Million to Houston—Press Release," May 10, 2005, http://www.visithoustontexas.com/media/press_releases.php?id=25&category=12856 (accessed September 20, 2007).
2. Maxine Golding, "Trends for Religious Conventions," *Expo Web*, September 2006, http://www.expoweb.com/Trends/0609Religioustrends.htm (accessed September 19, 2007).
3. Utah Idaho Southern Baptist Convention, "Website—Homepage," http://www.uisbc.org/aboutus.htm (accessed September 20, 2007).
4. First Christian Church of Longwood, "Website: Newsletter—July 2006," July 2006, http://www.firstchristianlongwood.org/PraiseTheLordDetail.asp?PTLID=22 (accessed September 20, 2007).
5. Gospel Music Association, "Christian Festival Association, September 2006," press release, September 21, 2006 http://www.gospelmusic.org/newsmedia/OMNewswire_detail.aspx?iid=18284&tid=33, (accessed September 20, 2007).
6. Gospel Music Association, "Christian Festival Association, September 2006," press release, September 21, 2006 http://www.gospelmusic.org/newsmedia/OMNewswire_detail.aspx?iid=18284&tid=33, (accessed September 20, 2007).
7. Kingdom Bound Festival, press release, March 1, 2007 http://www.24-7pressrelease.com/view_press_release.php?rID=25110, (accessed September 25, 2007).
8. Evangelical Lutheran Church in America, "Website: Youth Gathering Ministries," http://www.elca.org/youth/gathering_about.html (accessed September 20, 2007).
9. Women of Faith, "Company Overview," http://www.womenoffaith.com/About/companyoverview.asp (accessed September 20, 2007).

10. Women of Faith, "About Us," http://www.womenoffaith.com/About/whatsthis.asp (accessed September 20, 2007).

11. The Learning Channel (TLC), "Fansites/The Monastery," http://tlc.discovery.com/fansites/monastery/monastery.html (accessed September 25, 2007).

12. The Abbey of Gethsemani, "Retreats Web page," http://www.monks.org/makeretreat.html (accessed September 19, 2007).

13. MP3.com, "Benedictine Monks of Santo Domingo de Silos," http://www.mp3.com/artist/benedictine-monks-of-santo-domingo-de-silos/summary/ (September 20, 2007).

14. Angel Records, "Benedictine Monks of Santo Domingo de Silos," http://www.angelrecords.com/bio.asp?ContributorID=4451 (accessed September 20, 2007).

Chapter 8

1. Sight & Sound Theatre, "About Us," http://www.sight-sound.com/WebSiteSS/gethistory.do (accessed September 14, 2007).

2. Sight & Sound Theatre, "Coming to Branson in 2008!" brochure.

3. Sight & Sound Theatres, "2007 Season" brochure.

4. Sight & Sound Theatres, "2007 Season" brochure.

5. Sight & Sound Theatres, "Daniel," http://www.sight-sound.com/WebSiteSS/getshowdetails.do?eventCD=DAN (accessed September 14, 2007).

6. The Miracle Theater, "Homepage," http://www.miracletheater.com (accessed September 14, 2007).

Chapter 9

1. Wilkening, David, "Targeting in Travel Is More Important than Ever," *Travel Mole* (April 24, 2007).

2. ITA Office of Travel & Tourism Industries, "2006 Survey of International Travelers," http://tinet.ita.doc.gov/ (accessed July 2007).

3. Holstein, William J., "Casting off the Myths of Cruises." *New York Times,* July 21, 2007.

4. Cheryl Coggins Frink, "Non-Profits and Churches Raise Much Needed Cash While Cruising the High Seas." *Austin American Statesman*, May 20, 2007, http://www.signature-journeys.com/NewsBrief.asp?NewsID=29 (accessed September 29, 2007).

BIBLIOGRAPHY

Bible Gateway, New King James Version. Gospel Communications International, 2007.

Blake, Everett C., and Anna G. Edmonds. *Biblical Sites in Turkey.* Istanbul, Turkey: Sev Yay A.S., 1997.

Bramlett, Perry C., and Ronald W. Higdon. *Touring C.S. Lewis' Ireland and England .* Macon, GA: Smyth and Helwys Publishing Inc., 1998.

Cimok, Fatih. *A Guide to the Seven Churches.* Istanbul, Turkey: A Turizm Yayinlari Ltd., 1998.

"East of the Jordan, Toward the Sun Rising" (Joshua 1:15): Biblical Jordan at a Glance. Amman, Jordan: Jordan Tourism Board, 2006.

Dyer, Charles H., and Gregory A. Hatteberg. *The New Christian Traveler's Guide to the Holy Land.* Chicago, IL: Moody Publishers, 2006.

Edmonds, Anna G. *Turkey's Religious Sites.* Turkey: Damko A.S., 1997.

Eyewitness Travel Guides: Egypt. NY: DK Publishing, 2001.

Eyewitness Travel Guides: Greece, Athens and the Mainland. NY: DK Publishing, 1997.

Eyewitness Travel Guides: Jerusalem and the Holy Land. NY: DK Publishing, 2000.

Eyewitness Travel Guides: Rome. NY: DK Publishing, 1993.

Fann, Anne-Geri, and Greg Taylor. *How to Get Ready for Short-Term Missions.* Nashville, TN: Thomas Nelson, 2006.

Greene, Leon H., M.D. *A Guide to Short-Term Missions.* Waynesboro, GA: Gabriel Publishing, 2003.

Gretzschel, Matthias, and Toma Babovic. *In Martin Luther's Footsteps.* Hamburg, Germany: Ellert and Richter Verlag, 1996.

Hoffmann, Wolfgang. *Luther: A Practical Travel Guide to the Most Significant Sites in Germany Associated with the Great Reformer.* Germany: Schmidt–Buch–Verlag, 1995.

In The Footsteps of Paul the Apostle in Greece. Athens, Greece: Greek National Tourism Organization, 2003.

Jordan: Religion and Faith: Biblical Jordan. Amman, Jordan: Jordan Tourism Board, 2006.

Jordan: Visitor's Guide. Amman, Jordan: Jordan Tourism Board, 2006.

Kirby, Scott. *Equipped for Adventure: A Practical Guide to Short-Term Mission Trips.* Birmingham, AL: New Hope Publishers, 2006.

Kurian, George Thomas. *Nelson's Dictionary of Christianity.* Nashville, TN: Thomas Nelson, 2005.

Meadows, Carl. *How to Organize Group Travel for Fun and Profit.* Shawnee Mission, KS: Group Travel Business Institute, 2000.

Moreau, Scott A., Gary R. Corwin, and Gary B. McGee. *Introducing World Missions.* Grand Rapids, MI: Baker Academic, 2004.

Palmer, Martin, and Nigel Palmer. *The Spiritual Traveler: The Guide to Sacred Sites and Pilgrim Routes in Britain.* Mahwah, NJ: HiddenSpring, 2000.

Pilgrimage and Christian Tourism. Israel: Israel Ministry of Tourism, 2004.

Pocock Michael, Gailyn Van Rheenen, and Douglas McConnell. *The Changing Face of World Missions.* Grand Rapids, MI: Baker Academic, 2005.

Routes to Luther: Lutheran Sites in Eisenach, Erfurt, Schmalkalden, Eisleben, Wittenberg, and Torgau. Germany: Wege zu Luther e.V., 2005.

Ward, Douglas. *Berlitz Complete Guide to Cruising and Cruise Ships 2007.* London, UK: Apa Publications GmbH and Co., 2007.

Wareham, Norman, and Jill Gill. *Shrines of the Holy Land: A Pilgrim's Travel Guide.* Liguori, MO: Liguori Publications, 1998.

Wright, Kevin J. *Catholic Shrines of Western Europe: A Pilgrim's Travel Guide.* Liguori, MO: Liguori Publications, 1997.

Wright, Kevin J. *Europe's Monastery and Convent Guesthouses: A Pilgrim's Travel Guide.* Liguori, MO: Liguori Publications, 2000.

INDEX

Illustrations are indicated by *italics*.

4/14 Window, 189, *189*
10/40 Window, 188–89, 192, 194, 195, 210

A

Abbey of Gethsemani, 290–92
Abbey of Monte Cassino, 296–97
Abbeys of Saint Peter and Saint Cecelia, *284*, 292–93
Abu Ghosh, Israel, 44
Acre (Akko), Israel, 40–41
adventure vacations
    advantages and disadvantages, 246–47
    African safaris, 13, 249–50, 385–86
    "at a glance," 243–44
    costs, 243, 247
    as fellowship vacations, 9, 13, 244, 246, *248*
    inspirational stories, 248–49
    learning vacations, 221, 250–52
    preparing for, 247–48
    reasons to choose, 243, *243*, 244, 245
    types of, 245–46
    web sites and resources, 360, 385–86
    See also Christian camps
affinity-based conferences, 265–66
affinity-group retreats, 274
Africa
    missionary travel, 189, 191, 206–7, *207*
    safaris, 13, 249–50, 385–86
Akhisar (Thyatira), Turkey, 77, 81–82
Akko (Acre), Israel, 40–41
Alasehir (Philadelphia), Turkey, 77, 83
Alaska, 237–38, 251, 252
Amman, Jordan, 57
Amphipolis, Greece, 100–101
Anata (Anathoth), Israel, 44
Anathoth (Anata), Israel, 44
Anjara, Jordan, 56–57
Antakya (Antioch), Turkey, 70, 71, 85–86, *86*
Antioch (Antakya), Turkey, 70, 71, 85–86, *86*
Antipatris (Aphek, Afek), Israel, 44
Aphek (Afek, Antipatris), Israel, 44
Apollonia, Greece, 101–2
Arkansas, 15, 222–25, 326–27
Armageddon (Megiddo), Israel, 39
As Salt, Jordan, 57
Ashdod, Israel, 44, 239

Asia

India, 191, 207, 210, 231–33
missionary travel, 189, 191, 207–8, 210
See also China
Assisi, Italy, 118, 128–29
Athens, Greece, 91, 92–95, *93*
attractions, Christian. *See* Christian attractions
Augsburg, Germany, 156

B

Bahamas, 226–28, *226*
Banias/Panias (Caesarea Philippi), Israel, 38
Baptism Archaeological Park, 51–54
Bede's World, 133
Beersheba (Beersheva), Israel, 46
Belgium, 251
Berea (Veria), Greece, 105
Bergama (Pergamum), Turkey, 77, 80–81
Bet Sahur, Israel, 44
Beth Shan, Israel, 38
Bethany (Jerusalem), 35
Bethany Beyond the Jordan, 51–54, *51*
Bethel, Israel, 44
Bethlehem, Israel, 30, 42
Bethphage Church, 35
Bethsaida, Israel, 37–38
biblical lands
    advantages and disadvantages, 22–23
    "at a glance," 20
    Christian cruises, 78, 91, 92, 107, 239
    costs, 20, 23–24
    inspirational stories, 30
    learning vacations, 251
    as pilgrimage, 9, 10–11, 21
    preparing for, 24–26
    reasons to choose, 20, 21–22
    See also individual countries
biblical parks and interactive centers, 305–10
Billy Graham Library, 316–17
boat travel. *See* Christian cruises; *individual countries*
Branson, Missouri, *14*, 15, 222–25, 323–25
Britain. *See* England
Britain's abbeys and cathedrals, 134
Buckfast Abbey, 294–95

C

Caesarea, Israel, 43
Caesarea Philippi (Banias/Panias), Israel, 38

Cairo, Egypt, 68, 239
California, 310–12, *311*, 312–15, 345
Cambodia, 210
camps, Christian. *See* Christian camps
Cana (Kefer Kana), Israel, 38
Canada, 195, 238, 251, 252, 384
Canterbury, England, 5, 136–37, *137*, 190
Capernaum, Israel, 38–39, *39*
Cappadocia, Turkey, 70, *85*, 86–87
Caribbean, 208, 226–28, *226*, 238
catacombs (Rome), 120, *125*
Cenchreae, Greece, 96
Charters
    adventure vacations, 246
    airline, 8
    cruise lines, 241
    European river cruises, 239
    "magic number" for, 370
    popularity of, 13, *235*
    preparing for, 240
China
    faith missions, 189
    leisure vacations, 229–30
    missionary travel, 191, 207, 208
    web sites, 379
Chorazin, Israel, 38
Christian attractions
    advantages and disadvantages, 303
    "at a glance," 300
    biblical parks and interactive centers, 305–10
    costs, 300, 303
    mega-churches, 310–15, *311*
    museums, 316–23
    as new trend in Christian travel, 14–15
    preparing for, 303–4
    reasons to choose, 300, 301–2
    theaters and performances, *14*, 15, 323–29
    web sites and resources, 389
    welcome centers, 329–33
Christian camps
    advantages and disadvantages, 277
    adventure camps, 13, 246, 385, 386, 388
    "at a glance," 275
    choosing the right camp, 276–77
    as Christian travel type, 6, 14, 277, *281*, *282*
    costs, 275, 277–78
    opportunities, 279–81
    preparing for, 278–79
    reasons to choose, 254, 275, 276
    web sites and resources, 385, 388
Christian cruises
    advantages and disadvantages, 235–36
    "at a glance," 233

biblical lands, 78, 91, 92, 107, 239
    choosing the type of cruise, 235, *235*
    costs, 233, 236–37
    cruise lines, selecting, 241–43
    cruise lines, working with, 356, 357, 359
    destinations and styles, 237–39, *239*
    as fellowship vacations, 9, 12–13, 236, 241
    as fund-raising program, 340–42
    inspirational stories, 240–41
    preparing for, 239–41
    reasons to choose, 233–34
    web sites and resources, 241–43, 385, 397
Christian event vacations
    advantages and disadvantages, 257
    affinity-based conferences, 265–66
    "at a glance," 254–55
    choosing the type of event, 257
    as Christian travel type, 13, 254
    conventions for denominations and Christian
        organizations, 260–61, 387
    costs, 255, 257
    inspirational stories, 259
    marketplace conventions, 264–65
    preparing for, 258–59
    reasons to choose, 254, 255–56
    web sites and resources, 386–87
    See also crusades, rallies, and entertainment
        events
Christian festivals
    on Christian cruises, 263
    Germany, 148, 149, 158
    Jamaica, 228
    North America, 262–63
    preparing for, 258
    web sites, 387
Christian leisure vacations. *See* leisure vacations
Christian Quarter (Jerusalem), 32
Christian retreats
    advantages and disadvantages, 269–70
    "at a glance," 267
    as Christian travel type, 6, 13–14, *13*, 254, *273*
    costs, 267, 270
    preparing for, 270–71
    reasons to choose, 254, 266–69
    types of, 272–74
    web sites and resources, 388
    See also monastic guest-stay vacations
Christian travel ministries
    asking and obtaining permission for, 348–50
    choosing a "home base," 351
    conducting a travel survey, 352–53
    conventions on, 265, 395–96
    Crystal Cathedral's program for, 311, 345

Holy Family's flight to Egypt, 69
Holy Land Experience, The, 15, 225, 308–10
Holy Lands. *See* biblical lands
Horns of Hittin, Israel, 41

I

India, 191, 207, 210, 231–33
insurance, travel, 204, 394
interactive centers and biblical parks, 305–10
Iona Abbey, Scotland, 160, 162–65, *165*, 190
Iran, 210
Iraq, 210
Ireland and Northern Ireland, 169–70, 190, 191
Israel
    background, 29
    central Israel, 42–45, *42*
    Christian cruises, 239
    inspirational stories, 30
    learning vacations, 251
    lodgings, 36–37
    map, 27
    northern Israel, 37–41, *37*, *39*
    reasons to visit, 21–22, 28, *28*
    southern Israel, 45–46, *46*
    tourism, modern, 8
    tourism in ancient times, 4, 5
    transportation, 29, 35–36
    traveler's tips, 30, 35
    See also Jerusalem
Istanbul (Constantinople), Turkey, 73–75, *73*
Italy, 251, 296–97
    See also Rome, Italy
Izmir (Smyrna), Turkey, 77, 79–80
Iznik (Nicea), Turkey, 70, 76

J

Jaffa (Joppa), Israel, 44–45
Jamaica, 228
Japan, 191
Jerash, Jordan, 57, *57*
Jericho, Israel, 30, 43
Jerusalem, Israel
    Christian cruises, 239
    Pope John Paul II, visit by, 8
    reasons to visit, 30–31
    sites and activities, *31*, 32–35, *33*
    tourism in ancient times, 4, 5
    travel planning and lodgings, 35–37
JESUS Film Project Master Studio Tours, 15, 225, 332–33
Jezreel Valley, Israel, 41
Joppa (Jaffa), Israel, 44–45
Jordan

background, 49–50
Bethany Beyond the Jordan, 51–54, *51*
inspirational stories, 50–51
map, 47
more biblical sites, 56–59, *57*
Mount Nebo, 55–56
reasons to visit, 21–22, 48, *48*, 50, 55
transportation, 49–50
Jordan River, Israel, 30
Jordan River, Jordan, 51–54, *51*
Judean Desert, Israel, 45
Julian of Norwich, 133–34

K

Karak, Jordan, 57
Kavala (Neapolis), Greece, 102–3, *102*
Kazakhstan, 210
Kefer Kana (Cana), Israel, 38
Kentucky, 251, 290–92, 318–20, *318*
Kiriat Yearim (Abu Ghosh), Israel, 44
Kishon River, Israel, 41
Kusadasi, Turkey, 78–79, 239

L

lake and river cruising, American, 238
Lancaster, Pennsylvania, *14*, 15, 225, 323–25
Laodicea (Eskihisar), Turkey, 77, 84–85, *84*
Latin America, 191, 209–10, 251, 384
learning vacations, 221, 250–52
leisure vacations
    advantages and disadvantages, 219
    "at a glance," 216–17
    choosing the type of trip, 218–19
    costs, 216, 220
    as fellowship vacations, 9, 12, *12*, 216, 218, 219
    inspirational stories, 221, 224, 227–28
    international, 226–33
    preparing for, 220, 222
    reasons to choose, 216, 217–18
    students and youth, *221*, 221
    United States, 222–25
    web sites and resources, 384–85, 397
    See also Christian attractions
Lincoln, Epworth, and York, England, 142
Lindisfarne, The Holy Island, 133
lodging industry, resources on, 359
London, England, 134–36, *134*
long-term missions, 187, 207
Lot's Cave, Jordan, 58–59

M

Machaerus (Mukawir), Jordan, 58
Madaba, Jordan, 58

Kevin J. Wright is North America's most recognized Christian travel authority and one of the world's most sought-after faith tourism experts. A fifteen-year veteran of Christian travel, Kevin is the founder and president of the *World Religious Travel Association* (WRTA)—the leading global community for faith tourism. The organization hosts the *WRTA Social Network*, the world's first online social network for Christian and faith-based travel.

Kevin is also the founder of the *World Religious Travel Expo and Educational Conference*, an international tradeshow and convention for churches, organizations, group planners, travel providers, tourist boards, travel agencies, and individuals involved in religious travel. In addition, Kevin is president of the *Religious Marketing Consulting Group*, a team of independent professionals who assist companies with entering or expanding their presence in Christian and faith-based tourism.

In the mid-1990s, Kevin introduced the concept of religious travel guidebooks into the publishing industry and is today an award-winning author. In 2004, Kevin launched the high-profile religious travel division at Globus, one of the world's largest tour operators. In 2005, he pioneered the country's first-ever national religious travel conference designed to educate tourism professionals about Christian and faith-based travel. He has journeyed to almost thirty countries, visited more than three hundred major places of pilgrimage, embarked on full-ship Christian cruises, participated in short-term missions, attended dozens of Christian events, toured Christian attractions, stayed overnight in monasteries, and much more.

Kevin has been interviewed by *The Early Show* on CBS, *TIME* magazine, *USA TODAY*, *Wall Street Journal*, *New York Times*, *Los Angeles Times*, *Denver Business Journal*, *El Pais* (Spain's leading daily newspaper), *Financial Express* (India), *Travel Weekly*, *Travel Agent Magazine*, *Travel Age West*, *Christianity Today*, *Church Executive*, *Going on Faith*, *Leisure Group Travel*, and dozens of other news, travel, and religious media outlets.